S0-BYD-064

Accounting
Information System

I. Eugene McNeill
University of Houston

GOODYEAR PUBLISHING COMPANY, INC.

Current printing (last digit):
10 9 8 7 6 5 4 3 2 1

0-87620-305-5

Library of Congress Catalog Card Number 79-131485

Printed in the United States of America

Contents

Preface

This textbook is designed for a one-semester course in financial accounting to meet the academic needs of:

1. Students who will take only one semester of accounting to obtain a good understanding of financial information such as that appearing on standard financial reports.
2. Students who will take one semester of financial accounting followed by a semester of managerial accounting for an understanding of both external and internal reports.
3. Students who will continue in the study of accounting in intermediate and cost courses.

The concepts and their application in this book provide a strong background for the student who will take only one course; they should give the accounting major such a depth of understanding as to make the intermediate accounting courses much less rigorous than students usually find them.

Systems Approach

Accounting is an information system providing financial information for use in making decisions. Studying accounting as a system makes many topics more meaningful and understandable. The role of information in decision making and the concept of the flow system with feedback and controls are presented in chapters 1 and 2 as a setting for a deeper understanding of accounting.

The systems approach allows the student to see relationships from the very beginning; he does not have to study segmented procedures and principles, but sees them as an integrated whole from their first introduction. This allows the development of deeper insights during the study of the traditional accounting procedures and reporting practices.

To make the systems approach a more complete one, contributions from the behavioral sciences are used, particularly in the first three chapters. Accounting is related to human interaction; knowledge about individual and collective human behavior is essential to the development of a functioning system. For this reason, material has been drawn from the appropriate literature in psychology and sociology.

Special Features

From a broad systems view, this text synthesizes and clarifies several topics. Of special note are the treatment of the following:

1. Introductory chapters provide an orientation to decision making and flow systems as a setting for the further study of financial information.
2. Accounting concepts are included in the overall information system as qualitative standards for determining the desired information output and, therefore, the data input to the system.
3. Revenue is conceptually defined as the earned inflow of resources (chapter 6); criteria for revenue recognition and the timing of revenue reporting are presented and applied to specific situations.
4. Expenses are conceptually defined as the consumption of resources (chapter 7); criteria for expense recognition and the timing of expense reporting are presented and applied.
5. The funds-committed concept is presented as a clarification and explanation of the traditional cost concept. This allows a clear distinction between funds committed in assets and the value of such assets.
6. The procedural aspects of accounting are presented in terms of processing data either manually or electronically, since classifying, transferring, storing, summarizing, and reporting are the functional stages in processing data, whatever means may be used. Traditional ledger

and journal devices are presented in chapters 4 and 5, but in a broad and realistic setting.

7. Topics are treated cohesively. For example, revenue allocation between periods results from the application of criteria for revenue reporting and, therefore, is presented in the chapter on revenue as a part of that topic. Expense allocation, similarly, results from the application of criteria for expense reporting and is presented in the chapter on expenses.
8. For the first time, working capital is conceptually defined as funds in current asset form that come from long-term sources (including earnings), funds that the firm provides to finance its own operations. This conceptual definition is provided in addition to the computational definition (the excess of current assets over current liabilities); it leads to a clarifying distinction between working capital and other funds on the funds statement prepared according to AICPA standards (chapter 14).
9. The preceding and other clarifications lead the student to see equities on the balance sheet primarily as the source of the firm's financial resources and assets as those resources committed in specific items. This view is consistent with the concept of reporting assets as the amount of funds committed in them.
10. The income statement is seen as a report of the earned inflow of resources matched with the consumption of resources for the period, resulting in net income as the net increase in resources from the firm's operations. All items on the income statement are stated on a funds-committed basis consistent with the presentation of items on the balance sheet.

These definitions and clarifications bring the traditional accounting concepts into sharp focus, making them more meaningful and useful. The application of the traditional concepts is emphasized throughout the text.

Organization of Material

The first two chapters of the text on accounting as a financial information system may be used as a reading assignment or they may be given full attention in lecture sessions, according to the preference of individual instructors. All chapters are arranged in the recommended sequence except for the following:

1. Chapter 9 on the special problems of depreciation is written to be independent of the remainder of the text material. If an instructor does not care to treat the topic in its full depth this chapter might be omitted, since basic depreciation computations are included in chapter 7 with the general treatment of expenses.
2. Chapters 9 and 10 may be reversed in order if the instructor prefers

that students study the development of asset costs before they treat depreciation in greater depth.

3. The last topic in chapter 10 is written as an independent section so that it may be omitted. The author is aware that in some programs the use of index numbers is introduced after the first course in accounting and that the instructor may wish to leave the topic for a later course.

Each chapter includes:

1. A set of preview questions on the first page of the chapter, designed to sensitize the student to the major points of the chapter and provide a basis for later review.
2. Questions and exercises at the end of each chapter for student study and class use.
3. Procedural problems that emphasize the procedural and computational techniques related to chapter topics.
4. Conceptual problems that emphasize a deeper understanding of concepts and their applications.

Supplementary Materials

This text is accompanied by a complete set of supplementary study and teaching materials, including:

1. A programmed instruction book, providing for students a structured learning process that virtually assures their mastery of the material. Both linear and branching programming are used, each with the material to which it seems best suited. Small program steps are used to teach concepts and techniques; large program steps are provided as problems with solutions available for self-checking by the student. The program reinforces the student's learning from the text by repetition, special emphasis, and elaboration, and it is recommended especially for use with accounting students at the freshman and sophomore levels.
2. Demonstration Problems and Notes, to provide the student with orderly note-taking materials and the instructor with selected questions and problems around which to develop his lectures. The Demonstration Problems and Notes have these special features:
   a. Special spacing and binding so that the instructor can make transparencies from the note material for projection during the lecture.
   b. An instructor's manual containing suggested solutions to all demonstration problems and, also, suggestions for content and special emphasis of lectures.
3. Short practice set giving data processed manually in traditional journals and ledgers for one month and by computer for the next month. A program is provided free to instructors using the practice set. Both parts may be used, or either part may be used without the other.

4. An examination booklet containing a range of problems, both objective and subjective in nature.
5. A solutions manual, with helpful orientation to the concepts and structure of the text and programmed material, and solutions to all questions, exercises, and problems in the text and examinations. Loose-leaf binding allows easy preparation of transparencies.
6. Accounting forms for student use in solving assigned problems.

Author's Background

This textbook and its related teaching materials represent a culmination of the author's many years of teaching experience at both the graduate and undergraduate levels.

In addition to the teaching of accounting subject matter under university classroom conditions (classroom lecture method), my experience includes preparation of a series of television lectures for the teaching of the introductory and professional development courses at the University of Houston. This resulted in the development of additional teaching materials to enhance the student's learning process, one of the more successful items thus developed being the supporting programmed text which accompanies *Financial Accounting.* The presentation and sequencing of the subject matter in a systems format is an attempt to provide a thorough understanding of the firm's financial information models, to emphasize their relevancy to decision making, and to bring the meaning of accounting information into sharper focus for students.

Acknowledgements

A very real indebtedness must be recognized to professional colleagues who have contributed in many ways to the development of significant ideas and techniques. The following are among those to whom appreciation is extended for their helpful comments on the manuscript:

Allan R. Bailey, San Diego State College
Teddy L. Coe, Texas A & M University
Dennis Gordon, University of Akron
Charles Griffin, The University of Texas at Austin
Arthur Hardy, San Jacinto College
James M. Harris, California State College at Long Beach
Frank Kaulback, University of Virginia
Robert A. Kelley, Corning Community College

Kevin M. Lightner, San Diego State College
Carlton Stolle, Texas A & M University
William H. Talbert, The University of Texas at Austin
Joe Thomas, South Texas College

Special thanks are extended to Professor Teddy L. Coe, Texas A & M University, Professor Arthur Hardy, San Jacinto College, and Mr. David Smith, The University of Houston, for their contributions to the development of problem material. Personal appreciation is expressed for the tireless and patient work of my secretary, Mrs. Catherine Parker, in preparing the manuscript.

Although this is exceptional, I must express appreciation for the quality of support and encouragement afforded by personnel of Goodyear Publishing Company, Mr. Alfred W. Goodyear, Mr. James P. Levy, and especially Mr. Bennett Parr, who gave the manuscript his close attention from its inception. Mr. Harvey Schloss made his valuable contribution to the styling and production of the finished book, and Mrs. Karen Christenson did an imaginative and strengthening job of copy editing.

More than to anyone else, however, I feel gratitude to my wife, Edith, and to Laurie, our daughter remaining at home, for their support and understanding during the long months devoted almost exclusively to this work rather than to them.

Financial Accounting

A Decision Information System

1 Business Decisions and Information

Preview Questions

As you study look for the answers to the following questions:

- **What is a decision?**
- **What are the three steps involved in decision making?**
- **What are the differences between group decisions and personal decisions?**
- **What is the relationship between information and decision making?**
- **Who makes major decisions in business?**
- **How is financial information provided?**
- **What are the common information models (also called financial reports)?**
- **What kinds of information do these financial reports contain?**

All activities, including those of a business firm, are accomplished by making a series of decisions, communicating these decisions to others, and performing the resulting tasks.

STRUCTURE OF DECISIONS

Decisions in Business

In any study of an organization's decision-making process the emphasis is usually on planning and control decisions made by management. In fact, the term *management decisions* is commonly used. Actually, important business decisions include those made by many different people at many different levels:

Decisions of investors concerning the purchase or sale of company shares or bonds.

Decisions of creditors about granting credit and about collection procedures.

Decisions of top management in planning both operations and financing.

Decisions of all levels of management in interpreting and communicating the results of top management decisions.

Decisions of lower management and workers in planning and performing duties.

Decisions of management at all levels in evaluating performance.

Decisions of management at all levels in reviewing and revising decision and communications.

Decisions of persons concerning employment.

Decisions of persons in government agencies concerning compliance with regulations.

Functional Structure of a Decision

What is a decision? What is involved in making a decision? A decision is a choice among alternatives. **When alternative actions are available or, realistically, when alternatives are *known* to be available, a choice must be made.** The alternatives may be in any area of a firm—alternative sources of funds for financing a building expansion, alternative physical arrangements of production facilities, alternative sales programs, an individual's employment alternatives.

That choice among alternatives which we call a decision is actually the culmination of a series of steps involving several decisions. One must first accept the existence of alternatives, that is, recognize that there is a reason to consider more than one course of action. This recognition may be caused by the realization of possible benefits obtainable through alternative actions. Likewise, the decision to consider alternatives may be made because of an awareness that the present action is not producing acceptable results and, therefore, that some change is needed. In order to make an intelligent decision one needs information about the alternatives among which he must choose. In terms of the firm, accounting furnishes information about the financial results of past actions and about the possibility of better results from alternative actions.

Identifying criteria for success The question of acceptable results indicates another decision which must be made: what results will one accept as adequate for any action? Put more formally, **for each action someone must develop or identify criteria for success.** He must provide an answer to the question: what is acceptable as a result of this action? If the criteria are established and the results of present action are measured against them, then it may become obvious that some change in action is needed. This realization may stimulate a search for alternative actions which will meet the criteria for success. Accounting develops information about desirable and reasonable objectives and about actual results of present actions.

Interaction among decision elements If one begins the decision-making process by establishing criteria for successful results, comparing them with present performance may cause him to decide between continuing the present action and seeking alternatives. On the other hand, one may begin his decision making by becoming aware of alternatives; this approach may cause him to specifically define his criteria for success to give him some basis for choice among the alternatives. Note that if one is aware of criteria for success and does not investigate alternatives to present action, he has decided that present action is preferred (perhaps unconsciously) to searching for better alternatives; he has chosen between the alternatives of seeking better alternatives and continuing the present action. Also, if one is aware of alternatives but does not identify criteria for success as a basis for choosing among them, he has chosen between the alternatives of identifying success criteria and continuing the present action. Of course, one might change his course of action without identifying criteria for acceptable results; in so doing, he may use criteria not consciously recognized or he may select them almost at random, with the decisive factor being some emotional appeal. It is assumed that success in business does not follow from making decisions in this manner.

Elements of the decision set There appears to be a set of three decisions actually involved in the phenomenon we call a decision:

1. **The decision to seek alternatives**
2. **The decision upon criteria for success**
3. **The actual choice among alternatives to meet the criteria most fully.**

In an organization each of these three decisions can be made by a different person or group. The office manager may decide to seek alternative methods for making copies of printed materials. He may then delegate to a person or a committee the task of identifying criteria for successful reproduction. Based on these criteria he may choose a reproducing device, or he may designate someone to compare performances of various devices and select the one that most nearly meets the identified success criteria. Establishing criteria and comparing performances require information. For many decisions, such information is provided by the financial information, or accounting, system.

In many instances the first two of the three decisions may be implied by the act of examining alternatives, and in many instances the decision to seek the best alternative and to use certain criteria for success will be made without any conscious awareness of them as separate decisions. However, a few attempts to make primary decisions completely skipping the first two steps will present persuasive evidence that the two preliminary decisions are very important. It may be that in most business situations the preliminary decision to seek the best alternative is considered a criterion of good management and, therefore, is not consciously considered a decision to be made. The practice of identifying criteria for success to measure alternatives does not appear to be so uniformly followed. Some facets of this problem will receive attention later as we examine the structure of a decision in greater detail.

Behavioral Structure of a Decision

Because business decisions are made by persons, they are examples of human behavior. An examination of behavior may therefore aid our understanding of decisions.

Decisions as behavior of individuals Decisions that appear to be made by a group (a consensus, or combined opinion of a professional, political, or other group) are actually composed of the decisions of individuals within the group. Sometimes group decisions are the decision of the group leader, accepted by the other members of the group; sometimes the group decision may be the result of combining decisions made by individuals based on their separate considerations of the question at hand. Whatever the formation of the decision, it appears that ultimately the decision-making process is a behavior of the individual. This does not mean that the person is not influenced by others in making the decision; he will probably be strongly influenced by the current general attitudes of others, and he will be influenced by his knowledge of previous attitudes of others concerning the specific point of decision or concerning things which he relates to it.

Stimuli and behavior What is the decision-making behavior of an individual? It appears that it can be described in the same terms as other behavior.

Behavior is action which occurs in response to stimuli; it may be physical (muscular or glandular), or it may be mental (thought). Stimuli are energies impinging on a subject. These energies may be external or internal to the subject, and they may be derived from physical (sensory) or mental (thought) sources. Responses to stimuli apparently are developed in relation to providing pleasure or satisfaction, or to avoiding pain. Every act has a cause; stimuli cause action. A stimulus may be physical in origin: the nervous system's signal that a hand has touched something very cold or that a sound vibration has reached the ear. Or, the stimulus may be mental in origin: the thought of a delicious food, or of an act that should be done. The thought of a sum of money or his purpose for wanting money might stimulate a salesman to make greater efforts in selling merchandise on which he will earn a commission. The thought of going to a ball game might stimulate a student to put aside his studying, or the thought of future success in business might stimulate greater interest and attention to studying.

Complex responses Responses to stimuli may be very automatic in some cases. If while moving a file cabinet one injures his foot he may groan aloud with pain, shout profanities and epithets, and hop about grasping the injured foot. These things he might do without thought or specific encouragement at the time, especially if he is alone in the office. However, if the injury occurs in the presence of his coworkers, the impulse to react to pain in a violent fashion might be overcome by fears of embarrassment or loss of status by creating a disturbance and "looking foolish." These thoughts, in turn, might stimulate control of the first impulse so that he reacts to the pain not by hopping about and shouting, but by groaning or muttering softly and grasping the injured foot. Other responses, too, may be made primarily as a result of mental stimuli and may involve the interaction of many thoughts and emotional drives. The self-image of the person (how he perceives himself) and his continuing awareness of his physical and social environment affect his responses to specific stimuli. Most business decisions are complex responses to stimuli.

Belief, preference, bias It should be noted that every person develops a hierarchy of values which strongly flavors his responses. The kind and strength of a person's responses may indicate his attitudes toward various stimuli.

One's beliefs are those bits of information he accepts as fact, as truly depicting the reality of a subject. This acceptance can be described as belief. As used here, belief is not an emotional response; it is a mental acceptance of something as fact. It does not involve a matter of liking, disliking, or of identifying.

Like, dislike, and identification, on the other hand, may be described as preference. One may like one object or act or even one bit of information better than others; he prefers the liked thing to others. Since one may like things to a greater or lesser degree and dislike other things also to different degrees, preference is scalar. With complicated objects (such as other people) one may like some aspects and dislike others; one may experience a preference both for and against the object, an ambivalence. The degree of one's preference may range from very mild to very strong.

When a person is deeply influenced in his responses by one thing, we may call this influence a bias. The thing for or against which one holds a bias receives a great deal of his attention and so, in responding to stimuli, a person may relate the stimuli to the object of his bias. Thus, his behavior in general can be affected by the bias. One's bias may be for the goodness of mothers or for the integrity of businessmen or the dishonesty of certain salesmen. Experiences which strongly affect one's self-image may develop biases which in turn will affect behavior.

Group decisions Decisions a person makes when acting alone may be different and reveal different values from decisions made by that same person acting for or as a part of a group. For example, a person may be strongly biased toward giving to the poor and toward being lenient and understanding with irrational or deviant behavior. This bias might be the result of his valuing the individual; his self-image might be that of a kind, understanding, and helpful person, especially when dealing with those less advantaged than he. However, when acting as manager for a company a person may be affected by other biases and another self-image. In this setting he may assign greater values to efficiency, proper use of resources, and production of a profit for the owners or shareholders. He may view himself as an efficient manager who respects his responsibility to owners and investors and who works hard at his job, and he may insist that all other employees conform to a similar image for employees. It would be expected that these varied values and self-images would result in quite different behavior when he acted as a manager than when he acted as an individual.

A normally responsible individual who personally respects the values of law and order may participate, as a member of a group, in acts of violence or destruction because he wants to be accepted and belong. His self-image as an individual differs from his self-image as a member of a group.

Being a member of a business organization may allow a person to adopt values different from his own in making decisions concerning organization matters. As a matter of fact, criteria for success, which would involve value standards, may be determined by someone else and communicated to the decision maker. He may have the responsibility of measuring persons or things against the predetermined criteria without having the opportunity to influence the criteria by his own values. With the self-image of a cooperative organization man he may accept organization-determined criteria or criteria specified by his superiors without questioning the values inherent in them.

As mentioned above, in some situations one person or group specifies the success criteria, another identifies critical aspects of various alternatives, and a third person or group decides which available alternative best conforms to the criteria and, therefore, should be chosen for the firm. Note that, in group decisions, the person making the critical decision on criteria for success is not specifying criteria for a decision he, as an indivdual, will make; in fact, the criteria he specifies may not be used by him at all—they may be to help others make an organizational decision. It appears that he is, therefore, quite able to act with substantial freedom from his personal preferences, biases, and value standards. His image of himself as a good manager may enable him to fully adopt those value preferences called for in the specific situation.

These phenomena involved in depersonalizing organizational decisions indicate that decisions made for organizations may be reached more rationally and objectively than personal decisions, which lack the screen of the organization to reduce the effect of values and biases.

INFORMATION AND DECISIONS

In order to make an intelligent decision one must have access to relevant information. This is true whether he is acting for himself or for an organization. And this is where the accountant's function becomes essential for the success of the decision-making process in business.

Functions of Information

Development of criteria for success implies that there is adequate information about desired outcomes. **Choosing among alternatives implies that there is information which will allow comparison between probable outcomes of each alternative and desired outcomes, or criteria.** The availability of this kind of information makes decisions possible; however, information may do more than describe criteria and alternatives. **The presence of certain information, coupled with one's self-image and the drives which motivate him, may serve as the stimulus for making decisions.** Reading good reviews of a new musical group and learning of its appearance on campus next weekend might stimulate a student to reexamine his plans for spending every evening in the library with his term paper. Information that the company's delivery costs are greater than expected may stimulate a manager to seek alternatives to the present delivery equipment and procedures. Information about new and more efficient delivery equipment may stimulate a manager to inquire into its efficiency compared to that of presently used equipment and equipment available from other sources. In decision behavior information can provide both stimulus and comparative description or measure of alternatives.

Information and Data

From the preceding discussion of objectivity in group decisions and the importance of information in decisions, it becomes apparent that information may play a critical role in business operations where so many decisions are made for the business firm (organization) according to firm (group) criteria. This explains the great effort business firms expend to provide information to those given the responsibility for making company decisions. As used in the context of business decisions there is an important distinction between "information" and "data," or "facts." **Information is described as data relevant to a decision. Data, in order to be considered decision information, must bear on some aspect of criteria or alternatives related to that decision.** As seen earlier, this information about criteria or alternatives may stimulate decision action or help in choosing the best among alternative actions, or it may do both of these. Such information (relevant data) for one decision may not be relevant to another decision. One of the major problems in business is determining which information will be needed for decisions and providing that information when it is needed.

Function of Accounting

The great size of business firms and the high speed and extreme complexity of operations have increased the difficulty of specifying the information needed by management. Also, great size and complexity complicate the problems of obtaining that information and providing the appropriate persons with it. Information is often needed on a wide range of subjects: the number of employees and their abilities, the capacity of warehouse storage areas, the number and specifications of production machines, the money required to pay for services and goods, the monetary results of the company's activities, to suggest a few.

Accounting has developed as a partial response to this need; it provides information about financial aspects of the business. It is true that accounting often provides nonfinancial information, and probably should provide more, but the primary service of the accounting function has been the supplying of financial information. This information is provided for the use of all those who make decisions concerning business firms: investors, management, employees, and government.

Specific Decisions

The nature of decisions may be treated in generalizations, but decisions themselves are not general or abstract—each one is specific. **A decision, as a response to stimuli and information, involves a specific choice among specific alternatives.** In business as elsewhere one cannot function by responding that "in general" or "generally" he would choose a type of action—he must make a specific choice among alternatives, based upon specific information under specific circumstances. Investors, business managers, and owners alike must decide in favor of the preferred alternative; these decisions will be the basis of action. The investor, for example, may have to decide

What kind of return on my investment do I want: currently available income, long-term growth in value, or some combination of these?

What rate of return do I desire on my investment? Of possible rates of return, what rate shall I seek?

What degree of risk (of loss) am I willing to bear? Among the investment alternatives available, how much risk am I willing to take in order to increase the possible rate of return?

What degree of liquidity is necessary or desired? Do I want to be able to obtain my capital in cash at any time? If not at any time, then for what period am I willing to have my capital committed and, thus, not available for alternative investments?

What kind of investment will suit my needs? Shall I invest in mortgage bonds or debentures, or in preferred stock or common stock?

What kind of industry will provide the rate of return and degree of risk that I prefer? Should I invest in one of the mining or extractive industries, in manufacturing, in a service industry, in the financial area?

Which company in the chosen industry should I invest in? Which specific company will provide the return and risk I prefer?

Shall I continue my investment in the present company, or will some other company provide a better combination of risk and return on capital?

The typical manager will probably face decisions such as these.

What organization structure should we adopt for the company? Shall we have centralized authority, or decentralized? Shall we provide for "top level" decisions or group decisions? Should all duties be spelled out in job descriptions, or will persons perform better with less prescription?

Which lines of product should the company emphasize? Which products will be demanded by customers? Which, for a long period of time? Which products provide the best margin of profit (excess of selling price over cost)? Which combination of products will provide efficient and economical production?

Are the financial results of management action satisfactory? How profitable is the company? Are any regions or lines of product more profitable than others? Has the company made tne profit we expected it to make? What facets of operations need special attention?

What personnel changes should be made? Whom should we promote to positions of greater responsibility? To whom should we give increases in pay? What kind of person should we hire? Should we ask this person to accept a transfer to other tasks in which he might be more successful? Should we dismiss this person from the employ of the firm?

How shall we perform this assembly operation? Should it be a manual operation, or shall we inquire into automated equipment for this task? What degree of control should we maintain over the quality of work done?

Is our information system functioning well? What information is needed by managers, employees, investors, and others? How frequently and how soon is this information needed? Is the information being provided? Is it provided on time?

Since the term "owner" is usually applied to the investor who takes an active part in the operation of the business, the owner is a combination investor and manager; his decisions would include those in both the preceding lists. His combination of responsibilities might cause him to approach the problems differently, setting different criteria or giving different emphasis to various elements of information. Employees, government agencies, and many others must continuously make decisions concerning specific business firms.

·inancial Information for Decisions

Each person who makes a decision in business should have full information concerning the criteria for success and the various alternatives for attaining the desired success. The decisions of investors and management mentioned above indicate that a wide range of information is needed.

The first investor decision listed above requires information about the investor himself: his money needs for current expenditures, his desire to save on income taxes by deferring the reporting of income until he sells the investment and by reporting long-term capital gains (which are taxed at lower rates than ordinary income). Information on all these is needed in order for the investor to make the first decision. The second decision requires that the investor have information about available rates of return as well as about his personal needs for income. Decisions listed later in the group require information about earnings and dividends in various industries, and about earnings, dividends, and financial strength of specific companies.

The first managerial decision listed requires a good knowledge of human group behavior and of the wide range of organization types or structures adaptable for the company's best performance. Other decisions listed require information about probable customer response to the various products, about costs to produce the products, about efficiency of specific operations and performance of individuals, and about many other facets of the firm. Note that some substantial amount of this information is financial in nature; that is, it is expressed in terms of money. It is the task of accounting to provide this financial and closely related nonfinancial information.

Information for investors The problems of management and investors are generally different; however, management necessarily is interested in the decisions which face investors and in getting investors the necessary information. It is management's responsibility to provide information to all those who have legitimate interests in the firm; one means of doing this is through periodic financial reports, prepared by the accounting department. These financial reports have each been developed into a standard format and content so that basic financial information about the firm will be available consistently.

Standard financial reports Information most commonly needed about a firm falls into three general classes related to the firm's financial status, its profitability, and its sources of funds for current use.

Three specific financial reports contain these different kinds of information. The *balance sheet* reveals a firm's financial status by presenting information about the amount and original sources of funds committed (or tied up) in the firm's assets. The *income statement* reports a firm's profitability through information about revenue, expenses, and the net income resulting from the firm's business activities. Information about the current sources and uses of funds is provided by the *funds statement*.

These three are the standard financial reports normally sent to stockholders, creditors, and others interested in a company's financial affairs. Most of this book is concerned with developing the information for these reports.

Balance sheet This report is composed of two listings: first, a list of the assets, or resources, of the firm; assets are things of value to the firm. This list is paralleled by a list of equities, the sources of the assets. This latter list is often thought of as a list of the claims against the firm, since those who provide assets or funds with which assets are obtained

ABLE BAKER CORPORATION
Balance Sheet
December 31, 1968

ASSETS		EQUITIES	
Cash	$ 10,000	Liabilities:	
Accounts receivable	30,000	Accounts payable	$ 20,000
Merchandise	112,000	Taxes payable	4,000
Equipment	90,000	Mortgage notes payable	130,000
Building	120,000	Total	$154,000
Land	18,000	Shareholders' equity:	
		Paid-in capital	$160,000
		Capital from earnings	66,000
		Total	226,000
Total assets	$380,000	Total equities	$380,000

will normally claim benefits in return. **The balance sheet presents the firm as a grouping of assets in which specified amounts of funds are committed, with the providers of these funds exerting claims of an equal amount against the firm as creditors or stockholders.**

This report presents the financial position of the firm and is often entitled the "statement of financial position." Note that the balance sheet is a static model of the firm; it presents information as of a specific date and, therefore, represents the firm's position *on that date only*. For many decisions it is important to know the firm's total assets or resources and their composition. Also, it is often important to know the sources of the firm's assets because of the different kinds of claims that may be exerted. Those who provide the credit reflected in the liabilities on the balance sheet will claim repayment. Those who have invested in the firm the amount shown as "paid-in capital" normally do not claim repayment but expect to be paid a return on their investment out of the earnings of the business. Continued attention will be given to items on this financial model of the firm in later chapters.

Income statement **This financial report presents information about the results of the company's activities or operations *for a specified period.*** The period of time included is normally one year, although it is not uncommon for income statements to be made for a period of a month or a quarter. The income statement is often entitled the "statement of operations" or the "operating statement." For information about a firm's profitability—"how well" the firm did financially—one looks to the income statement. Company operations are reflected as inflow

ABLE BAKER CORPORATION
Income Statement
For the Year Ended December 31, 1968

Revenue:		
Sale of merchandise and services		$320,000
Expenses:		
Cost of merchandise that was sold	$190,000	
Salaries and wages	56,000	
Utilities	10,000	
Taxes expense	15,000	
Depreciation of building and equipment	9,000	
Other expenses	10,000	
Total expenses		290,000
Net income		$ 30,000

of assets (*revenue*) and consumption of assets (*expenses*). The excess of revenue over expenses is termed *income*, or *net income*. Net income, accumulated through the years, is represented on the balance sheet (see preceding illustration) as "capital from earnings," often referred to as "retained earnings." The net income of $30,000 on this report evidently was added to a net income of $36,000 from prior years to make the total of $66,000 reported on the balance sheet above as capital from earnings.

Funds statement The success of management in providing funds needed by the company to purchase services and goods and to pay claims of creditors is reflected in the "funds statement," often referred to as the "funds flow statement" or as the "statement of source and application of funds." In this report funds are normally understood to be available assets, that is, assets which can be used by management to meet company needs. In a later chapter we shall distinguish between uncommitted company funds (working capital) and other kinds of funds. For the present, an example of fund reporting can be seen in the following funds statement.

ABLE BAKER CORPORATION
Funds Statement
For the Year Ended December 31, 1968

Funds were provided by:		
Sale of services and goods	$320,000	
Less current expenditures for goods sold and operating expenses	275,000	$45,000
Sale of old equipment		12,000
Additional investment by shareholders		20,000
Total funds provided		$77,000
Funds were used for:		
Payment of mortgage note	$ 25,000	
Purchase of additional equipment for cash	30,000	
Total funds used		55,000
Increase in funds from beginning of the year		$22,000

The report reveals the inflow of assets from business operations ($45,000) and from other events. The outflow of funds ($55,000) is deducted from the total inflow to indicate the amount of the increase in funds during the year. This report is a very good indicator of management's success in financing the firm during the year.

These three reports (balance sheet, income statement, and funds statement) contain the standard financial information which normally is provided to shareholders at least annually. The remaining chapters of this book are devoted to developing an understanding of this information, from its origin to its use in making investment and management decisions.

General and specific information models The investors' information needs have been somewhat generalized in developing the financial information reports normally provided. The balance sheet, income statement, and funds statement contain standard information which will suffice for most of the decisions made by investors. Since they provide general information not limited to any specific decision, these reports might be termed "general information models." For some specific decision such as might arise in the course of a merger with another company, information not included in the standard reports might be needed. For this decision special information might be obtained and assembled to form a specific view of the firm; this would be termed a "specific information model." Information may be taken from the general models, analyzed, restructured for special purposes, and thus made into specific models.

With analysis the information contained in the standard reports, or general information models, should serve the information needs of most investors. Should this become untrue the accounting profession must act, changing the models so that they provide the needed information.

QUESTIONS AND EXERCISES

1-A. Define the term *decision*.

1-B. What are the differences between the functional structure and the behavioral structure of a decision?

1-C. Are the functional structure and behavioral structure mutually exclusive in describing a decision?

1-D. What is a group decision? In what sense can group decisions be described as personal decisions? How are they different?

1-E. What is the relationship between information and the three functional stages in a decision?

1-F. How is information related to a decision as human behavior?

1-G. Everyone in business activities must make decisions of some sort. What two groups are identified, however, as the major decisionmakers in business?

1-H. Once an investor has decided on the degree of risk and the rate of return he prefers, he can choose one or more industries that provide acceptable investments. What further decision must he make before investing?

1- I. What kind of financial information about a specific firm does one need to decide whether to invest in its shares?

1- J. What kind of information is reported on the balance sheet? On the income statement?

1-K. What kind of information does the funds statement provide?

PROCEDURAL PROBLEMS

1-1. Mr. McDermot has asked his wife to buy him a jacket to wear on winter trips to his farm. What criteria would he logically set to guide her in making a selection?

1-2. For his course in business finance, John Fahla needs a thorough but concise description of the operations of the bond market on which a business firm might buy bonds, temporarily investing funds unneeded until later in the year. When he goes to the library what criteria will he use to select books for cursory examination? On what criteria will he consider books to check out for detailed study? How will he finally decide which one book to check out?

1-3. Mr. Jones, Mr. Cozmetski, and Mr. Moreno are being considered for promotion to head of their accounting department in the 3-R Corporation. Mr. Hertzfeld, the company's controller, has suggested that the three men serve as a committee to determine what criteria he should use in making the promotion. What problems should he expect them to encounter in attempting to set criteria?

1-4. The executive committee of the company (composed of the president, two senior vice presidents, the treasurer, and the controller) have decided on criteria for investment projects. Each project in which funds will be committed for more than one year should have annual earnings of at least 30 percent of the investment to contribute toward company administrative expenses and net income. A screening committee composed of the controller and two vice presidents finds that it does not agree with this criterion. Might it find it possible to screen projects even though it disagrees with the criterion for project acceptance? Explain.

1-5. Mrs. Evelyn Parks is looking for an investment in the utility industry. Since most utility companies are well financed and financially sound, she looks first to profitability in selecting companies for further attention. What financial report will she use as the primary source for the companies' income? Which report will tell her whether a company has difficulty obtaining enough funds from company operations to pay for operating expenses? Which financial report probably will be of greatest value to her in examining utility companies as potential investments?

CONCEPTUAL PROBLEMS

1-6. John Graham experienced difficulty in getting to his university classes when he and his family moved across town from the campus. Cross-town public transportation is very poor, and John found that he would have to allow two hours to get to class from his new home. Commuting for at least four hours each day will not allow him time for the part-time job at which he has been working to help pay his expenses. The relatively high cost of transportation, $1.25 each way from his home to the campus, will require him to use a substantial amount of his savings since he will not be able to work.

John resolved his problem by buying a two-year-old Chevord which he will drive to the campus each day, taking two other students who will pay $1 each per day. Current operating expenses are expected to be about $40 a month. The Chevord is very economical to operate and seats four people fairly comfortably. It should lose very little each year in market value because it changes very little in style from year to year. This is important in case John's needs change after graduation next year. With the automobile transportation, John can continue to work part-time on campus and will not have to use his savings except for paying a part of the cost of the auto. Also, he concludes that a substantial part of the automobile's cost should be considered still in savings because the car will be useful for many years.

a. What criteria did John Graham apparently use in seeking an alternative to public transportation?
b. What criteria did he apparently use in selecting the particular automobile?
c. What information probably stimulated his search for an alternative to public transportation?
d. What information about specific automobiles did John probably use in selecting the Chevord from available automobiles?

1-7. The office manager received by mail an announcement of the new Nordic duplicator that will reproduce pictures, drawings, and documents in color for approximately three cents per copy. Immediately he asked for information about the cost of using the present Zero duplicating equipment for the past quarter and the number of copies produced. Since this information indicated an average cost of nearly four cents per black and white copy (including the cost of materials at about two cents per copy, rental on the equipment, and an estimate of the cost of clerical time to operate the equipment), the office manager called the Nordic representative to obtain more information and a demonstration of the new equipment.

The demonstration went well; copies were produced quickly and were sharp, clear, and reasonably true to the colors of original documents. The Nordic representative showed a price list on which the cost of materials needed for reproducing in color was 3.25 cents per copy. Monthly rental on the Nordic equipment was 50 percent more than on the old Zero equipment, and the rollers and guides on the equipment required cleaning at the close of each day, using about a half hour of one person's time.

The office manager responded that the total cost was much more than the advertising had led him to believe; copies produced by the old Zero equipment were accurate duplicates of the originals, except that colors were reproduced as shades of grey; and while color copies are nice, they are frills that do not merit the extra expenditure. The Nordic equipment was not ordered.

a. What information stimulated the office manager's request for information about the operating costs of the old Zero equipment?

b. The comparison of what two information items led the office manager to ask for a demonstration of the Nordic duplicator? Were these items of information compared appropriately? At that time did he have full information about the Nordic duplicating equipment?
c. The comparison of what information finally led the office manager to reject the Nordic duplicator?
d. Was color reproduction a criterion for successful operation of office duplicating equipment in the office manager's view?
e. What apparently were the primary criteria for successful office duplicating?

1-8. Based on information in the following income statements, Frank Nordgren decided to invest in shares of Ulto Enterprises.

INCOME STATEMENTS
For the Year Ended June 30, 1971

	Tip-Top Corporation	Ulto Enterprises
Revenue from sales of goods and services	$3,556,200	$970,400
Total operating expenses	2,971,900	643,800
Net income	$ 584,300	$326,600
Net income per share of stock	$ 5.84	$ 3.27
Market price per share of stock	97.25	46.75
Percent of net income to market price of shares	6%	7%

a. Does the total amount of income appear to be the most important criterion for selection?
b. Is net income per share of stock the most critical measure of a successful investment?
c. What influence did the percent of net income to market price per share appear to have on Mr. Nordgren's decision?

2 The Financial Information System

Preview Questions

As you study look for the answers to the following questions:

- **What is a system?**
- **What types of systems are there?**
- **What are the stages in an information system?**
- **How are data checked?**
- **What is feedback?**
- **What are quantitative standards?**
- **What are qualitative standards?**
- **What concepts compose the qualitative standards?**
- **How is the financial information system made up?**
- **What is the relationship between quantitative standards and other elements of the financial information system?**
- **What is the relationship between qualitative standards and other elements of the financial information system?**
- **What are the meanings of *debit* and *credit*?**

Most information needed in business is related to finances. The basic purpose that information serves in business is to describe alternatives in some way, making it possible for one to compare these alternatives with criteria for success. Information may also serve as a part of the stimuli for making a decision. The provision of full, relevant information adds to the possibility of reaching an objective decision; possession of less than full information inclines toward subjectivity in the decision.

Information is not just facts—it is facts related to a decision. Unrelated facts, no matter how interesting, do not qualify in the decision-making context as information; they are simply data. In order to provide information one must acquire facts, relate these facts to one another and to factors in the decision, and transmit the resulting information to the decisionmaker. This process of acquiring, relating, and transmitting implies an organization of actions or things; it is called a system.

Financial information is provided through the accounting system. The accounting system involves many steps: specifying what financial information is needed and from what data such information can be developed, processing those data, and actually producing reports containing the needed information. In order to understand the accounting system for producing financial information, we shall briefly examine systems in general.

TYPES OF SYSTEMS

A system is a group of things which are interrelated in function.

Studying a few specific types of systems will provide a good basis for understanding the financial information system.

Equilibrium System

One such interrelated grouping is the equilibrium system. The elements or forces are so related that an equilibrium is developed, usually within identifiable limits. For example, a building, the air outside the building, the air inside, and the thermostatically controlled heating device can be described as an equilibrium system. When the temperature of the outside air drops, this decrease affects the temperature of the air inside the building, which in turn affects the thermostatic control. At a predetermined temperature, this device activates the heating element to produce and supply heat to the inside of the building. As the temperature rises the thermostat is again affected, this time causing the heating element to reduce the heat produced or to cease producing heat. The inside temperature, still affected by the lower temperature outside, will decrease by the transfer of heat through the walls, roof, windows, and doors (especially through open windows or doors!) until the control device again activates the heating unit to repeat the cycle. The continued interactions maintain an equilibrium within the range of temperatures at which the heating unit is activated and deactivated. Systems of the equilibrium type are used frequently in business and industry to maintain temperatures and pressures. They are common in the operating systems of living organisms.

Flow System

Another interrelated group is the flow system. This type is seen practically everywhere since flow is common to so much activity. For example, the heating device in the equilibrium system described above involves flow of heat and heated air and, therefore, can be called a flow system within the equilibrium system. Included in the flow system would be the fan or blower and the ducts or channels through which the air passes.

Flow systems are common in living organisms—the respiratory system and the circulatory system are examples. Flow systems are common in business, also. An assembly line in a factory is a rather involved flow system, including the movement of all the parts to the assembly locations and the movement of the major component as parts are added to it. **The movement of information in a business firm provides another example of a very involved flow system.**

Input-Output System

When major attention is focused on what is put into a flow system and on what is put out by the system, then the system itself is often referred to as an input-output system. In one type of system the input is specified, for example, crude oil into a refinery or ore into a smelter, the flow manipulation is controlled, and the output is the planned result of the available input and the flow manipulation. In another type the output is specified, and both the input and flow are controlled to produce the specified output.

The financial information system has some aspects of both types of input-output systems. When the system is planned, the output (desired information) is specified by description and quality. Then the sources of data are determined and the flow system developed to manipulate the available data into the desired or specified information as output. At this stage it has the appearance of the second type of system, with output specified and input and flow controlled. Once the system is in operation the input is specified (to conform to the planned flow, manipulation, and specified output), the flow is controlled, and the output is the result of the data available for input and the controlled flow. The information output is controlled in quality, but in quantity it is dependent on what happens in the firm to generate data as input. This is characteristic of the first type of system described above.

ELEMENTS OF AN INFORMATION SYSTEM

Development of an information system involves the following stages:

- Specification of information needed
- Identification of data for information development
- Data processing
  - Recording
  - Transmitting
  - Classifying
  - Storing
  - Summarizing
- Reporting the resulting information.

These stages can be seen in detail in the development of financial information in the accounting system.

Specification of Information Needs

It is important to focus attention on information needed for specific decisions. Information needs must not be confused with present supply or present use of information. Information now used may be, simply, whatever is available, and the information now supplied may not be what is best for the immediate decisions. To determine the information which will be needed one must study all decisions which are likely to be made. Standard financial reports have been structured on the premise that the information they contain is the information needed for most investor decisions. It is expected that the information available may not be adequate for special decisions and that special effort may be necessary to generate, summarize, and report the needed information.

Identification of Data

When information needs have been specified (including quality, quantity, and timing) one looks to data sources to identify those data necessary for the required information. Most data about a business firm concern changes; that is, things that have happened in the firm. These happenings are *transactions* (actions with others) and *actions* (activities within the firm).

Data Processing

In order that they can be captured and used, data are recorded on documents or business papers. Sales slips, deposit tickets, cash register tapes, check stubs or copies, purchase order forms, and receipts given for cash collected are but a few of the hundreds of different business documents on which data are initially recorded.

The data flow, or processing portion of the information system, works from the original data to the information reported for use in making decisions. The stages involved in this flow system are

1. **Recording** of data in business documents. Sometimes data are recorded on business documents and put simultaneously into electronic transmitting, classifying, and storage devices.
2. **Transmitting** or moving of data from locations at which they were first recorded to a central location. This may be done by transferring documents, transferring data in condensed form on punched cards, punched paper tape or magnetic tape, or transferring data electronically by wire or radio with input to the transmitter from cards, paper tape, or magnetic tape.
3. **Classifying** data into predetermined classes. These classes of data are determined by the kinds of information which will be developed from them.
4. **Summarizing** data into totals by classes and groups of classes.
5. **Storing** data by classes preparatory to use of these data in the preparation of financial reports.
6. **Reporting** information in the form of standard financial statements and special reports.

Validity and Accuracy Checks

The validity and accuracy of data are checked periodically in the flow process to assure that data output from the system conforms to the planned output, that it represents in the desired way the changes in the business. Data are valid when no extraneous data have been put into the system. Data are considered accurate when *all* specified data have been put into the system and no inaccuracies have been introduced in data manipulation. When an error is detected, the source of the inaccuracy is determined and correction is made.

An interesting example of the validity check is the use of a cash register with a charge plate attachment. When merchandise is sold to a customer the clerk registers each item, and the price is displayed on the register in large numbers readily visible to the customer. This procedure is dependent on the effort of the clerk in getting valid data recorded, and it also provides for a check of the recording by the customer. Resulting data should include the quantity and price of the items with very few errors. Use of the customer charge plate, containing information about the type of credit extended to the customer as well as correct name and address, prevents errors in billing. There should be no data errors on the plate regarding the customer charging merchandise. Wherever data are put into the system, similar techniques to control validity of information are used.

One type of check for data accuracy is seen in the transferring of data to individual customer records for monthly billing. Sales slips prepared when the sales were first recorded (as in the preceding example) are accumulated and arranged in alphabetical order, and a total is obtained. Entries are then made on the record of each customer for whom there is a charge. The records of these customers will show an increased amount owed to the company. But how can one be sure that no error was made in transferring amounts from the sales slips to customer records or in computing the new amounts owed by the customers?

One procedure will check for errors in both operations. A total is obtained for the new balances in the customer accounts, and the previous balances are subtracted. The resulting amount should be the same as the initial total of the sales slips. If any error has been made these two amounts will not be equal, and an immediate search and correction can set things right.

Summary of Data Processing

In summary, the financial information system (accounting system) includes devices for recording and manipulating data, storing of such data, and procedures for checking their validity and accuracy before they are put into the system and processed. All systems of data processing, whether manual or machine based, provide for these same operations. The devices used may make the operation of systems appear quite different; for example, the accumulation of data on records kept manually may appear to be totally different from the accumulation of similar data on records prepared through the use of an electronic computer. In both cases, however, a well-planned system will include the basic stages or operations of an information system.

Feedback

Information provided as the result of an action and which is useful in controlling the conduct of that action is termed *feedback*. Flow systems of all types, controlled systems, that is, provide feedback as information on which control action is based. In the accuracy check example above, the amount resulting from the subtraction of the old balance total from the new balance total in customer accounts is feedback. This information can be used to decide whether the data are accurately manipulated or some corrective action is needed.

It is interesting to note that the financial information provided as an output from the financial information system serves, among other purposes, as feedback in the overall management system and the investment system. Managers make decisions about company operations, and investors make decisions about buying, selling, or holding investments on the basis of this information. Following these decisions, the firm continues its operations, feeding data about operations into the information system and receiving more output as information for management and investors. Managers can use this information to decide whether their preceding decisions were best and whether company operations should continue as they have been or be changed in some way; investors can use the information to decide whether their original decisions obtained the desired results and, again, whether to buy, sell, or hold investments. In each case, the one who made a decision gets, from the result of that decision, feedback which can help him in making future decisions.

Quantitative Standards for Information

The two quantitative standards for information are that data input be complete: that is, that *all* specified data relative to a specific subject or action be put into the system; and that all manipulation of data be done accurately. Recording, transferring, computing, and reporting should be done without error.

Complete data input Devices and procedures mentioned earlier in this chapter in connection with validity checks as means assuring the validity of data input to the system also assure that all appropriate data are included. For example, the use of a cash register for recording sales, both for cash and on credit, provides an assurance that all sales will be recorded. All money collected from customers for cash sales and all sales slips, including those for sales on credit, must be placed in a drawer of the cash register. The drawer will not open unless the cash register is operated, and operating the cash register records data for the transaction.

Getting complete information about transactions occurring in outlying locations away from supervisory personnel who would insist that full information be reported may be difficult. The persons completing the transactions must be persuaded that full information is important. Many devices and procedures other than the cash register are used to assure the recording of complete information on all transactions.

Accuracy of processing One special procedure for checking the accuracy of data handling (checking the sales slip totals against balances in customers' records) was discussed earlier in this chapter. Throughout the information system these accuracy control procedures, both in manual and more sophisticated computer systems, are performed as a part of the data handling so that one using information developed from the data can be sure of its validity and accuracy.

Qualitative Standards for Information

The qualitative standards relate to the kind or character of information and data. The terms indicate that what is desired is not just any information about a topic, but information of a specific kind.

Example of available data The amount at which a recently acquired delivery truck is to be reported on the balance sheet must be determined by a decision. There are several alternatives, based on the following information:

The list price of the truck was $2,800. The dealer agreed to a lower price of $2,500 and allowed a trade-in credit of $1,100 for an old delivery truck, leaving $1,400 to be paid in cash.

In prior efforts to sell the old truck the best offer was $1,000, indicating an advantage of $100 in obtaining the trade-in value of $1,100.

The old truck was reported on the balance sheet at an amount of $920 just before it was traded. This truck plus the $1,400 cash were given in exchange for the new truck.

After the new truck is used for three months it is not worth as much as when it was purchased.

Because different kinds of financial data are available concerning the trucks, a choice must be made among the data. The criteria for this choice relate to what *kind* of information will be needed. **Standards that specify the kind of information and data needed are qualitative standards.**

In selecting from the data generated by changes occurring within a firm, such as in the above example, the major factor to consider is the kind of information needed to represent the changes. What information will be needed about the purchase of a delivery truck? What information will be needed about the sale of merchandise? What information will be needed to report the combining or merging of one company with another? Answers to these questions should logically be based on the kinds of decisions for which the information will be used. Since information on the standard general financial models (balance sheet, income statement, and funds statement) will be used for many different kinds of decisions, specifying the information needed on these reports becomes even more difficult. Rather than using needs for specific decisions, we use general concepts as standards for specifying information to include in the general information models.

Concepts as qualitative standards Qualitative standards are composed of the concepts of the firm, property, income, and so forth, which are involved in making decisions. These concepts guide the specification of information needed and the selection of data for the system. **Specific concepts act as qualitative standards, giving guidance concerning which of many possible amounts is most useful as information; they provide guidance in selecting data to represent changes occasioned by a transaction; and they guide in determining which factors in a firm can be measured financially.** Concepts such as those in the following list will be examined critically as they are considered in later chapters.

1. *Concept of the firm* indicates the kind of action required for success of the firm—purely financial or a combination of financial and social. This provides a general guide to the kind of information needed to measure success.
2. The *continuity*, or going-concern, concept indicates that the firm

should be treated as if it will continue indefinitely unless there is evidence to the contrary.

3. The *cost*, or *funds committed*, concept indicates that the most meaningful amounts, those that are reported for assets, are the amounts of funds committed or "tied up" in the assets.
4. The *stable-dollar* concept indicates that the dollar is sufficiently stable in value to be used, without adjustment for changes in its purchasing power, in reporting assets, equities, and income.
5. The *periodicity* concept indicates that economic activity of the firm can be identified with specific periods of time and that revenues and expenses can be matched within regular time periods so as to measure income.
6. *Consistency* indicates that when there are acceptable alternative methods of measurement the method selected should be used continuously in order that information for any period will be consistent with that for other periods.
7. *Materiality* indicates that significant effects of transactions and internal actions are to be recorded and reported. Effects which are insignificant may be ignored.
8. *Conservatism* indicates that overly optimistic interpretations should not prevail. When alternative amounts are available, the lesser amounts for assets and income generally are preferred.
9. *Full disclosure* indicates the reporting of all significant information, even if not normally included in the system. Explanations and footnotes to other information may be needed for full disclosure.
10. *Objective evidence* as a concept indicates that each change in amounts is to be based as far as possible on objective, verifiable information. Subjectively determined measurements of changes are not acceptable.

Influences on the application of qualitative standards Getting useful and dependable information to investors is vitally important in developing and maintaining an active and widespread market for company shares, such as exists in the United States and other well-developed countries having capitalistically oriented economies. Once the holding of shares has become widespread, getting useful and dependable information to investors, who may make up a sizeable segment of the population, becomes a matter of social and political significance. Since investors are the greatest users of general financial reports, the information needs of investors must have a strong influence on qualitative standards and their application. Accountants, whose professional responsibility is centered on financial information, reflect their concern through personal performance and professional standards. Many organizations in the United States have influenced the development of standards for information reported to investors: the Financial Executives Institute, American Accounting Association, National Association of Accountants, among others. However, the greatest direct influence on standards for reporting financial information has come from the following:

American Institute of Certified Public Accountants, through many special studies, standards for conducting audits, and the continuing identification and development of "generally accepted accounting principles" for financial reporting.

Securities Exchange Commission, an agency of the federal government, by setting standards for reporting to investors and enforcing those standards.

New York Stock Exchange and other exchanges, in insisting on conformity to standards by the companies whose shares are traded on the exchanges.

In later chapters we will emphasize the kind of information apparently needed for investor decisions and the application of various concepts which act as standards in determining the information reported to investors.

Summary of Data Flow

Data are selected according to some predetermined standards of relevance or quality. These data, in a business firm, concern financial

FLOW CHART—ELEMENTS OF THE ACCOUNTING SYSTEM

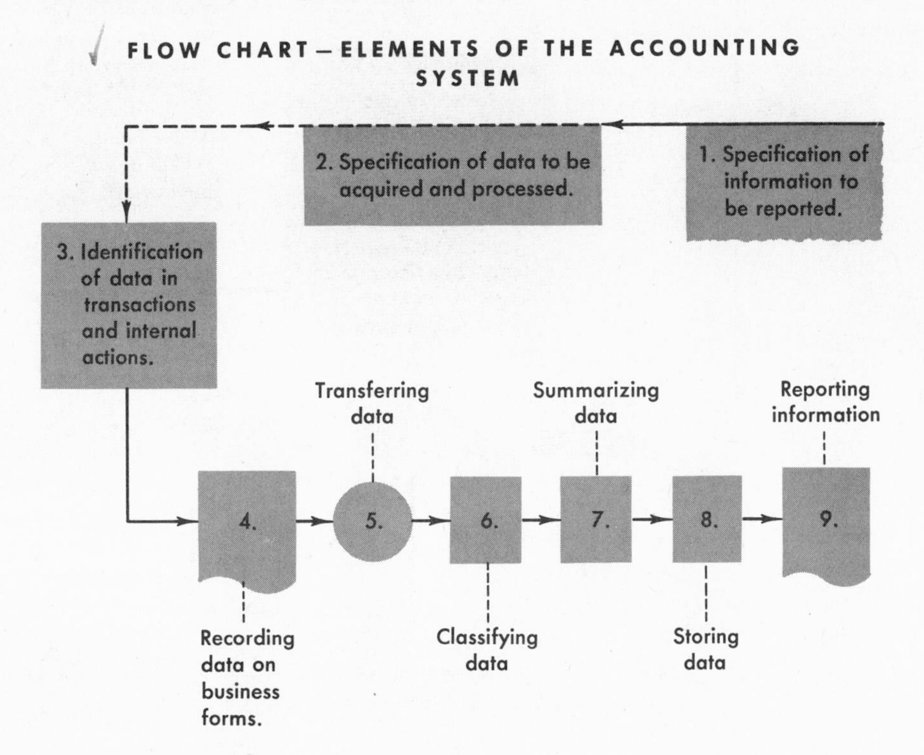

changes occurring through significant financial events, either transactions or actions within the firm. The data are input to the system from business papers, or as a part of preparing the business papers as records of the events. The data are classified, transmitted, summarized and stored. They are related to other data and to factors involved in decisions, and the resulting decision information is the output from the system in the form of financial reports. This is pictured in the flow chart, Elements of the Accounting System.

Qualitative controls are effective in specifying the information to be reported as output from the financial information system and, therefore, the data selected for input to the system. They are effective, also, in classifying data and reporting information. Quantitative controls are effective throughout the system in maintaining the validity and accuracy of the data. The relationship of standards to the other elements of the system is shown in the flow chart below.

QUALITATIVE AND QUANTITATIVE STANDARDS RELATED TO OTHER ELEMENTS OF THE ACCOUNTING SYSTEM

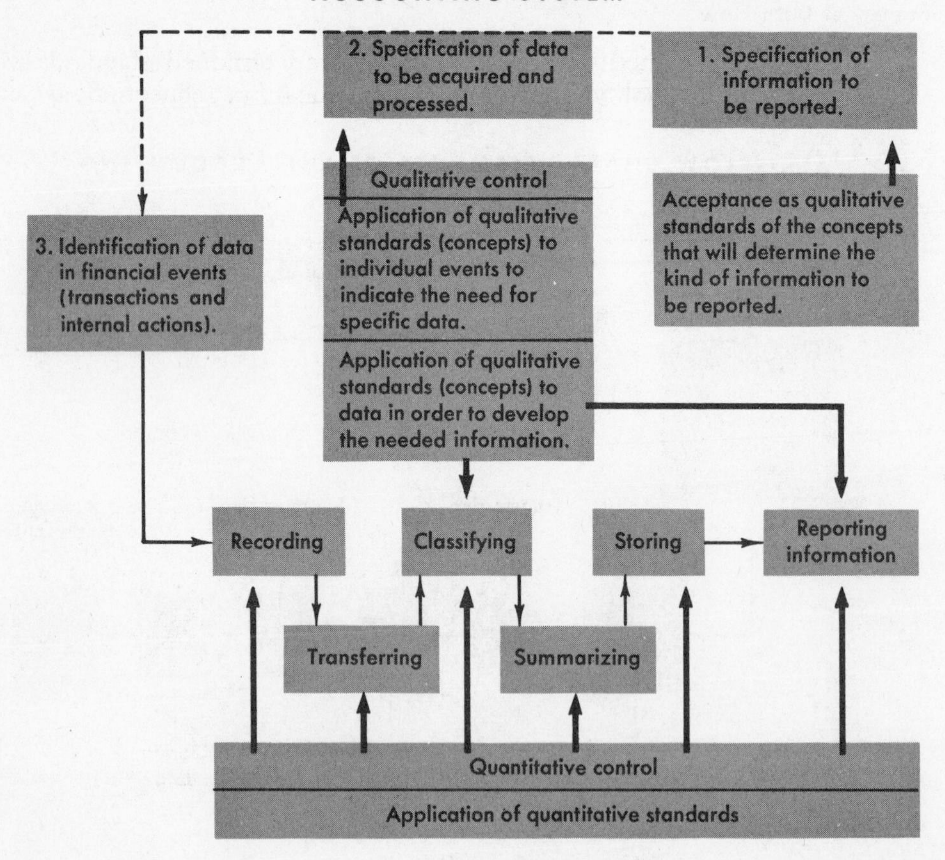

Subsystems in the FIS

The financial information (accounting) system is composed of many subsystems, two of which stand out as unique. As mentioned in the preceding chapter, information normally required by investors concerns two general aspects of the business firm: the assets of the firm, and the sources of assets, or claims against the firm (equities). To emphasize these aspects, the two leading financial reports, the balance sheet and the income statement, contain information structured in two subsystems: assets (resources) and equities (claims). At the first stage of recording, financial data are classified to provide input into the two subsystems in whatever detail is needed. The data are then manipulated within the two subsystems, with certain relationships always prevailing between the two. These unique subsystems can be included in the flow chart of the accounting system as shown below.

The effects of this dual subsystem arrangement for processing financial data will be seen in the identification of data from transactions in chapter 3 and, thereafter, in the recording and summarizing of data in the illustrations. Two special words, directly related to the dual subsystem arrangement of data, will be introduced. *Debit* is used to identify positive inputs into the assets, or resources, subsystem, and *credit* to identify positive inputs into the equities, or claims, subsystem. In an interesting frugality of words, opposite meanings are assigned to debit in the equities subsystem and credit in the assets subsystem. *Debit* identifies negative inputs to the eq-

DUAL SUBSYSTEMS OF THE ACCOUNTING SYSTEM

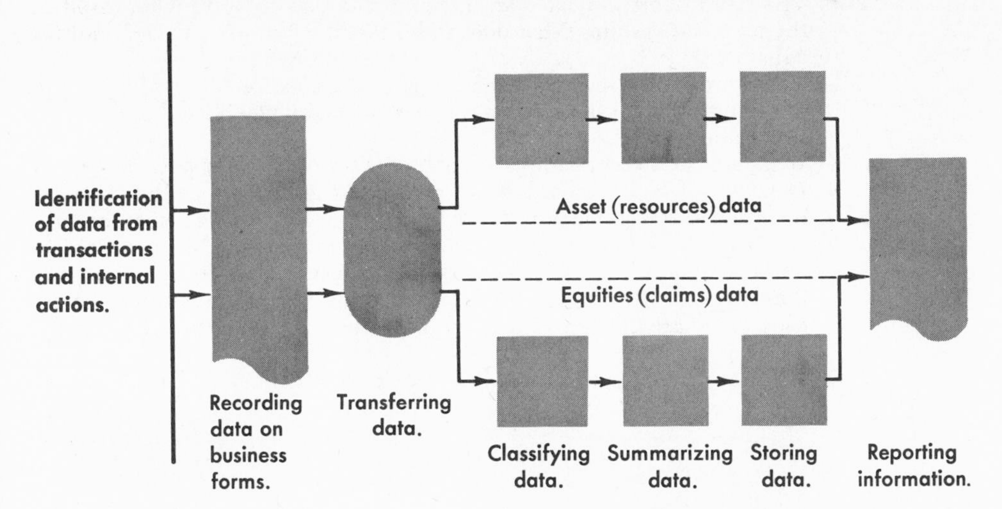

uities subsystem and *credit* negative inputs to the assets subsystem. Interesting and efficient controls provided by the dual subsystem structure also will be seen in later chapters.

QUESTIONS AND EXERCISES

2-A. What term is used to indicate a group of things that are interrelated functionally?

2-B. Give an example of an equilibrium system; of a flow system.

2-C. In some flow systems, emphasis is placed on the input to the system or on its output. What is such a flow system called?

2-D. Quantitative standards are very specific; all specified data should be put into the system, and data manipulation should be done accurately. Qualitative standards are expressed less directly. How are qualitative standards presented?

2-E. There are ten concepts which influence the kind of information reported and, therefore, the kind of data acquired and processed. These concepts serve as qualitative standards in the accounting system. List the ten concepts. (pp 27-28)

2-F. At what points in the accounting system does the application of qualitative standards exercise qualitative control over data and information?

2-G. At what points in the accounting system are the quantitative standards applied through quantitative controls of completeness and accuracy?

2-H. Which comes first in a data system, the specification of the information to be reported or the recording of data?

2-I. Which seems more reasonable, that the steps of transferring, classifying, summarizing, and storing data must always be done strictly in that order, or that these steps may be arranged in the sequence that provides greatest efficiency?

2-J. Data related to assets and equities are processed as different kinds of data in two subsystems of the total accounting system. In which steps of data processing are these two subsystems seen most clearly?

2-K. The word *debit* indicates an increase in a class of data when used in the asset subsystem. What does *debit* mean when used in the equities subsystem? decrease

2-L. The word *credit* indicates an increase in a class of data when used in the equities subsystem. What does *credit* mean when used in the asset subsystem? decrease

2-M. What are the two meanings of each of the words, *debit* and *credit*? (pp. 31-32)

2-N. Data normally are recorded on business documents, but they may be recorded through machines such as cash registers. Data may be processed by writing the data in classes, summarizing, and preparing reports manually. Also, computers may process data by manipulating them according to programmed instructions. Regardless of the method used, what are the steps involved in processing data so that information may be reported?

2-O. What are the standard financial reports that contain information produced by the accounting system?
balance sheet, income statement, funds statement

PROCEDURAL PROBLEMS

2-1. As chairman of the student information committee, Mark Davis has been asked to recommend a system that will provide information representative and descriptive of the student body. What steps should Mark follow in planning the system?

2-2. David Marks, a certified public accountant, has been engaged to plan an accounting system for the Holiday Shops which sell gifts and party supplies. What steps should Mr. Marks follow in planning the accounting system?

2-3. In chapter 1 you learned that the balance sheet is composed of two lists, one of assets and one of equities. Explain what happens to each group of data in an accounting system's data processing stages.

2-4. The accounting system in Kitty Parker's Kindness Loan Company operates as follows: data about completed loans are recorded on loan forms; these forms are transferred from all the branches to the central office; data from the loan forms are classified and stored by writing them on list-type records, one such list for each class of data; the classes of data are summarized each week by totaling the items on each list; financial reports are prepared from the summarized data.

As Miss Parker's loan company grows, the transferring of large numbers of loan forms from the various branches to the central office becomes a burden. The physical handling of the forms to prevent damage or loss becomes a problem. Also, the branch managers find that they need to retain the loan forms for reference in dealing with their loan customers.

Can you suggest a change that would improve the system's sequence of operations? Describe how the system would operate after your changes.

CONCEPTUAL PROBLEMS

2-5. The Student Organization for Tutoring (SOT) provides college students as free tutors for elementary school children who cannot keep up with their classes and whose families cannot afford tutoring service. The greatest need is for tutors in reading, math, spelling, grammar, and basic science. Before acceptance as tutors, college students must express an interest in tutoring and agree to maintain a regular schedule of tutoring sessions with their assigned students. Also, each prospective tutor must be approved by a committee of two teachers after a conference of the teachers and the student. Students are assigned to tutor only those subjects in which they indicate an interest.

The tutoring activities have been so rewarding to past participants that the program is to be enlarged for next semester. SOT's executive committee has permission to obtain from all students during registration the information it needs in order to select, contact, and assign tutors to elementary students at various city schools.

In order to plan its activities, the executive committee needs to know how many students are approved for tutoring and how many approved tutors are available for each subject.

a. What are the criteria for selecting a tutor?
b. What additional criterion is helpful in making specific tutoring assignments?
c. What information does the SOT executive committee need from each college student?
d. How do you suggest that the information be acquired? Orally or written? In what format?
e. Suggest steps in the system to develop the information needed by the executive committee.

2-6. Tim Warro has just paid his university $100 each for the exclusive privilege of operating four food and drink concession stands in the new fieldhouse during the basketball season. His concession agreement with the university includes a provision that he will pay to the university within two weeks after the last home basketball game an additional amount equal to 20 percent of the profit from operating the concession stands. Profit is to be measured by deducting all operating expenses (cost of food and drinks served, ice, other supplies, and wages paid to Tim Warro's assistants) from the amounts collected for sales. No provision is made for Tim's own salary; his only income is to be his 80 percent of the concession profits. The university will provide all preparation and serving equipment (but not supplies) and a cash register at each stand.

Tim is required to maintain adequate records to support the figures he reports to the university. Also, he wants accurate records to determine whether he should purchase the concession rights for the next year.

a. What information will Tim Warro need in order to measure his profit?
b. What data from the concession stands' operations will he need to develop the information?
c. Suggest some basic steps that he might use to collect and process the data.

3 Identifying and Recording Financial Data

Preview Questions

As you study look for the answers to the following questions:

- **What do data represent in terms of the firm?**
- **Where do financial data originate?**
- **How can one specify data needed to indicate changes in the firm?**
- **What general classes of information are needed from the accounting system?**
- **How does one identify the essential data in transactions?**
- **What concepts affect the information and data needed?**
- **What is the first step in operating the financial information system?**
- **What is the next step, and what does it require?**
- **What step follows the identification of needed data?**

Financial data used as inputs to the financial information system represent changes in the firm. If no changes occur, no data inputs are needed; the data already in the system will represent the firm until some financial change occurs. When changes do occur, data must be identified and recorded for input to the system.

SOURCES OF FINANCIAL DATA

Two kinds of events, transactions and actions within the firm, cause changes in the firm and therefore are sources of financial data.

A businessman can recognize clearly his need for information for making decisions about the firm's management and the stockholders' information needs for decisions about investments in the firm's shares. An accounting system may be set up to accumulate and process data for reporting the needed information. However, no information will be forthcoming unless data representing financial changes in the firm are recognized and put into the system. Recognition of essential data generated by significant events (both transactions and actions within the firm) is the crucial first step in the data processing stage of the accounting system. It requires a thorough understanding of all the firm's transactions and operations.

Transactions as Sources of Data

Financial events that occur between the firm and others outside it are known as transactions.

Changes that occur through transactions must be interpreted financially, and the financial data thus specified are recorded for input to the information system.

The receipt of the original investment in the firm is a transaction; it is a financial change from the firm's having no resources invested in it. The receipt of each additional investment is a financial change; each investment transaction is the source of data reflecting the change. Transactions involve many kinds of financial changes: the purchase of land and buildings, payment of liabilities, and receipt of revenues. Analysis of the transactions provides the data to reflect the changes in the information system.

Internal Actions as Source of Data

Once resources have been acquired, the use of those resources by the firm may generate changes which should be reflected in data input to the information system.

The kinds of changes which can occur are numerous; examination of a few will demonstrate how input data are developed from them.

When a cabinet manufacturer buys lumber, it is easy to see that the transaction increases the amount of lumber available for building cabinets and decreases the amount of cash (if payment was made upon delivery). Data for these changes would be input to the system. When 1,000 board feet of this lumber is transferred from the materials storage area into the factory and is shaped and assembled into cabinets, another change has occurred, even though the lumber has not been transferred to anyone. Data reflecting this change should be put into the information system, because it is significant that the firm now has finished cabinets rather than raw lumber. These would be data from an internal action.

Another illustration of an internal action which causes change and, therefore, generates data for the system is seen in insurance. At the time an annual property insurance premium is paid in advance (an asset called prepaid or unexpired insurance), the firm acquires protection from property loss for the next year in exchange for cash. Changes from this transaction would be recorded. The input data from the transaction would reflect the acquisition of prepaid insurance and the disposition of cash. The protection for the future is an asset or resource; it has value which the company can utilize by using the protection, or which can be converted into cash by cancelling the policy and obtaining a refund. In many instances this asset can be transferred by sale if the insured property is sold. The amount of future insurance protection decreases each day until, at the end of a year, the asset is totally dissipated. A change has occurred without an additional transaction because of the continuous action of insurance expiring daily; data are needed as input to reflect the change.

Data representing changes occurring within the firm may be recorded as input at the time the changes occur, or the data may be summarized or computed at the end of a financial period and changes for the whole period recorded with one input of data. The change of lumber into finished cabinets might be recorded on a date within the year; however, the change in insurance protection caused by the expiring of protection with time might be summarized and recorded only at the end of the period.

SPECIFICATION OF INFORMATION AND DATA NEEDED

In an information system, data for individual transactions can be recorded only if someone has specified the kind of data that are to be recorded for each kind of transaction. The specific data needed for each type of transaction depend on the information that is to be provided by the system.

The question of what information is needed about an event turns us back again to the specific decisions that will be based on the information. Financial information from the accounting system will be used mostly to prepare financial models of the firm in the form of financial reports (such as the balance sheet, funds statement, and income statement, illustrated in chapter 1) from which information will be available for analysis. The reports are structured to contain information for a number of different types of decisions; however, emphasis is placed on decisions of the investor. Daily and periodic information for management and information for government agencies must also be included in the needed financial information.

Asset Information

The amount of funds committed to (tied up in) different kinds of assets is needed for a good analysis of the financial stability and liquidity (cash availability) of the firm by investors. Management needs this kind of information for planning and projecting net income, or earnings, of the business, and governmental agencies regularly require it.

The amount sold on credit to each customer and the amount collected from each is needed by management so that bills can be sent to encourage customers to pay the firm. The dates that sales are made is needed for this purpose and to provide information for management decisions about the kinds of collection efforts to use.

The preceding are but a few specific illustrations of information needed about assets; other information about the many different kinds of assets is needed in both summary and detailed form.

Liability Information

The amounts of short-term and long-term liabilities (amounts owed by the firm, or creditors' claims) are needed by investors because these reveal the source of a specific amount of the firm's capital, and they indicate the amount of claims for repayment that the firm must satisfy. Dates of purchasing on credit and credit terms afforded by specific creditors are important to management in assuring that creditors are paid early enough so that all discounts for paying early can be taken, and so that cash will be available to pay others as they become due. These mentioned needs will serve to illustrate some kinds of information needed about liabilities; much additional information is required for management, investor, tax, and other needs.

Owners' Equity Information

This information shows how much capital was invested and how much has been earned by the firm. It is needed only in summary form for most uses. Management needs detailed information about the number of shares owned by each investor; this information is used in assigning weights to votes of shareholders at meetings and in computing the amount of dividends to be paid to each shareholder. The amount of accumulated or retained earnings is one of the factors in management decisions relating to the amount of dividends to declare, and it is of critical importance in some income tax questions. The types of information indicated here are only indicative of the many uses of a great mass of information about shareholders' or owners' equity used by investors, management, and governmental agencies.

Net Income Information

Net income is the net inflow or increase in earned resources of the firm. It is computed as the excess of the gross inflow of earned resources (revenue) over the resources consumed in obtaining that inflow (expenses).

Therefore, data from which net income information is computed are both revenue and expense data. Refer to the income statement in chapter 1 for a review of the information used in deriving net income.

Net income is the most widely used measure of success of business firms. Investors, brokers, and investment analysts use net income as a direct indicator of success for the year. Management, especially central, or top management, knows that its own success in managing is measured to a large extent by the net income of the firm. As a measure of the earnings of the firm for the year, net income is related to total *capital* (financial resources) of the firm and to shareholders' equity to obtain percentages of return on these measures of capital.

Revenue Information

In analyzing the way in which a firm makes a profit, or net income, revenue information is very important to managers and investors. The portion of revenue that was used for various kinds of expenses and the part that remained as net income are computed by comparing each of these items with revenue. The trend of these relationships indicates the progress being made toward efficiency in various phases of the company, or the lack of progress. Revenue information is used by investors in their attempts to predict the future success of the firm.

The "production" of revenue is the responsibility of the sales organization in the firm. The amount of revenue expected for a period is forecast by management, and other operations are geared to the expected level of revenue. Actual revenue resulting from operations is compared with the forecast at frequent intervals to determine whether budgets for various phases of operations must be adjusted, either upward or downward. A complete chapter is devoted later to the measurement and reporting of revenue.

Expense Information

The consuming of assets (resources) by the firm in its operations results directly from management decisions and the efficiency of management and other employees of the firm. Expense information is used by investors to estimate the relative efficiency of the firm and to aid in predicting what the firm will accomplish in the future. The efficiency of operations and, therefore, the success of management are reflected in the increase or decrease of expenses from one period to the next. An understanding of expense information is essential in the study of accounting. A full chapter is devoted to this topic later.

Each item of expense is budgeted, based on the level of activity forecast and an assumed mode of operation and degree of efficiency. Management compares actual consumption of assets (expenses) with the budget at frequent intervals so that changes in operations can be made if actual expenses vary too greatly from the planned expenses.

Management needs detailed information about expenses in each area of the firm's operations. Investors normally need only summary information about expenses. The Internal Revenue Service may require different measures of some items of revenue and expenses than those used by management and investors. Government regulatory agencies may require still differently measured or structured information about expenses.

Summary of Information Needs

It would be impossible to present here a description of all information about the firm needed by the many users of such information. However, when the financial information system is planned for a firm, full information needs must be specified. This detailed statement of needed information guides in specifying the data to be recorded for different kinds of transactions and other events. It guides, also, in classifying those data and in accumulating and summarizing them to produce the needed information.

DATA REQUIRED FOR INFORMATION DEVELOPMENT

Once the full information needs are specified, one can look to the changes occurring in the firm—transactions and internal actions—to specify the data that can be combined to produce the desired information. Data available from each type of event are examined, and those items useful in information development are specified as data to be recorded and input to the accounting system. It should be remembered that recognition of relevant financial data is crucial for the student's understanding of later stages in accounting, as well as for the accountant's operation of the entire financial information system. Examination of useful data from a few types of transactions will indicate the steps involved in this process.

Investment Transaction

This type of transaction occurs when a company receives assets and gives to the investors shares of stock in the company. Useful data that would be recorded for each such transaction are as follows:

1. Amount of each kind of asset received. Such data are used in accumulating information about the dollar amount of each kind of asset on hand.

2. Total amount of capital contributed. These data are used to accumulate information showing the sources of the firm's resources, including amount of resources invested.
3. Name and address of the investor, for sending notices of shareholder meetings, ballots for shareholder voting, information about dividends, financial and operating reports from management, and other communications.
4. Number of shares issued to each investor. These data are accumulated for each investor so that his vote can be weighted properly and so that his dividends can be computed accurately.
5. Date of the transaction, to aid in identifying the transaction and assuring accuracy of recording and accumulating data.

These data about an investment in the firm probably will be recorded on a variety of records, letters, memoranda, etc; some of them will appear on the stub or other record of the stock certificates issued. As we shall see later in this chapter, someone must be able to recognize and identify these data on the records and input the appropriate data into the financial information system. This is one of the accountant's tasks.

Asset Acquisition for Cash

When the firm purchases assets and pays cash for them there are changes in at least two assets, cash and the asset or assets acquired. There are no changes in equities in this kind of transaction. Data needed for information development are

1. Amount of money paid for each class of assets purchased and the total paid out. These data can be used to accumulate the amount of funds committed in each kind of asset acquired as well as the amount of cash on hand.
2. Date of the transaction, to aid in identifying the transaction for later reference.

These data may be on purchase orders, shipping tickets from suppliers, invoices, and check records or copies of checks.

Asset Acquisition on Credit

The purchase of assets on credit creates changes in assets and in liabilities. Data needed from each transaction for development of information include:

1. Price and kind of the assets acquired. This helps in accumulating data about the amount of funds committed in various assets and about lia-

bilities. Price data can be checked against a price list and the order to assure their accuracy.

2. Name and address of the supplier from whom the assets were purchased. Data must be accumulated for total liabilities and, also, for the amount owed each supplier, so that payment can be made correctly and on time. The address is needed for contacting the supplier about adjustments or terms and for sending payment properly.
3. Credit terms of the purchase are important to aid management in paying on time and enabling it to take advantage of any discounts allowed for prompt payment. Also, management can check the terms against the terms agreed upon to assure their correctness.
4. The date of the transaction is needed to determine the due date and period during which discounts may be taken.

These data, as with purchases for cash, may be on purchase orders, shipping tickets from suppliers or receiving reports, and invoices.

Payment to a Creditor

When a payment is made, cash is decreased and the claims of the creditor are reduced. There may be a discount involved for paying early; if so, the creditor's claim is reduced by more than the amount of cash paid out. Data that should be recorded for each such transaction include:

1. Name of the creditor being paid. This makes it possible to change the data indicating the amount owed to this specific creditor.
2. The amount of cash paid. This is needed so that changes in cash may be accumulated and the amount of cash remaining may be reported.
3. The amount of discount allowed, if any, serves to adjust the amount of funds committed in the items purchased from this supplier. A discount indicates that a lesser amount than the original price is paid.
4. The amount of the liability reduction caused by the payment. This may be the amount of the cash paid or it may be more if a discount is taken for early payment.
5. The date of the transaction is used for reference if the data must be reexamined.

Copies of checks or records of checks are the usual documents for recording data about cash payments. Such records should contain all the needed data for this type of transaction.

Other Transactions

The preceding specifications of data needed for certain transactions are provided as examples of the relationship between information needed and data specified for recording transactions. Of course there are many more kinds of transactions. The data to be recorded for each kind are specified by the accountant or manager, or the accountant-manager team which plans the information system. Some of these transactions include paying for personal services in advance, using services after they are paid for, using services before payment (on credit), using materials, performing service for clients for cash, performing services on credit, selling goods for cash, selling goods on credit, and collecting from customers. There are still other transactions that we shall consider as we encounter them in the study of the financial information system.

CONCEPTS AFFECTING INFORMATION AND DATA

The concepts serving as qualitative standards presented in chapter 2 are important in specifying the information needed and the data to be recorded for transactions. Comments on some of the concepts should provide an understanding of their influence.

Cost, or Funds-Committed, Concept

There are various amounts that might be used to represent an asset in the financial information system. For an automobile there is the suggested or "window" price, advertised price, a price with a trade-in, a cash price, a value computed on the basis of service expected from the automobile, and others. **The cost concept indicates that the funds committed in an asset should be the amount reported for that asset.** When assets are bought, the amount reported is the cash price. When assets other than cash are received as investments, the fair value (what they could have been bought for) is interpreted as the best funds measure of the assets invested. This concept will be examined in much greater detail in later chapters dealing specifically with asset reporting.

Continuity, or Going-Concern, Concept

This is the assumption of continuity of the firm—that the firm will continue in operations similar to those of the present long enough for it to obtain the benefit from its assets and to pay to creditors the amounts of their claims against the firm. Without this assumption it would be meaningless to report the funds committed to many assets which have utility only in consumption by the firm. An example of this is letterhead supplies; these can be used only by the firm for which they were printed, having practically no value if offered for sale. Such supplies normally are reported at their cost to the firm, based on the transaction in which they were obtained, on the assumption that the firm will continue in business and use the supplies. The continuity assumption often is termed the *going-concern* concept. Without making the assumption one could not support the interpretation of many supply items as assets.

Periodicity Concept

This is the concept that it is meaningful to identify financial changes with specific periods of time and to report financial information at regular periodic intervals. Most firms report annually, with some of these providing interim reports quarterly. Business operations are conducted on a continuous basis; operations do not come to a stop at the end of each year or quarter. However, in order that information about the operations of a firm may be compared to prior operations of the same firm and to operations of other firms, it has been helpful to accept the proposition that operations can be broken into time segments and that information will be reported for uniform time segments or fiscal periods. The effect of this concept is seen in the allocation of insurance premiums over the periods of time that insurance protection is in force. The portion of the premium applicable to the protection afforded during a fiscal period (expiring during that period) is reported as a change for the period. The amount of the premium applicable to future periods is continued as an asset, with changes for future expiration to be reported in future periods.

Materiality Concept

This concept relates to the relative importance of items of data. If an amount is large enough to affect one's judgment of the financial strength or operating success of a firm, it is material. Financial changes involving the amount must be analyzed carefully and data representing them properly classified. Generally accepted accounting principles would be followed in reporting a material financial amount. If an amount would not affect one's opinion of the firm, the amount is not material, and it is not essential that generally accepted accounting principles be followed in reporting it. This concept places on the accountant the burden of exercising insight and judgment in determining which amounts may be reported according to management's desires or instructions and which must be reported according to accepted standards, even if these standards should be contrary to expressed interpretations of the firm's managers.

Other Concepts

Other concepts listed in chapter 2 influence the interpretation of transactions and actions. The choice of data to represent or measure financial changes and the classification of these data are guided and structured by such broad concepts as one's image of the firm and by such specific concepts as funds committed in (or cost of) assets. Concepts of revenue, expenses, and net income will be added in later chapters.

IDENTIFICATION OF DATA FROM RECORDS

In order for an accountant to identify data for transactions and input those data to the processing part of the system, he must be acquainted with the various business forms on which data are recorded.

Records of Transaction Data

Data for transactions are recorded on business forms or documents of some type. Sales on credit are recorded on sales tickets or sales invoices similar to those in Figures 3-1 and 3-2. These forms are pictured because they are so commonly used and because they contain data about the kind of transaction that occurs most frequently in many firms: a sale.

The receipt of cash as an investment is recorded in a letter acknowledging receipt of the money or on a receipt form. Data for the receipt of cash for cash sales may be recorded on cash register tapes or on copies of cash sales tickets given to customers. Data for cash collections from credit customers are recorded on copies of receipt forms given to customers, on special billing forms that the customers return to the firm with their payments, or on memoranda or notation forms for customer checks received without either of the other forms.

Purchases of merchandise, supplies, or equipment will be recorded on several documents: a copy of the purchase order on which the firm ordered the goods; a packing slip or a receiving report, giving evidence that the goods were received; and an invoice from the supplier, indicating the amount and price of the goods with a total that the supplier expects to receive for the shipment. Purchase orders and invoices are very common business forms; they are illustrated in Figures 3-3 and 3-4.

Figure 3-1

SALES TICKET

No. 09417 Date *Dec. 13, 19--*

ABC COMPANY
Sales Ticket

Sold to: *James P. Brown*

Address: *1440 Avenue D*

Greenville, Ind.

Credit clearance *1B* Salesperson *T.C.C.*

Catalog No.	Description	Quantity	Price	Amount
A4176	*Flange, 3/4"*	*7*	*1.10*	*7.70*
AA4177	*Brace, 6"*	*7*	*.80*	*5.60*
D1011	*Packing, Size C*	*1*	*2.60*	*2.60*
	Sales Tax			*.32*
	Total			*16.22*

Items listed above received in good condition.

Customer
Signature *J. P. Brown*

Other actions and transactions are recorded on employee time tickets and payroll records, copies of checks or check stubs, deposit tickets, cash register tapes, and other forms. The important point at this stage in the study of the financial information system is to know that data for each transaction are recorded and that specific forms have been developed for recording data for the different kinds of transactions.

Identification of Data from Transaction Records

After transaction data are recorded on business forms or documents, someone with a thorough knowledge of the accounting system must

Figure 3-2

SALES INVOICE

No. 125034 Date *Dec. 13, 19--*

Invoice
ABC COMPANY

To: *James P. Brown* Terms: *2/10, n/60*

1440 Avenue D Shipment: *Railway express Collect*

Greenville, Ind.

Quantity	Catalog No.	Description	Back Ordered	Quan. Shipped	Price	Amount
10	*A4176*	*Flange, 3/4"*	*3*	*7*	*1.10*	*7.70*
7	*AA4177*	*Brace, 6"*		*7*	*.80*	*5.60*
1	*D1011*	*Packing, Size C*		*1*	*2.60*	*2.60*
		Sales Tax				*.32*
		Total				*16.22*

identify and classify the data for input into the financial information system. Both good performance by the accountant and management's understanding of the accountant's task are vital to efficient operation of the financial information system and the business firm. In the remaining chapters we will emphasize identification, classification, and processing of data for the three financial statements: the balance sheet, income statement, and funds statement. Other data will be given only passing note.

From the data flow illustrated in chapter 2, it is evident that changes involved in a transaction may affect either or both of the subsystems (assets and equities) which constitute the processing part of the financial information system. From the transaction one must identify changes in either the firm's assets or equities, or in both of these. This requires a thorough knowledge of the various types of transactions and of the business forms on which data for them are recorded. Reviewing a few kinds of transactions for which data were specified earlier in the chapter may be helpful in describing the identification of data.

Figure 3-3
PURCHASE ORDER

Purchase Order
CITY SUPPLIERS
909 Oval Street
The Heights, Conn.

No. 36093

Date: *Mar. 8*, 19--

To: *Central Wholesalers*
123 Center Street
Central City, Conn.

Terms: *2/10, n/30*

Shipping Instructions: *Deliver*

Quantity	Catalog No.	Description	Price	Amount
3 doz.	*S403*	*Case, attaché, brown leather*	*$ 60.00*	*$180.00*
2 ea.	*S811*	*Cabinet, folding display*	*274.00*	*548.00*

Investment transaction The changes that occur are an increase in cash or other asset received by the firm as an investment, and an increase in paid-in capital. These are classifications of information on the balance sheet; data in the transaction are recognized as affecting these classifications. The effect (increase or decrease) on the classifications, the amount of each, and the date are the data one needs to identify for an investment transaction.

Asset acquisition for cash The decrease in cash and the corresponding increase in the asset or assets received are the basic data needed from this type of transaction. The amount of change in each asset and the date complete the basic data needed.

Asset acquisition on credit From the purchase order, packing slip or receiving report, and invoice, the accountant should identify the supplier who

Figure 3-4
INVOICE

Invoice
CENTRAL WHOLESALERS
123 Center Avenue
Central City, Conn.

No. C6102

To: *City Suppliers*
909 Oval Street
The Heights, Conn.

Date: *March 14, 19--*
Shipping Instructions: *Our truck*

Terms: *2/10, n/30*

Quantity	Description	Catalog No.	Back Ordered	Shipped	Price	Amount
3 doz.	*Cases, attaché, brown*	*S403*		*3 doz.*	*60.00*	*180.00*
	leather					
2 ea.	*Cabinets, display,*	*S811*		*2 ea.*	*274.00*	*548.00*
	folding					
	Total					*728.00*

provided the goods on credit, the kind or kinds of assets acquired and total price of each kind, the total owed the creditor, the date, and the credit terms. The most critical data are the kinds and amounts of asset increases and the amount of liability increase; these are used in classifying financial data for input to the data processing stage of the system.

Payment to creditor The accountant should be able to identify from copies of checks or records of checks written the amount of decrease in creditor claims (liabilities), the decrease in cash, and any discount deducted for early payment. These data are input to the system as changes in the different classes of data. The name of the individual creditor who was paid must be identified so that the data indicating the amount of his claim can be changed.

Other transactions The same basic process is followed for all transactions. One determines which classes of information are affected by the transaction; he identifies these classes and the amount by which each is affected. Data for all sorts of revenue earning, asset consumption (expense), receipt and payment of cash, and other transactions can be identified in this same fashion from the business documents on which the data are recorded.

SUMMARY

In the planning stages of a financial information system, the information that will be needed from the system must be specified. From this, the data to be input to the system from various transactions can be specified. The first step in operating the system is the recording of the specified information for each transaction. Someone must then identify the data on the various business forms for input to each subsystem and segment of the overall accounting system; a knowledge of the accounting system is needed here. The next stage involves classification of data, which is emphasized in chapter 4.

QUESTIONS AND EXERCISES

3-A. The accounting system handles great masses of data. What do these data indicate in relation to the firm?

3-B. What two significant kinds of events cause changes in the firm and, therefore, provide data for the accounting system?

3-C. Which of the following events are transactions?
  a. Received $10,000 invested in the firm.
  b. Purchased and received $200 worth of office supplies.
  c. Used $150 worth of the supplies in the office.
  d. Paid insurance premiums for a year in advance.

3-D. Which of the following events are internal actions?
  a. Purchased and received $200 worth of advertising supplies.
  b. Used $120 worth of the advertising supplies.
  c. Paid insurance premiums for three years in advance.
  d. One year of the insurance coverage expired.
  e. Material issued from the warehouse was used in building shelves for the sales area.

3-E. In planning a financial information system, what serves as the basis for specifying the data to be recorded for each type of transaction?

3-F. What are the major classes of information reported on the balance sheet? On the income statement?

3-G. Define the following terms:
Asset
Liability
Owners' equity
Revenue
Expenses
Net income

3-H. The funds-committed or cost concept serves as a qualitative standard in defining the data reported for assets. Explain.

3-I. Using the funds committed to represent assets, which of the following amounts would be recorded for a delivery truck just purchased for cash?
a. The vehicle's list price or window price.
b. The price agreed to before considering a discount for paying cash.
c. The actual amount of cash paid, after discount, for the truck.

3-J. The continuity concept compels one to interpret data as though the firm would indefinitely continue essentially unchanged unless there is contrary evidence. What effect does this have on the data reported for special assets such as letterhead supplies?

3-K. One of two documents is normally used to record a sale. What are these documents?

3-L. Three documents, two prepared by the buyer and one prepared by the seller, contain data about a credit purchase. What are the documents?

PROCEDURAL PROBLEMS

3-1. For each of the following transactions indicate the kind of *assets* affected and the amount of the increase or decrease.
a. Borrowing $1,000 from the bank, giving a ninety-day, 8 percent note payable to the bank.
b. Performing service for a customer and billing him for $500.
c. Purchasing merchandise for $300 on thirty-day credit.
d. Collecting $300 from the customer in (b) above.
e. Paying $200 for an initial stock of office supplies.

3-2. Provide the financial data indicated for each transaction.
a. Receiving $10,000 cash as investment in the firm:
Kind of asset increased and amount
Amount of increase in invested capital
b. Paying $600 for office equipment:
Kind of asset increased and amount
Kind of asset decreased and amount
c. Purchasing shop equipment, giving a sixty-day note for $900:
Kind of asset increased and amount
Kind of liability increased and amount
d. Paying $450 cash on the note given in (c) above:
Kind of liability decreased and amount
Kind of asset decreased and amount

3-3. For each transaction below, indicate the kind of asset, liability, revenue, or expense affected, and the amount.

a. Paying $400 for supplies.
b. Performing service and billing the customer for $250.
c. Using $100 worth of supplies in performing service in (b).
d. Collecting $150 from the customer in (b).
e. Completing the performance of service for a customer and receiving $400 payment immediately.
f. Paying $300 for labor used in performance of service in (b) and (e).
g. Receiving a bill for delivery of supplies to the work site in (b); the bill is for $10 and is payable at the end of the month.

3-4. On what business documents will one find the following recorded?
a. Sale on credit.
b. Sale for cash.
c. Purchase on credit.
d. Collection from credit customer.
e. Payment to creditor.

3-5. Which of the qualitative control concepts relates to each of the following?
a. The idea that the firm will operate long enough to consume its resources and pay its liabilities.
b. The idea that very small amounts may not be worth the use of a great deal of time to analyze and to contest, but that large amounts should be treated carefully.
c. The idea of measuring and reporting financial changes at regular, periodic intervals.

CONCEPTUAL PROBLEMS

3-6. The Acme Service Company is replanning its financial information system. From the following list of system activities, indicate which ones fall within the planning stage and which ones occur in the system's operation.
a. Writing financial reports.
b. Deciding exactly what kind of information is desired on standard financial reports and on special reports.
c. Recording data on sales tickets.
d. Specifying the data that will be needed from various types of transactions.
e. Identifying data already recorded on documents such as checks, sales invoices, and purchase orders.
f. Classifying data according to the items affected by the event.
g. Storing data for later use.
h. Summarizing data preparatory to writing financial reports.

3-7. Mayton's Cash Grocery has decided to sell on credit to customers with approved credit. What additional information now will be reported on the firms's balance sheet and income statement? What data from the credit sales will be needed to develop the information?

3-8. Sales invoices for the Porter Company were planned when no discounts were offered for paying cash. Now the Porter Company offers customers who have normal thirty-day credit a discount of 1 percent for paying within ten days from the date of the sale. It offers customers who have sixty-day credit terms a discount of 2 percent for paying within ten days. Occasionally a special discount of 1 percent for paying within fifteen days is offered.

What changes do the Porter Company accountants need to make in sales tickets so that data will be properly recorded?

4 The Use of Accounts in Data Processing and Control

Preview Questions

As you study look for the answers to the following questions:

- **What is the classifying of data?**
- **What is an account?**
- **How is the debit-credit notation used?**
- **How are data for each transaction classified?**
- **What is the balance of an account?**
- **What is the trial balance?**

In planning a system to provide financial information, these are the first three steps the accountant normally takes:

1. Determine which decisions will be made by the users of the information,
2. Specify which information will be needed to match the criteria for success in the decisions, and
3. Specify the data which are to be collected and organized into the needed information.

In the third step the data are specified in detail; later, data will be classified and then stored and summarized by classes.

USE OF ACCOUNTS

Classifying data is determining their effect on specific items of information reported on financial statements. The record of each data classification is called an *account*.

Each account is a record of positive and negative inputs affecting a specific classification of data, for example: cash, accounts receivable by the firm, building, equipment, accounts payable by the firm, or invested capital. A group of accounts is called a *ledger*. For ease in working and demonstrating, the two-column account often is presented in an abbreviated "T" form (as in Figure 4-2) with positive inputs (increases) on one side and negative inputs (decreases) on the other side.

Accounts used with manual procedures (not utilizing machines) for handling data in the financial information, or accounting, system have been developed over hundreds of years into generally standard formats. A manual model of the system and each of its parts will be used throughout this book as the primary basis for studying the system. It is important, as each part of the system is studied, that its performance is understood in each data-keeping method: in the manual system, the unit record (punched card), and the stored program (computer) systems which we will discuss in this chapter.

Debit and Credit Notation

The significance of these words was touched on briefly in a preceding chapter. Debit refers to a positive input into any account in the subsystem of asset accounts; credit refers to a positive input into any account in the subsystem of equity accounts. These terms have opposite meanings when used with the opposite subsystems: debit refers to a negative input (decrease) in any equity account, while credit refers to a negative input (decrease) in any asset account. Each word, therefore, is given a dual meaning:

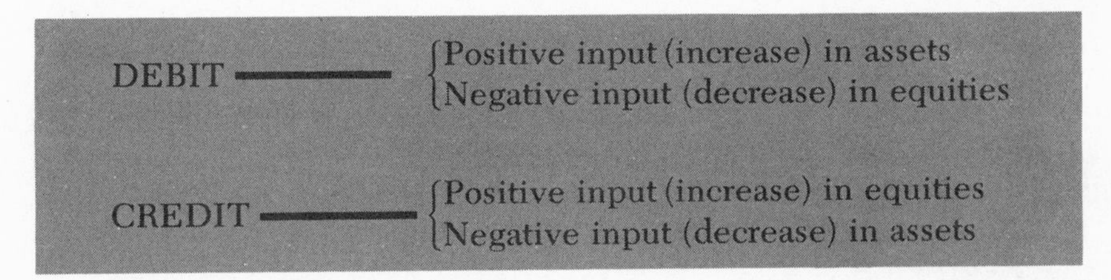

This usage of the words debit and credit has no significance outside the financial information system. Within the system it has great value, especially when coupled with the conventional procedure in the manual system of placing debits on the left side of an account and credits on the right side. When the use of debit and credit in accounts has been demonstrated we shall look more closely at the specific good which comes from the word usage and the left- and right-hand locations.

Use of the debit-credit notation can be demonstrated by applying it to data from transactions. If the firm receives $10,000 as an investment after issuing shares of stock to the investors, there is an increase of $10,000 in the data classification "Cash," and an equal increase in the claims, or equities, of shareholders. Cash is an asset and, therefore, the data classification for cash is in the asset subsystem; an increase in an asset account is placed on the debit, or left-hand side, as illustrated in this T-account:

Cash

Debit (+)	Credit (−)
10,000	

The equities of shareholders derived from their investing in the firm are shown in the data classification for invested capital in the equities subsystem with the title "Capital Stock." An increase in this classification of data is shown as a credit, on the right side of the following T-account:

Capital Stock

Debit (−)	Credit (+)
	10,000

Transaction Data in Asset and Equity Accounts

Asset and equity accounts contain data accumulated for each of the items on the balance sheet, which was illustrated in chapter 1. A more complete illustration is provided in Figure 4-1 as a reminder of the kinds of accounts included in the asset and equities subsystems.

Figure 4-1

ACME GLASS COMPANY
Balance Sheet
December 31, 1971

ASSETS			EQUITIES		
Current assets:			Current liabilities:		
Cash		$ 3,110	Accounts payable	$17,271	
Accounts receivable		16,088	Notes payable	11,000	
Notes receivable		8,771	Salaries payable	2,122	
Merchandise		37,404	Taxes payable	1,721	
Supplies		5,962	Total current liabilities		$ 32,114
Total current assets		$ 71,335	Long-term liabilities:		
Plant assets:			Notes payable (5 years to maturity date)		35,000
Equipment	$32,339		Stockholders' equity:		
Building	45,000		Capital stock	$80,000	
Land	20,000		Retained earnings	21,560	
Total plant assets		97,339	Total stockholders' equity		101,560
Total assets		$168,674	Total equities		$168,674

The grouping of asset and liability items into current assets, plant assets, current liabilities, and long-term liabilities is included in Figure 4-1 only to make the balance sheet realistic. These groupings are not important in learning to classify and record data in accounts. Their significance will become evident later as we study the reporting of financial information.

The classifying of data and the use of the debit-credit notation in inputting those data into individual accounts within the asset and equity subsystems are illustrated in the following transactions and the T-accounts in Figure 4-2.

May 1 The firm received $5,000 cash as an investment and issued shares of stock.
The $5,000 amount should be classified as an increase in the asset "cash" and in the invested capital "capital stock." The increase in cash is classified further as a debit to the Cash account and the increase in capital stock is classified as a credit to the Capital Stock account. Refer to the entries dated May 1 in these two accounts in Figure 4-2.

2 The firm paid $200 for supplies to be used in the office.
The $200 should be classified as an increase in the asset "supplies" and a decrease in the asset "cash." The increase in supplies is classified further as a debit to the Supplies account, and the decrease in cash is classified as a credit to the Cash account. Refer to the entries dated May 2 in these accounts in Figure 4-2.

4 Office equipment is purchased for $900 on credit (to be paid at the end of the month).
The $900 is classified as an increase in the asset "office equipment" and as an increase in the equity of creditors, "accounts payable." The increase in office equipment is a debit to that account, and the increase in accounts payable is a credit to that account. Refer to the accounts in Figure 4-2.

11 Additional office equipment was purchased for $1,200, with $400 paid in cash and the remaining $800 to be paid by the end of the month.
The asset "office equipment" is increased by $1,200; the asset "cash" is decreased by $400; and the equity of creditors, "accounts payable," is increased by $800. The increase in office equipment is a debit to that account; the decrease in cash is a credit to that account; and the increase in accounts payable is a credit to the Accounts Payable account.

30 The firm paid the $900 owed for office equipment purchased on May 4.
This $900 is a decrease in accounts payable and a decrease in cash. The decrease in accounts payable is input as a debit, since Accounts Payable is a classification within equities; the decrease in cash is input as a credit, since Cash is a classification within assets.

Figure 4-2

TRANSACTION DATA IN ASSETS AND EQUITY ACCOUNTS

Accounts in the **ASSET SUBSYSTEM**

Cash

Debit (+)		Credit (−)	
(May 1)	5,000	(May 2)	200
		(May 11)	400
		(May 30)	900

Office Supplies

Debit (+)		Credit (−)	
(May 2)	200		

Office Equipment

Debit (+)		Credit (−)	
(May 4)	900		
(May 11)	1,200		

Accounts in the **EQUITIES SUBSYSTEM**

Accounts Payable

Debit (−)		Credit (+)	
(May 30)	900	(May 4)	900
		(May 11)	800

Capital Stock

Debit (−)		Credit (+)	
		(May 1)	5,000

System Steps Involved in Using Accounts

Processing data in accounts involves three of the general steps in processing data into information. First, data are classified as to which accounts are affected and how the accounts are affected. Next the data are entered, or input, into the accounts and stored there, with each item now associated with other data affecting the same account. Following these steps of classification and storage, the data are summarized for use in reports. Summarizing the data involves finding the excess of positive inputs over negative inputs in each account. In the Cash account in Figure 4-2 the only positive input (debit in this asset account) is $5,000; the negative inputs (credits in the Cash account) total $1,500. The excess of positive inputs over negative inputs (debits over credits) is $3,500; this amount is called the balance of the Cash account.

The Office Supplies account has only one positive input in it, so the debit balance of this account is $200.

The Office Equipment account has two positive inputs (debits) and no credits in it. Therefore, the balance of this account is the total of the debits, or a debit balance of $2,100.

In the Accounts Payable account there are two positive inputs (credits, since this account is in the equities subsystem) and one negative input (debit). The balance of the account is the total of the credits, $1,700, minus the debit of $900, or $800 as a credit balance.

There is only one input in the Capital Stock account. This is positive input of $5,000 (a credit) and, therefore, the account has a credit balance of $5,000.

The Trial Balance

The summarizing process of computing each account's balance provides data showing the result of all changes for the period. The summary data, or account balances, can be reported in the convenient form called a trial balance:

TRIAL BALANCE
May 31, 1970

	Debit	Credit
Cash	$3,500	
Office supplies	200	
Office equipment	2,100	
Accounts payable		$ 800
Capital stock		5,000
	$5,800	$5,800

The very interesting result that debit balances equal credit balances provides accounting personnel with information for a decision concerning control over processing data. If the total of debit balances were not the same as the total of credit balances, one would know that some error such as the following had occurred:

An item of data from a transaction had been classified incorrectly as to its effect, and therefore as to whether it was a debit or credit in an account, or

An amount had been input into an account incorrectly. For example, if the original $5,000 in the Cash account had been erroneously input as $5,500, the debit balance of the Cash account would have been $500 more, or $4,000, and the total of the debit balances would have been

$6,300. The inequality between this amount and the $5,800 total of credit balances would have indicated that an error had occurred and should be found and corrected, or

A computational error had been made, or some input had been overlooked in summarizing, or

The balance of some account had been listed incorrectly on the trial balance.

This checking for equality of debit and credit amounts is an important quantitative control in the financial information system.

The trial balance shown above is orderly and arranged as a rather formal report. As one might surmise, this listing of debit and credit balances is often done on an adding machine without indicating the account titles. A variation is to enter all balances of one kind (debit or credit) in the adding machine as positive amounts and to enter the other balances as negative amounts; a total of all amounts should then be zero. Any amount other than zero would indicate a lack of equality and signal that an error should be corrected. This convenient method of providing feedback information about the accuracy of data in the system is possible because of the debit-credit notation used in classifying and storing data.

Revenue and Expense Accounts

Certain changes occurring in assets and equities during a period are occasioned by "business operations" of that period. Data from these changes are needed to provide information about the firm's profitability. The changes in equities, or claims, of investors resulting from operations are classified as revenues or expenses. Revenues are earned inflows of assets; the source of the assets is recorded by positive inputs to special shareholder equity accounts. Expenses are the consumption of assets; they are recorded as negative inputs to special shareholder equity accounts.

In Figure 1-1 (chapter 1) it was indicated that the shareholders' equity information is reported as paid-in capital and capital from earnings. Data which will make up this latter category of information are classified in detailed revenue and expense accounts so that the detailed data can be used to prepare the income statement (Figures 1-2 and 4-3); in other words, the revenue and expense accounts make up a secondary subsystem within the equities subsystem of data. Revenue and expense accounts contain data accumulated for each item on the income statement, which was illustrated in chapter 1. A more detailed income statement is shown in Figure 4-3 as a reminder of the accounts that are used to accumulate data for this report.

Figure 4-3

ACME GLASS COMPANY
Income Statement
For the Year Ended December 31, 1971

Revenue:		
Service revenue		$96,615
Expenses:		
Salaries and wages	$37,420	
Supplies used	3,116	
Rent expense	9,600	
Utilities	2,797	
Advertising	6,983	
Depreciation	4,410	
Miscellaneous expense	1,201	
Total expenses		65,527
Net income		$31,088

The use of revenue and expense accounts is illustrated in the following transactions and the accounts in Figure 4-4:

June 1 The firm received $1,000 cash upon completion of a specified service for a customer.
The $1,000 is classified as an increase in cash (debit to the Cash account) and as an increase in capital from earnings. This increase is recorded in a revenue account to provide data for the income statement; it is classified as an increase in capital from earnings and is credited to the Service Revenue account. See Figure 4-4.

9 After completing a service for a customer, the firm sent an invoice for $1,300 with the agreement that the customer would pay $800 within the month of June and the remaining $500 within the month of July.
The $1,300 is classified as an increase in assets (accounts receivable) and in capital from earnings (service revenue). The increase in accounts receivable is debited to that account, and the increase in service revenue is credited to the Service Revenue account. See Figure 4-4.

11 The firm paid $600 for labor used on the above job which was completed and collected for on June 1.
The $600 is a decrease in assets (cash) and is credited to the Cash account. It is a decrease in capital from earnings (offsetting the increase of June 1) and is debited to the Wages Expense account.

18 The accounting office received issue slips from the supplies storeroom indicating that $120 worth of supplies were used on the two jobs completed on June 1 and June 9.

Figure 4-4

Accounts in the

ASSET SUBSYSTEM

Cash

Debit			Credit
(6-1 Bal.)	3,500	(June 11)	600
(June 1)	1,000	(June 27)	700
(June 30)	800		

Accounts Receivable

Debit			Credit
(June 9)	1,300	(June 30)	800

Office Supplies

Debit			Credit
(6-1 Bal.)	200	(June 18)	120

Office Equipment

Debit			Credit
(6-1 Bal.)	2,100		

Accounts in the

EQUITIES SUBSYSTEM

Accounts Payable

Debit			Credit
		(6-1 Bal.)	800

Capital Stock

Debit			Credit
		(6-1 Bal.)	5,000

Retained Earnings

Debit			Credit

Service Revenue

Debit			Credit
		(June 1)	1,000
		(June 9)	1,300

Supplies Expense

Debit			Credit
(June 18)	120		

Wages Expense

Debit			Credit
(June 11)	600		
(June 27)	700		

This $120 is a decrease in assets (office supplies) and a decrease in capital from earnings (supplies expense). The decrease in assets is shown as a credit in the Office Supplies account, and the decrease in capital from earnings is shown as a debit in the Supplies Expense account.

27 The firm paid $700 labor for the job completed on June 9.
As for the June 11 payment, this is a decrease in the asset "cash" and a decrease in capital from earnings, classified as wages expense. The $700 is credited to the Cash account and debited to the Wages Expense account.

30 Received $800 cash from the customer for whom a job was completed on June 9. The check was accompanied by a memorandum from the customer asking that it be "applied on my account."
This $800 is an increase (debit) to Cash and a decrease (credit) to Accounts Receivable. It does not affect capital from earnings nor, of course, the Service Revenue account—that change was recorded on June 9.

Transaction Data in Revenue and Expense Accounts

When the data in the accounts shown in Figure 4-4 are summarized (balances in asset and equity accounts are brought over from the transactions recorded in Figure 4-2), they can be presented in a trial balance as of June 30 as follows:

TRIAL BALANCE
June 30, 1970

	Debit	Credit
Cash	$4,000	
Accounts receivable	500	
Office supplies	80	
Office equipment	2,100	
Accounts payable		$ 800
Capital stock		5,000
Service revenue		2,300
Wages expense	1,300	
Supplies expense	120	
	$8,100	$8,100

Data in the revenue and expense accounts represent changes which will be summarized further and entered in the record of capital from earnings. Revenues are increases in capital from earnings and are, therefore, credits. Expenses are decreases in capital from earnings and, since decreases in all classes of data in the equities subsystem are debits, expenses are entered as debits.

FORM OF ACCOUNTS

Manual Account Forms

Accounts which one might see in a manual system are of two general forms. The form from which the T-account is derived is illustrated in Figure 4-5. When one eliminates from the two-column account all lines except the topmost horizontal line and the central vertical line, he has the skeleton or T-account form. In this form, debits are entered on the left side and credits on the right. The form illustrated is for Accounts Receivable; therefore, the debits are positive inputs to the account and the credits are negative inputs. When such an account form is used for an account in the equities subsystem (Accounts Payable or Capital Stock, for example) positive inputs are on the credit side and negative inputs are debits. Note that the form provides for date and other data to identify the input to the account.

Figure 4-5

TWO-COLUMN ACCOUNT FORM

Accounts Receivable

Date		Explanation		Debit	Date		Explanation		Credit
June	9			1300 00	June	30			800 00
July	7			1100 00					

Figure 4-6

BALANCE-COLUMN ACCOUNT FORM

Accounts Receivable

Date		Explanation	Debit	Credit	Balance
June	9		1300 00		1300 00
	30			800 00	500 00
July	7		1100 00		1600 00

The other account form in general use is the three-column, or balance-column, form. The major difference between this form and the T-account form is that both the debit and credit columns, along with a balance column, are on the right portion of the account; each input is written on a separate line, and the balance of the account is computed and entered after each input entry. This form is illustrated in Figure 4-6.

Accounts on Punched Cards

When punched cards are used in the processing of financial data through the classifying, summarizing, and storing steps, the process is begun in the same manner as in a manual system. Data from transactions are classified as to their effects on classes established for assets and equities. Then, through use of a key-punch machine, a card is punched with these data in a coded pattern so that the data can be read by other machines. Usually a card is punched with all items of numerical data, including the account affected, the kind of transaction, the date, an indication of whether the numerical data are positive or negative input, and, of course, the amount. A card with such data punched in it is illustrated in Figure 4-7. Accounts are identified by numbers instead of names in this process. Data cards for a day's transactions are arranged in numerical order of account numbers on a high-speed "sorter." If management wants a daily report, these cards can be run through a "tabulator" or "accounting machine" to print out the data in a predetermined format.

The deck of cards for any day's transactions, arranged in numerical order of the accounts affected, can be combined with other cards for those accounts by running all the cards together through another machine, known as the "collator." This machine merges the two decks of cards by account number. In this state the cards are available for further processing with cards from later transactions, or for printing a list of individual cards by account number or totals of cards by account number.

One can see that punching data into the cards, sorting the resulting cards by account number, and merging them with cards of prior days' transactions accomplishes basically the same steps of classifying and storing as does the manual system. When the cards are run through the tabulator to print out a summary by account number, the summarizing step is accomplished very much as it is in the manual process. Specific procedures with punched cards will be discussed with their equivalent manual processes in later chapters.

Figure 4-7
DATA IN THE PUNCHED CARD

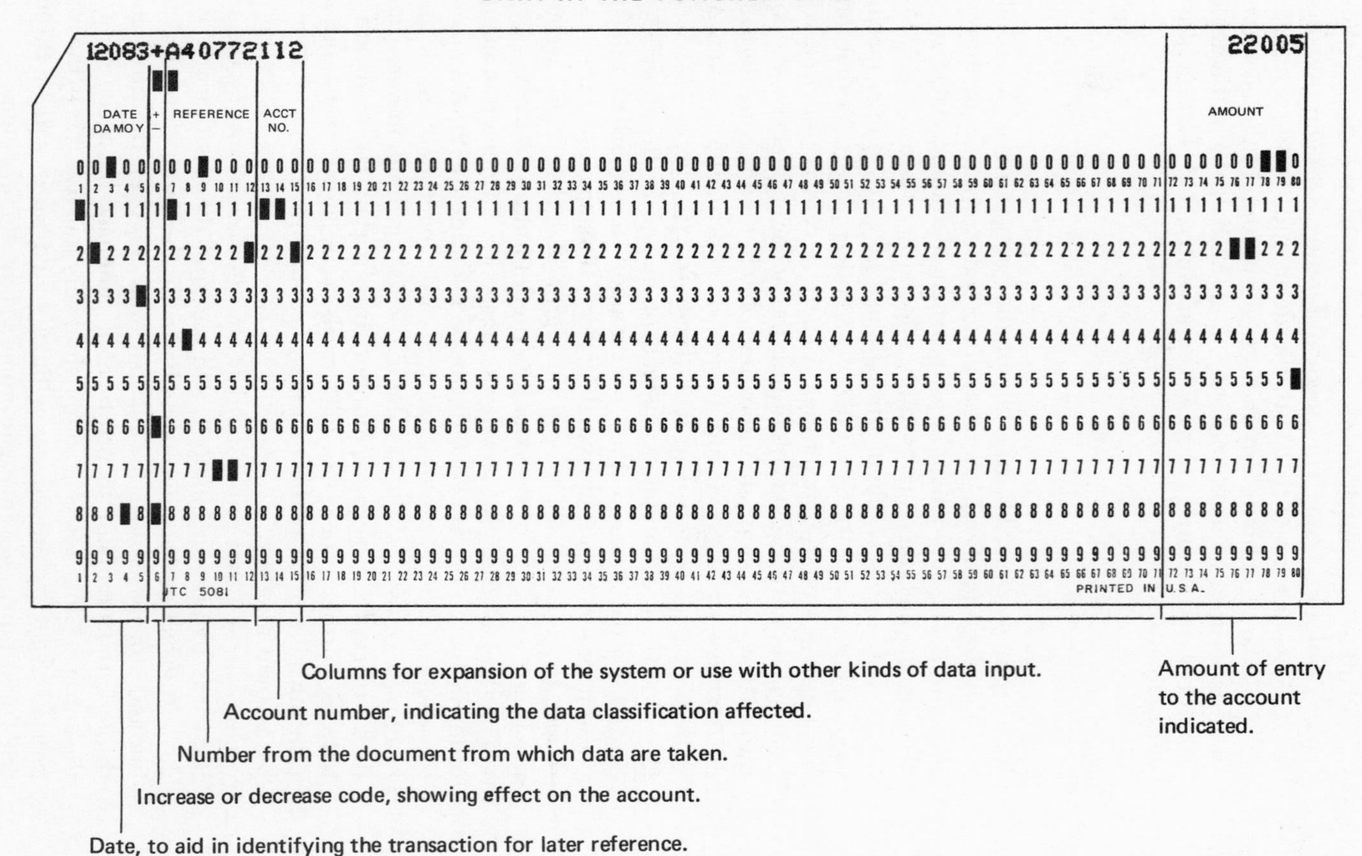

Accounts on Magnetic Tapes and Discs

When stored program electronic processors (computers) are used to increase the speed of processing data, it is important that data be fed into the processing operation at great speed. Since there is a physical limit in the movement of punched cards which keeps their input speed at an almost infinitesimal fraction of the input speed of magnetic tape it is common to transfer data from the originally punched cards to magnetic impulses on a special plastic tape. This tape, in turn, feeds data into the computer at a speed more comparable to the computer's operating speed.

When magnetic tapes or discs are used for data storage, data about individual accounts in the asset and equities subsystems are stored in preassigned areas of each tape or disc. These data can then be read at great speed to be collated with other data or summarized and printed in report form. The computer operates according to instructions called a "program"; the program data are fed into the computer and stored in a special instruction or program area before the inputting of data to be processed. Impulses in the stored program guide the computer in taking the proper steps to process the input data. The processing steps, as in other data processing methods, are classifying, storing, and summarizing data to prepare it for printing in some report format.

QUESTIONS AND EXERCISES

4-A. What are accounts? What function do they perform? What form or appearance may they take? What is a ledger?

4-B. In referring to the subsystem of asset accounts, what meaning does the word *debit* have? In this subsystem of accounts, what is the meaning of *credit?*

4-C. In the subsystem of equity accounts, what is the meaning of *debit?* Of *credit?*

4-D. Combine the thoughts in questions 4-B and 4-C to give a full statement of the meaning of *debit* and *credit.*

4-E. Analyze the following events and enter the appropriate amounts in the "+" and "–" sides of the accounts indicated. Letter each amount to identify it.

a. Received $9,900 from the issue of shares of stock in the company.
b. Paid $1,200 for equipment.
c. Purchased additional equipment for $3,000, paying $800 cash and signing a note payable in ninety days for $2,200.

Asset accounts to be used: Cash, Equipment.
Equity accounts to be used: Notes Payable, Capital Stock.

4-F. Analyze the following events and enter data representing them in the debit and credit sides of the accounts indicated. Identify each amount with the letter of the event it represents.

a. Received $8,000 from the issue of stock shares in the company.
b. Paid $700 cash for equipment.
c. Borrowed $2,000 from the bank and signed a note payable in three months.
d. Paid employees $900 wages for services performed.
e. Received $1,600 revenue from a customer for services completed.
f. Employees provided an additional $200 of service, and the company agreed to pay them when that job is finished or at the end of the month.

Asset accounts: Cash, Equipment.
Equity accounts: Notes Payable, Wages Payable, Capital Stock, Service Revenue, Wages Expense.

Prepare a trial balance from the balances of the accounts.

4-G. For the following events, tell whether the account named in parentheses is debited or credited, and why.

a. Purchased equipment for cash (Equipment).
b. Purchased supplies on credit (Accounts Payable).
c. Paid the creditor for the supplies purchased in (b) (Accounts Payable).
d. Sold excess equipment for cash. (Equipment).
e. Used some of the supplies (Supplies Expense).

4-H. Describe a transaction that will result in the following (one transaction for each lettered item).

a. A debit to an asset and a credit to an owners' equity.
b. A debit to an asset and a credit to a liability.
c. A debit to an asset and a credit to an asset.
d. A debit to a liability and a credit to an asset.

4- I. What kind of balance (debit or credit) does each of the following accounts normally have?

a. Cash
b. Accounts Receivable
c. Equipment
d. Capital Stock
e. Accounts Payable
f. Notes Payable
g. Service Revenue
h. Salaries Expense
i. Notes Receivable

PROCEDURAL PROBLEMS

4-1. The Willis Bros. organized their business January 1, 1969. Record the corporation's transactions in T-accounts for Cash, Repair Supplies, Office Supplies, Truck, Equipment, Accounts Payable, and Capital Stock. Prepare a trial balance at the end of the month.

Jan. 1 Issued capital stock for $10,000.
2 Purchased equipment for $3,000 on account.
10 Purchased $400 worth of office supplies and $700 worth of repair supplies for cash.
22 Purchased a truck to be used in the business; paid $2,000 cash and agreed to pay $2,000 more at the end of the year.
31 Paid $600 owed for the equipment.

4-2. The Rhine Company was organized on July 1. Record its transactions in T-accounts for Cash, Cleaning Supplies, Furniture, Building, Accounts Payable, and Capital Stock. Prepare a balance sheet as of July 31.

July 1 Issued capital stock for $10,000 cash.
4 Purchased furniture on account for $2,000.
10 Made a cash payment of $1,000 owed on the furniture.
15 Purchased cleaning supplies worth $400, paying $100 cash with the balance on account.
22 Issued $12,000 in capital stock in exchange for a building.
30 Paid $200 owed for cleaning supplies.

4-3. The following transactions are for the Ace Novelty Company:

Aug. 1 Capital stock was issued for $75,000.
4 Land was purchased for $10,000 and a building for $30,000; the company paid $6,000 cash and assumed a mortgage note payable for $34,000.
10 Office equipment was purchased for $4,000 on account.
11 Paid $200 cash for office supplies.
17 The company made a cash payment of $2,000 on the office equipment account and $4,000 on the mortgage note.
30 The company issued $30,000 additional capital stock in payment of the land and building mortgage note.

Record the transactions in T-accounts and prepare a trial balance as of August 31, 1969.

4-4. The Scott Furniture Company was organized May 1. Record the following transactions in T-accounts. Prepare a trial balance as of May 31.

May 1 $20,000 of capital stock was issued for cash.
1 Manufacturing equipment was purchased on account for $6,000.
4 Office equipment (price $800) and office supplies (price $300) were purchased for cash.
12 Paid $4,000 on the amount owed for the manufacturing equipment.
18 Borrowed $6,000 from the bank and gave a note payable.
25 Purchased a factory building for $8,000 cash.
31 Repaid $1,000 of the amount borrowed from the bank.

4-5. The R. J. Blake Company had the following transactions during June:

June 1 Received $20,000 for capital stock issued.
1 Paid $600 for rent for the month.
1 Leased a truck for $400 a month. Payment will be made at the end of each month.
4 Purchased office furniture on account for $1,400 and paid $200 cash for office supplies.
6 Billed Tommy's Market $700 for services performed.
11 Paid $120 cash for insurance for the month.
14 Collected $300 from Morgan Electric Supply for work completed.
16 Paid $300 cash for cleaning supplies.
22 Completed additional work for Tommy's Market and submitted a bill for $400.
27 Collected $600 from Tommy's Market on account.
30 Examined the supplies on hand and determined that $60 worth of office supplies and $130 worth of cleaning supplies had been used during the month.
30 Paid the $400 truck rental.
30 Paid salaries of $700.

Record the transactions in T-accounts and prepare a trial balance.

4-6. The Johnson Equipment Repair Company had the following transactions in February:

Feb. 3 Received $20,000 for capital stock.
6 Purchased repair parts for $1,400.
6 Mr. Johnson completed repair work and billed the customer $120.
9 The company paid $30 to rent a special tool required to complete a job.
10 Mailed a customer a statement for $200 for work completed.
16 Paid $200 rent for the shop.
17 Received $100 on account.
19 Completed emergency repairs for a client and received $800 cash.
23 Paid $40 for cleaning supplies which were used immediately.
28 Determined that parts costing $200 had been used to make repairs during the month.

Record the transactions in T-accounts and prepare a trial balance.

4-7. The Dyna-Flow Corporation had the following transactions during September. Record the transactions in T-accounts and take a trial balance.

Sept. 1 Issued capital stock for $20,000.
2 Paid $600 rent for the office.

Sept. 4 Borrowed $10,000 from the local bank to purchase equipment. Gave the bank a note payable.
7 Purchased equipment for $20,000 cash.
8 Completed service contract for Jackson Bros. and billed them $3,500.
10 $600 office supplies purchased on account.
14 Collected $4,000 cash fee from Lane, Inc. for services completed.
15 Paid salaries of $800.
21 Purchased furniture and fixtures on account, $1,100.
24 Billed Dubrey Co. $7,000 for work performed.
29 Paid $700 on account, $500 for furniture and $200 for supplies.
30 Collected $6,000 from Dubrey Co. on account.
30 Examined office supplies and determined that $300 worth of supplies had been used during this month.
30 Repaid bank $1,050, $1,000 on the note and $50 interest for the month.
30 Paid $800 salaries.

4-8. The Morgan Toy Company was organized May 1. Record its May transactions in T-accounts and prepare a trial balance as of May 31.

May 1 Issued capital stock for $50,000.
1 Purchased newspaper advertising for $400.
1 The company purchased on account toys for resale costing $12,000. Toys purchased for resale are charged to the Merchandise Inventory account.
2 Paid store rent for the month, $600.
3 The company sold toys for $3,500 on account; the toys sold cost $2,500. (The company removes the cost of toys sold from the Inventory account and charges it to the expense account, Cost of Goods Sold, as sales are made.)
6 Purchased $600 of office supplies on account.
8 Made a credit sale of $4,000; these toys had cost $3,000.
14 Collected $1,500 cash on account.
15 Paid salaries of $1,500.
22 Paid miscellaneous expense of $30.
31 Examined office supplies on hand and determined that supplies costing $200 had been used during the month.
31 Paid salaries of $1,500.
31 Received a bill from the city for utilities for May of $300. The bill was paid June 3.

4-9. Presented below is a trial balance of Clyde J. Key, Inc., prepared as of February 1, 1971.

a. Enter these balances into general ledger accounts, and record the transactions that occur during February. Note that you may require additional ledger accounts to record these transactions.

b. Prepare a February 28, 1971, trial balance.

CLYDE J. KEY, INC.
Trial Balance
February 1, 1971

	Debit	Credit
Cash	$ 18,000	
Accounts receivable	9,000	
Office supplies	800	
Merchandise inventory	9,000	
Building	25,000	
Land	40,000	
Accounts payable		$ 3,500
Salary payable		4,000
Mortgage payable		18,000
Capital stock		60,000
Sales revenue		83,400
Cost of goods sold	62,700	
Salary expense	4,000	
Insurance expense	400	
	$168,900	$168,900

Feb. 2 Made a credit sale of $4,000. The merchandise sold had cost $2,800.
3 Paid the salary due for January.
6 Purchased merchandise on account for $14,000.
9 Purchased a delivery truck for $9,000 cash.
11 Made a cash sale of $900. Cost of merchandise sold was $700.
11 We exchanged $20,000 of our land for an additional building, valued at $20,000.
14 One of our customers converted his $4,000 account with us for a 6 percent interest, sixty-day note.
15 Received an advertising bill for $700.
17 Made a credit sale of $9,000. Merchandise sold had cost $7,200.
18 Collected $2,000 on account.
21 Paid the advertising bill received on February 15.
21 Made a $1,400 cash purchase of merchandise.
24 Made a $1,000 payment on our mortgage with the bank.
25 Received a $400 bill for our February insurance.
28 Made an $11,000 credit sale of merchandise that had cost $8,500.

Feb. 28 February salaries to be paid on March 3 are $6,000.
28 Office supplies used during the month cost $200.
28 Received $25 as interest income on our note receivable.

4-10. On November 1, 1971, Sam Kent organized a corporation, Vend-Matic Candy Company, by transferring to the corporation $4,000 of his personal cash in exchange for shares of stock. On November 4 he purchased for the corporation from Sanders Machine Company ten coin-operated vending machines for $800 cash each. He also rented six machines for $40 each per month, to be paid the first day of the following month. To pay for the machines and provide operating capital the company borrowed $12,000 from First National Bank, giving a two-year note payable.

The company purchased on account candy costing $7,000 to stock the machines. The company also purchased a used truck for $900 to be used by Billy Williams, a company employee, who was paid $400 a month to stock the machines and collect the money. Fuel expense for the month was $40, paid in cash.

Total candy sales for the month were $7,000, with the cost of the candy sold being $5,400.

On November 28 the company paid the first $500 installment on the mortgage along with a $10 interest payment. On November 30 the company paid Billy Williams and also paid Mr. Kent $500 for serving as president of the company.

a. Establish T-accounts for Cash, Candy Inventory, Machines, Truck, Machine Rental Payable, Mortgage Payable, Capital Stock, Sales Revenue, Cost of Goods Sold, Salary Expense, Fuel Expense, Interest Expense, and Machinery Rental Expense, and record the company's transactions for the month.
b. Prepare a trial balance for the company as of November 30, 1971.

4-11. On March 1, Shaw Corporation had the following account balances. Establish T-accounts with these beginning balances, record the March transactions, and prepare a March 31, 1971, trial balance.

March 3 Collected $3,000 on account.
7 Paid the rent payable.
8 Performed services for $6,000 cash.
11 Purchased additional office furniture for $2,000 on account.
11 Received a bill for March insurance of $400.
15 Recorded and paid salary expense for March 1–March 15 of $700.
19 Paid $800 on account payable.
23 Billed a client $4,000 for services completed.
25 Made a $1,050 cash payment ($1,000 was paid on the mortgage, and $50 was paid as interest for March).
29 Determined that cleaning supplies which cost $75 had been used during the month.
31 Paid the March rent of $1,000.
31 Paid March salaries of $2,000.

SHAW CORPORATION

Trial Balance

March 1, 1971

	Debit	Credit
Cash	$ 22,000	
Accounts receivable	41,000	
Office supplies	4,300	
Cleaning supplies	300	
Office furniture	16,500	
Automotive equipment	24,030	
Accounts payable		$ 19,800
Rent payable		1,200
Mortgage payable		30,000
Capital stock		20,000
Service revenue		68,200
Rent expense	2,400	
Interest expense	1,950	
Salary expense	22,000	
Cleaning supplies expense	420	
Office supplies expense	900	
Insurance expense	3,400	
	$139,200	$139,200

4-12. Presented below are a set of general ledger accounts of Lincoln Manufacturing Company in which are recorded transactions for the month of August. Related amounts are indicated by letters. Examine the entries in the ledger accounts and prepare an explanation or description of each transaction.

Cash

(a)	10,000	(e)	120
(h)	2,000	(j)	825
(i)	1,500	(k)	1,200
		(l)	500

Accounts Payable

(l)	500	(b)	6,000
		(f)	11,000
		(g)	400

Accounts Receivable

(d)	14,000	(i)	1,500

Note Payable

(j)	800	(c)	40,000

Repair Parts

(f)	11,000	(m)	1,400

Delivery Equipment

(b)	6,000		

Factory Building

(c)	40,000		

Land

(a)	20,000		

Insurance Expense

(g)	400		

Interest Expense

(j)	25		

Salary Expense

(k)	1,200		

Repair Parts Expense

(m)	1,400		

Capital Stock

		(a)	30,000

Service Revenue

		(d)	14,000
		(h)	2,000

Advertising Expense

(e)	120		

CONCEPTUAL PROBLEMS

4-13. Peter Bandy has just organized a new firm called Bandy Office Services. He wants an accounting system that will provide information from which an income statement, a balance sheet, and a retained earnings statement similar to the following can be prepared.

BANDY OFFICE SERVICES
Income Statement
For the Year Ended November 30, 19--

Revenue:		
Service revenue		$x,xxx.xx
Miscellaneous revenue		xxx.xx
Total revenue		$x,xxx.xx
Expenses:		
Salaries	$x,xxx.xx	
Supplies	xxx.xx	
Taxes	xxx.xx	
Rent	xxx.xx	
Utilities	xx.xx	
Telephone	xx.xx	
Miscellaneous expenses	xx.xx	
Total expenses		x,xxx.xx
Net income		$x,xxx.xx

BANDY OFFICE SERVICES
Balance Sheet
November 30, 19--

ASSETS		EQUITIES		
Cash	$ xxx.xx	Liabilities:		
Accounts receivable	x,xxx.xx	Accounts payable		$ xxx.xx
Supplies	xxx.xx	Taxes payable		xx.xx
Equipment	x,xxx.xx	Notes payable		xxx.xx
Other assets	xx.xx	Total		$x,xxx.xx
		Owners' Equity:		
		Capital stock	$x,xxx.xx	
		Retained earnings	xxx.xx	
		Total		x,xxx.xx
Total assets	$x,xxx.xx	Total equities		$x,xxx.xx

BANDY OFFICE SERVICES
Statement of Retained Earnings
For the Year Ended November 30, 19--

Retained earnings at beginning of year	$ xxx.xx
Add net income	xxx.xx
	x,xxx.xx
Deduct dividends declared during the year	xxx.xx
Retained earnings at November 30	$ xxx.xx

a. Prepare a list of accounts that will be needed in the Bandy Office Services accounting system (financial information system).
b. What changes in the accounts would be needed to provide separate information about revenues from typing, filing, and other office work instead of simply one amount for service revenue?

4-14. The L & L Company provides a variety of yard and lawn services, classified as mowing and trimming, planting and bedding, landscaping, tree trimming and removal, and miscellaneous work. The company operates in three different locations in a major city.
a. How many revenue accounts are needed if the amount of revenue is to be reported for each class of service?
b. How many revenue accounts are needed if the amount of revenue for each class of service is to be reported separately for each of the three business locations?
c. What titles do you suggest for the revenue accounts used to classify and accumulate revenue data separately for the classes of service at the different locations?

4-15. The L & L Company consumes different kinds of resources in providing service to customers and, therefore, reports different kinds of expenses. Expense accounts used by the company are Administrative Salaries, Rent, Utilities, Labor, Supplies, Depreciation of Equipment, Taxes, Transportation, and Miscellaneous Expenses.
a. If data for the first three expense classifications are to be kept just for the central office, and if data for all other expenses are to be accumulated for the central office and also separately for each of the three business locations, how many expense accounts will be needed? Prepare a list of these accounts.
b. If, in addition to the classification of expense data indicated above, data for both Labor and Supplies are to be classified separately for each type of service performed (mowing and trimming, planting and bedding, landscaping, tree trimming and removal, and miscellaneous work) at each business location, how will the previous list of accounts be changed?

4-16. Buck Strong's Automotive Repair Service classifies revenue data in accounts for Towing Revenue, Road Service, and Shop Repairs. On sales tickets the firm's personnel have been writing such items as "Service on 1971 Buick," and "General Service to Auto." In order that data may be available for recording in the revenue accounts, what suggestions would you make as to better preparation of the sales slips?

5 The Use of Journals in Data Processing and Control

Preview Questions

As you study look for the answers to the following questions:

- **What is a journal?**
- **What are the functions of the journal?**
- **How are entries made in a two-column journal?**
- **What is done with data from a journal?**
- **What are special journals?**
- **How are frequent transactions handled in a journal?**
- **What is the purpose of subsidiary ledgers, and how are they used?**
- **What are the most frequently occurring transactions in a firm?**
- **What are some of the most frequently used journals in a business firm?**

In the use of accounts to classify, store, and summarize data, two shortcomings become apparent. First, it can be seen that with a large number of transactions and the attendant volume of data it would be most difficult not to make errors when entering data to the accounts, and second, the process can prove very inefficient.

FUNCTIONAL NEED FOR THE JOURNAL

Errors can be made by entering an amount in the wrong account, entering an amount on the wrong side of an account (debit or credit), or writing an amount incorrectly. Common errors in entering amounts stem from reading the original amount incorrectly and from writing incorrectly by transposing digits in the number or writing an incorrect number of cyphers; any of these errors would result in inaccurate data. Errors which affect the data quantitatively might be discovered by making a trial balance. Qualitative errors such as entering data in the wrong account would not be detected by the trial balance procedure. Correcting errors detected by examination when a trial balance does not balance is both time-consuming and expensive; it would be much better if such errors could be prevented.

A primary function of the journal is the prevention of both qualitative and quantitative errors in data input and processing.

A problem always present in a data processing system with any sizeable volume of data input is the matter of efficient handling. The earlier the data can be summarized in the processing the smaller the volume of data will be and, therefore, the smaller the task of storing the data. In chapter 4 we examined the ledger account as a place to store and summarize data by specified classes. When there are large volumes of data of one class to be recorded in one account those data may be summarized before inputting them to ledger accounts. The journal, when specially planned and arranged, serves this summarizing function.

In its simplest form the journal serves only the function of providing qualitative and quantitative control; this form will be examined first. Special arrangement or adaptation of the journal to aid in the summarizing function will be considered after the basic form and its functions have been considered.

TWO-COLUMN JOURNAL

The journal's primary function is to serve as a place where classified data from transactions may be written and examined for accuracy of classification and amount before they are entered in ledger accounts. The journal normally is manually prepared and may serve as a source of input to ledger accounts in a manual system or, in special transactions, as a source from which cards are punched for input to a punched-card or computer system.

Preparing the Journal Entry

A simple two-column journal is pictured in Figure 5-1. Standard notation is used in the format of the entry so that it may be read accurately by any person with a basic knowledge of accounting. The date the journal entry is prepared is entered in the date column. The transaction is then examined to determine the changes involved. The data for such changes are classified according to the accounts affected and the effect on each account. The titles of these accounts and their inputs make up the body of the journal entry. It is customary to list the accounts which have debit inputs first, followed by those which have credit inputs. Note that the titles of the accounts debited begin immediately adjacent to the date column, while the titles of accounts credited are indented to the right a few spaces. This special placement of account titles serves as a check on accuracy when one transfers data from the journal to accounts. Amounts for which the accounts are debited are written in the debit column, and amounts for which accounts are credited are written in the credit column.

Figure 5-1
TRANSACTION DATA IN A TWO-COLUMN JOURNAL

Date		Accounts and Explanation	P.R.	Debit	Credit
May	19	Office Equipment		2400 00	
		Office Supplies		380 00	
		Cash			2780 00
		BP Supply Co. invoice E1143,			
		dated May 18; Check No. 3071			

As one can easily imagine, through the long period of the manual accounting system's development, the most common and troublesome error in entering data in accounts probably was writing the amount on the wrong side of the account; this error changes the effect on the account from positive to negative, or vice versa. The arrangement of the journal entry provides a double visual cue for the person entering these data in the ledger accounts after the journal entry is completed. As he reads the title of the first account in the entry, its location should cue him that the account is to be debited. He next finds the account among all those which make up the ledger and again looks to the journal entry to determine the amount to enter; he sees the amount in the debit column, again cueing him that the amount should be entered as a debit. The cueing process occurs again in the entering of credit amounts.

Posting from the Journal to Ledger Accounts

When data from the transaction have been classified and the journal entry completed, the quantitative control of checking for equality of debits and credits can be applied to the journal entry; for each entry the total of debit amounts should equal the total of credits. Entering data in accounts from the journal is called "posting." One posts a journal entry by entering in the appropriate ledger accounts the amounts indicated for those accounts in the journal entry. One can see in Figure 5-2 that complete cross-referencing is done as the amounts are entered; the page number of the journal is entered in the posting reference (P.R.) column in each ledger account to which an item is posted. This aids in future reference to the full journal entry and to the business documents for the transaction. The account number of each account to which posting is done is entered in the posting reference column of the journal on the same line with the amount posted to that account; this aids later in determining that journal entries were posted correctly.

Qualitative and Quantitative Controls Provided by the Journal

Use of the journal gives some control to the critical function of classifying financial data for processing. One can prepare the journal entry, showing his analysis of the transaction, and review it or have it reviewed before inputting data to the accounts. For very involved or disputable transactions the opportunity for review provided by the journal is especially valuable.

Figure 5-2

POSTING: TWO-COLUMN JOURNAL TO ACCOUNTS

Page 14

Date		Accounts and Explanation	P.R.	Debit	Credit
May	22	Office Equipment	212	3100 00	
		Office Supplies	112	410 00	
		Notes Payable	410		2000 00
		Cash	101		1510 00
		BP Supply Co. invoice E2191,			
		dated May 20; 60-day note date			
		May 20; Check no. 3102.			

Cash

No. 101

Date			P.R.	Debit	Date			P.R.	Credit
xxx	x		x	xxx xx	May	22		14	1500 00

Office Supplies

No. 112

Date			P.R.	Debit	Date			P.R.	Credit
May	22		14	410 00					

Office Equipment

No. 212

Date			P.R.	Debit	Date			P.R.	Credit
May	22		14	3100 00					

Notes Payable

No. 401

Date			P.R.	Debit	Date			P.R.	Credit
					May	22		14	2000 00

Even when a relatively small number of transactions are involved, use of a journal reduces error. It is very easy to input only a part of the data by simply forgetting or overlooking some of the effects of the transaction, or by forgetting how much of the data had been recorded when work is resumed after an interruption. Because of the automatic cross-referencing with posting, use of the journal allows one to assure himself, first, that all data are properly classified, and second, that all data are entered in the appropriate ledger accounts.

SPECIAL JOURNALS

There are a few types of transactions which are repeated in great volume, dozens, hundreds, or thousands of times each month. Each time a transaction recurs it has the same kind of effect on the same assets or equities, and, therefore, data from all similar transactions will be classified in the same fashion. Two hundred collections of cash during one month could result in the writing and posting of two hundred journal entries to the accounts affected, with the Cash account debited in each of the entries. Making two hundred entries in the Cash account involves a great amount of work; moreover, with the boredom and fatigue accompanying repetitive routine actions, a greater probability of error develops. **There are especially planned journals with special columns to summarize such highly repetitive data before taking it to the ledger account. Time and effort (therefore, cost) and the probability of error are reduced by summarizing data in these special journals.** The efficiency and control they provide can be seen by examining their use.

Sales Journal

Sales on credit are the most frequent transaction in many firms. All credit sales have the same effect: they increase the asset, "accounts receivable," and increase the equity, "sales revenue." For each transaction the Accounts Receivable account is debited and the Sales Revenue account is credited. Figure 5-3 pictures a highly specialized journal form, the Sales Journal, used only for recording data from credit sales. Note that data for each sale are written on one line, and that included in these data is the name of the customer but not the accounts affected by the transaction. Even a moderately busy firm which sells on credit could hardly operate a manual information system without the efficiencies of journals such as this. More details about posting from this journal and others will be discussed later.

Figure 5-3

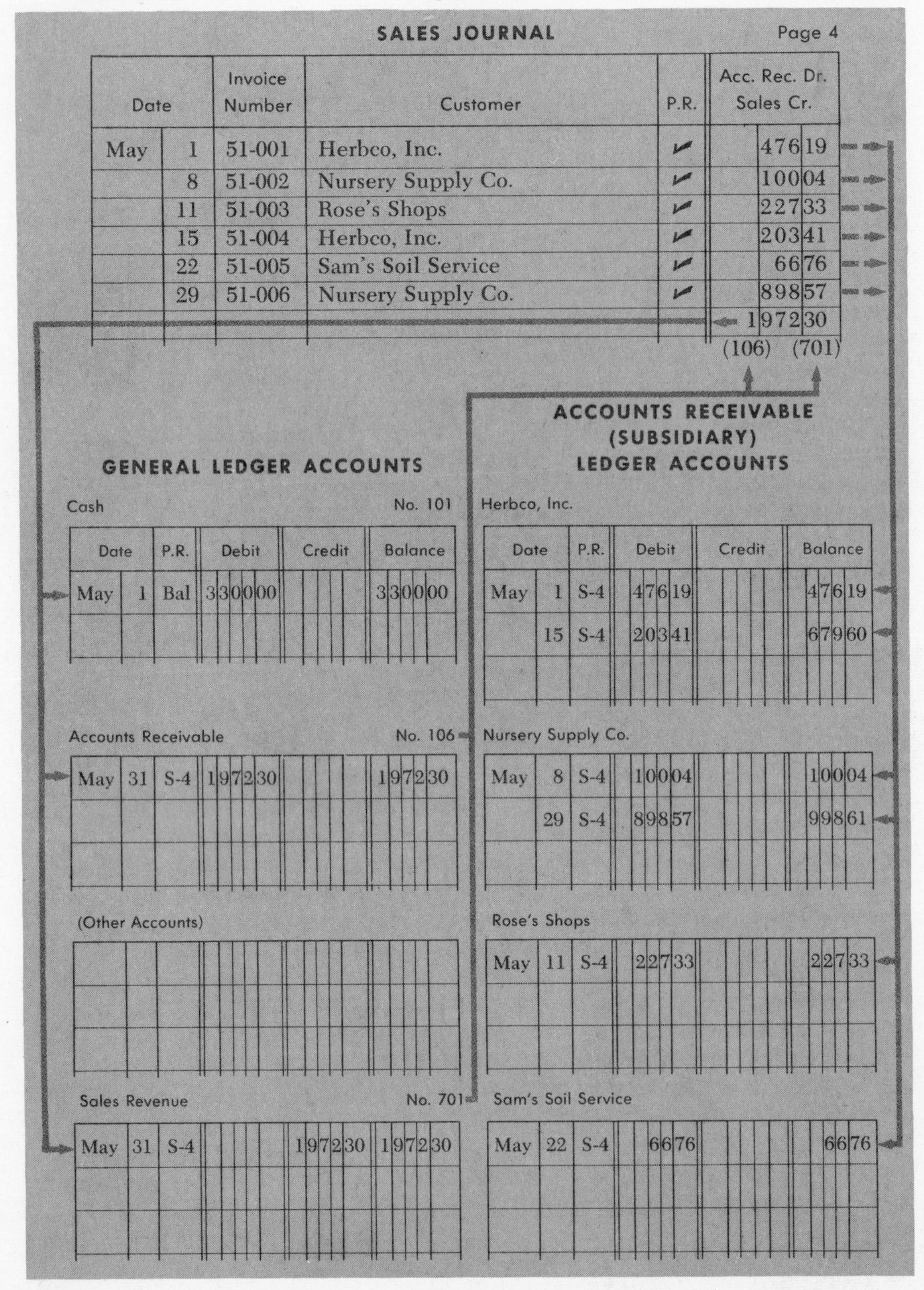

SALES JOURNAL Page 4

Date		Invoice Number	Customer	P.R.	Acc. Rec. Dr. Sales Cr.
May	1	51-001	Herbco, Inc.	✓	476 19
	8	51-002	Nursery Supply Co.	✓	100 04
	11	51-003	Rose's Shops	✓	227 33
	15	51-004	Herbco, Inc.	✓	203 41
	22	51-005	Sam's Soil Service	✓	66 76
	29	51-006	Nursery Supply Co.	✓	898 57
					1972 30
					(106) (701)

GENERAL LEDGER ACCOUNTS

Cash No. 101

Date		P.R.	Debit	Credit	Balance
May	1	Bal	3300 00		3300 00

Accounts Receivable No. 106

Date		P.R.	Debit	Credit	Balance
May	31	S-4	1972 30		1972 30

(Other Accounts)

Date		P.R.	Debit	Credit	Balance

Sales Revenue No. 701

Date		P.R.	Debit	Credit	Balance
May	31	S-4		1972 30	1972 30

ACCOUNTS RECEIVABLE (SUBSIDIARY) LEDGER ACCOUNTS

Herbco, Inc.

Date		P.R.	Debit	Credit	Balance
May	1	S-4	476 19		476 19
	15	S-4	203 41		679 60

Nursery Supply Co.

Date		P.R.	Debit	Credit	Balance
May	8	S-4	100 04		100 04
	29	S-4	898 57		998 61

Rose's Shops

Date		P.R.	Debit	Credit	Balance
May	11	S-4	227 33		227 33

Sam's Soil Service

Date		P.R.	Debit	Credit	Balance
May	22	S-4	66 76		66 76

Cash Receipts Journal

Other types of special journals are planned for groups of transactions which affect one account in the same way, but which also affect many other accounts. In Figure 5-4 each transaction has the effect of increasing cash and, therefore, data for each transaction include some amount entered in the Cash Debit column. The Cash Receipts Journal is especially planned for manual recording of data from cash receipt transactions; only data from these transactions are recorded in this journal. To record the data for a cash receipt in the Cash Receipts Journal, one classifies the data from the transaction and enters the amount of the debit to cash in the Cash Debit column after writing other descriptive data about the transaction. If there are columns which describe the effect of the transaction on other accounts, the appropriate amounts are written in those columns. Should data from the transaction affect some account for which a column has not been provided, that account title is written in the Explanation column and the amount involved is entered in the Sundry Credit column. Note that columns used to summarize data are already headed with account titles and, therefore, only the total is posted from each of such columns. Since data in the Sundry Accounts column affect several accounts, they are entered in the accounts one by one and the total, as a conglomerate of the changes in several accounts, is not used.

Subsidiary Ledgers

There are other special journals to be examined, but, at this point, attention should be given to the subsidiary ledger in Figures 5-3 and 5-4. In these figures the subsidiary ledger is made up of accounts for individual customers, or individual accounts receivable. Note that details from the single column in the Sales Journal and from the Accounts Receivable column of the Cash Receipts Journal are entered in the appropriate accounts in the subsidiary ledger. These accounts provide data for use in preparing monthly bills to customers and for management to use in determining whether special collection efforts are needed. Also, individual customer accounts provide information which is helpful in deciding whether to refuse further credit to a customer or to encourage him to use his credit for larger purchases.

The arrangement of data in the Accounts Receivable account in the general ledger and in the accounts receivable subsidiary ledger accounts provides a valuable proof of quantitative accuracy in processing the data through this stage. Note in Figures 5-3 and 5-4 that the

Figure 5-4

CASH RECEIPTS JOURNAL

Page 6

Date		Account Credited ~~Explanation~~	P.R.	Sundry Credit	Acc. Rec. Credit	Sales Credit	Sales Dis. Debit	Cash Debit
May	1	Cash Sales	✓			202 02		202 02
	12	Herbco, Inc.	✓		476 19			476 19
	14	Nursery Supply Co.	✓		100 04		1 00	99 04
	24	Herbco, Inc.	✓		203 41		2 03	201 38
	25	Cash Sales	✓			611 21		611 21
	29	Notes Receivable	118	200 00				204 50
		Interest Income	801	4 50				
				204 50	779 64	813 23	3 03	1794 34
				(✓)	(117)	(601)	(602)	(101)

GENERAL LEDGER ACCOUNTS

Cash — No. 101

Date		P.R.	Debit	Credit	Balance
May	1	Bal	3300 00		3300 00
	31	CR6	1794 34		5094 34

Accounts Receivable — No. 117

Date		P.R.	Debit	Credit	Balance
May	31	S-4	1972 30		1972 30
	31	CR6		779 64	1192 66

Notes Receivable — No. 118

Date		P.R.	Debit	Credit	Balance
May	1	Bal	500 00		500 00
	29	CR6		200 00	300 00

Sales — No. 601

Date		P.R.	Debit	Credit	Balance
May	31	S-4		1972 30	1972 30
	31	CR6		813 23	2785 53

Sales Discounts — No. 602

Date		P.R.	Debit	Credit	Balance
May	31	CR6	3 03		3 03

Interest Income — No. 801

Date		P.R.	Debit	Credit	Balance
May	31	CR6		4 50	4 50

ACCOUNTS RECEIVABLE (SUBSIDIARY) LEDGER ACCOUNTS

Herbco, Inc.

Date		P.R.	Debit	Credit	Balance
May	1	S-4	476 19		476 19
	15	S-4	203 41		679 60
	12	CR6		476 19	203 41
	24	CR6		203 41	—

Nursery Supply Co.

Date		P.R.	Debit	Credit	Balance
May	8	S-4	100 04		100 04
	29	S-4	898 57		998 61
	14	CR6		100 04	898 57

Rose's Shops

Date		P.R.	Debit	Credit	Balance
May	11	S-4	227 33		227 33

Sam's Soil Service

Date		P.R.	Debit	Credit	Balance
May	22	S-4	66 76		66 76

totals of the columns from which details are posted to customers' accounts in the subsidiary ledger are posted to the Accounts Receivable account. **This means that whenever all data from a journal have been posted to the subsidiary ledger and to the appropriate accounts in the general ledger, the total of the balances in all customers' accounts in the subsidiary ledger should equal the balance in the Accounts Receivable account, since the same data are involved in both.** Should any quantitative error have been made in posting to the customers' accounts or to the Accounts Receivable account, performing the proof should indicate an inequality which would serve as a cue to find and correct the error.

Purchases Journal

Data for each purchase on credit are recorded in the Purchases Journal, with an amount from each transaction being entered in the Accounts Payable column. The account to be debited for each transaction is determined and the amount for that account is entered in the appropriate column; if there is no special column for the account, the account title and amount are written in the Sundry Accounts column. All column totals are posted except for the Sundry Accounts column, where the total is a conglomerate and is not used. Individual amounts are posted from the Sundry Accounts column to the accounts indicated. Details are posted from the Accounts Payable column to the creditors' accounts in the subsidiary ledger.

Transactions in which goods or services are purchased on credit have in common the fact that they all increase accounts payable. Classification of data for each such transaction will include a credit to the Accounts Payable account. The debits will be to various accounts, many of them to Merchandise (or Purchases, as an alternate account title) and Supplies, and a few to miscellaneous accounts not often affected. Recording credit purchases in and posting from the Purchases Journal are illustrated in Figure 5-5, where the Accounts Payable column is the source of data to be posted to individual creditor accounts in the subsidiary ledger and the total of that column is to be posted to the Accounts Payable account. The use of the subsidiary ledger and the Accounts Payable control accounts are similar to the handling of accounts receivable in preceding illustrations.

Cash Payments Journal

Data from all payments of cash are entered and summarized in the Cash Payments Journal. Since cash is decreased by each payment, the data for each payment transaction include an amount credited

Figure 5-5

PURCHASES JOURNAL

Page 36

Date		Account ~~Debited~~ Credited	P.R.	Acc. Pay. Credit	Merchandise Debit	Supplies Debit	Sundry Debit		
							Account	P.R.	Amount
May	1	Hinson Company	✓	420 40	420 40				
	4	Abco, Inc.	✓	611 96	550 00	61 96			
	9	Hinson Company	✓	288 15	288 15				
	16	City Distributers	✓	134 37			Ofc. Equip.	211	134 37
	24	Mather Bros.	✓	360 00	360 00				
	29	Abco, Inc.	✓	395 52	200 50	95 02	Store Equip.	221	100 00
				2210 40	1819 05	156 98			234 37
				(401)	(121)	(131)			

GENERAL LEDGER ACCOUNTS

Cash 111

Date		P.R.	Debit	Credit	Balance

Merchandise 121

Date		P.R.	Debit	Credit	Balance
May	31	P36	1819 05		1819 05

Supplies 131

Date		P.R.	Debit	Credit	Balance
May	31	P36	156 98		156 98

Office Equipment 211

Date		P.R.	Debit	Credit	Balance
May	16	P36	134 37		134 37

Store Equipment 221

Date		P.R.	Debit	Credit	Balance
May	29	P36	100 00		100 00

Accounts Payable 401

Date		P.R.	Debit	Credit	Balance
May	31	P36		2210 40	2210 40

ACCOUNTS PAYABLE SUBSIDIARY LEDGER ACCOUNTS

Abco, Inc.

Date		P.R.	Debit	Credit	Balance
May	4	P36		611 96	611 96
	29	P36		395 52	1007 48

City Distributers

Date		P.R.	Debit	Credit	Balance
May	16	P36		134 37	134 37

Hinson Company

Date		P.R.	Debit	Credit	Balance
May	1	P36		420 40	420 40
	9	P36		288 15	708 55

Mather Bros.

Date		P.R.	Debit	Credit	Balance
May	24	P36		360 00	360 00

Figure 5-6

CASH PAYMENTS JOURNAL

Page 41

Date		Account Debited	P.R.	Sundry Debit	Acc. Pay. Debit	Mdse. Debit	Pur. Dis. Credit	Cash Credit
May	7	Store Equipment	231	120 00				120 00
	13	Hinson Company	✓		420 40			420 40
	14	Abco, Inc.	✓		611 96		12 24	599 72
	19	Hinson Company	✓		288 15		5 76	282 39
	24	Cash purchase	✓			163 07		163 07
	25	City Distributers	✓		134 37		1 34	133 03
	28	Supplies	131	77 50				77 50
				197 50	1454 88	163 07	19 34	1796 11
				(✓)	(401)	(121)	(712)	(111)

GENERAL LEDGER ACCOUNTS

Cash 111

Date		P.R.	Debit	Credit	Balance
May	1	Bal	4000 00		4000 00
	31	CP41		1796 11	2203 89

Merchandise 121

Date		P.R.	Debit	Credit	Balance
May	31	P36	1819 05		1819 05
	31	CP41	163 07		1982 12

Supplies 131

Date		P.R.	Debit	Credit	Balance
May	31	P36	156 98		156 98
	28	CP41	77 50		234 48

Office Equipment 211

Date		P.R.	Debit	Credit	Balance
May	16	P36	134 37		134 37

Store Equipment 221

Date		P.R.	Debit	Credit	Balance
May	29	P36	100 00		100 00
	7	CP41	120 00		220 00

Accounts Payable 401

Date		P.R.	Debit	Credit	Balance
May	31	P36		2210 40	2210 40
			1454 88		755 52

Purchase Discounts 712

Date		P.R.	Debit	Credit	Balance
May	31	CP41		19 34	19 34

ACCOUNTS PAYABLE SUBSIDIARY LEDGER ACCOUNTS

Abco, Inc.

Date		P.R.	Debit	Credit	Balance
May	4	P36		611 96	611 96
	29	P36		395 52	1007 48
	14	CP41	611 96		395 52

City Distributers

Date		P.R.	Debit	Credit	Balance
May	16	P36		134 37	134 37
	25	CP41	134 37		--

Hinson Company

Date		P.R.	Debit	Credit	Balance
May	1	P36		420 40	420 40
	9	P36		288 15	708 55
	13	CP41	420 40		288 15
	19	CP41	288 15		--

Mather Bros.

Date		P.R.	Debit	Credit	Balance
May	24	P36		360 00	360 00

to the Cash account. Debits are to various accounts, but, as can be seen in Figure 5-6, accounts commonly debited are Accounts Payable and Merchandise (or Purchases). When it is expected that an account will be debited many times during a period, a column for summarizing the many debits to that account can be added and only the total entered in the account. Debits to accounts for which there are not special columns are entered in the Sundry Accounts column. Posting from the Cash Payments Journal follows the same pattern as from other special journals. In studying this journal the transactions in Figure 5-6 should be analyzed, the data traced into the journal, and posting traced to the general ledger and the subsidiary ledger.

Other Special Journals

We have discussed the use of special journals for frequent transactions—sales on credit, cash receipts, purchases on credit, and cash payments. The principle involved is this:

special journals are planned to suit the data handling needs of the firm. Whenever, in an individual firm, a transaction occurs frequently and regularly, a column may be added to an existing special journal or a new journal may be formed to handle it.

If there are frequent purchases of office supplies on credit, a column may be added to the Purchases Journal so that the debits to the Office Supplies account can be summarized and posted as one amount. If, in a large number of transactions, notes payable are given to suppliers and creditors, one might initiate a Notes Payable Journal, providing a Notes Payable Credit column and whatever debit columns are needed to accommodate the data from transactions involving notes. If customers return large numbers of items sold on credit, a Sales Return Journal with a single column for the debit to Sales Returns and the credit to Accounts Receivable can be used. Posting from this journal would be similar to posting from the single-column Sales Journal. If all these journals appear fairly standard in arrangement it is because certain transactions are fairly common among business firms.

The General Journal

Although special journals are provided for frequently occurring transactions, there are a few transactions that do not fit into these journals;

these are recorded in the two-column journal, commonly called the general journal to distinguish it from the various special journals. The general journal is expected to have relatively few entries and may consist of separate sheets, with each sheet planned to contain the data for only one transaction. Such forms are generally called journal vouchers. One form of journal voucher is shown in Figure 5-7; here

Date *Oct. 13* , 19-- Voucher No. *106091*

JOURNAL VOUCHER

File Reference:
Weekly Summary (Form 416B) Oct. 7–11, 19--
Southeast branch

Accounts:	Debit	Credit
Cash	*8077 51*	
Accounts receivable	*5811 26*	
Supplies	*300 00*	
Sales—Dept. A		*3037 75*
Sales—Dept. B		*10491 02*
Sales—Dept. C		*660 00*
Explanation:		
Payment for office supplies from current receipts		
authorized by telephone (E. J. Brown Oct. 8, 19--).		

Prepared by: *H. Little* Reviewed: *B. Crew* Approved: *T. Mann*

Date: *10/13/--* Date: *10/13/--* Date: *10/14/--*

Figure 5-7 The journal voucher normally contains space for recording one transaction or a summary of transactions for some specific period—in both instances, only one journal entry with proper explanation and approval. Journal vouchers are used for special transactions and for transferring information from branch offices and from separate departments or stores. After posting, they are filed and are used as a journal. This journal voucher records a weekly summary of sales and collections by the Southeast branch store.

it can be seen that the entry is made on the journal voucher just as it would be on a two-column journal form and that data are posted from the voucher to ledger accounts. Journal vouchers are accumulated in a binder file to make up the general journal.

Internal Actions and the Journals

Only data from transactions have been used to demonstrate the various journals and their uses. Actions within the firm create changes in assets and equities and, therefore, call for data inputs to the information system. Many of these actions, such as accumulation of interest and expiration of insurance, occur gradually and are recorded in summary form at the end of the reporting period. These data are handled so infrequently that there is no special journal; data for such actions are recorded in the general journal. More detailed attention will be given to this topic in later chapters.

There are some frequently occurring actions within the firm, the effects of which are needed currently in the information system. Such actions are found most often in manufacturing operations; examples are the issue of materials from the stock room and the transfer of finished goods from the factory to the finished goods warehouse. Detailed data from these internal actions are used almost solely by management in the control of manufacturing and other physical operations; these data are treated in detail, therefore, in studies of management, or managerial, accounting. For the study of data related to financial decisions it appears appropriate to consider only those internal actions which have direct financial effects; data inputs in this study will be almost solely from transactions, with only summary data from internal actions.

Journals in Punched-Card and Computer Systems

In manual systems where data handling is limited to human speeds and in which human error is so probable, journals serve a dual purpose of providing efficiency through summarizing data and providing control of accuracy through qualitative and quantitative controls. In punched-card and electronic systems these needs are not present, and journals are not prepared as they are in manual systems. In these high speed, relatively accurate systems, a card is normally punched with the data coded in holes; this card causes the same impulses whenever it is "read" by a machine, and it can be handled at a rate of from hundreds to thousands of cards per minute. When data from cards are transferred to magnetic tape, reading can be done from the tape at a rate equivalent to tens of thousands of cards per minute. Accuracy controls and summarizing are not needed as much in these systems; however, when cards are sorted in like groups to be merged with other similar cards or to have data transferred to magnetic tape, lists, sometimes in summary form, are printed so that there will be available a copy of the input data in readable form. These lists, or "hard copy" printouts, are often called journals, although they do not serve the functions common to journals in manual systems.

QUESTIONS AND EXERCISES

5- A. What are the uses of the ledger account studied in the preceding chapter?

5- B. What needs in the accounting system are filled by the journal?

5- C. In an accounting system using a two-column journal for recording data from all financial events, what criticism might be appropriate if there are great numbers of transactions?

5- D. Explain the use of each of the lettered columns (A through E) in the following two-column journal form.

A		B	C	D	E

5- E. What conditions might cause one to add Cash Debit and Cash Credit columns to the two-column journal?

5- F. What conditions would cause one to use separate journals to record cash receipts, cash payments, sales on credit, and purchases on credit?

5- G. Joe Brown and his son, Joe, Jr., have organized a small business to trade in classic and antique automobiles. For the first seven months of operations, the firm has been involved in very few transactions. A manual accounting system is used, with a two-column journal. What kind of changes might the system need if business activities increase so that there are several cash payments each day and an average of several cash collections per week?

5- H. What purpose is served by the "posting reference" columns in the journal and the ledger accounts?

5- I. Assume that the four-column journal illustrated below is to be used for recording the following events. Indicate for each event the columns (A through D) that would be used for entering debit and credit amounts.

Date	Accounts	P.R.	Sundry		Cash	
			Debit (A)	Credit (B)	Debit (C)	Credit (D)

a. Received cash as an investment in the business.
b. Paid cash for one month's rent.
c. Purchased supplies on credit.
d. Used a part of the supplies in performing service for a customer.
e. Billed a customer for service performed.
f. Received cash from a customer in payment for services previously provided and billed.

5- J. Assume that five journals are used by the firm—Cash Receipts Journal, Cash Payments Journal, Sales Journal, Purchases Journal (multi-column), and two-column general journal. In which of the journals would each of the following events be recorded?
a. Receipt of cash as an investment in the firm.
b. Purchase of merchandise on credit.
c. Receipt of cash for a cash sale.
d. Sale of merchandise to a customer on credit.
e. Purchase of office supplies on credit.
f. Use of one-third of the office supplies during the month.
g. Payment to a creditor for merchandise purchased earlier.
h. Sale of merchandise for cash.
i. Purchase of merchandise for cash.

5- K. Indicate which journal is described by each item (a) through (e) below.
a. Headings on the four money columns are Cash Debit, Sales Credit, Accounts Receivable Credit, and General Credit.
b. Only one column, the total of which is posted as a debit to Accounts Receivable and as a credit to Sales.
c. Only two columns, with the headings simply Debit and Credit.
d. Headings on the four money columns are Accounts Payable Credit, Purchases Debit, Supplies Debit, and Sundry Debit.
e. Five money columns with the headings Sundry Debit, Supplies Debit, Purchases Debit, Accounts Payable Debit, and Cash Credit.

5- L. From the journal form below, indicate the account to which each of the lettered items is to be posted. What kind of journal is this?

Date		P.R.	Sundry Credit	Acc.Rec. Credit	Sales Credit	Cash Debit
			(H)	(G)	(F)	(E)
			(A)	(B)	(C)	(D)

a. Item A, the total of the Sundry Credit column.
b. Item B, the total of the Accounts Receivable Credit column.
c. Item C, the total of the Sales Credit column.
d. Item D, the total of the Cash Debit column.
e. Item E, individual item in the Cash Debit column.
f. Item F, individual item in the Sales Credit column.
g. Item G, individual item in the Accounts Receivable Credit column.
h. Item H, individual item in the Sundry Credit column.

5-M. What is a subsidiary ledger? How is a subsidiary ledger related to accounts in the General Ledger?

5-N. What information for control is provided by a subsidiary ledger and the related control account?

5-O. The Jones Company has seven thousand credit customers with accounts in the firm's Accounts Receivable Subsidiary Ledger. If the total of the balances in these individual customers' accounts is $62,115, what balance would you hope to find in the Accounts Receivable control account? What are some of the errors that might cause the total of the account balances in the subsidiary ledger to differ from the balance of the control account?

5-P. What kinds of errors might still be in the subsidiary ledger when the total of the account balances in that ledger equals the balance in the related General Ledger control account?

PROCEDURAL PROBLEMS

5-1. Record the transactions of the Sherman Furniture Company in a two-column journal. Use page 8 as the page number of the journal. Post to General Ledger accounts and prepare a trial balance. Use accounts and account numbers from the list following the transactions.

May 1 Issued 200 shares of capital stock to Michael Sherman for $10,000.

3 Purchased office furniture on account from R. M. Reynolds Co. for $2,000. Invoice no. J1164, dated May 2.

4 Paid insurance of $400 for the month to the Robert Morgan Agency. Their invoice N612, dated May 1, our check no. 210.

7 Borrowed $15,000 from First National Bank, giving a 7 percent, 18-month note payable.

10 Purchased merchandise for $12,000 on account from Morris Bros. Invoice no. BB104762, dated May 7. (The company charges this to the asset account, Merchandise.)

12 Purchased office supplies for $600 from Anderson Inc. Invoice no. E 7122, dated May 12. Our check no. 211.

14 Made a credit sale to Higgins Furniture Co. for $7,000. Our invoice no. 001, dated May 14 (cost of all sales is computed and recorded at the end of the period).

14 Purchased a delivery truck for $6,000 from Modern Motors. We gave our check no. 212 for $2,000 and agreed to pay the balance over the next 12 months. Invoice no. MM 12-4126.

May 19 Made a cash purchase of merchandise from Hartford Furniture Company for $4,000. Invoice no. JR 104414, dated May 19. Our check no. 213.

21 Received a check from Higgins Furniture Company for $3,000 on our invoice no. 001.

25 Made a cash sale of $2,400 to Ware Furniture. Our Invoice no. 002.

31 Made the following cash disbursements
$600 to R. M. Reynolds; check no. 214, invoice no. RJR 7194.
$875 to First National Bank; $75 was interest for May. Check no. 215; $800 was paid on a note.
$1600 to Morris Bros. $50 was interest. Check no. 216, their invoice no. 44717.
$800 rent for May to Morgan Realty Co. Check 217.

Accounts	Number
Cash	101
Accounts receivable	111
Merchandise	112
Office supplies	121
Office furniture	131
Delivery truck	135
Accounts payable	201
Notes payable	220
Capital stock	301
Sales revenue	401
Insurance expense	511
Interest expense	512
Rent expense	513

5-2. Presented below is a partial list of General Ledger accounts of the Northshore Development Company with balances as of August 1. Also presented is a list of balances in the Accounts Receivable Subsidiary Ledger as of the same date.

	Debit	Credit
Cash	$2175.75	
Accounts receivable	4401.84	
Capital stock		$1500.00
Sales		9432.50
Sales discounts	164.50	

Accounts Receivable Subsidiary Ledger balances:

Foster Construction	$ 726.32
Mitchell Inc.	1740.40
Scheyes Corp.	491.75
Simmons Bros.	323.17
Wray Inc.	1120.20
	$4401.84

Record the following transactions of Northshore Development Company in a Cash Receipts Journal similar to the one in Figure 5-4. Use page 22 as the page number of this journal. Then post the transactions to the General Ledger accounts and Accounts Receivable Subsidiary Ledger.

Aug. 3 Received $224.00 from Foster Construction.

8 Simmons Bros. paid $107.33 cash and received $1.67 discount.

10 Made a cash sale of $44.20.

17 Issued 60 shares of capital stock for $6,000.

20 Scheyes Corp. closed their account, paying $488.22 and taking a discount of $3.53.

24 Made a cash sale to Mitchell, Inc., receiving $106.16.

29 Wray, Inc. paid $318.10.

5-3. Presented below is a partial list of General Ledger accounts and an Accounts Receivable Subsidiary Ledger of the Williams Manufacturing Co. with balances as of February 1.

General Ledger Accounts

101	Cash	$ 4,674.50
121	Accounts receivable	5,879.82
151	Delivery equipment	14,321.25
401	Sales	23,410.45 Cr.
404	Sales discounts	386.16

Accounts Receivable Subsidiary Ledger

Hayes Inc.	$4655.40
Morgan Electric Inc.	126.28
Saimes Co.	426.64
Wright Foundry Co.	671.50

Record the following transactions on page 21 of a Cash Receipts Journal similar to the illustration in Figure 5-4. Post to the General Ledger accounts and to the Accounts Receivable Subsidiary Ledger.

Feb. 4 Wright Foundry Co. paid $396.30 after receiving a $3.70 discount.

9 Sold a used delivery truck at salvage value of $685.

11 Collected $2210 from Hayes Inc.

20 Made a cash sale of $71.30.

22 Received $424.20 from Saimes Co. after they deducted a sales discount of $2.44.

25 Received $604.40 from Hayes Inc.

5-4. The following is a partial list of transactions of the Abey Corporation. Record the transactions on page 12 of a Purchases Journal similar to the one illustrated in Figure 5-5. Post to General Ledger accounts and to the Accounts Payable Subsidiary Ledger.

Nov. 3 Purchased merchandise for $2,100 from Ridgeway Inc.
6 Purchased merchandise from Martin Co. for $600.
11 Purchased office furniture on account from Steinway Inc. for $2,400.
13 Office supplies costing $400 were acquired on account from James Supplies Inc.
19 Merchandise was purchased from Martin Co. for $900.
23 Purchased cleaning supplies from Holmes Industrial Supplies for $200. Supplies are to be used immediately.
27 Purchased merchandise from Raines Inc. for $1,400.
29 Additional office supplies costing $400 were purchased from Layne Inc.

5-5. Below is a partial list of General Ledger accounts and an Accounts Payable Subsidiary Ledger of Ware Products, Inc., with balances as of June 1.

General Ledger Accounts			**Accounts Payable Subsidiary Ledger**	
101	Cash	$14,400	ABCD, Inc.	$1200
111	Office supplies	150	Anson Bros.	1725
131	Office furniture	6,500	Shaw Corp.	1010
201	Accounts payable	7,785	Verritt, Inc.	730
401	Merchandise purchases	7,220	Wilson Supplies Corp.	3120
404	Purchase discounts	6		$7785

Record the following transactions of Ware Products, Inc. on page 40 of a Cash Payments Journal as illustrated in Figure 5-6. Then post to General Ledger accounts and Accounts Payable Subsidiary Ledger.

June 6 Paid $400 to Verritt Inc.
10 Purchased additional office furniture for $700.
12 Paid the Shaw Corp. account in full, receiving a $40 discount.
17 Purchased merchandise for cash from Wayne Products for $625.
20 Paid Anson Bros. $225 on account.
23 Paid Wilson Supplies Corp. $2,000.
25 Office supplies were purchased for $60 cash.
29 Paid the ABCD balance in full, receiving a 1 percent discount.

5-6. Record the transactions of Ranger Enterprises on page 16 of a two-column journal. Post to General Ledger accounts and prepare a trial balance as of April 30.

Apr. 1 Received $20,000 from Jim Hart for 200 shares of capital stock.
1 Paid rent for the month to Granger Realty Co. $700. Invoice no. 4-102. Our check no. 712.

6 Purchased factory equipment on account for $3,000 from Mitchell Tool Company. Invoice no. A61644.

9 Billed R. T. Wright $925 after completing work for him. Our invoice APR 1061.

14 Purchased office supplies for $400 from McCamy Inc. Invoice no. 14038. Our check no. 713.

16 Billed James Hollis Inc. $420 and Rob's Service Co. $660 for services completed. Our invoices no. APR 1062 and APR 1063.

20 Received $600 from W. T. Wright on his account.

24 Paid $60 to the Daily Bulletin for newspaper advertising to April 15. Check no. 714.

29 Paid $725 to Mitchell Tool Company on account. Their invoice A61644. Our check no. 715.

General Ledger accounts that may be used in this problem are:

101 Cash
110 Office supplies
104 Accounts receivable
121 Factory equipment
201 Accounts payable
301 Capital stock
401 Service revenue
511 Rent expense
512 Advertising expense

5-7. Record the transactions of Layne Lumber Co. in a Purchases Journal, page 20. Use column headings: Accounts Payable Credit, Merchandise Debit, Equipment Debit, and Sundry Debit. Post to General Ledger accounts and an Accounts Payable Subsidiary Ledger. Prepare a list of individual accounts payable as of November 30 and check the total against the balance of the Accounts Payable account.

Nov. 2 Purchased lumber for resale on account from Southeastern Tree Farms for $7,122.50.

6 Acquired on account from Watson Machine Co. mill equipment costing $16,277.14.

8 Purchased on account unprocessed timber from Frontier Land Company for $2,750.11.

13 Purchased additional milling equipment on credit from Watson Machine Co. for $6,125.25.

19 Purchased window frames, doors, and cabinets on credit for resale from Lyndon Cabinet Shop for $1,244.50.

20 Additional lumber costing $4,372.17 was purchased on account from Southeastern Tree Farms.

24 Purchased fuel for the mill on account for $461.30, from Industrial Fuels Inc. This fuel is to be used immediately.

General Ledger accounts that may be used in this problem are:

121 Merchandise ~~inventory~~
123 Mill equipment
201 Accounts payable
512 Fuel expense

5-8. Below is a partial list of transactions of the Bell Company for September. Record these transactions on page 6 of a Cash Payments Journal as illustrated in Figure 5-6. Post to General Ledger accounts and prepare an Accounts Payable Subsidiary Ledger as of September 30.

Sept. 3 Purchased merchandise for cash from Shepherd Inc. $1,026.36.
8 Paid Wayne Products $198.40 cash and received $1.20 discount.
10 Paid $306.00 for office furniture.
16 Paid the Cabot Bros. Inc. account, receiving a 2 percent discount.
19 Paid Shepherd $481.30 on account.
24 Paid Wayne Products $322.50.
30 Paid City Electric Co. $77.35 for utilities for September.

Following is a partial list of General Ledger accounts and an Accounts Payable Subsidiary Ledger with balances as of September 1:

General Ledger Accounts			Accounts Payable Subsidiary Ledger	
101	Cash	$11,472.24	Bost Enterprises	$ 471.17
121	Merchandise	14,981.20	Cabot Bros. Inc.	620.00
122	Merchandise discounts	216.88	Shepherd Inc.	715.35
131	Office furniture	6,218.47	Wayne Products Inc.	612.20
201	Accounts payable	2,418.72		$2,418.72
511	Utilities expense	-0-		

5-9. Mattco Corporation records its credit sales in a one-column Sales Journal and uses a Cash Receipts Journal with columns for Accounts Receivable, Sales, Sales Discounts, Sundry Credit, and Cash. Listed below are balances taken from the company's General Ledger and Accounts Receivable Subsidiary Ledger as of June 1. Enter these balances in ledger accounts and record the June transactions in the Sales Journal and Cash Receipts Journal. Post to the General Ledger accounts, and prepare a June 30 Accounts Receivable Subsidiary Ledger trial balance. Use 14 as the page number of the Sales Journal and 44 as the page number of the Cash Receipts Journal to record transactions.

General Ledger Accounts			Accounts Receivable Subsidiary Ledger	
101	Cash	$ 9,106.20	Gowan, Inc.	$ 2,140.36
121	Accounts receivable	25,734.03	Harms Co.	4,000.00
401	Sales	51,329.71	Lowery Machine Co.	13,422,12
401A	Sales discounts	2,027.42	Prince Industries	6,171.55
402	Interest income	3,488.19		$25,734.03

June 2 Collected from Harms Company their account in full after deduction of a 2 percent discount.

4 Made a $2,316.40 credit sale to Lowery Machine Company, inv. no. J416.

6 Received $60 as interest income.

7 Made a $243.63 cash sale to Prince Industries.

10 Collected $400 from Gowan, Inc.

13 Made a $3,371.39 credit sale to Harms Company, inv. no. J417.

19 Collected $2,120.30 from Prince Industries after a discount of $19.60.

22 Credit sales were Lowery Machine Company, $1,912.40, inv. no. J418; Gowan Company, $3,693.10, inv. no. J419.

27 Interest income received was $44.50.

29 Made a $63.72 cash sale.

30 Collected $2,819.31 from Lowery Machine Company.

5-10. The January transactions of Haltom Corporation are to be recorded on page 16 of a Cash Receipts Journal with columns headed Sundry Credit, Accounts Receivable, Sales, Sales Discounts, and Cash. Post to General Ledger accounts and Accounts Receivable Subsidiary Ledger accounts. Prepare a January 31 schedule of Accounts Receivable Subsidiary accounts.

General Ledger Accounts			Accounts Receivable Subsidiary Ledger	
101	Cash	$ 9,360.21	Gentry Motors	$ 9,280.67
121	Accounts receivable	21,725.68	Hageman Appliance	2,000.00
300	Capital stock	50,000.00	Lewis Supply	3,320.40
500	Sales	-0-	Reynolds, Inc.	7,124.61
500A	Sales discounts	-0-		$21,725.68

Jan. 6 Issued additional capital stock for $60,000.

9 Made a cash sale for $423.60 to Gentry Motors.

11 Hageman Appliance Company took a 2 percent discount and paid their bill in full.

14 Collected $2,132.40 from Lewis Supply.

19 Reynolds Corporation took a $31.65 discount and made a cash payment of $2,931.80.

23 Made a cash sale for $114.23.

29 Cash collections on account:

Gentry Motors	$4,167.28
Lewis Supply	$ 924.70

5-11. Presented below are a partial trial balance of Global Corporation, prepared on August 1, and an Accounts Payable Subsidiary Ledger for the same date. The transactions shown below represent the company's

August cash disbursements. Record these transactions on page 9 of the Cash Payments Journal, then post to the General Ledger and Subsidiary Ledger. Prepare a schedule of the Accounts Payable Subsidiary Ledger and compare that total with the control account.

General Ledger Accounts			Accounts Payable Subsidiary Ledger	
100	Cash	$41,322.40	Chatham, Inc.	$ 7,135.50
120	Merchandise	16,140.12	Graham Brothers, Inc.	6,000.00
121	Merchandise discounts	1,071.43	Jordan Corporation	13,241.12
130	Delivery equipment	30,200.00		$26,376.62
200	Accounts payable	26,376.62		
500	Rent expense	-0-		

Aug. 4 Paid $9,120.20 to Wingate Motor Company for cash purchase of delivery equipment.

8 Paid Chatham, Inc. $918.00 cash to apply on account and received a $19.20 discount.

10 Purchased merchandise for cash for $311.41.

14 Paid the Graham Brothers account, taking a 2 percent discount.

19 Paid $1,366.53 to Jordan Corporation.

23 Purchased merchandise for cash from Graham Brothers, Inc. for $1,908.20.

28 Paid Chatham, Inc. $2,020.10.

31 Paid August rent of $800.00.

5-12. Jarmon, Inc. uses a Purchases Journal to record all credit purchases. They have special columns for Merchandise and Supplies; other purchases are recorded in the Sundry column. The company also uses a Cash Payments Journal with special columns for Accounts Payable, Supplies, and Purchase Discounts. Any other cash purchase is recorded in the Sundry column.

Presented below is a partial list of General Ledger accounts and Accounts Payable Subsidiary Ledger with the November 1 balances. Record these balances in ledger accounts; record the transactions in the journals; post the journals to the ledger accounts.

General Ledger Accounts			Accounts Payable Subsidiary Ledger	
101	Cash	$29,321.71	Durr Pipe Manufacturing	$ 3,011.35
106	Supplies	1,974.20	Jasso Auto Company	16,120.00
120	Merchandise	71,320.00	Laake Machine Shop	4,812.19
120A	Merchandise discounts	2,326.30	Mire Industrial Products	9,129.63
131	Store equipment	41,152.12		$33,073.17
200	Accounts payable	33,073.17		
500	Insurance expense	-0-		

Nov. 4 Paid $2,000 to Jasso Auto Company.

8 Paid $3,200 to Mire Products. This consisted of $2,000 on account and $1,200 for a cash purchase of merchandise.

10 Purchased merchandise on account from Durr Pipe Manufacturing, $2,316.41.

10 Made a cash purchase of cleaning supplies for $211.25.

14 Paid Jasso Auto Company $1,580 on account, taking a $20 discount.

15 Purchased store equipment on account for $934.62 from Mire Industrial Products.

21 Paid the November insurance premium of $329.50 to Lacy Insurance Agency.

23 Made credit purchases of merchandise from

Laake Machine Shop ....$ 344.20
Durr Pipe Mfg. $1,462.90

24 Paid $914.00 for full payment of the store equipment purchased November 15, taking a discount for the balance.

27 Purchased cleaning supplies on account from Mire Industrial Products for $923.60.

30 Paid Durr Pipe Manufacturing $1,523.35 on account.

5-13. The Blackmon Corporation was organized on February 1 when it issued capital stock of $200,000. The company immediately began purchasing on account factory equipment and inventory. Set up a Purchases Journal with these column headings: Accounts Payable Credit, Merchandise, Factory Equipment, and Sundry Debit. Record the following transactions, post to General Ledger accounts and Accounts Payable Subsidiary accounts, and at the end of the month prepare a schedule of the Accounts Payable Subsidiary Ledger. General Ledger accounts are

1611 Merchandise
1810 Factory equipment
2020 Accounts payable
2821 Insurance expense

The transactions are to be recorded on page 1 of the journal.

Feb. 3 Purchased factory equipment for $23,193.40 from Finch, Inc.

5 Inventory costing $8,263.16 was purchased from Gryder Corporation.

12 Factory equipment was purchased from Kneale Corporation for $9,319.30.

16 Inventory purchases were made:

Gryder Corporation $3,141.67
Moye Corporation $6,629.80

19 Purchased additional factory equipment from Finch, Inc. for $6,920.20.

23 Purchased factory equipment for $16,120.92 from Kneale Corporation.

28 The company received an insurance bill for $244.50 from Rogers Agency for February insurance.

CONCEPTUAL PROBLEMS

5-14. In the accounting system of the Edith R. Manufacturing Company, data are classified on business documents, with pencilled notations made to indicate the accounts affected by the events. Amounts are transferred from the documents to the ledger accounts affected. Some difficulties have been encountered with this accounting system, revealed most clearly by the fact that the trial balance for December 31, 1971, does not balance. Auditors who were brought in to help put the system in order found $5,000 debited in the Retained Earnings account with the notation, "Cash payments from past periods." Examination of the Cash account does not reveal any payment of $5,000. No document can be found that appears to relate to this item. Fourteen other items in various accounts cannot be related to any business documents in the company files.

a. In addition to the fifteen items in various accounts that do not appear to relate to available business documents, what other kinds of errors might you expect to find in this system?

b. What change in the system do you recommend as a logical step to eliminate such errors in the future?

5-15. The Sally Ho! Pleasure Boat Company operates four sightseeing boats that provide different degrees of comfort and luxury to passengers while covering approximately the same scenic river routes near the city. Sally First, the original open boat, provides a slow trip with open air, wind, spray, and all the vagaries of nature for its passengers. Sally Second, Sally Third, and Sally Fourth provide increasing degrees of luxury, the latter ship being fitted with a plastic sightseeing dome covering the deck and containing an air-conditioned lounge and deck restaurant. So that the profitability of each boat can be measured, it has been decided to accumulate separate data for revenue and operating expenses of each boat. About one-third of the trips of all four boats are on a charter basis, with the customer (a business firm or an individual) being billed for the basic charter fee plus services the day after the chartered tour. Tickets for nonchartered tours are sold at the dock office for cash; a notation of the starting and ending numbers for each day on the prenumbered tickets makes it possible to determine how much of the cash collected each day is for each boat. Revenue from chartered tours is recorded in the Charter Sales Journal. Revenue from cash sales of tickets is recorded in the Cash Receipts Journal.

a. Why might the Sally Ho! Pleasure Boat Company's management want information on revenue from cash sales of tour tickets and chartered tours reported separately?

b. Assuming that revenue from chartered tours and cash ticket sales is to be reported separately for each boat, what headings do you suggest for revenue columns in the Charter Sales Journal and the Cash Receipts Journal? Explain how posting to revenue accounts from these journals should be done.

5-16. Bob Grinfield is bookkeeper for his father's business, the Grinfield Emporium. In maintaining accounts with credit customers, Bob posts amounts from individual credit sales tickets to the customers' accounts in the Accounts Receivable Ledger. He then adds the balances in all accounts in the Accounts Receivable Ledger to obtain the total amount owed the Emporium by credit customers. He compares this amount with the balance in the Accounts Receivable control account and reasons that the difference is the total of the amounts he has just posted to the customers' accounts. This difference is recorded with a journal entry debiting Accounts Receivable and crediting Sales Revenue. This procedure always maintains the balancing status between the total of the accounts in the Subsidiary Ledger and the balance in the Accounts Receivable control account.

The bookkeeping procedure devised by Bob Grinfield apparently works nicely; there is never a discrepancy between the total of the customers' individual accounts and the balance in the control account. However, Mr. Grinfield is bothered constantly by customers complaining about incorrect amounts (for which they are billed at the end of the month) posted to their accounts. Frequently the errors are caused by Bob's or his assistant's transposing digits in numbers or transplacing the digits by adding or dropping a cipher in the number. For example, $23.37 may be written as $32.37 or as $23.73, and $1.00 is sometimes posted as $10.00 or as $.10. Occasionally, an amount is posted twice to the same customer's account or omitted entirely from the posting.

a. Explain why these errors are not revealed by the information provided by the accounting system.

b. Prepare instructions for young Bob Grinfield, detailing a procedure whereby errors in posting to customers' accounts will be revealed each day so that they may be corrected before monthly bills are sent out.

6 Periodic Reporting of Revenue

Preview Questions

As you study look for the answers to the following questions:

- **What is revenue?**
- **Why must revenue be measured?**
- **What criteria are used to determine when revenue is reported?**
- **At what operating stages may revenue be reported?**
- **Under what conditions is revenue allocated between years?**
- **How is revenue measured through reductions in revenue?**

In developing and using information about a firm's activities, one finds the terms *revenue, expenses*, and *net income* to be closely related. This chapter presents the basic concepts of net income and revenue and the qualitative standards which guide in the reporting of revenues. Expenses are treated in chapter 7.

BASIC CONCEPT OF REVENUE

The concept of net income or profit is probably more commonly used and understood than is the idea of revenue. Net income is computed by comparing the earned inflows of resources with the consumption, or using up, of resources; the excess of the earned inflows is net income.

> ***Revenue* is the term applied to the total of the earned inflows of resources to a firm.**

Net Income: Definition and Description

Net income is the firm's increase in resources from its own activities. This is measured as the excess of the earned inflow of resources over the consumption of resources used in earning that inflow. This excludes the inflows of resources which come from investors and creditors and most outflows paid to them.

Information about net income is vital to decisions about the firm's financial success. The board of directors may be strongly influenced by the amount of net income when considering whether the management team has been successful as managers. Investors use information about net income in their judgment of the past success of a firm and their estimates of the likelihood of its future success. Decisions about investing in shares or selling such shares depend largely on these estimates of the company's success (growth and ability to pay dividends) and, therefore, on information about net income of the company.

Net income or earnings of a firm is reported in two categories: that coming from *normal operations* (normal business activities), and that from *extraordinary* sources. Net income from normal operations can be described as follows:

From

Revenue: Inflows of resources from the sale of goods and services in the general effort to produce a profit (service to customers, merchandise), or *earned* inflows of resources.

Deduct

Expenses: Consumption of resources in the effort to produce a greater inflow from the sale of goods and services (wages, supplies used, cost of merchandise sold, rent, utilities, wearing out of equipment).

Result:

Excess of revenue over expenses is income from operations (operating income)—an increase in company resources coming from business operations.

Excess of expenses over revenue is loss from operations (operating loss)—a decrease in company resources from business operations.

Additions to company resources or reductions in resources from extraordinary activities (those not considered a part of normal business activities) may come from sources such as the following:

Additions: Inflows of resources from gains on the sale of assets which normally are used by the firm rather than normally sold by it (equipment, building) and other nonordinary events such as collection of insurance benefits upon the death of an insured officer.

Reductions: Outflows or consumption of resources such as losses on the sale or destruction of assets normally used by the firm (buildings, machinery, equipment) and the loss or destruction of goods normally sold.

Net income is usually reported in connection with its sources. The following summary indicates the kind of information normally included when reporting net income:

INCOME STATEMENT

For a Specified Period of Time

Revenue for the specified period of time		$100,000
Minus expenses for the same period		80,000
Result: Income (or loss) from normal operations for the period—net increase (or decrease) in resources from ordinary business activities		$ 20,000
Plus extraordinary gains for the period	$7,000	
Minus extraordinary losses for the period	2,000	5,000
Result: Net income (or loss)—net earned increase (or decrease) in resources from all company activities		$ 25,000

Revenue: Definition and Description

The first class of resource inflows, those from the sale of goods or services in the effort to produce a profit, is called "revenue"; the consumption of resources which is matched with revenue to compute income from operations is called "expenses." Expenses are considered in detail in chapter 7.

The magnitude of revenue is a gauge of management's success in sales and promotion efforts. The increase or decrease of revenue from year to year indicates to management the success of its efforts and provides investors with information to help predict the firm's future financial success. The amount of revenue is important as information in itself and, also, as data to be used in computing net income. The remainder of this chapter will be devoted to the identification and measure of revenue.

The second kind of resource inflow and outflow (those from extraordinary sources) is made up of miscellaneous items which are less useful in predicting future profits; some of these will be noted in later chapters.

Classification of Revenue Data

Data for the increase in assets affected by revenue are classified and stored as increases, or debits, in the appropriate asset accounts. If cash is received from the sale, the Cash account is debited; if credit is granted to the customer and, rather than cash, a claim against that customer is received, the Accounts Receivable account is debited. In either situation, the related increase in capital from earnings is stored in (credited to) a "revenue" account; the title of this account might be Service Revenue or (for the sale of merchandise) Sales Revenue. Variously classified information may be needed by management, investors, or others concerning sources of revenue:

From sales of different types of merchandise or different services,

From sales of either merchandise or services in various districts or territories, or

From sales to various types of customers.

Many different revenue accounts may be used to store data classified to satisfy these information needs.

Net income is the earned increase in resources; revenue is the total inflow of earned resources. Data for the resources are stored in asset accounts; data for the ownership (from earning) of the resources are stored in revenue accounts. The earning of resources by a firm is not accomplished in a single transaction; consumption of resources represented by salaries and rent and other required services occurs over a period of time, culminating in sales or service transactions from which an inflow of resources is received. This revenue results from decisions and actions in a broad area of business operations, and it is offset by the cost of these operations in computing the net income. Revenue data are classified tentatively as increases in equity (earned capital) on the assumption that they will be offset by data concerning the outflow of resources (expenses). Accounting for revenue is the first stage in determining and reporting net income.

Matching Revenues and Expenses

The measurement of net income (profit) is very important in developing information about the firm, and great effort is made to match the reporting of revenue and expense for this purpose. If revenue were reported in one year and expenses related to that revenue were not reported until the following year, net income would be measured incorrectly in both years. Without deduction of the expenses the first year, net income (normally revenue minus the related expenses) would be reported at too great an amount. In the second year, when the expenses were reported without the related revenue (which was reported the preceding year), net income would be understated. The point is that reliable information about periodic earnings of the firm is provided only when revenues and related expenses are matched in the same year and reported together.

Some expenses, such as the cost of goods sold and the commissions paid for selling merchandise or services, can be easily related to specific revenue. Other expenses are more indirectly related to the production of revenue. The problems encountered in matching expenses to revenues are treated in chapter 7.

STANDARDS FOR REPORTING REVENUE

Many data normally are available about revenues of a firm. A basic problem related to these data, however, is how to determine when to report revenue.

Criteria for Revenue Reporting

Which of the revenue data indicate that specific revenues relate to the current period and should be reported (along with appropriate expenses) on the income statement of this period? This question is answered by applying three criteria generally observed in current reporting:

1. The principal revenue producing activity has been performed. This carries the inference that the revenue stream of assets has been earned.

2. The amount which will be received in cash, or its equivalent, for performance of the activity has been determined or can be estimated with reasonable accuracy.

3. Expenses which were directly involved in creation of the revenue have been determined or can be estimated with reasonable accuracy.

It should be noted that the first two criteria pertain to the revenue itself—that it has been "earned" by performance and that the amount ultimately to be received is determinable—while the last criterion pertains to expenses which must be matched with the revenue to measure net income. If these expenses cannot be determined, then both the expenses and the related revenue are deferred until the time when they can be reported together. It is clear from these criteria for revenue recognition that the net income concept is primary and that measurement and reporting of net income is a principal purpose of the financial information system.

Accrual Basis for Reporting Net Income

When the aforementioned generally accepted criteria for revenue recognition are followed, reporting is said to be on the *accrual basis*. The word *accrual* indicates that revenues and expenses are reported as they occur or develop, rather than as they are collected or paid. Reporting on the basis of collections and payments is *cash basis* reporting, examined below. Accrual accounting requires inputs to the information system as soon as the revenue recognition criteria are met, so that revenue and expenses are reported as soon as they can be measured or estimated closely. As we shall see, this means that revenues from such things as rents, interest, and commissions usually are reported as they are earned (either before or after their collection) because all three criteria are first met at the time of earning. The remainder of this chapter, except for a brief treatment of cash basis reporting, will be devoted to several measurement problems involved in accrual reporting of revenue.

Cash Basis Reporting

Some individuals and small firms may measure revenue and expenses on a cash basis, taking into account the inflow of assets and the consumption or outflow only at the time that cash is affected. For the firm or person who is concerned primarily with the flow of cash and with maintaining an adequate supply of cash to meet anticipated needs, measurement and reporting on an accrual basis might not provide information as critically important as changes in cash. However, in most firms information developed on the accrual basis appears to represent net income in its most useful concept, the earnings inflow and outflow streams of assets—not just cash.

Cash basis reporting of income is familiar to all individuals who prepare their personal federal and state income tax reports. This may explain in part why many persons appear to think of revenue and expenses as the inflow and outflow of cash. If most transactions are on a cash basis, if there is not a material investment in depreciable assets, and if the inventory of merchandise and supplies is not substantial in amount, then cash basis reporting may measure quite adequately the net income of the firm. However, most firms do have substantial investment in assets which depreciate and in inventories, and engage generally in transactions involving credit rather than cash; therefore, the accrual basis for reporting revenue and expense is used almost universally in business firms. Our further consideration of measuring and reporting net income will refer to the accrual basis.

When to Report Revenue

The use of qualitative standards for revenue data, as seen in the criteria for revenue reporting, means that these criteria must be applied to specific situations in which revenue is earned.

The first two criteria for revenue recognition generally determine when specific revenue is reported. By the time that (1) the revenue-producing activity has been performed and (2) the amount which will be received has been determined, the amount of expenses related to producing the revenue will almost always be determinable. It is often said, therefore, that revenue is reported when it is "realized," meaning when something of measureable value has been earned and received. The thing received need not be cash, but it must have a determinable cash value to satisfy the second criterion. Applications of these criteria are seen in the following situations.

When goods are produced In most business firms it is not clearly determined at the time goods are produced how much will be received for them when they are sold, and it may not even be determined whether they will be sold. Therefore, revenue is not normally reported at the time goods are produced. There are some exceptions, however, to this normal practice.

Firms producing precious metals for which there is an established market and a guaranteed or controlled price can know that their products will be sold and how much they will receive. These firms normally report their inventory of precious metals at market price and treat this as the amount received for the production activity, thus reporting revenue in the same period that production of a quantity of the metal is completed, even though it may be sold and the amount collected during a later period.

Farmers often report their inventory of farm products at market price and, thus, report revenue in the period in which production is completed. Many farm products have some type of "guaranteed" price through the operation of the parity price system, and there are established markets and published prices for most farm products. Therefore, the criteria for revenue recognition appear to be met when production is completed.

When production on a contract basis requires a long period of time, revenue may be recognized for the part of the contract completed each period if eventual collection of the contract amount is reasonably assured. For example, Company M may be constructing a section of highway for an agreed total price, and the time required for construction may be three years. If the total contract price is $24,000,000 and at the end of the first year an engineering estimate indicates that the project is one-sixth completed, the firm may report a revenue of $4,000,000 for the year. This is a reasonable allocation of the total revenue to be derived from the contract; it meets the revenue recognition criteria if it is assumed that a valid claim to $4,000,000 exists because of the work already done, or if it is clearly probable that the contract will be completed and, therefore, that the company's claim for the amount currently earned will be enforceable later.

Data for recognition of revenue on a long-term contract based on the *percentage of completion* method, as discussed in the preceding paragraph, are input to the accounting system by a journal entry like the following:

Dec. 31	Receivable from Construction Contract....................................	4,000,000	
	Construction Revenue		4,000,000
	To record revenue recognized on contract no. XT407A on the basis of engineering reports showing approximately $16\frac{2}{3}$ percent completion.		

When goods are sold Much revenue of business firms is derived from the sale of goods. It is common practice to recognize revenue from such sales when the sales are completed; that is, when the goods have been delivered and a valid claim exists against the customer for the sales price. The inputting of transaction data from sales invoices in earlier chapters (debiting Accounts Receivable and crediting Sales) was premised on the fact that the sales invoice was prepared at the time of delivery or just afterward—that it represented a completed sale.

For most sales the terms are simple, and it is easy to determine when the transaction is completed, that is, when it results in the collection of cash for a cash sale or the existence of an enforceable claim from a credit sale. Sales on *special order* for which goods are specially fabricated may be enforceable when the product is completed, but before delivery; in some instances, therefore, revenue is recognized before delivery. In contrast, *sales on approval* are not complete until the customer has examined the goods and approved them; revenue recognition is delayed beyond the time of delivery until there is evidence that the goods have been approved. Other special terms may be included in sales agreements; in all cases, when a claim against the customer becomes enforceable, revenue should be recognized and revenue data recorded in the accounting system.

When cash is collected Some firms sell appliances, clothing, and other goods on the *installment basis* to customers whose poor credit standing raises the question of whether the sales agreement is, in fact, enforceable against them. In some such cases it may be considered that the second criterion for revenue recognition has not been met until cash is collected. Revenue is not recorded in this situation when the goods are delivered, but it is recorded piecemeal as collections are made. In matching revenue and expenses, the cost of the goods sold on the installment basis must be treated as expense in the periods that collections are made and in proper proportion to the collections. To accomplish this there has been developed a procedure to match cost price and sales price when the sale is made and to defer the combined effect, or gross margin, rather than deferring both separately. The following journal entries with their notations explain this procedure:

Sept. 26	Installment Receivables	600	
	Installment Sales		600
	To record installment sale. (An entry like this is made in a special Installment Sales Register, or Journal, for each installment sale for which the revenue is to be deferred.)		

Date	Account	Debit	Credit
Sept. 26	Cost of Installment Sales	400	
	Merchandise (or Purchases)....................		400
	To record the cost of an installment sale. (An entry like this is made in special columns of the Installment Sales Register for each sale or for the total installment sales for a period.)		
Nov. 15 and Dec. 15	Cash..	60	
	Installment Receivables.........................		60
	To record cash collections from installment customers on these dates. (Each collection would be recorded in the Cash Receipts Journal.)		
Dec. 31	Installment Sales	600	
	Cost of Installment Sales		400
	Deferred Gross Profit on Installment Sales		200
	To close out the sales and cost accounts for installment sales and to record the gross profit deferred until collections are made. (This entry is shown for one sale. It would include, of course, the total of all installment sales for the year.)		
Dec. 31	Deferred Gross Profit on Installment Sales	40	
	Realized Gross Profit............................		40
	To record the gross profit—in this case, one-third of sales price collected—on installments collected within the year. (This entry is shown for collections on one sale. Such entry would normally include the gross profit applicable to all collections for the year on all installment sales.)		

Revenue and cost of goods sold (gross profit) on installment sales may sometimes be deferred when they should not be. The profit on certain installment sales may be deferred for purposes of computing the federal income tax of the firm; this may have encouraged firms to defer the gross profit for financial reporting even when all criteria for revenue recognition are met at the time of the sale. **It is clear that gross profit should be deferred on only those installment sales for which collections are highly questionable.**

Allocation of Revenue Between Periods

Many transactions result in the earning of revenue over a period of time, often with collection of the revenue specified at the end of a long period or at intervals. For example, money may be lent on long term with the agreement that interest is to be paid each six months. If such a loan of $100,000 were made at 6 percent on November 1, interest would have been earned for two months by the end of the year, and all criteria for revenue recognition would have been met. Therefore, interest for two months ($1,000) would be recorded as an asset, representing the valid claim against the debtor (a new asset), and as a revenue, representing the earning of that amount. The journal entry would be as follows:

Dec. 31	Interest Receivable	1,000	
	Interest Revenue		1,000
	To record the accrual of interest earned for two months at 6 percent on a loan of $100,000.		

Later, when the interest is collected for the full six months, interest for four months will be recorded as revenue in that period and the interest accrued for two months of the preceding year will not be treated as revenue, but as the collection of a receivable (an asset). The journal entry is:

May 1	Cash	3,000	
	Interest Receivable		1,000
	Interest Revenue		2,000
	To record collection of interest at 6 percent for the past six-month period.		

This handling of the data for the interest revenue results in reporting revenue in the period when all revenue criteria are met. The procedure is applicable to all revenues which accrue over a period of time and are collected at the end of the period, for example, commissions, leases, and rental payments collected at the end of an agreed period.

Allocation of Revenue Collected in Advance

Revenue of several types is collected before it is earned. Examples are rent and lease payments collected in advance, insurance premiums, magazine subscriptions, and interest in some situations. If rent of $1,200 is collected in advance each quarter, the amount collected is not earned until the lessee has used the space; if a fire were to destroy the leased building, the amount not yet earned normally would have to be returned to the lessee.

Recorded as a liability when collected One might classify the precollected rent as a liability owed to the lessee until it is earned, at which time it becomes revenue. At the time revenue is collected in advance it may be recorded as follows:

Nov. 1	Cash	1,200	
	Unearned Rent Collected		1,200
	Rent collected in advance for November, December, and January.		

By December 31 two months have passed, and $800 of the rent has been earned. In order to have this $800 reported as revenue in the current year, this amount should be removed from the Unearned Rent Collected account and stored in the Rent Revenue account. The journal entry to accomplish this is:

Dec. 31	Unearned Rent Collected	800	
	Rent Revenue		800
	To record the earning of two months' of the three months' rent collected on November 1.		

Sometime during the following year, perhaps not until financial reports are to be made at the end of the first quarter of the year, the $400 rent for January will be transferred from the Unearned Rent Collected account to the Rent Revenue account.

Recorded as revenue when collected Much of the revenue collected in advance for short periods such as a month to a quarter will be earned and properly classified as revenue long before the end of the year. It is very common to find such collections classified as revenue at the time the first data are input to the accounting system. If this were done, the procedures presented above would be changed; the journal entry at the time of collection would be:

Nov. 1	Cash	1,200	
	Rent Revenue		1,200
	To record the collection of rent for November, December, and January.		

At the end of the year it must be recognized that one-third of the rent (the amount for January) has not been earned and should not be reported as revenue, but as a liability. The journal entry to remove $400 from the Rent Revenue account and record it in the Unearned Rent Collected account is:

Dec. 31	Rent Revenue	400	
	Unearned Rent Collected		400
	To record as unearned one month's rent collected for January.		

Both of these procedures (recording as a liability or as revenue, with proper *adjustments*) will result in our reporting $400 as a liability and $800 as revenue at the end of the year; therefore, they are both acceptable. In each case the revenue collected in advance is analyzed at the end of the period to determine how much of it is earned, and the accounts are adjusted to reflect the revenue recognition status at the end of the year.

Revenue Reductions

Use of the qualitative standards for revenue information which are seen in the criteria for revenue recognition affects the measure of revenue in specific situations.

Sales returns and allowances When merchandise or services are sold there is an inflow of assets (an increase). In earlier chapters we saw that such transactions are recorded with data inputs such as those shown in the following journal entry:

Cash (or Accounts Receivable)	900	
Sales Revenue		900

This journal entry inputs the $900 amount into the asset subsystem Cash account as a positive amount (increase) and into the equities subsystem Sales Revenue account with a similar effect (increase). There is a clearly measured inflow of assets, and revenue is recognized in the amount of $900.

If cash is returned to the customer or if an allowance is made which decreases the amount collectible from him following the sale, this is a decrease in assets derived from the sale and, therefore, a decrease in the revenue previously recognized. A refund of cash or an allowance on a customer's account would stem from the customer's return of merchandise or the firm's acknowledgement of faulty or inferior merchandise or services. Either of these situations results in a decrease in the price or inflow of assets received from the sale. Data to reflect the transaction must be classified as a decrease in the appropriate asset and a decrease in revenue. The decrease in cash or accounts receivable is classified as a credit to the appropriate asset account, and the decrease in revenue could be classified and stored as a decrease (debit) in the Sales Revenue account. However, the total amount of such price adjustments to customers is important information for management. Therefore, the decrease in revenue is stored in a separate account, Sales Returns and Allowances, so that such data can be summarized and reported as a separate item of information. The journal entry for input of data about a return of merchandise or other allowance is:

Sales Returns and Allowances....................................	100	
Cash (or Accounts Receivable).............................		100

Recording sales returns and allowances The entry is written in general journal form in the above illustration, and the General Journal might be used for a return or allowance which is applied against a customer's account. A refund of cash is a cash payment and would be recorded in the Cash Payments Journal in a manual model of the system; input of the data into a punched-card or computer-based model of the system would follow the pattern for all cash-payment input data.

If credit against customers' accounts is given frequently for returns or allowances on sales, a special procedure might be established for efficient handling of these data inputs. In a manual system, a special single-column journal might be used, since each transaction is interpreted as a debit to Sales Returns and Allowances and a credit to Accounts Receivable. Such a journal might appear as shown in Figure 6-1. Note in that illustration that individual amounts are posted to customers' individual accounts as credits, and the total of the column is posted to the Sales Returns and Allowances account as a debit and to the Accounts Receivable account as a credit.

The business document normally used for recording this transaction is the credit memorandum. This is a memorandum from the firm to its customer informing the customer that his account has been credited for the amount indicated, as an allowance off the invoice amount of the sale because of merchandise return or faulty merchandise or service. This credit memo may be used in a unit record (punched-card) system as a source of data to be punched into special transaction cards, with a separate card containing the account number

Figure 6-1

SALES RETURNS AND ALLOWANCES JOURNAL

Date		Account Credited	C/M No.	P.R.	Amount
May	7	Frederick W. Tilden	E-001	✓	55 00
	11	Alma T. Weeks	E-002	✓	16 00
	13	Joseph M. Carillo	E-003	✓	69 00
	19	Cumo U. Bowro	E-004	✓	21 00
	31	Eugene E. Massey	E-102	✓	2 40
		Sales Returns & Allowances Dr/Accounts Receivable CR		820/111	1745 75

for each of the accounts affected and the amount and nature (positive or negative) of the effect. These cards, along with other cards for the day, are then sorted by account number to summarize the changes in accounts. In a computer centered system one input card may be punched to indicate the type of transaction, the customer involved, and the amount; the computer program then guides the internal action of the computer to update stored data for all accounts affected.

Reporting sales returns and allowances The amount accumulated for sales returns and allowances for the period is shown as a deduction from sales in reporting revenue on the income statement. A detailed income statement might contain a revenue section presented as follows:

Revenue:	
Sales of goods and services	$946,408
Less returns and price allowances	13,772
Net revenue from sales	$932,636
Expenses:	
(Operating expenses deducted here)	

By definition, returns and allowances must be deducted in computing the amount of revenue. If revenue is an inflow of assets, then any offset or adjustment in that flow must be reflected in the information presenting the amount of revenue. The emphasis placed on periodic matching of revenues and expenses by the criteria for revenue recognition necessitates that returns and allowances be reported with the original revenue amounts to which they apply insofar as is possible. Since returns and allowances normally are quite immaterial in amount, it is common to see these adjustments reported in the period in which they occur, rather than in the period in which the related basic revenue is reported. In situations in which returns and allowances are material, estimates of the amount of present-period sales to be returned or adjusted must be made and the resulting reduction in accounts receivable and revenue must be input to the information system. In journal entry form this input would be:

Sales Returns and Allowances	2,000	
Allowance for Returns and Adjustments		2,000
To record the estimated merchandise returns and adjustments to be allowed next year on sales made late in the current year.		

This estimate would be deducted from sales revenue along with amounts accumulated from actual returns. The Allowance for Returns and Adjustments is a reduction in the amount expected to be collected from accounts receivable and is subtracted from the balance in the Accounts Receivable account to determine the amount reportable for this asset on the balance sheet. This adjustment is not common, but it provides a classic example of the application of qualitative standards in identifying data to be used in developing financial information.

Cash discounts on sales Discounts are often offered to credit customers to encourage them to pay before the normal term of credit expires. For example, an invoice from a manufacturer to a wholesaler or from a wholesaler to a retailer may indicate credit terms of "2 percent discount if paid within ten days; later the full amount is to be considered net (no discount deducted) and due within thirty days." This would be abbreviated, "2/10,n/30" and would be read, "Two ten, net thirty." These credit terms would permit a customer to deduct 2 percent, or $10, from an invoice of $500 and pay the invoice in full with a check for $490 within a ten-day period from the date of the invoice. Since the charge to the customer and the revenue would have been recorded at the full invoice amount, $500 in this case, the discount must be regarded as a reduction in price and classified so as to decrease the amount of revenue from $500 to the amount actually received, $490.

Recording sales discounts The original sale for $500 referred to in the preceding paragraph would appear this way in general journal form:

Accounts Receivable	500	
Sales		500

The collection of $490 in full payment of the $500 invoice would be classified as follows:

Cash	490	
Sales Discounts	10	
Accounts Receivable		500

This classification of data normally would not appear in the general journal in a manual system but would be entered in the Cash Receipts journal in the following format.

CASH RECEIPTS JOURNAL

Date		Account Credited	P.R.	Sundry Credit	Accounts Rec. Cr.	Sales Cr.	Sales Disc. Dr.	Cash Dr.
Oct	8	City Suppliers			500 00		10 00	490 00

Reporting sales discounts When the above data are posted to the ledger accounts, the Sales account will contain an accumulation of revenues from sales, and the Sales Discount account will contain an accumulation of reductions in revenue because of reductions in price for paying early. Sales and the related reductions are reported on a detailed income statement as follows:

Revenue:		
Sales of goods and services		$946,408
Less: Discounts on sales	$13,772	
Returns and price allowances	10,444	24,216
Net revenue from sales		$924,192

Since revenue is defined as an inflow of assets, the reduction in the amount actually received because of granting a reduction in price for early payment must be deducted from the revenue, which was already tentatively recorded at the full amount of the sales invoice.

Consistent interpretation of the business situation requires that we estimate the amount of cash discount most probably to be taken by customers on the amounts charged to them at the end of the fiscal period. We should then input the amount of the estimate as an additional amount of sales discount and as a reduction in the amount of accounts receivable. In journal entry form, this data input would appear as follows:

Sales Discounts	1,100	
Allowance for Sales Discounts		1,100
To record the estimated amount of discounts to be taken by customers on charges still subject to discount.		

This adjustment is posted to the Sales Discount account and included with the accumulated amounts actually deducted as discounts by customers. The Allowance for Sales Discounts represents an amount of accounts receivable not expected to be collected; therefore, this amount is deducted from the balance of Accounts Receivable reported on the balance sheet. Frequently, the amount of discounts available to be taken on accounts outstanding at the end of the period is so negligible in amount that the adjustment is not computed and recorded.

Uncollectible accounts receivable When sales are made on credit, the date of collection is postponed from the date of sale to some future date, usually within thirty to ninety days. This postponement raises the question of whether the firm will be able to collect for all the sales. The decision made when the credit is granted that a person will be able and willing to pay later could be wrong in some instances; in some cases the situation may change so that the customer's ability to pay diminishes. Experience of firms that sell on credit indicates that, on the average, a small percentage of credit granted will never be collected. This means that for all credit sales the amount to be collected and the amount of revenue that should be reported is slightly less than the total amount of the sales. Of course, if it were known in advance which customers would not pay, sales would not be made on credit to those customers. Since this information is not known, we must estimate the amount which probably will not be collected and deduct it from both the assets and the revenue derived from credit sales, if we are to avoid reporting amounts too great for accounts receivable and for revenue.

Estimating uncollectibles based on credit sales If customers are granted credit based on standards related to income and their history of debt-paying, it may be possible for a firm to determine from its own experience and that of similar firms (usually through information from trade associations) the percent of credit sales which probably will not be collected. This can be the basis for computing and recording the amount of the estimated uncollectible accounts receivable (reduction in sales revenue and accounts receivable).

Assume that Company X made $100,000 of credit sales to customers and collected $80,000 of this during the period. Data for the sales would have been recorded in the Sales Journal, and collection data would have been recorded in the Cash Receipts Journal. The resulting data in the ledger accounts would be as follows:

Cash

Debit	Credit
80,000	

Accounts Receivable

Debit		Credit
(from prior year)	15,000	80,000
	100,000	
(balance 35,000)		

Sales Revenue

Debit	Credit
	100,000

Allowance for Uncollectible Accounts

Debit	Credit	
	(from prior year)	500

If it is estimated that 1 percent of credit sales will not be collected, then $1,000 (1 percent of $100,000) of the amount added this year to the Accounts Receivable account should not be reported as an asset, and $1,000 of the amount in the Sales Revenue account should not be reported as revenue.

Recording the estimate of uncollectibles based on sales Since the gross amount of sales revenue and the gross amount of accounts receivable are important data for management and investor analysis, the reduction in these amounts because of probable uncollectibility is recorded in two additional accounts:

1. The reduction in accounts receivable is recorded as a credit in an account, Allowance for Uncollectible Accounts. The balance in this account is deducted from accounts receivable in computing the amount to be reported as an asset on the balance sheet.
2. The reduction in revenue is recorded as a debit in an account, Credit Losses. The balance in this account is deducted from sales revenue in computing the amount of revenue to report on the income statement.

Data in Allowance for Uncollectible Accounts have the effect of reducing an asset; therefore amounts are entered in this account as credits. Data in the Credit Losses account have the effect of reducing revenue (or capital from earnings); therefore amounts are entered in this account as debits. A journal entry to record the $1,000 estimate of uncollectibles from the preceding illustration is

		Debit	Credit
Dec. 31	Credit Losses	1,000	
	Allowance for Uncollectible Accounts		1,000

Following this journal entry the accounts from the illustration would appear as follows:

Cash

Debit	Credit
80,000	

Accounts Receivable

Debit		Credit
(from prior year)	15,000	80,000
	100,000	
(balance 35,000)		

Sales Revenue

Debit	Credit
	100,000

Allowance for Uncollectible Accounts

Debit	Credit	
	(from prior year)	500
		1,000

Credit Losses

Debit	Credit
1,000	

Writeoff of individual accounts At the end of each year when the estimate of uncollectible accounts is recorded, a negative input (reduction) is entered in accounts in both the assets subsystem and equities subsystem of financial data, as seen in the preceding journal entry. This reduces the amount of accounts receivable and the amount of capital from earnings.

When it is decided that a specific account cannot be collected, data for that account are removed from the system; the account is no longer included among the assets. No "loss" or reduction in revenue is recorded, however, because this was recorded in the preceding year-end estimate. This clearing of data from the individual account is called "writing off" the account. If a customer, Lunar Trade Company, cannot pay its account, which has a balance of $110, and this account is to be written off, the following entry will be made:

	Debit	Credit
Allowance for Uncollectible Accounts	110	
Accounts Receivable—Lunar Trade Co.		110

The credit removes $110 from the Accounts Receivable account and from the individual account of Lunar Trade Company, since it is now considered that this amount does not, in fact, represent a valid asset. The debit to Allowance for Uncollectible Accounts removes the $110 from that account, on the assumption that $110 of the amount entered as the estimate at the end of the preceding year has now been proven to apply to the specific account removed from the system. It should be noted that this action does not reduce the net amount reported for accounts receivable. The allowance for Uncollectible Accounts is deducted from accounts receivable; reducing both the allowance and accounts receivable by $110 does not affect the difference. The writeoff of an account, then, is only the removal of data no longer appropriately carried in the information system: it does not change the net amount of assets, nor does it affect any equity account.

Estimating uncollectibles based on age of accounts receivable An estimate of the amount of accounts receivable, but probably not collectible, can be based on the age (time past the due date) of the amounts still due from customers. Individual amounts in all customer accounts are classified in groups such as the following:

Not yet due
1 to 30 days past due
31 to 60 days past due
61 to 120 days past due
121 to 180 days past due
181 days to 1 year past due
More than 1 year past due

Based on the experience of the firm or that of other firms having similar policies for granting credit and procedures for collection, percents of probable losses can be determined for each of the age classes. Naturally, one would expect that the percentage of loss would increase with the time interval since the due date. The percentage of probable uncollectibles for each age class is applied to the amount in that class; the total from all these computations is the estimate of total uncollectible accounts resulting from sales of both the current year and prior years, since all accounts receivable, regardless of age, are included in the aging analysis. This means that the amount computed is the total amount which should appear as the balance in the account, Allowance for Uncollectible Accounts.

Recording the estimate of uncollectibles based on aged accounts receivable For use in illustrating the recording process, the accounts used in a prior illustration are repeated here:

Cash	
80,000	

Accounts Receivable	
(from prior year) 15,000	80,000
100,000	

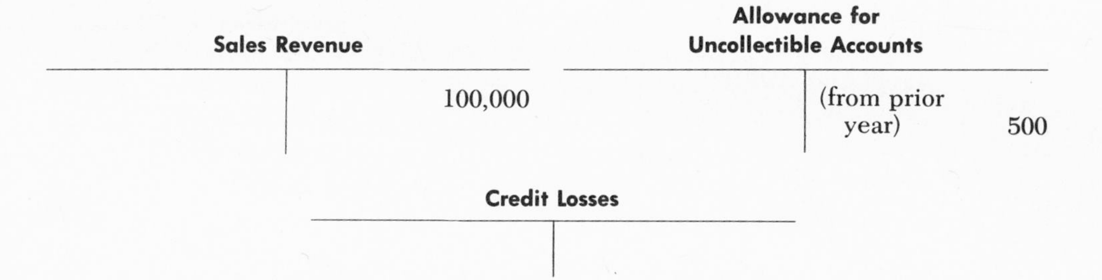

Assume that when accounts receivable are aged and the experience percents of probable uncollectible amounts applied to the various age groups, the resulting estimate of total uncollectibles is $1,480. This is the total amount which we should deduct from accounts receivable as an estimate of the accounts which are uncollectible. There is a balance of $500 remaining in the Allowance for Uncollectible Accounts from the preceding year. Since the $1,480 is the total estimate including aged accounts receivable carried from the previous year, we must deduct $500 from it to avoid counting last year's balance twice. The resulting amount of $980 is recorded as a reduction in revenue and accounts receivable by the following journal entry:

Dec. 31	Credit Losses	980	
	Allowance for Uncollectible Accounts		980

This computation and recording of the estimate of uncollectible accounts receivable results in the following data in the accounts:

Cash

Debit	Credit
80,000	

Accounts Receivable

Debit	Credit
(from prior year) 15,000	80,000
100,000	

Sales Revenue

Debit	Credit
	100,000

Allowance for Uncollectible Accounts

Debit	Credit
	(from prior year) 500
	980

Credit Losses

Debit	Credit
980	

It should be noted that the balance in the Allowance for Uncollectible Accounts is now $1,480, the amount estimated in the preceding section. The amount reported as a reduction in revenue (Credit Losses) for this period is $980. The difference of $500 is the amount recorded in the preceding year as estimated uncollectible amounts, and which has not yet been cancelled out by actual writeoff of individual accounts receivable.

Reporting the estimate of uncollectible accounts As a result of entering the amount of the estimated uncollectible accounts receivable in the accounting system, revenue will be reported as follows on the income statement:

Revenue:		
Sales of goods and services		$100,000
Less: Estimated credit losses	$ 980	
Returns and price allowances	1,020	
Discounts on sales	700	2,700
Net Revenue from sales		$ 97,300

($1,020 and $700 for returns and discounts are hypothetical amounts.)

This illustration uses the previously developed figure, $980, based on aging the accounts receivable, for estimated credit losses for the current period. If the estimate based on a percentage of credit sales were used, the presentation would be the same except that the $1,000 estimate would be used instead of the $980 amount.

Accounts receivable are presented on the balance sheet as follows:

ASSETS

Cash		$ xxx
Accounts receivable	$35,000	
Less estimated uncollectible accounts	1,480	33,520
Merchandise		xxx

Information concerning the gross amount of accounts receivable is reported, but only the amount estimated to be collected is added with other assets to obtain the total of all asset amounts.

Credit losses as revenue reduction or expenses Estimated credit losses for the period are reported by some firms as an expense rather than as a reduction in revenue. When this is done, the title "Bad Debts," or "Bad Debt Expense," is commonly used, and the amount is reported as one of the operating expenses. This procedure has merit in some situations, but it appears to be used more widely than is warranted.

If credit-granting standards and collection procedures are well planned, they must be presumed to result in losses which can be estimated from past experience. It therefore appears clear that since credit sales are made with the knowledge that not all of them will result in collections, the revenue is best measured by the amount management actually expects to collect. Following this argument, estimated credit losses would be reported as a reduction in revenue, as illustrated in the preceding sections of this chapter.

If credit is granted only rarely, and then to customers from whom it is expected that full collection will be made, and if it is determined later that some amounts probably will not be collected because of poor treatment of customers or poor collection procedures, then the expected loss might be interpreted as being the direct result of operations other than credit-granting. In this situation, reporting the estimated loss as a type of collection expense rather than as a reduction in revenue might provide a better understanding of the firm's operations. This situation appears to be an exception rather than the rule, and it appears that estimated credit losses normally are best reported as deductions from gross revenue. It is recognized, however, that this item is commonly reported as an expense.

Criticism of Revenue Recognition Standards

The standards presented in this chapter for recognizing and reporting revenue are applied with reasonable uniformity. Some firms may defer income improperly by using the *installment sales* method when there is little doubt as to collectibility of the accounts and all criteria or standards are actually met in the period in which the goods are sold. Not all contractors use the *percent of completion* method in reporting revenue from long-term contracts; some wait until the contract is complete to report the revenue. These are the relatively few exceptions; the vast majority of firms report most revenue in accordance with the standards.

Not everyone, however, agrees that the standards for reporting revenue are totally appropriate. It is argued that value is produced by all activities of the firm, not just by the sales activity, and that revenue should be recognized as value is produced and not just when the goods or services are sold. This argument holds that most manufactured goods are saleable and have a value to the manufacturer above his cost of production. Therefore, it is argued that the goods should be reported at the market value less what it will cost to sell them, with this value reported as revenue when the goods are produced rather than when they are sold. Such argument holds that the present standards give too much emphasis to the availability of funds from the sale and do not report the economic value at the time it is developed in the firm.

The arguments which have prevailed and have maintained the present definition of revenue and the present standards for its recognition are:

> The principle financial problem in many firms is the flow of funds—the development of funds in free form for paying the operating costs of the firm. Recognizing revenue when funds (cash or other specific value) are received from the sale provides information of an important financial nature.
>
> It is not possible to judge with accuracy how much will be received for many products before the goods are sold. Sales may be in bulk lot at a lower price, or demand may increase so that sales may be made at a higher price.
>
> Revenue reported as the development of economic value in the firm would not provide information of any great utility to management. Also, revenue reported on this basis would give less information than presently reported revenue (as a part of net income) as to the availability of funds for dividends to stockholders.
>
> Measurement of revenue as now reported can be made quite objectively, whereas determining revenue on the basis of development of economic value would involve judgment to a greater extent.

The arguments can be countered to some extent with a recitation of the weaknesses of the present standards, but they do prevail, and it appears that revenue will be reported for some time in the future without change from the current definition and standards. If change in revenue reporting does come, it will no doubt provide for reporting the present *realized* revenue as a clearly distinguishable element of the total economic value revenue.

QUESTIONS AND EXERCISES

6- A. What is revenue? How is revenue related to net income?

6- B. Revenue is recognized when cash and accounts receivable are received in exchange for merchandise or services.

a. Why is revenue normally not recognized when equipment is received in exchange for cash or a promise to pay cash later?
b. Under what circumstances, if any, would you favor recognition of revenue upon the purchase of an asset?

6-C. Explain the purpose and use of the account, Allowance for Uncollectible Accounts. When is this account credited? When is it debited? What other accounts are affected by these changes?

6-D. What is meant by "aging" accounts receivable? Why is this done?

6-E. Does the recording of credit losses on the basis of estimates, rather than at the time of actual loss of individual accounts, reflect extreme conservatism? Explain your answer.

6-F. Why are credit losses estimated and reported for each fiscal period? Why is an adjusting entry made to record the estimated amount of credit losses? Why is this done rather than waiting until the time of the proven loss for each individual account and reporting each such loss with a debit to the Credit Losses account?

6-G. CCC Corporation estimated on December 31, 1971, that it would lose 1 percent of its 1971 credit sales because the accounts would be uncollectible. CCC Corporation's credit sales for the year were $979,400; what journal entry would be used to record the predicted loss?

6-H. The following is a summary of the "aging" schedule for the DDD Company's accounts receivable at the end of the fiscal year:

0–30 days	$311,412
31–60 days	190,055
61–90 days	41,202
Over 90 days	4,188
Total	$546,857

Experience indicates that only 40 percent of bills over ninety days old are collected, while 80 percent are collected from those sixty-one to ninety days old, 96 percent from those thirty-one to sixty days old, and 99 percent from those less than thirty-one days old. Allowance for Uncollectible Accounts has a credit balance of $12,222.13; what adjustment, if any, is needed?

6-I. Explain how the criteria for recognizing and reporting revenue are related to the "funds committed" concept of reporting asset data.

6-J. Distinguish between the accrual basis and the cash basis of reporting revenue and expenses.

6-K. Would it be possible to operate the financial information system so that year-end adjustments of revenue would not be needed? Explain.

6-L. Why is it usually necessary to adjust the revenue accounts at year end before using information from the system to report revenue?

6-M. A B Company's total sales for the year were $887,400. It allowed customers' discounts of $8,610 from total sales, accepted $15,100 of merchandise returned by customers, and expects to be unable to collect approximately $3,700 of credit sales. Show how revenue would be reported on an income statement for A B Company for the year.

PROCEDURAL PROBLEMS

6-1. The William Cramer Company records its transactions in a sales journal, a sales returns and allowances journal, a cash receipts journal (column headings: Sundry Credit, Accounts Receivable Credit, Sales Credit, Sales Discount Debit, Cash Debit), and a general journal. Record the following transactions in the appropriate journals.

Dec. 2 Sold $612.50 of merchandise on credit to Mike Ryan and Co. Sales invoice 12-001.

4 Sold Morris Bros. merchandise for $1,273.30 on account. Invoice no. 12-002.

4 Sold Helen Ames merchandise for $162.15 on account. Invoice no. 12-003.

5 Morris Bros. returned merchandise sold to them for $22.60. Credit memo M-001.

8 Made a credit sale of merchandise to Kenneth Hales, Inc. for $412.00. Sales invoice no. 12-004.

9 Made a credit sale to Mandel's Shops, Inc. for $1,650. Invoice 12-005.

11 Mike Ryan and Co. paid $396.30 cash and took a discount of $2.40.

11 Made a credit sale of merchandise for $210.10 to Simpson, Inc. Invoice 12-006.

13 Mandel's Shops, Inc. returned defective merchandise for credit of $30.00. Credit memo M-002.

14 Made a credit sale of $432.55 to Shaw, Inc. Invoice 12-007.

14 Simpson, Inc. was allowed a credit of $15.35 after they notified us of a defect in merchandise we delivered to them. Credit memo M-003.

17 Made a cash sale of $46.50 to Mandel's Shops, Inc.

19 Made a credit sale of merchandise to R. T. Burke Co. for $794.00. Invoice no. 12-008.

21 Received a payment of $159.10 from Helen Ames, Inc. after they took a discount of $2.05.

22 R. T. Burke returned merchandise for credit for $40.00. Credit memo M-004.

24 Kenneth Hales, Inc. paid their entire balance, taking a 1 percent discount.

25 Made a cash sale to Street Co. of merchandise for $27.35.

28 Received $46.45 cash from Simpson, Inc. and allowed them a $1.14 discount on account.

29 Shaw, Inc. took a sales discount of $1.75 and made a cash payment of $98.40 on account.

31 Made a credit sale of merchandise for $271.14 to Mike Ryan and Co.

a. Prepare adjusting entries to record an allowance for sales discount equal to the one percent of December credit sales and an allowance for sales returns and adjustments of $75.00.
b. Prepare the revenue section of an income statement to determine net revenue from sales.

6-2. The Mehrtens Publishing Co. publishes a monthly magazine. They received the subscriptions below and collected the revenue.

Jan. 1, 1968	One-year subscription	$12.00
June 1, 1968	Three-year subscription	23.40
Nov. 1, 1968	One-year subscription	12.00
April 1, 1969	Two-year subscription	19.60

a. Assuming Mehrtens Publishing Company records subscriptions as a liability when received, prepare the adjusting entries for December 31, 1968, and December 31, 1969.
b. Assuming Mehrtens Publishing Company records subscriptions as revenue when received, prepare the necessary adjusting entry for December 31, 1968.

6-3. The Johnson-Sineway Construction Co. has a contract (contract no. KAN. P10748) with the state of Kansas for work on three projects. The company will compute revenue separately on each project. Prepare the adjusting entries for December 31, 1968, and December 31, 1969, to record revenue for work completed during the year. Show supporting computations.

		Percentage Completed as of Dec. 31	
Project	Total Contract Price	1968	1969
A	$ 645,000	40	100
B	3,225,000	12	65
C	1,325,000	34	77

6-4. The Safari Motorcycle Sales Co. uses the installment basis to recognize revenue from sales to individuals.
a. Record the transactions in a two-column journal.
b. Prepare the adjusting entries at the end of the month to record deferred gross profit and realized gross profit.

July 3 Sold to James Wray for $1,200 on account a motorcycle with a cost to us of $800.

7 Sold Mickey Simpson a motor bike that had cost us $600, for $800 on account.

12 Received $210 on account from James Wray.

21 A motorcycle that cost us $700 was sold to C. K. Roth for $1,000 on account.

July 24 Mickey Simpson paid us $380 on his account.
31 Received $160 on account from C. K. Roth.

6-5. The credit department of Wilson Wholesale Grocery has prepared the schedule of accounts receivable balances as of December 31.

Amount	When Due	Percent Estimated Uncollectible
$47,280	Current	1
11,460	1–30 days past due	3
7,600	31–60 days "	8
3,210	61–90 days "	12
4,160	91–180 days "	26
1,720	Over 180 days"	70
$75,430		

The current balance of allowance for doubtful accounts is $321.12. Compute the amount of estimated uncollectible accounts and prepare the adjusting journal entry.

6-6. The Rand Company has the following account balances as of December 31.

Accounts Receivable	$ 77,140.00
Allowance for Uncollectible Accounts	367.68
Credit Sales for the year were	246,500.00

Two individual accounts are considered uncollectible:

Zenith Warehouse, Inc.	$71.20
Ray Auto Supply	16.38

a. Prepare the journal entry to record the writing off of the uncollectible accounts.
b. Prepare the journal entry to record the estimate of uncollectible accounts if the amount is to be 1 percent of credit sales for the year; 2 percent of account receivables as of December 31.

6-7. The following information was taken from the books of Lavidage, Inc. as of December 31, 1971.

Accounts receivable	$ 39,800.00
Allowance for uncollectible accounts	723.40
Credit sales (includes $42,000 for December)	511,000.00

The credit losses for December are estimated to be 2 percent of credit sales for December. The sales discounts on December sales to be taken in January are estimated to be one-half of one percent of December credit sales. It is estimated that merchandise representing 1 percent of accounts receivable will be returned.

a. Prepare adjusting entries.
b. Prepare a partial balance sheet to show net accounts receivable after all adjustments.

6-8. Shane Appliances, Inc. has $118,200 of accounts receivable which has been broken down into the following aging schedule. The current balance of allowance for uncollectible accounts is $2,732.45.

Prior to preparing its year-end adjusting entries, the company decides to write off all accounts over 180 days old.

a. Prepare the entry to write off the 180-day past due accounts.
b. Prepare the adjusting entry to record estimated uncollectible accounts.

Amount	When Due	Percent Estimated Uncollectible
$ 71,220	Current	1
14,830	1–30 days past due	4
21,200	30–60 "	19
6,710	60–90 "	30
3,520	90–180 "	50
720	Over 180 "	100
$118,200		

6-9. The Thompson Appliance Company sells television sets on the installment basis. All the sets cost $300 each and are sold for $400. During the month of February the company sold twenty-one sets and collected $7,200 cash from prior installment sales.

Prepare the February 28 entries to record deferred gross profit and realized gross profit for the month.

6-10. The Saxon Realty Company began operations in 1971 with four buildings which they leased to tenants under rental contracts described below. The rental fee was collected when the lease was signed.

A. N. Mitchell leased building 2 on April 1, 1971, for a two-year period at $300 per month. Buildings 3 and 4 were leased to Sineway, Inc., on August 1, 1971. They paid $2,400 for a two-year lease on building 3 and $3,600 for a one-year lease on building 4.

a. Assuming Saxon Realty Company records rental collections as revenue when received, prepare the entries to record the contracts and the December 31, 1971, adjusting entry.
b. Assuming the collections on these contracts were originally recorded as liabilities by Saxon Realty Company, prepare the December 31, 1971, adjusting entry.

6-11. The Hampton Island Shipyards, Inc., is constructing two ships under a contract that allows the company to recognize revenue for the percentage of work completed during each year. Revenue is computed for each ship.

Prepare the December 31, 1970, and December 31, 1971, entries to record revenues earned during each of those years.

Ship Number	Total Contract Price	Percentage Completed During the Year Ended December 31	
		1970	1971
311	$1,400,000	30	45
312	$3,700,000	65	35

CONCEPTUAL PROBLEMS

6-12. Reported credit losses are based on the prices due from customers. The real loss to the seller from an uncollected sale is the cost of the merchandise, plus any incremental handling and selling expenses. How can you justify current practice in face of these facts?

6-13. Three different companies recognize revenue as follows:

Building contractor—at the time of production.
Wholesale grocer—at the time of shipment to customers.
Retail installment seller of small appliances—at the time of collection.

What statement of principles of revenue recognition and reporting justifies all three practices? What conditions must exist in each case if the practice is not to violate the principle?

6-14. The Egton Corporation began business on July 1. During the first quarter of operation it delivered to customers products with a total sales price of $100,400. The company officers had no prior experience on which to base an estimate of the collectibility of accounts receivable and, therefore, decided to use the industry average of 1½ percent of sales (all of which were on credit) until data could be obtained from the company's experience.

a. Prepare a journal entry for September 30 to record estimated credit losses for the quarter.
b. On September 16, City Suppliers was declared bankrupt. Egton Corporation collected $40 from the trustee as the total amount available for payment on the $90 owed them by City Suppliers. Prepare the entry for the $40 collection and the writeoff of the remaining $50.
c. On September 30, an analysis of accounts receivable showed the following:

0–30 days old	$15,000
31–60 days old	5,000
61 days and over...........	3,000

Based on experience of local firms granting credit on the same basis as Egton Corporation, the company's auditors suggested that the following percentages be used to compute the amount that would probably prove uncollectible from the first quarter's sales: zero–thirty days, 1 percent; thirty-one–sixty days, 5 percent; more than sixty days, 20 percent. Prepare a journal entry to adjust data in the accounts to this basis.

6-15. The Gambling Equipment Corporation sells gambling paraphernalia to illegal operators of gaming houses. This equipment carries a high markup over cost and usually is sold on terms of one-sixth in cash and the remainder in five equal, monthly payments.

In highly sporadic raids by law officers and in gangland skirmishes for control of gambling territories the equipment may be confiscated or destroyed before all payments have been made. It is customary (and custom is law in this market) for the seller to make no effort to collect unpaid installments when the equipment is destroyed or stolen by outsiders; this is understood to be a fair sharing by him in the risks of the trade.

Because of the risks, the GE Corporation recognizes revenue when cash is collected. Following are data for the month of October:

On October 1, the GE Corporation has in its warehouse a variety of gambling paraphernalia which cost $221,000. Customers owe the corporation $81,000 for equipment of various kinds that cost the corporation a total of $32,400.

Gambling paraphernalia of various types was purchased for $77,000.

Gambling equipment which cost $72,000 was sold for $180,000; $30,000 was collected in cash, and the equipment was released to customers' pick-up men.

Regular monthly collections of $36,000 were made.

Paraphernalia which had originally cost the GE Corporation $8,000, and on which customers still owed a total of $6,000, was confiscated or destroyed during the month under such conditions that the GE Corporation accepted the loss.

Administrative, selling, and collection expenses for the month, totaling $11,200, were paid.

a. Prepare an income statement for the Gambling Equipment Corporation for the month of October using the basis for revenue recognition adopted by the company.
b. On a balance sheet for October 31, at what amount would one report the equipment that is in the possession of customers, but for which full collection has not been received?
c. Why do you agree or disagree with the basis the GE Corporation uses for recognizing revenue?

7 Periodic Reporting of Expenses

Preview Questions

As you study look for the answers to the following questions:

- **What are expenses?**
- **What kinds of resources are consumed in producing a revenue inflow?**
- **What specific criteria are followed to determine when to report expenses?**
- **On what basis are expenses reported?**
- **How must expenses be adjusted before they are reported?**
- **How is the amount of merchandise cost considered expense identified?**
- **What is amortization? Depreciation?**
- **How are warranty and premium expenses measured?**

In the preceding chapter net income was seen as the resources added by a firm's activities. Revenue is one phase of a firm's adding to its resources—the inflow of earned resources. We are ready now to consider expenses, the other element in a firm's earning income.

BASIC CONCEPT OF EXPENSES

The consumption of resources in the conduct of the firm's activities (all generally in the effort to produce income) is termed *expenses.*

Generally all activities of a business firm are regarded as related to earning revenue either now or in the future. The question of goals and responsibilities of the firm will be considered in a later chapter. At this point, the general concept of expenses as the consumption of resources, including the outflow of goods sold, in the conduct of the firm's operations is adequate for our understanding and analysis of expenses.

Forms of Expense

Expenses are usually explained as the consumption of resources. There may be some basis for thinking of the cost of goods sold as an outflow of resources, but the concept of consumption appears to apply adequately even to that item. When wages are paid for employee service, money is paid for service (a resource), which has been consumed. When supplies are purchased a resource (supplies) is received, and the supplies are then consumed. There are two forms of expenses:

1. Consumption of services—salaries, interest, taxes, rent, and such.
2. Consumption of goods—cost of goods sold, supplies, depreciation of property, and such.

Qualitative Standards, or Criteria, for Reporting Expenses

Generally, an expense is reported when a resource has been consumed. There are additional qualifications or standards, however. The standards observed in current practice can be expressed in the following criteria for expense reporting:

1. Resources have been consumed.
   a. A resource of the firm, either goods or service, has been consumed or dissipated in the general activities in which the firm engages to produce revenue, either directly or indirectly. And,
   b. The activity in which the resource was consumed is not reasonably certain to produce a revenue in the future.

   Or,

2. Resources have not yet been consumed; however, revenue has been reported which is directly related to the future consumption of resources in an amount that is known or can be estimated with reasonable accuracy.

There is strong emphasis on matching the reporting of expenses with the reporting of related revenue. In criterion number 1, above, it is clear that resources may be consumed for the purpose of producing revenue, but if this activity is directly related to revenue which is reasonably certain to be reported in the future, the reporting of the expense will be delayed and matched with the reporting of the related revenue. In the second criterion, expense is reported before the consumption of resources if the activity producing the revenue is reasonably certain to cause a resource consumption in the future; thus, the reporting of revenue and expense is matched in the same period. To aid in understanding revenue and expenses, turn back to chapter 6 and relate the criteria for revenue reporting to these criteria for expense reporting. Note that revenue is measured by the amount of funds received and **expenses are measured by the amount of funds committed in the resources consumed.**

APPLICATION OF CRITERIA FOR EXPENSE REPORTING

The concept of matching expense and revenue is reasonable, but, just as there are some rather involved problems in applying the concept of revenue recognition (seen in chapter 6), so there are some problems in applying the concept of expense reporting. Several commonly encountered situations are examined below.

Distinguishing between Expense and Expenditures

Expenditures are payments. When made for goods or services, these payments may be made either before or after the goods or services are consumed. Some goods, such as land, may be paid for but never actually consumed, and, of course, it is possible for goods and services to be consumed and never paid for. The *consumption* of goods and services is expense; it is clear that this is not the same as expenditure, although most expenses do have a related expenditure.

When expenditures for resources are made in the same reporting period (month, quarter, or year) that the resources are consumed, the expenditure and consumption are reported together. For example, employees perform services for the firm and are paid for these services; normally these events occur within the same period and, therefore, data for the expenditure are classified as an expense and as a decrease in cash. In journal entry form this appears as follows:

July 8	Salary Expense	180	
	Cash		180

This is a very common occurrence, and many expenses are recorded in this way. The illustrations of classifying and processing transaction data in chapters 3 and 4 frequently used this situation.

There are other situations in which the resource is obtained on credit and consumed during the period in which a bill is received, but before an expenditure is due. In this case, data for the credit purchase of the resource are classified as an expense and an increase in a liability, as is illustrated in the following journal entry:

July 9	Legal Expense	400	
	Accounts Payable		400

The expenditure for the attorney's fees will be made in a later period and is not related directly to the expense at the time of expenditure. Payment of the attorney's fee which was recorded above would be classified as follows:

Aug. 14	Accounts Payable	400	
	Cash		400

Frequently, however, the consumption of the resource is considered separately from the purchase or the actual expenditure. Analysis of such situations will be treated in the remaining sections of this chapter.

When expenditures are classified and reported as if they were expenses, the reporting is said to be on a *cash basis*. Remarks about such reporting were included in chapter 6.

Reporting Accrued Expenses

When resources, normally services, are consumed before there has been a data input for their acquisition, either by credit or cash purchase, an expense has *accrued*. Expenses accrue day by day for the consumption of services represented by wages and salaries, interest, taxes, and such. These accrued expenses often are paid within the reporting period, and data for the payment are classified as an expense and a reduction in cash, as illustrated in the preceding section.

When accrued expenses are not paid within the reporting period in which they occur, special attention must be given to compute and input data for them into the system. To illustrate, assume that wages in the shop in the amount of $3,000 per week are paid each two weeks. If the fiscal, or reporting, year ends on Thursday following payday, the preceding Friday, wages will have accrued for four days. If the regular work week is five days, then wages in the amount of $2,400 ($600 per day for four days) have accrued, and data for this should be entered into the system. This $2,400 is the measure of the services consumed and, therefore, is an expense. It also measures the amount of liability to employees, who at this time are creditors of the firm. They have supplied resources to the firm for which they have not been paid; they have a claim against the firm for this amount. On the last day of the fiscal year (assume June 30) the following classification of data would be entered:

June 30	Wages Expense	2,400	
	Wages Payable		2,400

The wages expense will be posted to the Wages Expense account and reported on the income statement as a part of the total for the year. The wages payable will be posted and reported as a liability on the balance sheet for June 30.

Since data for the employee services consumed to June 30 but unpaid appear as a liability, on the following payday the payment of $6,000 for two weeks' wages will be classified as the payment of a liability of $2,400 and expenses for the next year of $3,600:

July 8	Wages Payable	2,400	
	Wages Expense	3,600	
	Cash		6,000

Computation and classification of data for all accrued expenses follow this general pattern.

Reporting Prepaid Expenses

Resources acquired before they are consumed are assets: supplies, merchandise, equipment, insurance protection, buildings purchased, and occupancy rights in rented buildings are examples. Certain of these resources which may have alternative uses, or the use of which depends on further management decision or action, are reported separately as assets; merchandise, equipment, and buildings from the preceding list are of this nature. Other resources which cost less, which normally are consumed day by day or in small amounts, and the consumption of which normally will not be changed significantly by management action are thought of and reported as *prepaid expenses.* In the preceding list, supplies, insurance protection, and occupancy rights in rented buildings might be combined and reported as prepaid expenses among the assets on the balance sheet.

There are two different patterns in which firms classify transaction data at the time payment is made for these prepaid expenses. Later inputs of data for consumption of the prepaid expenses are based on the original classification; therefore, these two patterns of data classification must be recognized.

Prepayment recorded as an asset When resources such as supplies, insurance protection, and occupancy rights in a building are paid for before they are consumed, they may quite properly be recorded as assets. The purchase of supplies for cash might be recorded as follows:

June 6	Supplies on Hand	120	
	Cash		120

The payment of insurance premiums might be recorded with a journal entry such as:

June 1	Prepaid Insurance	360	
	Cash		360

The payment of rent in advance for a quarter may be recorded as follows:

June 1	Prepaid Rent	900	
	Cash		900

The use of the accounts Supplies on Hand, Prepaid Insurance, and Prepaid Rent indicates that the resources purchased have not yet been consumed and are classified as assets.

Data representing the use or consumption of resources which were acquired in advance must be input to the system at the end of the period so that assets and expenses will be reported in the correct amount. Assume that fifty dollars of the supplies purchased on June 6 are used by the end of the month. A journal entry would be prepared adjusting the Supplies on Hand account and the Supplies Expense account for the supplies consumed. The entry would be:

June 30	Supplies Expense	50	
	Supplies on Hand		50

If the insurance premiums were prepaid for one year, then one-twelfth of the premium, or $30, would have expired or been consumed by use of the protection by June 30. The following journal entry would be made:

June 30	Insurance Expense	30	
	Prepaid Insurance		30

Since the rent was paid for three months, one-third of the $900 will have been consumed by occupying the building to June 30. The consumed or "expired" rent is recorded as follows:

June 30	Rent Expense	300	
	Prepaid Rent		300

Note that the criteria for expense reporting are met for only that portion of each of the original prepayments which is classified in the above entries as an expense; the criteria are not met for that portion which is left in the asset accounts as *prepaid* expenses.

Prepayment recorded as an expense When resources such as those considered in the preceding section are paid for before they are consumed, data for the payment may be classified as expenses, especially if the prepayment is for only a short period or if similar items often are consumed before payment is made. The advantage in classifying the acquisition of a small order of supplies as expense is that, when the supplies are consumed shortly, no further attention need be given the matter—the data are already classified as expense. However, when the fiscal period ends before the resource (supplies, in this case) is fully consumed, then a part of the cost of the resource should be reported as an asset rather than as expense. This requires a journal entry to adjust the data in the accounts.

Assume that the purchase of $120 of supplies has been recorded as follows in anticipation of their being used shortly:

June 6	Supplies Expense	120	
	Cash		120

Following this kind of recording, the $70 of supplies not yet used on June 30 ($120–$50 used, as recorded in the preceding section) would be recorded by a journal entry like the following:

June 30	Supplies on Hand	70	
	Supplies Expense		70

This adjustment of data results in $70 being reported as an asset and $50 being reported as expense, just as is done by the other pattern of entries for supplies in the preceding section. It should be noted that the next two items illustrated (insurance and rent) are adjusted so that the final amounts reported are the same as those in the preceding section also.

The payment of one year's insurance premium might have been recorded as an expense:

June 1	Insurance Expense	360	
	Cash		360

On June 30, the eleven months of insurance protection would be recorded as an asset by transferring eleven months of the premium from the Insurance Expense account to an asset account, Prepaid Insurance:

June 30	Prepaid Insurance	330	
	Insurance Expense		330

Following this pattern, the payment of three months' rent might have been recorded as follows:

June 1	Rent Expense	900	
	Cash		900

Likewise, on June 30 it would be necessary to transfer the two months' rent then still paid in advance to an asset account with the following journal entry:

June 30	Prepaid Rent	600	
	Rent Expense		600

The task confronting one in adjusting for a prepaid expense is to determine how the original payment for the resource was recorded, compute the amount that qualifies as an expense and the amount which should be reported as an asset, and then adjust the data in the accounts so that they will show this division between expense and asset. The amounts reported should be the same, regardless of the pattern of journal entries used.

Reporting the Consumption of Merchandise Sold

Merchandise is purchased, placed in stock, and sold. The cost of the merchandise sold is the measure of a consumption (or outflow) of resources in exchange for a normally greater inflow of other resources as revenue. If all merchandise purchased is recorded in the Merchandise account, the problem presented is very much like that of supplies in the preceding discussion: adjusting the accounts so that the cost of a resource acquired before consumption is divided between the amount on hand (an asset) and the amount consumed (an expense). In the case of merchandise, the cost is divided between the amount remaining on hand, or in *inventory* (an asset), and the amount that was sold (an expense).

For illustration, assume that a Merchandise account contains the following data:

Merchandise

Jan. 1 inventory	20,000	
Dec. 31 purchased	120,000	

It is customary to count merchandise in stock at the end of the year (take inventory) and multiply the quantity of each item by its cost price to determine the cost of the inventory; that is the amount of merchandise remaining as an asset. The remainder of all the merchandise that was in inventory at the beginning of the year and that was purchased during the year has been sold; the cost of this merchandise is reported as an expense, Cost of Goods Sold. Assume that the inventory on December 31 amounts to $24,000 at cost. Data in the accounts should show $24,000 of merchandise and $116,000 as cost of goods sold. The journal entry adjusting the accounts to reflect these amounts is:

Dec. 31	Cost of Goods Sold	116,000	
	Merchandise		116,000

After this journal entry is posted, the accounts appear as follows:

Merchandise

Jan. 1 bal.	20,000	Dec. 31	116,000
Dec. 31 pur.	120,000	Dec. 31 bal.	24,000
	140,000		140,000
Jan. 1 bal.	24,000		

Cost of Goods Sold

Dec. 31	116,000	

Cost of goods sold is reported at $116,000 as an expense on the income statement, and merchandise is reported at $24,000 (the Merchandise account now has this balance) as an asset on the balance sheet.

There are several ways of arriving at the price to use as the cost of the final inventory. The problems encountered in pricing inventory and reporting merchandise costs are of such proportion that all of chapter 8 is devoted to this topic.

Credit Losses as Expense

The estimated credit losses were viewed in chapter 6 as a cancellation of, or reduction in, revenues. This would mean that the resources provided by sales are considered to be the amount the firm actually expects to collect. This seems realistic: if at the time goods are sold you expect to collect only a part of the sales amount, it is rational to consider only that part an inflow of resources. Claims against customers which you do not think are collectible can hardly be called resources.

A different situation can exist, however. If at the time of the sales it is expected that all amounts will be collected, and later, because of failure of the collection personnel, it appears that some amounts will not be collected, the estimate of credit losses might be seen as an expense. The sales price would measure the resource (accounts receivable) received from the sale, since all of it is expected to be collected. Later, when some amount is lost because of poor collection procedures, the amount so lost is looked upon as a dissipation of resources and, therefore, as an expense. In this situation management would be better informed if the credit loss were reported as an expense for which collection personnel are responsible.

The procedures for estimating and recording credit losses as expense (often called bad debt expense) may be the same as those presented in chapter 6. In most firms, it appears that the specific failure of collection personnel is not the normal condition and that credit losses should therefore be reported as a reduction in revenue rather than as an expense.

Depreciation expense

Depreciation qualifies as an expense and is reported uniformly as such. It clearly represents the consumption of resources, but the measure of the amount consumed each period is not well defined. Terms and definitions will be considered first, and then attention will be given to methods of computing the amount of depreciation.

Amortization, depreciation, and depletion *Amortization* is a term generally used to indicate the spreading of some amount over a number of periods. In accounting and financial reporting, amortization indicates the spreading of the cost of a resource over the periods in which the resource is used. Normally the term is applied to long-life assets and refers to the transferring each period of a part of the cost of the assets to expense, following the same concept as in transferring the cost of supplies to expense as they are used.

The term *depreciation* is used to indicate the amortization or spreading of the cost of long-lived tangible assets which decline in use value but not in physical size—buildings, equipment, automobiles, etc.

Since tangible assets make up most of the long-life properties of many firms, depreciation is probably the most commonly used of the three terms which refer to the spreading of the asset cost. More detailed attention is given to the meaning of depreciation in chapter 9.

Depletion refers to the amortization of the cost of extractable assets such as coal, ores, oil and gas, gravel and sand, and other such assets which are removed piecemeal over a period of years.

The special use of the terms *depreciation* and *depletion* leaves amortization with two uses in accounting:

1. To indicate the general function of spreading an asset's cost over a period of years in transferring it to expense. With this use, depreciation and depletion are special cases of amortization.
2. To indicate the spreading of the cost of intangible assets over a period of years as this cost is transferred to expense. No special term is used for expensing intangible assets, so the general term amortization is applied.

One normally speaks of *depreciating* tangible long-life assets, *depleting* reserves of extractable assets, and *amortizing* intangible assets.

Percentage depletion For federal income tax purposes, firms in the extractive industries may compute and deduct an amount called *percentage depletion* in arriving at their taxable income. For tax purposes the term *depletion* may indicate the amortization of asset cost, but it is also used to refer to this percentage of revenue which may be deducted instead of cost depletion in computing taxable income. Percentage depletion (an allowed percentage of revenue) is deducted instead of cost depletion if it is greater for that period. Percentage depletion is purely an income tax provision—it is not used otherwise in financial reporting. When percentage depletion is used for tax computations, depletion of asset cost is still used in computing income on the income statement.

Computing and recording depreciation With terms and definitions clarified, attention can be given to various methods of computing the amount of depreciation each year. The usefulness and results of the various methods will be considered in chapter 9; the computations involved are presented on the following pages.

Straight-line depreciation The cost of an asset minus its expected salvage or scrap value at the end of its expected useful life to the firm is the amount to be depreciated. If it is desired that this amount be depreciated evenly over the years of usefulness, with the same amount transferred to depreciation expense each year regardless of the relative use of the asset or the relative benefit derived from that use, then "straight-line" depreciation is used. The computation of the amount reported as expense each year by straight-line depreciation is merely the depreciable amount (cost minus expected salvage value) divided by the number of years of expected useful life.

For an example of straight-line depreciation, assume that a machine is purchased at a cost of $26,000 and put into use early in 1971; that it has an expected useful life of eight years; and that its expected salvage value is $2,000. Depreciation per year is computed as follows:

Cost of machine	$26,000
Minus expected salvage value	2,000
Depreciable amount	$24,000
Expected useful life of machine	8 years
Depreciation per year ($24,000 ÷ 8 years)	$ 3,000

At the end of the first year, the machine is reported as an asset on the balance sheet at $23,000 (cost, $26,000, minus depreciation to date, $3,000), and depreciation expense of $3,000 is reported on the income statement. At the end of the fourth year, this machine is reported on the balance sheet at $14,000 (cost, $26,000, minus depreciation to date, $12,000), and depreciation expense is reported on the income statement at $3,000, the same amount each year.

Classifying and recording depreciation data Data for the annual depreciation ($3,000 in the preceding example) are classified as an expense and a reduction in the amount to be reported for the depreciated asset. The expense is recorded by a debit to the Depreciation Expense account. The reduction in the asset amount is not shown by a credit to the Machinery account, or other long-life asset account, but is classified as accumulated depreciation on machinery and is stored in an account with that title. The journal entry for the depreciation on the machine would be:

Dec. 31	Depreciation Expense	3,000	
	Accumulated Depreciation on Machinery		3,000

Depreciation expense is reported on the income statement with other expenses. The machinery is reported with other assets, with both the original cost and the accumulated depreciation shown as follows:

BALANCE SHEET

ASSETS

Cash		$ x,xxx
Merchandise		x,xxx
Etc.		xxx
Machinery	$26,000	
Accumulated depreciation	3,000	23,000

After four years of use, the machinery would be reported as follows on the balance sheet:

Machinery	$26,000	
Accumulated depreciation	12,000	14,000

This technique for recording depreciation data and for reporting those data on the income statement and balance sheet is used quite consistently regardless of the method employed in computing the amount of depreciation for each year.

Unit-of-production method Operating equipment sometimes is depreciated according to the service derived from it. A precision tooling and shaping machine may be expected to produce 100,000 units of product during its useful life. Using straight-line depreciation, a firm would report the same amount of depreciation in all years, regardless of the volume of production. Some firms would prefer to compute the depreciation per unit of expected production and then use this amount for each unit actually produced in a year to compute the depreciation for that year. This is the unit-of-production method; it is illustrated below, using the same data as in the preceding illustration, except that an expected production life of 100,000 units is substituted for an expected life of eight years, and production this year is assumed to be 12,000 units:

Cost of machine	$26,000
Minus expected salvage value	2,000
Depreciable amount	$24,000
Expected total production from machine	100,000 units
Depreciation per unit produced ($24,000 ÷ 100,000 units)	$ 0.24
Depreciation for the year ($0.24 × 12,000)	$ 2,880

At the end of the first year, the machine is reported on the balance sheet at $23,120 (cost, $26,000 – depreciation to date, $2,880), and depreciation expense is reported at $2,880. At the end of the second year, if production is 15,000 units, depreciation expense will be reported at $3,600 ($0.24 × 15,000), and the machine will be reported on the balance sheet at $19,520 (cost, $26,000 – depreciation to date, $6,480).

Both the straight-line and the unit-of-production methods assign the same amount of depreciation to all units, either time or product. There is a strong argument, presented in chapter 9, that a greater amount of depreciation should be assigned to the early years in the machine's life and less to the later years. This is called *accelerated depreciation*, and the methods presented next produce two different patterns of accelerated depreciation.

Declining balance method This method reports as expense each year a constant percentage of the declining, undepreciated cost of the asset. Depreciation amounts and undepreciated balances for all years of a five-year asset are presented in Figure 7-1. The depreciation rate to be used for a specific asset is found by the computation, $1 - \sqrt[n]{\frac{s}{c}}$, where n is the number of years expected life of the asset, s is the expected salvage value at the end of n years, and c is the original cost of the asset. The rate thus computed probably would be rounded to the nearest even percent except on assets of very long life, since its computation contains some amounts which may be estimated very roughly.

Figure 7-1

DECLINING BALANCE DEPRECIATION

(a) Year	(b) Undepreciated Asset Amount	(c) Depreciation at 40 percent	(d) Accumulated Depreciation to date	(e) Book "Value"
1	$50,000	$20,000	$20,000	$30,000
2	30,000	12,000	32,000	18,000
3	18,000	7,200	39,200	10,800
4	10,000	4,320	43,520	6,480
5	6,480	2,592	46,110	3,888

(a) Simply the year designation for each line of the table.
(b) Amount of the asset cost which is not yet depreciated at the beginning of the year. Computed by column (b) minus column (c) on the preceding line, or column (e) on the preceding line.
(c) Depreciation for each year. Computed as 40 percent of the amount in (b) on the same line.
(d) Depreciation accumulated for all past years.
(e) Book "value": original cost minus depreciation to date in column (d).

The depreciation is recorded annually for the amount shown in column (c) of Figure 7-1 in the same manner as described earlier. The entry for the first year is:

Dec. 31	Depreciation Expense	20,000	
	Accumulated Depreciation on Machinery		20,000

The journal entry to record depreciation for the fourth year would be:

Dec. 31	Depreciation Expense	4,320	
	Accumulated Depreciation on Machinery		4,320

After depreciation is entered for the fourth year, the Machinery account still has a balance of $50,000, and the Accumulated Depreciation on Machinery account has a balance of $43,520. The "book value" of this machinery at the end of the fourth year is the excess of cost over the accumulated depreciation, or $6,480, the amount shown in column (e) on line 4 and in column (d) on line 5.

Sum-of-years'-digits method Depreciation of the equipment treated by the declining balance method in Figure 7-1 is computed by the sum-of-years'-digits method in Figure 7-2. Note the assumption that the estimated salvage value is $2,500. The pattern of depreciation produced by this method is different from that of the declining balance method; both are highly accelerated compared to the straight-line method, however. Detailed examination of these patterns and their significance is treated in chapter 9.

Figure 7-2

SUM-OF-YEARS'-DIGITS DEPRECIATION

(a) Year	(b) Years Remaining Life/Sum of Years	(c) Depreciation	(d) Accumulated Depreciation	(e) Book "Value"
1	5/15	$12,500	$12,500	$27,500
2	4/15	10,000	22,500	17,500
3	3/15	7,500	30,000	10,000
4	2/15	5,000	35,000	5,000
5	1/15	2,500	37,500	2,500
15		$37,500		

Estimated useful life, 5 years.
Projected salvage value, $2,500.
(a) Year designation for each line with total of the numbers.
(b) Fraction for computing depreciation for the year. Number of years remaining life (from beginning of the year) over the total of the years' digits in column (a).
(c) Depreciation computed for each year: fraction in (b) multiplied by the depreciable amount of asset cost, $37,500 (cost less projected salvage value).
(d) Depreciation accumulated for all past years.
(e) Book "value": original cost minus depreciation to date in column (d).

The computation uses the fractions formed by dividing the number of years of projected life at the beginning of any year by the total of the numerals, or digits, representing the periods of total expected life; this is seen in columns (b) and (c) of Figure 7-2. The computation is designed to produce the specific pattern of depreciation seen in the amounts in column (c). The sum of the years' digits is meaningless as an amount, but it is useful when related to the years of remaining life to develop the series of fractions in column (b). It should be noted that if, for a study of projected expenses, the amount of depreciation is needed for some future year, that amount can be computed without computing depreciation for the intervening years.

The recording of depreciation uses the same procedures regardless of the method used to compute the annual depreciation amount. From the data in Figure 7-2, a journal entry would be made at the end of each year for the amount of depreciation for that year as shown in column (c). The Accumulated Depreciation account will develop balances year by year as indicated in column (d). The equipment is reported annually as an asset at its "book value," which is the original cost minus the depreciation accumulated to that date.

Other Expense Problems

The problems in the preceding sections are the ones most often encountered by a business firm in determining what expenses to report to determine net income. There are other situations, however, in which expenses for which future expenditures will be made must be estimated and reported with current revenue.

Warranty expenses When a firm sells products under a warranty, it commits itself to make expenditures for the future repairs or replacements specified under terms of the warranty. The expense represented by the future expenditures is estimated and matched currently with the revenue from the sales giving rise to the expense. Assume that the Major Company manufactures and sells a product with a warranty covering all moving parts for one year and all cast parts of the case for two years. Terms of the warranty call for the Major Company to repair or replace broken or faulty parts without charge during the warranty period. If sales this year are 10,000 units from which revenue of $180,000 is derived, it is reasonable to conclude that some expense has been generated, that the sale of 10,000 units will cause some amount of expenditure (consumption of resources) in the future. This means that the criteria for reporting an expense have been met; what is lacking is the amount of the expense and details for classifying its effect.

In the example of the Major Company, the company's experience has been that not every unit needs service under the warranty; in fact, only 10 percent of the units are presented for service under the warranty, but the average cost of parts and labor for each unit serviced is $6. The warranty expense which should be reported this period is computed as follows:

Number of units sold	10,000
Percent of units returned for service	10
Number of units projected to be serviced	1,000
Average cost to service a unit	$6.00
Total projected service expenditure from current year's sales	$6,000

The projected expenditure of $6,000 is entered both as an expense and as a liability (obligation to pay the amount in the future) because, even though the amount is estimated, it is reasonably certain that approximately this amount will be claimed by customers. The classification of these data is seen in the following journal entry, which is made for the estimated expense at the end of the year:

Dec. 31	Warranty Expense	6,000	
	Warranty Liability		6,000

When warranty expenditures are actually made in the future, the amounts are classified as a reduction in the liability, not as expense, because the expense was reported earlier with the revenue. The journal entry recording the expenditure of $20 for labor and the issue of $18 of parts in performing repair for a customer would be:

May 17	Warranty Liability	38	
	Parts on Hand		18
	Cash		20

In computing and reporting net income for the year, the $6,000 is reported as an expense along with other expenses. The Warranty Liability account balance will be reported on the balance sheet along with other liabilities such as accounts and notes payable.

Premium expenses Some firms issue coupons in packages, printed on the packages, or separately with purchases of some minimum size. The coupons are redeemable upon presentation (sometimes with a cash payment) for special goods, which are usually referred to as *premiums*. As in the case of warranties, an expense is incurred when sales are made and premium coupons are issued, because an expenditure will be required in the future when the coupons are presented. That expenditure must be estimated and reported currently with the revenue from the sales so that revenue and expense will be matched properly and the resulting net income will represent the results of the period's operations.

Assume that the manufacturers of Cheekos place a coupon in each Cheekos package. When ten coupons are mailed to the company with fifty cents, the company will send the customer a "descriptive plastic model of the solar system." This premium costs the company seventy cents, including packaging and mailing. It is estimated that only one out of each fifteen coupons issued will be returned. If the company sold 3,000,000 boxes of their product this period, the premium liability to be reported would be computed as follows:

Number of coupons issued		3,000,000
Fraction of coupons to be redeemed		1/15
Number of coupons estimated to be redeemed		200,000
Number of premiums to be issued (one for ten coupons)		20,000
Cost per premium:		
Total cost of premium	$0.70	
Payment from customer	.50	$ 0.20
Expected premium cost for three million coupons		$4,000

The estimated expense for the year and the liability for future issue of premiums is recorded in journal entry form as follows:

Dec. 31	Premium Expense	4,000	
	Premium Liability		4,000

When premiums are issued, the cost of the premium in excess of the payment received for it is classified as a reduction in the premium liability. The entry for the issue of 1,000 premiums, when 10,000 coupons and $500 cash are received, would be:

Jan. 26	Cash	500	
	Premium Liability	200	
	Premiums on Hand		700

There are many other circumstances in which expenses must be estimated and reported in order to match revenues and expenses in presenting net income on the income statement. Most of these have the general characteristics of the ones already examined. Estimates of expenses in the preceding sections serve well to demonstrate the problems involved in a firm's determining and reporting its expenses and its net income.

Special Problems in Expense Determination

Many expenses are closely related to specific expenditures or to estimates of future expenditures. These expenditures are often in the same period that the expense is reported or are expected to occur shortly afterward. There are two types of expenses (cost of goods sold and depreciation), however, for which the time of the expenditure and the time of reporting of the expense may be separated by as much as several months to many years. This long separation in time gives rise to problems of measurement, due chiefly to general inflation and changes in specific prices. These problems will be examined in detail: the general problems dealing with merchandise prices in chapter 8; those related to depreciation in chapter 9; and those dealing specifically with inflation in chapter 10.

QUESTIONS AND EXERCISES

7-A. Is the total amount paid for supplies during a year a good measure of the consumption of supplies during that year?

7-B. Is the amount of salaries paid an exact measure of the consumption of the resource, the time and skill of employees?

7-C. How are expenses related to revenue? What is the financial measure of expenses?

7-D. Expenses are defined as the consumption of the firm's resources. Explain the circumstances under which expenses may be reported when resources have not been consumed.

7-E. If supplies which cost $12,000 were on hand January 1, supplies totaling $43,000 were purchased during the year, and supplies costing $14,000 were on hand on December 31, what is the amount of supplies expense for the year?

7-F. Normally, expenses are reported in the period in which resources are consumed, not in the period in which expenditures are made for the resources. Explain how this statement is related to prepaid expenses and accrued expenses.

7-G. If, at the end of an accounting period, an asset account "Postage" has a debit balance of $445 and there is $65 worth of postage stamps on hand, what adjusting entry is needed?

7-H. If a firm's sales employees are paid a total of $3,000 per week for working Monday through Friday, what adjustment of the accounts is needed if the fiscal period ends on Wednesday? On Monday?

7-I. On September 1, the Toot-R Tutoring Service paid $180 for liability insurance for twelve months and debited the Prepaid Insurance account. Before preparing financial statements at December 31, what adjustment should the accountant make?

If the payment of $180 on September 1 had been recorded by a debit to Insurance Expense, what adjustment would be made on December 31?

7-J. The following data are available at the end of the fiscal year:

Interest paid in advance on January 1	$ 32
Interest expense accrued on January 1 but paid during the current year	22
Interest paid during the current year (total)......	209
Interest accrued at the end of the year	27
Interest paid in advance as of December 31.....	28

What amount should be reported as interest expense for the year?

7-K. An asset which cost $30,000 is expected to have a useful life of about four years and a salvage value of about $3,600. Compute depreciation for this asset for each of the four years by each of the following methods:

a. Straight-line
b. Sum-of-years'-digits
c. Declining balance at 40 percent

Prepare the journal entry for one year's depreciation by the straight-line method.

PROCEDURAL PROBLEMS

7-1. Prepare December 31 adjusting entries to record the following unpaid liabilities and related expense.

a. Salaries earned by employees during the last week in December but paid January 7, $700.00.
b. Received a bill on December 30 from City Utility Company for $200 for December utility service; paid the utility bill on January 10.
c. Borrowed $1,000 from mortgage loan company on December 1, interest to be paid when the loan is repaid but accrued as an expense monthly. The interest rate is 6 percent per year.

Prepare entries to record the following transactions which occurred subsequent to December 31.

d. January 7, paid employees' salaries for the two-week period ended January 7, $1,500.
e. January 10, paid the December utility bill.
f. December 1, repaid the $1,000 borrowed from mortgage loan company plus interest.

7-2. The following information has been taken from the records of Ames, Inc. for the current year.

1. The company purchased three insurance policies: two-year premium of $240 paid March 1; thirty-six-month premium of $540 paid August 1; one-year premium of $72 paid September 1.
2. On September 1 borrowed $8,000 from First National Bank on a two-year note; $600 interest was paid in advance.
3. An inventory of supplies was taken, and it was determined that $200 of supplies had been used during the year. Supplies costing $500 had been purchased during the year; no supplies were on hand at the beginning of the year.

a. Assuming that prepayments are recorded as assets, prepare the adjusting entries for December 31.
b. Assuming that prepayments are recorded as expenses, prepare the adjusting entries for December 31.

7-3. The Simpson Furniture Company had the following purchases of merchandise debited to the Merchandise account:

March 3, Purchase on account	$112,000
June 10, Purchase on account..................	44,000
August 22, Cash purchase	11,000
November 14, Purchase on account...........	27,000
	$194,000

The inventory on January 1 was $14,500, and the inventory on December 31 is $23,000.

Prepare the adjusting entry to record cost of goods sold for the year.

7-4. The Wright Manufacturing Company has just purchased a machine costing $40,000 with an estimated salvage value of $4,000 and an estimated life of ten years or 360,000 production units. The plant manager has asked you to prepare a depreciation schedule under each of the following methods, for the first four years (show depreciation expense, accumulated depreciation, and book value for each year).

a. Straight-line
b. Unit-of-production method

Production For The Four Years

Year	Units Produced
1	22,000
2	19,000
3	29,000
4	16,000

c. Declining balance (use a 20 percent rate)
d. Sum-of-years'-digits

7-5. The Williams Appliance Company manufactures and sells locally a small electric blender. They have asked you to prepare an adjusting entry for their probable liability to repair these products under their warranty. The company has the necessary information: sales for the year were 6,000 units; an estimated 4 percent of units sold will be returned for service; $7.00 is the estimated cost to repair an average returned blender.

Prepare the necessary December 31 adjusting entry.

7-6. The Fresh Brew Coffee Company issues one coupon with each one-pound package of coffee. For two coupons and twenty-five cents the customer will receive one coffee cup. The company sold 2,400,000 packages of coffee with coupons. They estimate that 5 percent of the coupons will be redeemed. The coffee cups cost the company forty cents each.

Prepare the December 31 entry for the premium liability for the year.

7-7. For each independent situation below compute the amount needed to complete the schedule.

	A	B	C
Beginning inventory	$14,000	$_____	$22,000
Purchases during year	37,000	52,000	67,000
Ending inventory	_____	11,000	18,000
Cost of goods sold	29,000	56,000	_____

7-8. Using the information presented in the Tower Company's unadjusted and adjusted trial balances dated April 30, below, prepare the adjusting journal entries.

	Unadjusted		Adjusted	
	Dr	Cr	Dr	Cr
Cash	$ 9,380		$ 9,380	
Accounts receivable	24,700		24,700	
Allowance for uncollectible accounts		$ 125		$ 335
Allowance for sales discounts				80
Prepaid insurance			800	
Prepaid rent	690		480	
Receivable from construction contract			7,300	
Merchandise	12,000		12,000	
Accounts payable		8,500		8,500
Salary payable		1,670		1,670
Subscriptions collected in advance				2,640
Capital stock		20,000		20,000
Subscription revenue		3,040		400
Sales		18,820		18,820
Construction revenue				7,300
Credit losses			210	
Sales discounts	210		290	
Salary expense	4,125		4,125	
Rent expense			210	
Insurance expense	1,050		250	
	$52,155	$52,155	$59,745	$59,745

7-9. Shown below are two trial balances prepared as of August 31 and reflecting transactions for the month of August for Wayne Appliance

Company. One trial balance has balances before adjustments; the other has the adjusted balances. By comparing the trial balances, prepare the August 31 adjusting entries.

	Unadjusted		Adjusted	
	Dr	Cr	Dr	Cr
Cash	$ 7,800		$ 7,800	
Accounts receivable	22,300		22,300	
Allowance for uncollectible accounts		$ 110		$ 435
Office supplies	1,400		1,125	
Plant machinery	35,000		35,000	
Accumulated depreciation-machinery		4,000		5,200
Delivery equipment	18,900		18,900	
Accumulated depreciation-del. equip.		2,700		3,340
Land	20,000		20,000	
Accounts payable		6,200		6,200
Mortgage payable		27,600		27,600
Interest payable				400
Salary payable				2,000
Capital stock		20,000		20,000
Sales		46,190		46,190
Credit losses			325	
Rent expense	1,400		1,400	
Salary expense			2,000	
Depreciation expense-machinery			1,200	
Depreciation expense-del. equip.			640	
Interest expense			400	
Office supplies expense			275	
	$106,800	$106,800	$111,365	$111,365

7-10. On January 2, 1967, Stilwell Corporation purchased for $12,000 a machine having an estimated life of five years or 130,000 units of production. Estimated salvage value was $1,600.

a. Using the straight-line depreciation method, what is the depreciation expense for 1969?

b. Assume production had been:

1967	18,000 units
1968	31,000 units
1969	49,200 units

What is the balance of the accumulated depreciation account after the December 31, 1969, adjusting entry, using unit-of-production depreciation?

c. Compute depreciation expense for 1970 if production is 28,400 units.
d. Using straight-line depreciation, what is the book value of the asset on January 2, 1972?
e. If this machine was depreciated using declining balance (40% annual rate) depreciation or sum-of-years'-digits depreciation which would produce the larger expense in 1967? 1969?
f. By what constant amount does sum-of-years'-digits depreciation method decrease depreciation expense each year?

7-11. Reynolds Appliance Company sells a small electric appliance and issues a warranty with each appliance that promises to repair any defect that occurs within three months of sale. The company closes its books on June 30. Sales records reveal that sales (in units) during April, May, and June were 4,100; 3,800; and 3,600, respectively. The company estimates that one percent of the units sold in April, two percent of units sold in May, and four percent of the units sold in June may be returned for repair (at an average repair cost of $4.50) during the next fiscal year.

a. Prepare the June 30 adjusting entry.
b. If the sales price per units has remained constant a company may, based on its past experience, be able to estimate its warranty costs as a percentage of its sales. Assume in this case the sale price has remained constant at $30 per unit and the company can expect to incur in the next fiscal year expense equal to one percent of the total sales of the three months ended June 30. Prepare the adjusting entry.

CONCEPTUAL PROBLEMS

7-12. Prepare journal entries to record the following in the accounts of Jackson Plumbing Supply Company.

June 13 Jackson Plumbing Supply Company ordered eight kitchen sinks from Storey Manufacturing Company at $32 each.

20 The sinks arrived. They were immediately delivered in the original crates to Vitillo Plumbing Company and billed to them at $48 each.

21 Mr. Vitillo notified Jackson Plumbing Supply that three of the sinks were damaged. The problem was resolved by Jackson's allowing Vitillo to deduct $10 from the price of each of the three damaged sinks.

27 Jackson Plumbing Supply received a notice from Storey Manufacturing Company that the same amount ($10 per sink) had been credited to Jackson's account.

7-13. The H H Construction Company has a contract to construct twenty miles of highway for the state of Ohio at a finished price of $200,000 per mile. Payments for each mile of highway are to be made according to this schedule: 40 percent at the time the concrete is poured; 50 percent at the time all work is completed on each mile; 10 percent when the full twenty miles of highway has been completed and accepted by the state engineers.

During the first period of construction, five miles of highway were completed and accepted, concrete was poured on a stretch of ten miles, and surveying and preliminary grading were completed on the final section of five miles.

The original estimate of cost was $160,000 per mile. Costs for the first period have been in line with the original estimates and have totaled $160,000 per mile on the completed stretch; $130,000 per mile on the second section of ten miles; and $20,000 per mile on the final section of five miles. It is estimated that work can be finished at the total cost of $160,000 per mile.

a. How much should the state of Ohio have paid the H H Construction Company within the first period of operations?
b. Show how you would report revenue and expense for the period.

7-14. The following data relate to wages expense for the year 1971:

Wages accrued at December 31, 1970	$ 2,000
Gross amount from all payrolls in 1971	198,000
Adjusting entry for wages accrued at December 31, 1971	6,000

a. What was the total wages expense for 1971?
b. What was the amount of wages paid during 1971?
c. What was the amount of wages paid during 1971, but included in expense during 1970?
d. What was the amount of wages paid during 1970, but included in expense during 1971?

7-15. On December 31, the unadjusted trial balance of the Hubner Company was as follows:

HUBNER COMPANY
Trial Balance
December 31, 1971

Cash	$ 56,000	
Accounts receivable	170,000	
Inventory	525,000	
Furniture and fixtures	210,000	
Accumulated depreciation on furniture and fixtures		$ 135,000
Prepaid insurance	2,000	
Prepaid rent	1,000	
Accounts payable		100,000
Capital stock		200,000
Retained earnings		104,000
Sales revenue		500,000
Wages expense	20,000	
Miscellaneous expenses	55,000	
	$1,039,000	$1,039,000

The following expenses are to be adjusted as applicable to the month of December:

Rent expense, $1,000.
Insurance expense, $175.
Depreciation – 1 percent of the cost of furniture and fixtures.
Wages earned by employees but not yet paid, $4,000.
Cost of goods sold – compute by using $225,000 as the amount of merchandise on hand on December 31.

a. Prepare journal entries to record the adjustments.
b. Prepare an income statement for the year and a balance sheet as of December 31.

8

Merchandise Reporting

Preview Questions

As you study look for the answers to the following questions:

- **How are merchandise costs recorded?**
- **How is inventory priced?**
- **How are inventory amounts estimated?**
- **What three concepts are essential in understanding merchandise reporting?**
- **What is the value of price level adjustment of inventory amounts?**

Information needed about merchandise may vary and, therefore, different uses of accounts for accumulating data may be seen.

THE SINGLE MERCHANDISE ACCOUNTS

In the preceding chapters changes in the asset, merchandise, were reflected in a Merchandise account. Maintaining a record of all changes in merchandise on a current basis is called the *perpetual inventory* procedure and entails steps such as those charted in Figure 8-1.

Figure 8-1

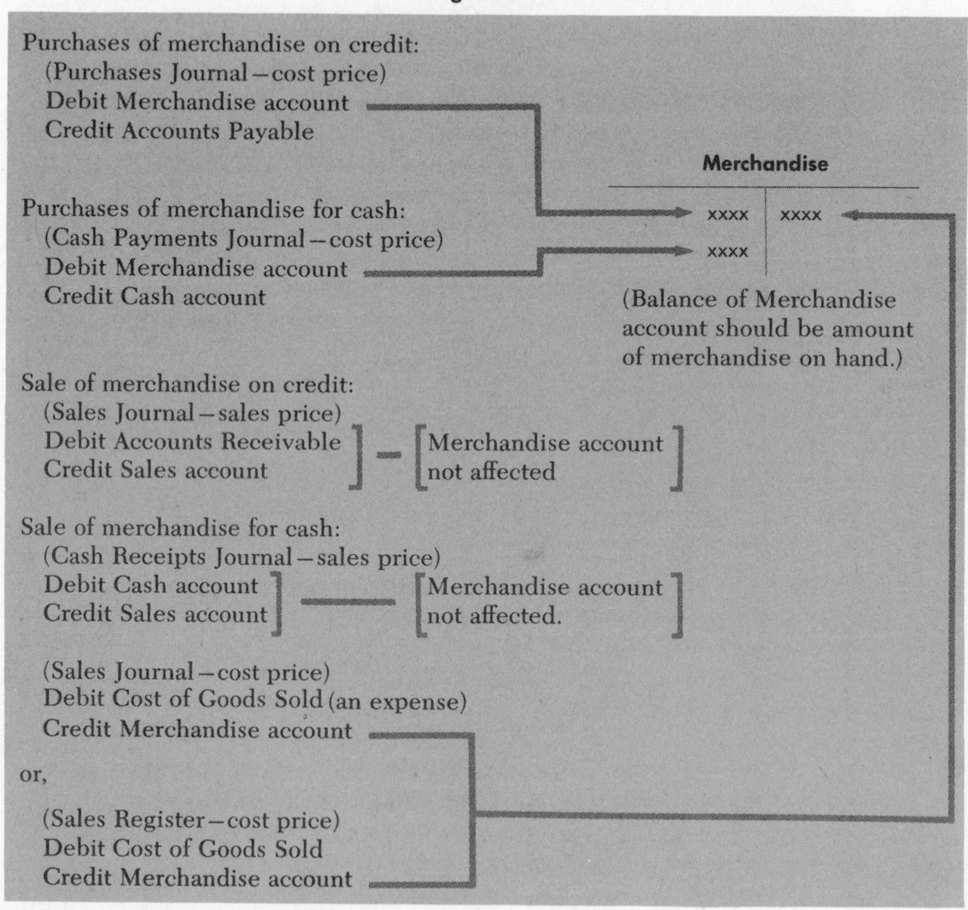

It will be noted that these procedures involve inputting data to record changes at both the retail or sales price and the cost price at the time merchandise is sold. For each sale an asset (either accounts receivable or cash) is increased and an equal increase in capital from earnings is recorded in the Sales account. This is only a part of the transaction; there is also a decrease in an asset (merchandise) and a corresponding decrease in capital from earnings, offsetting part of the increase which was recorded in the Sales account in the other part of the transaction. The decrease in capital from earnings is recorded as a debit in an expense account, Cost of Goods Sold.

The determination of cost at the time each sale is made involves referring to purchase documents or to cost records, either of which is time-consuming and costly. In the sale of relatively expensive items, such as automobiles and fine jewelry, this procedure has been found convenient and not too costly so that a full record of changes (at retail and cost prices) can be made for each sale. In other words, perpetual inventory procedures can be followed. However, when there are many sales of relatively inexpensive items, such as in a department store, one will find that the changes at retail price (accounts receivable and sales) are recorded in a sales journal, but that the changes at cost price (cost of goods sold and merchandise) are not recorded for each sale. Instead, the amount of these changes at cost price is computed for a period (month, quarter, year) and recorded in one journal entry at the end of that period. This is the *periodic inventory* procedure; it saves a large amount of cost in operating the information system and provides information on a periodic basis, as most financial information normally is provided.

Computing the Cost of Goods Sold

Maintaining a record of changes in merchandise with the cost of goods sold computed at the end of each period involves procedures such as those in Figure 8-2.

The computation of the cost of goods sold involves several operations:

1. Obtain a count of the items of merchandise on hand at the end of the period to determine the quantity of inventory (take the periodic inventory).
2. Determine the cost price which is applicable to this quantity of merchandise.
3. Multiply the quantity of each item by the applicable price to find the amount of the inventory at the end of the period (final inventory).
4. Add the amount of the inventory at the end of last period (the inventory with which the current period was begun) and the cost of all merchandise purchased during the current period. This amount should be

the balance in the Merchandise account at the end of the period before the cost of goods sold is credited to that account.

5. Subtract the amount of the inventory, found in step 3, from the total cost of merchandise available, found in step 4. The result is the cost of goods sold for the period.

Figure 8-2

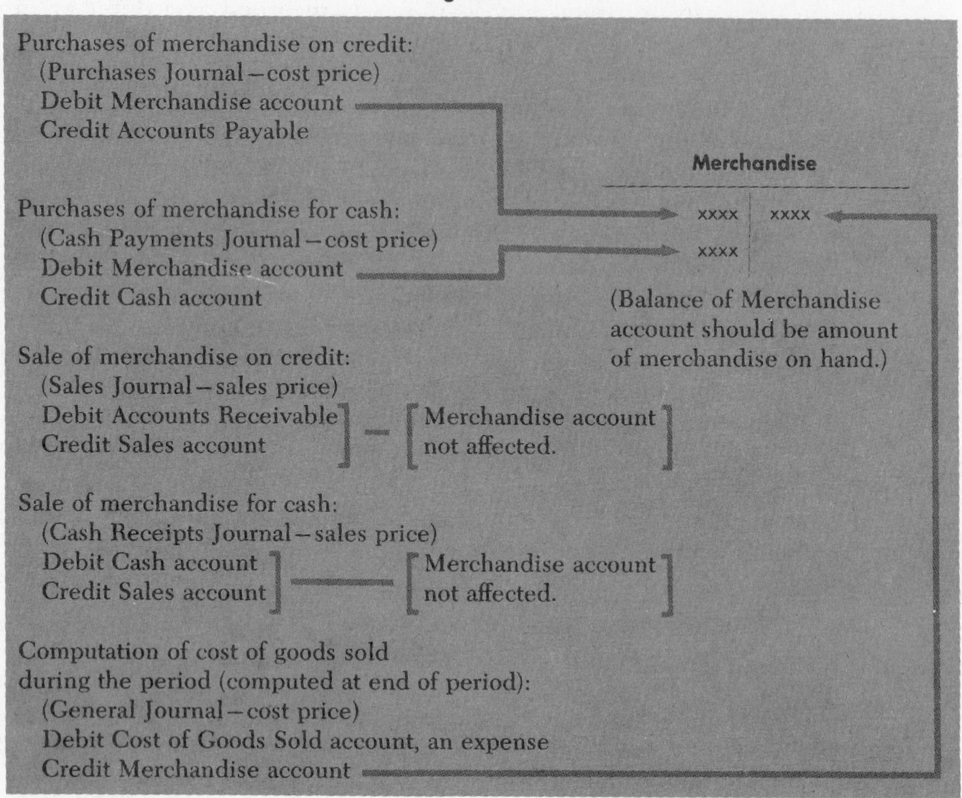

Assuming the following facts, the computation of the cost of goods sold would be as shown:

Inventory at end of last period, or beginning of current period, $12,000.
Total purchases of merchandise during period (cash and credit), $31,000.
Inventory at end of current period, $10,500.
Computation of cost of goods sold:

Beginning inventory	$12,000
Add purchases for the period	31,000
Total goods available for sale	43,000
Deduct ending inventory	10,500
Cost of goods sold	$32,500

The amount $32,500 would be used in the journal entry to record a negative input to the Merchandise account (to decrease that account) and a negative input to capital from earnings in the Cost of Goods Sold account.

Need for Other Information and Other Merchandise Accounts

The single Merchandise account used in the preceding paragraphs provides the data needed to compute the expense, cost of goods sold, which is adequate for preparation of the income statement. However, it does not easily provide other information needed by management in controlling operations of the firm. It does not provide information about purchases for the current period so that the amount is easily seen as the balance of an account; it does not provide a clear record of the inventory, period after period, so that data can be easily read off for comparative purposes. To provide these additional data in readily available format, the system may be adapted to use accounts for both Merchandise Inventory and Purchases instead of the single account, Merchandise.

MERCHANDISE INVENTORY AND PURCHASES ACCOUNTS

The Merchandise Inventory account is used to record data about the amount of merchandise on hand (inventory) at the end of each period, usually at the end of each year. Merchandise inventory is counted, priced, and totalled; the resulting amount is recorded in the Merchandise Inventory account.

The Purchases account (short title for merchandise purchases) is used to maintain a record of data representing the cost of merchandise purchased during the period. The invoice price of merchandise is recorded in the Purchases account; additional costs, such as freight and delivery costs from the supplier to the firm, can be recorded in an account, Freight In.

The separate accounts for inventory and purchases (and freight in, if applicable) contain the same data as would be debited to a single account for merchandise. When these accounts are used, the procedures involved in maintaining data about merchandise would be charted as in Figure 8-3.

Figure 8-3

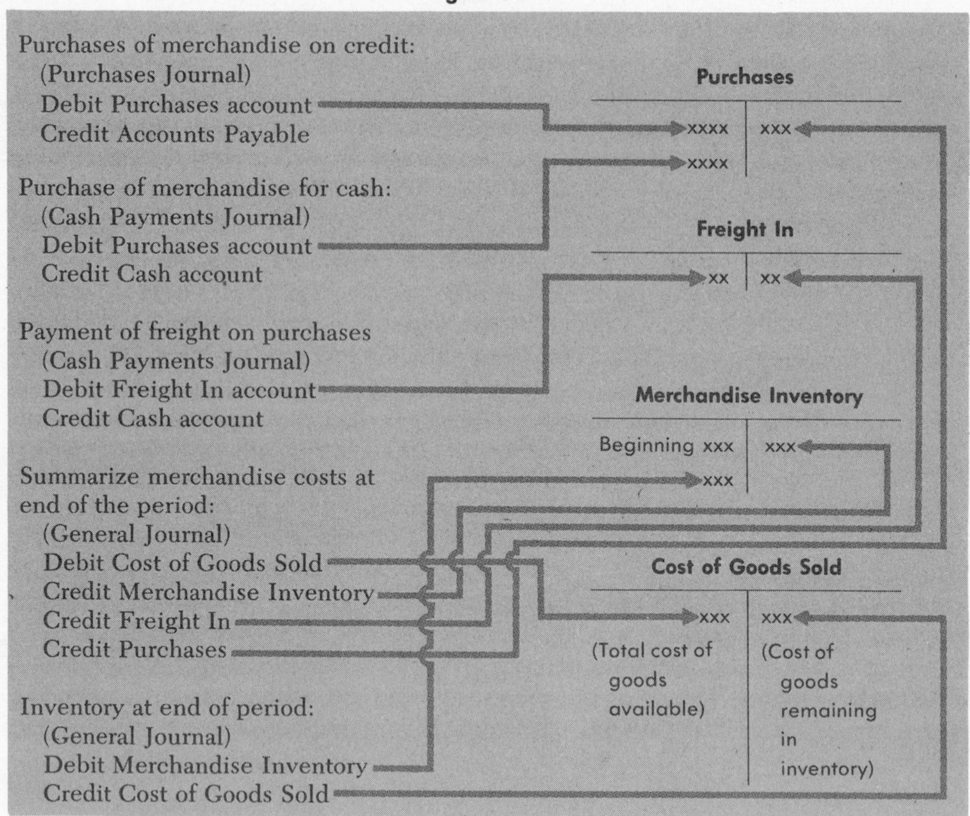

Using the same basic data, the three procedures (in the preceding three charts) will result in the same data reported as cost of goods sold and as merchandise inventory at the end of the period. The Cost of Goods Sold account contains the data used in computing cost of goods sold as illustrated.

ASSIGNING PRICES TO MERCHANDISE INVENTORY

In earlier paragraphs it was indicated that in order to compute the dollar amount of the inventory, merchandise must be accurately counted and priced. Many devices and procedures have been developed to count items of merchandise accurately—inventory sheets on which all items are listed and checked by a second counter, physical measure of bins of grain, prepunched cards marked by two different counters and read by computer, etc. None of these procedures contains any unique measures for quantitative or qualitative controls; they will not be considered in detail here. Measures now in use may be replaced by improved techniques, but the purpose will remain the same—to obtain an accurate count of goods in such places as warehouses, manufacturing plants, and stores.

The Problem of Inventory Prices

In determining the dollar amount of the inventory, there is one question which is of great importance in providing financial information: what price is used for the inventory? If prices have changed during the period, should the final inventory be reported at prices prevailing early in the period, those of late in the period, or some average of all prices? This question has been the subject of a great amount of thought and concern.

When the periodic reporting and matching concepts are combined with the cost, or funds committed, concept, there results a serious problem in assigning prices to merchandise which has been sold and to that still in inventory. Some prices from purchases of merchandise are matched as expense (Cost of Goods Sold) with current revenue, while other prices are assigned to merchandise still in inventory and will be matched with revenue of later periods. The question is: which prices are matched against revenue of which year? The problem is greater in times of inflation, when prices have increased significantly within the fiscal year. A firm may purchase goods, hold them for an average of several months, and sell them at prices which have increased during the holding period.

The difference between cost and selling price on a specific item may appear to indicate an exceptionally great profit. For example, consider an item which cost $8 on January 2 and which sold for $12 on that same date, cost $10 and sold for $15 on June 30, and cost $12 and sold for $18 on December 31. The margin on sales is 33⅓ percent of sales price throughout the period. If this item is purchased on January 2 and sold on approximately June 30, there would appear to be a margin of $7 ($15–$8), or 46⅔ percent of sales price. This apparent margin can be objected to on the assumption that the business will continue and that a replacement item will be purchased for $10 on about June 30. When the firm has purchased this new item, it then has in stock an item similar to the one it had on January 2, and it has $5 additional cash ($15 received from the sale minus $10 to replace the item sold). This $5 increase in resources, 33⅓ percent of selling price, is seen by some as a better measure of the profitability of the firm. They would argue that the firm does not gain by inflation so long as it continues to buy and sell, because the increased dollars of margin will be used in buying other units at the higher prices, and that the increase in dollars of profit is in direct proportion to the inflation, resulting in no real increase.

We can assume two more transactions in the above illustration and complete the situation as follows:

	Purchase Price	Sales Price
January 2, purchased one item	$ 8	
June 30, purchased one item, sold one item	10	$15
December 31, purchased one item, sold one item	12	18

With the generally accepted funds-committed basis for reporting, we have the three prices of merchandise to be assigned to the two items sold and to the one item on hand on December 31. If the $8 and $10 prices are assigned to items sold, the margin will be computed at $15 on the two, or more than 45 percent of the selling price; it can be argued that this is unrealistic. On the other hand, if the $10 and $12 prices are assigned to the items sold, the margin will be computed at $11 on the two, or 33⅓ percent of the selling price; this may appear to be a realistic profit margin, but it would result in reporting the one item on hand as an asset at the price of $8. This appears to be unrealistic, also, because a like item (perhaps that specific item) cost $12 on the date of the report. Of course, an average price might be used, assigning an average of $10 to each of the items. This would result in a profit margin of $13 (over 39 percent) on the two items sold and in reporting the one item on hand at $10. The profit margin appears to be only moderately overstated and the inventory value only slightly understated in relation to current cost prices; reporting on this compromise basis could not claim precision in measuring the amount of either the profit margin or the current price of assets.

If this appears to present a dilemma, appearances are not deceiving. The qualitative standards or guides now used for financial information do not provide for the problem of inflation, leaving persons to choose among the inventory pricing methods in their effort to make the reported net income and asset amounts as realistic as possible. One of the generally accepted standards for financial reporting is based on the premise that inflation in the United States is not material in its effect; the standard is that the dollar is adequately stable for use as a measurement in reporting.

Specific Item Inventory Pricing

When items of merchandise are not identical, and when the stock of goods is made up of a relatively small number of high-value items, one may find the inventory priced according to the price paid for each specific item still in stock at the end of the period. Automobiles, with various body styles, engines, and accessories, and each with its unique motor number, are an example of the type of merchandise which might be reported by the exact price of specific items. This requires that a record of each item be kept so that it will be known which items have been sold and which are still in inventory; since automobiles are identified and title is transferred by motor number, vehicles must be identified specifically when sold. It is quite simple to identify those in stock. This procedure is used with precious stones of high value, all types of registered vehicles, houses built for the market by residential builders, and other such high-cost items.

First-in, First-out Flow for Inventory Pricing

Firms in which merchandise is perishable or subject to damage, style change, or becoming shopworn normally attempt to move goods in a chain or queuing pattern. This results in a direct flow through, so that the first items of a particular good received by the firm are the first items sold. Pricing of goods may be matched with this chain or queuing flow in the first-in, first-out method of inventory pricing, commonly called the FIFO method. The goods remaining in inventory are the last goods of that quantity purchased.

For a demonstration of first-in, first-out inventory pricing, assume the following facts:

Inventory, March 1, ten items at $10 each	$100
March 8, purchased five items at $11 each	55
March 12, sold six items at $16 each	
March 19, purchased eight items at $12 each	96
March 27, sold six items at $17 each	
March 31, inventory count shows eleven items on hand.	

On a first-in, first-out basis the cost of the twelve items sold would be computed as follows:

Ten items in March 1 inventory, at $10	$100
Two items of the five purchased on March 8, at $11	22
Cost of goods sold (FIFO basis—first 12 items)	$122

The March 31 inventory of eleven items would be made up of the following:

Eight items purchased on March 19, at $12	$ 96
Three of the five items purchased on March 8, at $11	33
March 31 inventory at FIFO cost (last eleven items)	$129

Most merchandise flows in a chain or queuing pattern, and the first-in, first-out pricing of goods claims the virtue of matching the physical flow of goods. This appears to be of great importance to some, but others argue that the physical flow pattern is not relevant in assigning cost to goods. More of this argument will be seen in later paragraphs.

Last-in, First-out Flow for Inventory Pricing

The reverse queue flow pattern is seen in a few types of goods, but the last-in, first-out pricing method is not used in an attempt to match the physical flow of goods. The last-in, first-out (LIFO) method is used to match the most current cost with current selling prices in computing the margin on sales as a step in computing the net income for the period. Advocates of the LIFO method contend that, with continuing inflation, the margin on goods cannot be measured by deducting the cost of goods at prices of several months past from sales revenue at current prices. Therefore, regardless of the physical flow of goods, it is contended that the LIFO method should be used to match the most recent cost price with the current sales price in computing profit; thus the extreme misstatement of profit margin because of inflation can be avoided.

Using data from the preceding example, the last-in, first-out pricing of goods would result in the following cost for the twelve items sold:

Eight items purchased on March 19, at $12	$ 96
Four items of the five purchased on March 8, at $11	44
Cost of goods sold (LIFO basis—last twelve items)	$140

LIFO pricing of the March 31 inventory of eleven items would be:

Ten items in March 1 inventory, at $10	$100
One item of the five purchased on March 8, at $11	11
March 31 inventory at LIFO cost (first eleven items)	$111

It may be noted that the preceding computation used data for the full month, assigning the latest purchases to cost of goods sold regardless of the timing of purchases and sales. If records of inventory levels and prices are maintained currently, and if the cost of goods is computed as the goods are sold, the computation would differ:

LIFO PRICING ON CURRENT BASIS

	Sales (at cost)			Inventory		
	Units	Price	Amount	Units	Price	Amount
March 1 inventory (ten items)				10	$10	$100
March 8 purchase (five items)				10	$10	$100
				5	11	55
March 12 sale (six items)	5	$11	$ 55			
	1	10	10	9	$10	$ 90
March 19 purchase (eight items)...				9	$10	$ 90
				8	12	96
March 27 sale (six items)	6	$12	$ 72	9	$10	90
				2	12	24 $114
			$137			

Cost of goods sold:

Six items of the eight purchased on March 19, at $12 (sold March 27)	$ 72
Five items purchased March 8, at $11 (sold March 12)	55
One item from March 1 inventory, at $10 (sold March 12)	10
	$137

March 31 inventory:

Nine items from March 1 inventory, at $10	$ 90
Two items of eight purchased March 19, at $12	24
	$114

Advantages and shortcomings of LIFO LIFO pricing during periods of inflation assigns the later, higher prices to cost of goods sold and leaves the earlier, lower prices in inventory. The higher cost of goods sold results in a lower net income. This fact has caused many to urge last-in, first-out pricing as an equitable process for computing income subject to federal income taxes so that very unreal income from inflation would not be taxed. When the Internal Revenue Code admitted LIFO as an acceptable inventory pricing method for tax purposes, it provided that firms might use the LIFO method for tax computation if they use the same method for financial reporting to shareholders. This tax legislation is exceptional in relating tax computation procedures to financial reporting; its effect was to cause many firms to consider using last-in, first-out as a method for assigning prices in their financial information systems in order to obtain the tax savings from using it in their tax computations.

There are three significant problems which develop in the use of LIFO inventory pricing:

1. Prices for goods which remain in inventory are the earliest prices for the period during which the method has been used. If LIFO has been used for inventory pricing for eight years, then the final inventory will be reported chiefly at prices which are eight years old. With even modest inflation, the amount reported for the inventory is substantially different from its present value.
2. The matching of the most current cost prices with the current sales prices in the LIFO method works well until the inventory is reduced below the level at which the method was begun. When the volume of sales exceeds the volume of purchases and there is a reduction of inventory, the last-in, first-out method will assign some of the very old prices, applicable to the amount of the old inventory sold, to current cost of goods sold. This distortion is more severe than the price change in any one year and counteracts the purpose for using LIFO.
3. The end-of-period computation of LIFO prices assigns cost prices for the most recently purchased goods to cost of goods sold, regardless of whether any sales of goods have been made following those purchases. This allows management a certain degree of manipulation of reported net income; if earnings are exceptionally good and it is desired to defer reporting some of the earnings to a future period, the firm might accomplish this by making heavy purchases of goods very late in the year. Assuming continuing inflation, these late-year higher prices assigned to cost of goods sold by LIFO would cause the reported net income to be smaller that year. Of course, profit for the following year will be larger because of this operation. If net income appears to be smaller than desired, normal purchases may be delayed so that the late-year prices will *not* go into cost of goods sold. Of course, the effect of delaying purchases will be felt in smaller profits in the following period. This built-in device for affecting reported profit by purchasing or not purchasing goods late in the year is seen as a definite shortcoming for the LIFO pricing method.

These problems make it quite apparent that the last-in, first-out method of pricing inventories does an imperfect job of matching current cost and sales prices in computing net income and distorts the value reported for inventory on the balance sheet. Many people believe, however, that even with its shortcomings, during a period of continued inflation LIFO is better for inventory pricing than the other methods.

LIFO became much more popular in the years immediately after it was accepted in computing federal income taxes. The method is supported as a means of offsetting the inflationary effect on information used to compute net income, although, when it is used for this purpose, it seriously understates the price of the end-of-year inventory. It probably will continue as a popular method so long as our qualitative standards for financial information do not include some method of compensating for the effect of inflation in financial data. If the effect of inflation on prices were eliminated by the use of price level indexes, the greatest need for the LIFO method would no longer exist, and the method probably would loose some of its popularity.

Weighted Average Price

When an average price is used, it is not appropriate simply to average the prices paid without weighting them by the quantity of goods at each price; such simple average is not relevant to the goods in the specific quantities purchased by an individual firm. Using the preceding example, the weighted average price is computed:

$$\frac{\text{Cost of all goods available}}{\text{Number of items of goods available}} \text{ or } \frac{\$251}{23} = \$10.913$$

Cost of goods sold is twelve items at $10.913, or $130.96
March 31 inventory is eleven items at $10.913, or $120.04

Many liquids and grains of standard quality are physically mixed in storage so that those remaining are a mixture of all those which were in storage during the period; a weighted average price appears appropriately matched with the physical flow of goods. The weighted average price may be considered a compromise between the extremes of the other flow methods, for it is used by some firms with merchandise which does not mix in storage. The strongest argument, perhaps, is that the average is the most representative price and the compromise which will avoid the extremes in pricing and the problems seen in the use of both the FIFO and LIFO methods.

Moving Average Price

A weighted average of prices paid for goods, computed each time a new purchase of goods is received, is termed a moving average. A moving average is used when a current record is kept of all goods in inventory and when the cost of goods sold is computed as the sales are made. An average for the full period is not available until the end of the period; therefore, for current pricing it appears that an average cost on the date of each sale is appropriate.

Lower of Cost or Market Price

Following the convention of conservatism in reporting asset values, it has been customary to report merchandise at cost (determined by one of the preceding methods) whenever that cost is below current prices. When prices have suffered a decline and when the lower price level is expected to continue, then inventory is priced at its original cost or at the current price, whichever is lower. This is illustrated in the following:

Item	Cost Price	Current Price	Price Used for Inventory
O-Value	$ 4.75	$ 4.80	$ 4.75
A-Cup	.93	.90	.90
#12 THO	11.22	11.08	11.08
Flack	9.15	9.15	9.15

Estimating Inventory Amounts

Many firms prepare financial statements more frequently than once each year. Counting and pricing inventory more often than once annually would be a burden on personnel and quite expensive. For their *interim* statements, firms often estimate inventory amounts. Also, in situations in which the inventory cannot be counted (fire or storm loss, for example) an estimate must be made. Two methods frequently used for making this estimate are the *gross profit* method and the *retail* method.

Gross Profit Method

This estimate of inventory is based on the average markup or gross profit rate. Data normally are available concerning the total amount of merchandise on hand at the beginning and purchased during the period; these are the beginning inventory and purchase amounts. Also, data are available concerning the amount of goods sold; but these normally are the sales figures at sales price, which cannot be used in connection with cost-price data to compute the amount of goods remaining. The technique of this estimating method is to reduce the sales data to cost price (cost of goods sold) by using the average gross profit rate. Examine the following computation for this point:

Beginning merchandise inventory		$10,000
Purchases during the period (total cost)		40,000
Total		$50,000
Sales for the period	$63,000	
Average gross profit rate, 33⅓ percent		
*Estimated gross profit on sales	21,000	
Estimated cost of the goods sold during the period		42,000
Estimated ending inventory		$ 8,000

*Of course, the cost-of-goods-sold rate of 66⅔ percent might have been used with a direct computation to obtain the estimate of $42,000 for cost of goods sold.

Retail Inventory Method

This method of estimating inventory involves the same basic relationship as is used in the gross profit method, the percent of markup or gross profit. In the retail method one uses the actual markup data for the current period rather than relying on an average markup rate that would necessarily have come from data of prior periods.

In larger department stores the procedure for placing prices on merchandise (tagging operation) is closely controlled. As a part of this control a register is often kept of all price tags placed on merchandise, including the amount of markup from cost on the original tagging and the amount of markdowns or additional markups on retagging operations. These data allow management to act on a more informed basis in changing prices upward or downward to obtain the best combination of movement of goods and gross profit margin. These data also make it possible to obtain a cost-of-goods-sold rate, and conversely a markup rate, for the current period, which can be used in estimating the inventory remaining on hand at the end of the period. Observe the technique of using these data in the following illustration:

	At Cost Price	At Retail Price
Inventory at beginning of period	$10,000	$15,000
Purchases	40,000	59,000
Additional markups		3,000
Markdowns		(2,000)
Totals	$50,000	$75,000
Current cost percent of sales price: 50,000 ÷ 75,000 = 66⅔ percent		
Sales for the period		63,000
Estimated ending inventory at retail price		$12,000
Estimated ending inventory at cost price (12,000 × .66⅔)	$ 8,000	

The retail method is considered more reliable than the gross profit method because it uses current data. However, it does depend on an average rate, and it does not provide proof that the goods actually were on hand—that theft and pilferage, for example, had not occurred in substantial amounts. As estimates, however, these methods provide useful and sometimes essential information.

BASIC CONCEPTS RELATED TO INVENTORY PRICING

The problem of inventory pricing stems from some basic concepts which are effective as qualitative controls in developing financial information.

Periodic Reporting and Matching Concepts

A fundamental concept in information structuring is that of periodic reporting of information concerning the financial condition of the firm and the financial results of operations. We accept the point that managers, investors, and other users of financial information can gain more from analysis of the information and comparison of accomplishments if information is provided at regular intervals of time and if this information relates to changes for equal and consecutive periods of time. This concept of periodic reporting compels us to accept another, that of matching inflows and outflows, or revenues and expenses, for the period. Activities which produce revenue and which incur expenses are continuous for the most part; they do not stop and start at year's end. In order to provide information about activities of a year or a quarter (rather arbitrary time segments in the life of the firm) we must devise means of matching revenues and expenses to specific periods of time.

Asset Measurement Concept

Another concept which bears directly on the inventory problem is our concept of the measure of assets in terms of the data which are input to the financial information system. Industry, the accounting profession, and government agencies have all adopted the concept of funds committed as the acceptable input. This has resulted in the use of the original cost in reporting an asset, regardless of increases in value that may have occurred since its purchase. However, a significant decline in cost prices since the purchase of merchandise is interpreted as a loss of part of the funds committed by the purchase. In such a situation the lower current cost price is used instead of the original cost in pricing inventory.

Present Value Concept

For good communication, the symbols used in the communication process must have the same meaning to both the sender and receiver of information. It appears that persons who are not oriented to the theory of the "funds committed" or the "cost" concept normally may interpret the dollar amounts written beside classes of assets on the balance sheet as the "value" of those assets—with value being what they are worth on some ill-defined market, or what they are worth for use by the firm at the date of the report. Consideration of the various "values" obtainable for an inventory using different inventory pricing methods will demonstrate that the presently accepted qualitative standards of asset reporting do not result in information which reveals the present value of most goods. The reader of a financial report sees an amount for inventories, for example, which is derived by starting with the funds committed, or price paid, and then assigning that amount to goods sold and goods in inventory by one of several price flow concepts. Any increase in the value of the goods since they were purchased, either a change in market value or in use value to the firm, does not affect the amount reported. These increases since acquisition do not qualify as inputs to the information system.

Value of assets can be measured in terms of the market (the amount expressed by the price that would have to be paid to acquire a like asset currently) or in terms of the use to the firm (normally, the utility in producing revenue—the revenue it will produce minus the additional cost to produce that revenue). In a merchandising firm, the present value of the future revenues from sale of merchandise in inventory minus the additional cost of selling and collecting (including normal return on investment as a cost) should be very nearly the same as the present market value (cost to purchase) of the inventory. For merchandise there may be little or no difference between present market value and present utility value to the firm. The difference between these two determinations of present value will be more apparent when we consider the value of long-life assets.

Efforts toward present value It appears that many persons who deal with financial information have sensed the need to use a present value for merchandise. The last-in, first-out flow of costs is used in an attempt to match current cost prices with sales prices. The resulting "values" in inventory are acknowledged not to represent the utility or value of the goods—they are residual amounts left over after one has taken the most recently derived prices from an accumulation of transaction prices. The need for current prices in computing net income is deemed so important that, in order to use them, the resulting undesirable effect in the balance sheet is accepted.

For decades the continuing effects of inflation have been observed in the United States, but the need to adjust for inflation in financial information has not been critical. In some other nations inflation has become so severe on occasion that values in financial information have been updated by the use of price level indexes. If inflation had been 50 percent during the year, one would need to increase the beginning of the year inventory amount by 50 percent to compare it with the end of the year amount on an equivalent monetary basis. If inventory amounts were updated by a price level index there would be less need for the LIFO inventory pricing method, because amounts which were nearer the current value would be used for inventory items when sold and when reported as inventory at the end of the year.

Illustration of price level adjustment of inventories Assume that a firm has the following inventory amounts reported at the end of two consecutive years.

	December 31 1970	December 31 1971
Amount of inventory on FIFO basis	$450,000	$480,000

Assume, also, that the goods in the 1970 inventory were purchased at an average price level index of 150 and that the 1971 inventory was purchased at a price level of 165, which still prevails at the end of the year.

Casual observation of the reported inventory amounts would inform one that there had been a noticeable increase of $30,000 from December 31, 1970, to December 31, 1971. For a better comparison, one might adjust the earlier inventory to the same price level as the later one, as follows:

$$\$450{,}000 \times \frac{165}{150} = \$495{,}000.$$

Price level adjusted inventories would be stated:

	December 31 1970	December 31 1971
Amount of inventory, adjusted to December 31, 1971, price levels	$495,000	$480,000

This information gives a quite different impression of relative inventory amounts on the two dates. It now appears that there was a decrease in inventory of $15,000. Price level adjustment of cost prices would eliminate the effect of the monetary unit's changing value and allow comparisons as if the value of money had been constant at the present level.

Current Status of Price Level Adjustment

Adjusting inventory costs and other asset amounts for changes in the general price level would substantially affect the financial information normally provided to management and investors. Financial and investment periodicals in recent years have contained significant criticisms of financial information as it is now reported. The American Institute of Certified Public Accountants has studied in depth the general question of adjusting assets to the present value of the dollar. Statement Number 3 from the Accounting Principles Board (June,

1969) suggests that price level adjustments may be appropriate in some situations and that adjusted data may be reported as a supplement to basic unadjusted data. It appears that a total substitution of price level adjusted amounts for the unadjusted information which has been used in the past probably would create damaging confusion and lead to poor decisions and a disrupting of investment and financing markets. APB Statement Number 3 does not *recommend* reporting of adjusted data; it seems likely that any change recommended in the future might take the form of providing both unadjusted and price level adjusted information, at least for an interim experimental period. It must be recognized that no change from the present reporting may be considered desirable and that values not adjusted for changes in the value of the dollar may continue as the reporting standard.

QUESTIONS AND EXERCISES

8- A. When and how is cost of goods sold determined in a firm using perpetual inventory procedures?

8- B. When and how is cost of goods sold determined in a firm using periodic inventory procedures?

8- C. The purchase of which of the following results in a debit to the Purchases account for a grocery firm?
   a. Cash register for the store
   b. Ten gross of paper bags
   c. Newspaper advertising
   d. Five cases of vegetable soup

8- D. Using periodic inventory procedures, does the beginning or the ending inventory appear in the Merchandise Inventory account at the end of the accounting period before the accounts are adjusted?

8- E. During the first quarter of the year, a firm purchased merchandise costing $32,100. What was the firm's cost of goods sold for the quarter if there were
   a. No beginning inventory or ending inventory?
   b. A beginning inventory of $13,000 and no ending inventory?
   c. A beginning inventory of $14,000 and an ending inventory of $16,500?
   d. No beginning inventory and an ending inventory of $11,000?

8- F. What is summarized in the Cost of Goods Sold account? What items of data are involved?

8- G. What is the meaning of the phrase "lower of cost or market" as it is used with inventory pricing?

8- H. What are the meanings of the terms "FIFO" and "LIFO"?

8- I. If prices are rising, will the LIFO or the FIFO method of inventory pricing result in the higher cost of goods sold? The higher gross profit?

8- J. Why would a firm estimate its inventory?

8- K. What are two methods of estimating inventory at the end of a period?

8- L. The gross profit method and the retail method of estimating the dollar amount of inventory both use a markup, or gross profit, rate. What is the essential difference between the methods?

8-M. What kind of average, simple or weighted, is computed when an average price is used for pricing the ending inventory?

8-N. What is the difference between a weighted average price for a period and a moving average of prices during the period? How often is a new average price computed when a moving average is used?

8-O. In using the lower of original cost or current market price for inventory, indicate which price would be used for each of these items:

Item	Cost Price	Current Price
A	$ 3.19	$ 2.27
B	.99	.91
C	110.05	105.15
D	9.55	9.55

PROCEDURAL PROBLEMS

8-1. James Camera Shop sells two types of cameras, a low-priced Model A and an expensive Model B. On January 1 the shop had two Model B cameras on hand:

Serial JL1044 Cost $277.50
Serial MY721 Cost $293.00

There were no Model A cameras on hand. The shop had the following purchases and sales:

Jan. 2 Purchased four Model A cameras for $18.00 each.
4 Purchased one Model B camera, serial no. AX6140, for $265.25.
5 Purchased two Model A cameras for $21 each.
9 Sold one Model A camera.
12 Purchased four Model A cameras for $21.25 each.
14 Sold Model B camera, serial no. MY721.
17 Sold three Model A cameras.
21 Purchased two Model B cameras, serial no. BN4182, $303.30 and AQ3166, $281.20.
23 Purchased four Model A cameras for $22.50 each.
26 Sold two Model A cameras.
28 Sold Model B cameras, serial nos. AX6140 and AQ3166.
30 Sold three Model A cameras.

a. For Model A cameras compute the cost of goods sold and the January 31 inventory dollar amount using: (1) moving average, and (2) weighted average.

b. For Model B cameras compute the cost of goods sold and January 31 inventory amount using specific item inventory pricing.

8-2. The Merritt Grain Warehouse had a September 1 wheat inventory of 12,000 bushels made up of:

6,000 bushels purchased August 6 at $1.80 per bushel
3,000 bushels purchased August 14 at $2.10 per bushel
3,000 bushels purchased August 22 at $1.80 per bushel

During September the company made the following purchases and sales:

Sept. 3 Purchased 4,000 bushels at $2.00 per bushel.
8 Sold 4,000 bushels.
10 Purchased 2,000 bushels at $1.90 per bushel.
14 Sold 3,000 bushels.
19 Sold 4,000 bushels.
23 Purchased 3,000 bushels at $2.00 per bushel.
26 Sold 7,000 bushels.

Compute cost of goods sold and the dollar amount of ending inventory using
a. FIFO,
b. LIFO.

8-3. The Simpson Corporation had a December 1 inventory of 800 units with a unit cost of $4.00. During the month the following transactions occurred:

Dec. 3 Sold 300 units.
11 Purchased 200 units for $5.00 each.
16 Sold 250 units.
20 Sold 300 units.
22 Purchased 300 units for $7.00 each.
28 Sold 100 units.

Compute the cost of goods sold and the cost of the December 31 inventory by:
a. First in, first out.
b. Last in, first out.
c. Weighted average.

8-4. Lane Sporting Goods has taken a physical count of merchandise on hand on December 31. Using the cost and current market prices given, compute the dollar amount of inventory at lower of cost or market.

Item	Units on Hand	Cost Per Unit	Current Price Per Unit
Tennis rackets	12	$12.00	$11.50
Golf ball/per dozen	20	8.00	8.25
Rain jackets	16	18.00	17.00
Golf hats	10	4.50	4.50

8-5. The Slayne Corporation has asked you to estimate the February 28 inventory for use in interim financial statements. Using the following data and the gross profit method, calculate the February 28 inventory.
The February 1 inventory was $16,000 (physical count).
Purchases and sales during the month were

Feb. 4	Purchases	$ 8,000
11	Purchases	11,000
14	Sale (retail price)	18,000
16	Sale (retail price)	7,000
22	Purchases	4,000

The estimated gross profit rate on sales is 20 percent.

8-6. The Mitchell Appliance Company has provided the following inventory information:

	At Cost	At Retail
June 1 inventory	$12,000	$17,000
June purchases	48,000	60,000
Additional markups		4,000
Markdowns		(1,000)
June sales		65,000

Using this information, compute the estimated inventory at cost price for June 30 by the retail method.

8-7. The Tiger Toy Company began February operations with 200 units on hand at a cost of $18 per unit. Purchases were

Feb. 3	100 units at $20 per unit.
14	300 units at $21 per unit.
17	100 units at $22 per unit.
26	200 units at $23 per unit.

Sales (at a unit price of $30) were

Feb. 5	100 units
Feb. 16	200 units
Feb. 21	200 units

Compute gross profit on sales using
a. First in, first out.
b. LIFO determined at the end of the month.

8-8. Andrews Manufacturing, Inc., had a May 1 inventory of 200 units with a unit cost of $4.00. During May the following inventory transactions occurred.

May 4	Purchased 200 units for $6.00 each.
9	Sold 300 units.
10	Purchased 100 units at $5.00 each.
13	Sold 50 units.

May 16 Purchased 250 units at $4.00 each.
20 Sold 300 units.
24 Purchased 200 units at $7.00 each.
27 Sold 100 units.
30 Purchased 100 units at $4.00 each.

Compute the cost of goods sold and May 31 inventory cost using LIFO
a. Data for the complete month.
b. Computations as sales are made.

8-9. The Fisher Appliance Company had six units on hand on November 1. These had been purchased during October at a unit cost of $125.
November transactions were

Nov. 3 Sold four units.
7 Purchased seven units at $120 each.
14 Purchased two units at $110 each.
16 Sold three units.
19 Sold one unit.
23 Purchased three units for $135 each.

Compute the cost of goods sold and November 30 inventory cost using
a. FIFO.
b. Moving average.
c. Weighted average for the month.

8-10. To prepare April 30 financial statements Ennis Wholesale Corporation intends to use lower of cost or market inventory pricing. Using information given below, compute the inventory amount applying lower of cost or market to
a. Individual items.
b. Department totals.
c. Complete store total.

Dept. 1	Item	Units on Hand	Cost Per Unit	Current Price Per Unit
	A	6	$4.00	$4.25
	B	20	7.25	7.40
	C	9	4.50	4.30
Dept. 2	Item			
	D	24	$11.00	$14.00
	E	6	9.00	7.75

8-11. A. J. Petit, a men's clothing store, estimates its March 31 inventory by using the retail method and the data below. Compute the estimated cost of the March 31 inventory.

	Cost	Retail
March 1 inventory	$15,000	$ 30,000
March purchases	65,000	100,000
Additional markups............		none
Markdowns		(5,000)
March sales........................		75,000

8-12. Overseas International operates a division in Tasinza, a country subject to rapid price level changes. To eliminate the influence of these price level changes the company has selected 1962 as the base year, and they express all inventory values in 1962 prices (1962 = 100 percent).

The 1968 inventory, in 1968 prices, is $720,000; the 1969 inventory, in 1969 prices, is $628,000. The 1968 price index is 130, and 1969 index is 110.

a. Convert both of these inventories to 1962 prices.

b. Convert the 1968 inventory to 1969 prices.

8-13. On January 16, 1971, the Craft Company had a warehouse fire which partially destroyed its inventory. The remaining inventory has an estimated cost of $16,000. The company and insurance agents have agreed to determine the loss by estimating the inventory using the gross profit method.

The January 1 inventory at cost was $32,000. Purchases during January preceding the fire were $71,000, and sales at retail price were $90,000. The 1970 gross profit rate was 20 percent.

Calculate the inventory fire loss.

CONCEPTUAL PROBLEMS

8-14. The Parr Company uses a periodic inventory system. The following errors were found in the year-end inventories during a four-year period:

a. The December 31, 1968, inventory was understated by $3,000 because one crate of merchandise was overlooked during the annual physical stock-taking. The purchase of this merchandise had been recorded properly.

b. In costing one item in the December 31, 1969, inventory, a clerk transposed figures, producing an inventory total of $79,900, when the correct total would have been $82,600.

c. In computing the December 31, 1970, inventory, one lot of goods costing $1,100 was counted twice.

d. No errors were found in inventory computations for 1971. The December 31, 1967, inventory is accepted as correct, also.

The reported net income was:

1968...........	$60,000
1969...........	59,000
1970...........	64,000
1971...........	71,000

What was the correct net income figure for each year, and what was the amount of the error in the inventory figure reported on each balance sheet?

8-15. At the end of the year 1971, after the inventory was computed and recorded using periodic inventory procedures, the firm of Collins and Sons arranged for its first audit by a certified public accountant. In reviewing some of the more important items for several years past, the CPA detected the following errors:

1. Inventory of December 31, 1969, was understated by $4,000 because of an error in addition.
2. Merchandise that cost $3,300 was included twice in the inventory of December 31, 1970.
3. An item of merchandise that cost $3,000 was omitted from the December 31, 1971, inventory.

The reported net income for 1969 was $51,000; for 1970, $57,200; for 1971, $62,000.

a. What was the corrected net income for each year?
b. What was the amount of error (or errors) on each balance sheet?
c. What data input to the system is needed on December 31, 1971, to correct the errors so that the 1971 net income can be reported correctly from the accounts?

8-16. Al and Ben's Hardware Store has been in operation for several years. On the night of October 31 it burned, and everything except the accounting records, which were in the fireproof safe in the office, was destroyed or damaged too badly for sale. The firm wishes to file an insurance claim, but does not know the amount of inventory at the time of the fire. The following information is available from the accounting records:

1. Sales from the beginning of the fiscal year (July 1) through October 31 were $162,419.
2. Sales returns for the same period were $2,113.
3. Purchases from July 1 were $109,776.
4. Purchase returns from July 1 were $1,014.
5. Freight in on purchases was $2,228.
6. Merchandise inventory on July 1 was $41,171.
7. Average gross profit for the past three years (32 percent of net sales) appears appropriate for the four months of July through October.

Compute the estimated amount of inventory on October 31.

8-17. Catherine's Boutique is considering a public issue of stock to obtain funds for franchising its operations across the country. A public stock issue will require the firm to report several years' past operations with inventories priced on a consistent basis and will require that inventory pricing be done on a consistent basis in the future.

To aid in choosing between FIFO and LIFO pricing of year-end inventories, the firm has developed the following data:

Dec. 31	FIFO Cost	LIFO Cost
1962	$20,000	$20,400
1963	22,400	21,600
1964	23,000	22,200
1965	21,600	21,800
1966	20,600	21,600
1967	24,000	21,400
1968	24,400	20,800
1969	27,600	21,000
1970	30,000	23,800
1971	31,600	25,400

a. Which of the inventory pricing methods reported the greater cost of goods sold in 1962? Did that method report a higher or lower net income for 1962?

b. Which inventory pricing method resulted in lower net income for 1964? for 1965? for 1968? for 1971?

c. By which inventory method was the net income higher for the first five years? for the next five years? for the full ten-year period?

d. For years in which prices rise, FIFO yields a greater increase (or lesser decrease) in inventory and a greater net income than does LIFO. In which years was there apparently a price rise?

9 The Special Problem of Depreciation

Preview Questions

As you study look for the answers to the following questions:

- **What does *depreciation* mean in financial reporting?**
- **What are the methods of reporting depreciation?**
- **How do these methods differ?**
- **How does one select a depreciation method?**
- **What are the arguments for each method?**
- **What are the differences in computing depreciation for homogeneous and heterogeneous groups?**
- **What can change the depreciation computation?**

Depreciation is treated as a special problem in developing financial information because of the imprecise use and meaning both of the term and of data reported for it. Data for depreciation, however they are computed and interpreted, are reported as a measure of a resource consumed and, therefore, as an expense.

In approaching a new technical topic, it is best to first define terms to be used.

MEANING OF "DEPRECIATION"

Some of the difficulties in developing precise depreciation data which can be used well in financial analysis stem from the lack of a precise technical definition of the term.

The common social use of the word "depreciate" is indicated by the dictionary definition:

> To lessen in price or estimate value: lower the worth of—opposed to appreciate.[1]

This general meaning of a lessening or lowering in value is carried over into the financial use of the term. Here, however, the questions of what value is lessened and by how much apparently have prevented full concord in using the term. As a means of getting further into the topic, let us examine another definition.

Definition of Depreciation Accounting

The American Institute of Certified Public Accountants (AICPA) is the most influential professional body in determining qualitative standards for the development of financial information. This group has not defined depreciation in its publications, but it has provided a definition of depreciation accounting:

> . . . a system of accounting which aims to distribute the cost or other basic value of tangible capital assets, less salvage (if any), over the estimated useful life of the unit (which may be a group of assets) in a systematic and rational manner. It is a process of allocation, not of valuation. Deprecia-

[1] *Webster's Third New International Dictionary*, S.V. "depreciate."

tion for the year is the portion of the total charge under such a system that is allocated to the year.[2]

This AICPA definition of "depreciation accounting" includes the computation, processing, and reporting of data about depreciation of assets. In financial reporting, the word "depreciation" has taken on this same meaning, so that "depreciation" and "depreciation accounting" have become almost synonymous for financial purposes. Accountants speak of *depreciating* an asset, when actually they are referring to *accounting* for the depreciation or amortizing the cost of the asset.

Use of "Depreciation"

The imprecise use of terms has not helped to prevent or clarify confusion as to the meaning of the depreciation data included in financial statements. Managers may express concern as to whether the accounting depreciation matches *actual* depreciation, indicating that in their thinking depreciation still carries the general meaning of a lessening or lowering in value, with "value" being what something is *worth* currently. It might have been better if accountants had used the broad term "amortize" in financial reporting to mean the spreading of the original cost of an asset in a "systematic and rational manner" over the periods of its usefulness. This would have left the word "depreciate" with its original meaning of lowering in value, and the two terms could have been used separately. We must adjust ourselves to this dual meaning of "depreciate," however, if we are to understand its usage.

It is important to divorce the idea of value or worth from depreciation in financial reporting, because there it refers to spreading the original cost of an asset as an expense over the periods of use; it does not refer to reporting decreases in the current value of an asset. This will be pursued farther in chapter 10. In the present chapter we shall examine the system and rationale for deciding how an asset will be depreciated (or its cost amortized).

One rational approach to the problem of distributing the cost of an asset as an expense over its useful life is to seek to allocate cost to each year in proportion to that part of the total utility of the asset consumed during that year. To accomplish this, no direct reference need be made to market value during the life of the asset. Cost minus

[2] *Accounting Terminology Bulletin 1* (New York: American Institute of Certified Public Accountants, 1953), p. 25.

salvage value is distributed in some pattern, such as those produced by the computations already studied in chapter 7. The specific pattern is chosen because it appears to match the general consumption pattern of the asset's utility. This handling of depreciation conforms to the definition of expense and to the criteria for expense reporting.

DEPRECIATION METHODS

The concept of distributing the cost of an asset over its estimated useful life in a systematic and rational manner requires that there be a reason for distributing the cost in some particular manner. The methods most commonly used in computing the periodic depreciation amount were presented in chapter 7. They are the straight-line method, unit-of-production method, declining balance method, and sum-of-years'-digits method. Any of these methods may be applied to individual assets or to a group of assets treated as a unit.

In all methods of computing depreciation, the amount to be distributed as expense over the useful life of the asset is the total cost of the asset minus the expected salvage value at the end of that useful life. The useful life for computing depreciation must be the time that the particular firm expects to use the asset. Because of a firm's need for asset reliability or because of management's desire for a "modern" appearance, the end of an asset's useful life in one firm may find it quite useful to another. The time during which a particular firm expects to use an asset is, for purposes of computing depreciation, that asset's useful life to that firm. The estimated salvage value is based on the expected age and condition of the asset at the end of the projected useful life.

Straight-line Method

This method of computing depreciation assigns the same amount of depreciation expense to each period during the useful life of the asset. Early in the 1950s straight-line depreciation was widely used. Since that time other methods have grown in popularity.

Computation The following computation provides the annual depreciation amount using the straight-line method:

$$\frac{\text{(Total cost of asset) minus (estimated salvage)}}{\text{Estimated years of useful life}}$$

$$= \text{Annual depreciation amount}$$

For an asset which cost $8,000 and has an expected useful life of five years with an estimated salvage value of $500, the computation would be:

$$\frac{(\$8{,}000) - (\$500)}{5 \text{ years}} = \$1{,}500 \text{ per year.}$$

Recording this amount of depreciation each year reduces the amount at which the asset is represented in the information system, or its *book value* (from the manually kept "books" of record). The effects are shown in the following schedule:

Year	(a) Depreciation	(b) Accumulated Depreciation	(c) Book Value
0	—	—	$8,000
1	$1,500	$1,500	6,500
2	1,500	3,000	5,000
3	1,500	4,500	3,500
4	1,500	6,000	2,000
5	1,500	7,500	500

(a) Debited to Depreciation Expense, and credited to Accumulated Depreciation (contra account to the Equipment account).
(c) Equipment account balance minus Accumulated Depreciation balance.

It is important, for comparing this method of computing depreciation with other methods, to understand clearly the pattern taken by the annual depreciation. If the yearly depreciation amounts are indicated by points on a graph and these points are connected by a line, the line will be straight and horizontal (Figure 9-1). The method is named because of this pattern.

Rationale for and against straight-line depreciation Straight-line depreciation may be the most defensible of all methods in many situations. Arguments for the method are:

1. The useful life of many assets depends to a greater extent on age than on the amount of usage. With technological obsolescence becoming a greater factor, this may be increasingly true.
2. The utility derived from an asset year by year is very difficult to measure, and even harder to predict as a basis for some other method of computation; such prediction is not required for the straight-line computation.
3. The accuracy and validity of all methods may be challenged; straight-line is simpler to compute and easier to understand.

Figure 9-1

LINE CHART OF STRAIGHT-LINE DEPRECIATION

(Equipment cost, $8,000; life, 5 years; salvage, $500)

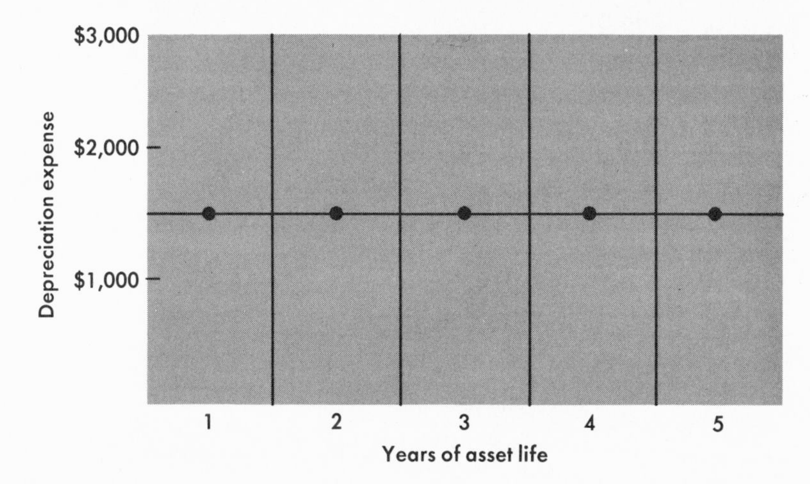

Arguments against straight-line depreciation are chiefly arguments for some other method, based on the identifying and emphasizing of specific use factors. These arguments will be discussed in later sections; briefly, some of them are

1. For some assets the utility value is clearly greater in early periods (operation is faster, production greater, performance more accurate); greater expense should be assigned these early periods.
2. Maintenance expense often increases as the asset ages. To offset this upward trend in expense and to maintain a more nearly stable total "use expense," the method used should provide higher depreciation in early years with a decreasing trend or pattern.
3. The degree of uncertainty as to possible use of equipment increases the farther into the future we project. The degree of certainty of use should influence the pattern of assigning total cost as depreciation; early years, in which the certainty of use is higher, should be assigned a greater part of the depreciation.
4. Some assets are used sporadically. Value is derived and therefore expense should be charged as the assets actually are used; the depreciation plan should reflect use and not passing of time.

It is clear that formidable arguments can be mustered for some method other than straight-line. The authors of one respected accounting text refer to the straight-line method as old-fashioned, one-horse-shay depreciation. The fact remains, despite these arguments, that the straight-line method is still widely used.

On the other hand, it is argued that accelerated depreciation often is unrealistic in that the expense during the early years is excessive. Perhaps the proponents of accelerated depreciation have chosen computation methods which are too accelerated and too rigid; other computations that would allow modification of the depreciation pattern might produce a more acceptable result. Computations other than the standard methods are not used frequently and will not be presented in this chapter.

Unit-of-Production Method

The unit-of-production method relates the amount of depreciation expense for a period to the service received from an asset. The computation requires an estimate of the total production to be obtained from the asset, rather than the number of years of service life.

Computation Use of actual year-by-year production volume and estimated total production in calculating depreciation is illustrated below:

Expected Total Production, 150,000.
Asset Cost, $325,000. Salvage, $10,000.

Year	(a) Units of Actual Production	(b) Depreciation at $2.10 Per Unit	(c) Accumulated Depreciation	(d) Book Value
0	—	—	—	$325,000
1	49,000	$102,900	$102,900	222,100
2	22,000	46,200	149,100	175,900
3	46,500	97,650	246,750	78,250
4	8,500	17,850	264,600	60,400
5	24,000	50,400	315,000	10,000
		$315,000		

(b) Computed as ($324,000 − $10,000) ÷ 150,000 units = $2.10 per unit.
(d) Original cost minus accumulated depreciation.

Actual production in the preceding table totals the amount that was expected. Normally the first projection of total production will not be accurate; the total expected production must be reviewed each year and adjusted to the best projection that can be made. The amount of depreciation per unit produced will change as the total expected production changes. It is necessary to adjust depreciation near the end of the asset's use so that the estimated salvage value is left undepreciated as book value.

Rationale for unit-of-production method This method of computing periodic depreciation appears appropriate under the following conditions:

1. The asset is used at irregular intervals of time or under varying conditions of stress.
2. Production by the asset can be measured in some type of units.
3. There is some basis for making an estimate of total units of production expected from the asset.
4. A rational manner of computation requires that depreciation for the period be related to the volume of product derived from the use of the asset.

The units of production may be expressed in terms of the number of units of goods processed (screws, nails, flanges, etc.), the units of service provided (hundreds of feet of metal cut, area of surface polished, etc.), or service in time units (hours operated). In the latter case the computation often is called the *service hours method* because of the emphasis on hours of service provided; the reasoning and computation is the same whether production is measured in units of goods, service, or time.

Assigning depreciation to periods on the basis of direct production from the assets involved does appear to be a rational manner of distributing the asset cost over the useful life. However, argument against the method holds that having the assets available for use is of value to the firm in providing the ability or capacity to do the work; this, in turn, aids in obtaining orders to be processed later. Holders of this view contend that the production assets in the shop provide utility in aiding many functions of the firm, not just the specific act of producing goods.

One would expect this method to be used when the period and degree of asset use is clearly sporadic, varying greatly from year to year, and when the assets involved are major items in the firm. This method is used consistently for computing depletion for extractable resources such as coal, sand, sulphur, and petroleum.

Accelerated Depreciation

Methods by which greater depreciation is assigned to earlier years of an asset's use are termed "accelerated" in comparison with the straight-line method. Many formulas and techniques could be divised for computing depreciation in some accelerated pattern. The two most common computations (the only two that have gained wide acceptance) are the declining balance and sum-of-years'-digits methods.

Declining balance method **The computation of the declining balance pattern of depreciation is based on the premise that the utility consumed by the use of an asset for any period is a fixed percent of the total remaining utility of the asset projected from the beginning of that period.** If the period in question is the first period, an asset's depreciation is some predetermined percent of its cost; for any succeeding period its depreciation is the same percent of its current book value (undepreciated cost). Details of the computation for an asset with a five-year life are given in chapter 7. Computations for an asset with a ten-year life are shown in the following schedule.

DECLINING BALANCE COMPUTATION

Asset Life, ten years

Year	(a) Undepreciated Cost at Start of Year	(b) Depreciation at 20 percent of (a)	(c) Accumulated Depreciation	(d) Book Value at End of Year
1	$45,000	$9,000	$ 9,000	$36,000
2	36,000	7,200	16,200	28,800
3	28,800	5,760	21,960	23,040
4	23,040	4,608	26,568	18,432
5	18,432	3,686	30,254	14,746
6	14,746	2,949	33,203	11,797
7	11,797	2,359	35,562	9,438
8	9,438	1,888	37,450	7,550
9	7,550	1,510	38,960	6,040
10	6,040	1,208	40,168	4,832

(a) Cost minus depreciation for prior years: $45,000 minus (c) for preceding year, or (a) for preceding year minus (d).

(b) The 20 percent rate is computed by the formula $1 - \sqrt[10]{\frac{5,000}{45,000}}$ and rounded to the nearest even percent. This results in a final $4,832 book value, which approximates the estimated $5,000 salvage value.

(c) Total of depreciation for current year and all prior years.

(d) $45,000 minus (c), or (a) minus (b).

Depreciation pattern The patterns of periodic depreciation expense and of the remaining undepreciated asset cost are similar with the declining balance computation. Since depreciation is based on undepreciated cost (book value) and is computed at the same rate each year, it follows that the book value will decrease by the depreciation percent each year. The patterns of both depreciation and remaining book value are shown in graph form in Figure 9–2, page 204.

Sum-of-years'-digits method **Computations involved in this method provide a pattern of depreciation that decreases by the same *amount* each year, as contrasted to the same *rate* in declining balance.** The total amount to be depreciated is distributed over the years of asset life by multiplying the total to be distributed by the following fraction each year:

$$\frac{\text{Useful life from beginning of year (in years)}}{\text{Sum of the digits representing years of life}}$$

The use of this computation is seen in the following schedule:

SUM-OF-YEARS'-DIGITS DEPRECIATION SCHEDULE

Asset Cost, $45,000

Estimated Life, ten years; Salvage, $5,000

(a) Year	(b) Depreciation Fraction	(c) Depreciation	(d) Accumulated Depreciation	(e) Book Value at End of Year
1	10/55	$7,273	$ 7,273	$37,727
2	9/55	6,545	13,818	31,182
3	8/55	5,818	19,636	25,364
4	7/55	5,091	24,727	20,273
5	6/55	4,364	29,091	15,909
6	5/55	3,636	32,727	12,273
7	4/55	2,909	35,636	9,364
8	3/55	2,182	37,818	7,182
9	2/55	1,455	39,273	5,727
10	1/55	727	40,000	5,000
55	55/55			

(b) Years' life from beginning of year ÷ sum of the digits representing the years.
(c) $40,000 × (b)
(d) Total of depreciation for current year and all prior years.
(e) $45,000 minus (d); or (e) for preceding year minus (c) for current year.

Depreciation pattern This method provides an acceleration of depreciation expense, but the expense decreases by the same amount every year. The patterns of depreciation expense and book value are seen in Figure 9-3.

Figure 9-2

DECLINING BALANCE DEPRECIATION PATTERN

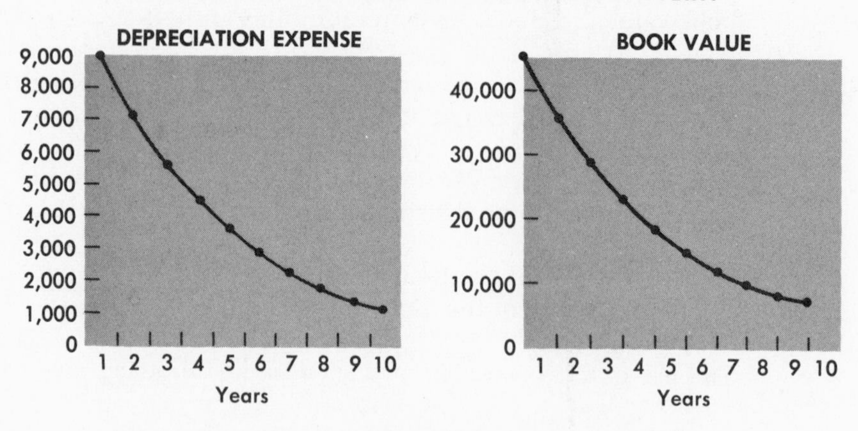

Figure 9-3

SUM-OF-YEARS'-DIGITS DEPRECIATION PATTERN

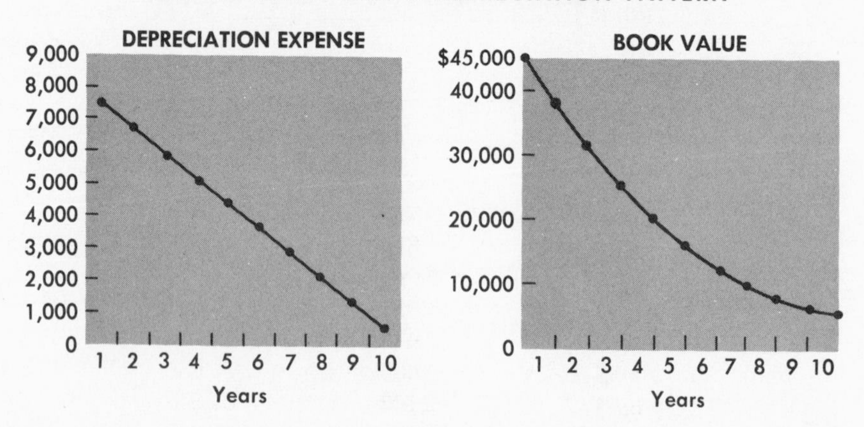

Book value of assets (undepreciated cost) declines in a curved pattern in both declining balance and sum-of-years'-digits depreciation. The slant of the curves is different, however. The patterns of depreciation and undepreciated cost for the three leading computation methods are shown in Figure 9-4.

It is clear that the declining balance method provides the greatest acceleration of depreciation for an asset with a ten-year life. With assets of longer life, the sum-of-years'-digits method provides the greater acceleration. It becomes apparent that choosing a depreciation method requires, first, identification of the general pattern of utility consumption and then computations to find the method most closely approximating that pattern.

Figure 9-4

DEPRECIATION PATTERNS OF THREE METHODS

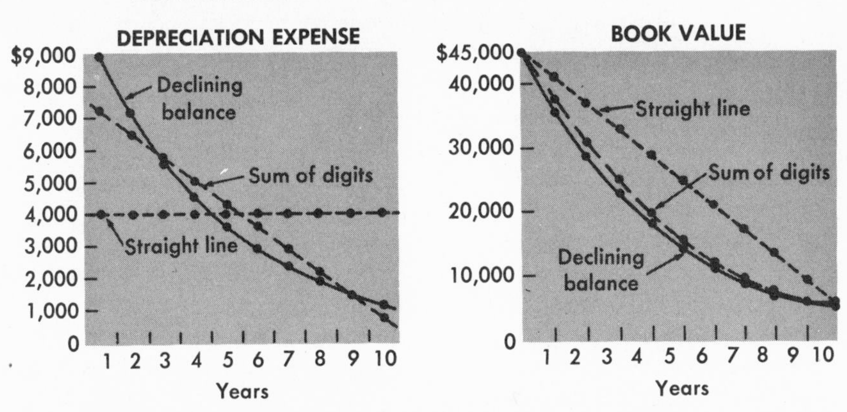

Selecting the Depreciation Method

In order to distribute the cost of an asset as expense over its life in proportion to the utility (or usefulness) consumed each year, it is necessary to identify the utilities (types of usefulness) of an asset and determine which of these are most important to the firm. Only then can the utility's pattern of consumption be estimated. For example, the utility of a tool storage shed is probably both accessible storage for tools and low maintenance cost. The utility of a pump may include the movement of a volume of liquid, low maintenance costs, and low operating cost. The utility of an exclusive furrier's delivery truck may include movement of goods, low maintenance and operating costs, degree of dependability, and degree of style. The pattern of utility consumption may be related to physical deterioration and increased maintenance requirements; to technological obsolescence and operating wear, which causes increased operating and maintenance cost; or to technological obsolescence, style obsolescence, physical age, and operating wear which affects dependability and operating and maintenance costs.

After identifying the types of utility received from an asset, one may find that none of them is easily measured. From experience and engineering projections one may establish expectations (some of which may be quite arbitrary or subjective) of utility consumption and match these with a pattern provided by some computation method. One does not often find precision in determining the pattern of utility consumption; instead, there is often a rather arbitrary choice between straight-line and accelerated depreciation. The method that will provide the fastest depreciation for income tax computation may be chosen, also, for financial reporting. Depreciation need not be the same for these purposes, but it is convenient when the same depreciation amounts are appropriate for both reporting uses. The greatest amount which may be deducted for tax computation may grossly misrepresent the consumption of asset utility. When it does, some better amount should be used for financial reporting.

Rationale for accelerated depreciation The considerations for selecting a depreciation method discussed in the preceding paragraphs may lead to the conclusion that much more of a particular asset's utility is consumed early in its life than in the later periods. This would argue for some method of accelerated depreciation.

Another very persuasive argument is based on the fact that operating and maintenance costs of many mechanical assets increase as they age. It seems that the total use cost of such assets should not increase as they get older; however, if operations and maintenance costs do increase, perhaps they should be matched with a decreasing depreciation charge to maintain a constant total use cost from year to year.

The effect of selecting accelerated depreciation for this purpose is pictured in Figure 9-5.

Figure 9-5

OPERATING AND MAINTENANCE COSTS PLUS DEPRECIATION

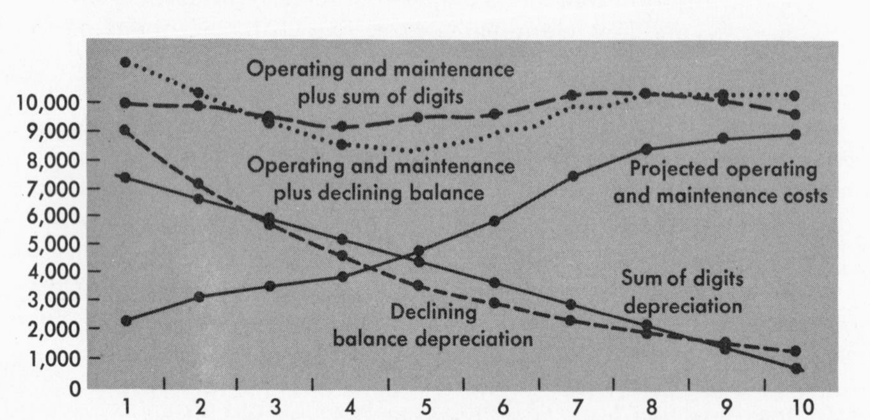

In this illustration the sum-of-years'-digits method provides a pattern which best matches the projected pattern of operating and maintenance expenses, resulting in an almost level line of total use costs for the equipment. Choosing the depreciation method in this way changes the emphasis from identifying specific utilities of the asset to specific use costs. Matching patterns to produce a constant total use cost seems to argue that original purchase and operating costs are not so clearly separable, that it is the total cost of using the machine that should be matched with its productivity. In some cases it might be desirable to obtain a total use-cost pattern that begins high and decreases as the asset provides less service, rather than a level (straight-line) pattern of total cost.

Arguments for the use of some method of accelerated depreciation would include the following:

1. In situations of increasing maintenance and operating costs an accelerated depreciation method will provide a decreasing pattern which, matched with those increasing costs, will maintain an approximately level total cost of usage. Wear in the early periods no doubt is often a direct cause of repairs in later periods; matching the patterns of depreciation and maintenance recognizes this fact.
2. Without regard to maintenance and operating expenses, it can be argued that greater utility is consumed early in the use of assets and, therefore, that greater expense should be reported in the early periods of use. The utility consumed might have contributed directly toward greater revenue in early periods, providing faster operation and, therefore, greater production. However, the utility might have contributed only indirectly to revenue in the present or in the future, such as the style utility provided by a new delivery truck.
3. If the market price is viewed as an indicator of an asset's remaining utility, and if the depreciation pattern is to be matched with the pattern of decreasing utility value (indicated by market price), then an accelerated depreciation method will provide an appropriate pattern in many cases. Assets generally lose market value faster in early years than in later periods.

Group Depreciation

Groups of assets may be treated as units for computing and recording depreciation. This affords two advantages:

1. It saves the time and cost of making many individual computations and the cost of maintaining data for individual items.
2. It provides a better statistical group, or sample, for computing the average life of such assets.

As you study data for both homogeneous and heterogeneous groups, these advantages will become apparent.

Group depreciation rate This term may be used to indicate the depreciation rate used for the total of any group, but generally it indicates the rate for a homogeneous group of assets. It is important that assets in a homogeneous group have the same expected lives and similar patterns of utility consumption. Usually, assets included in a homogeneous group have similar operational functions, although this is not necessary.

In a homogeneous group the expected life is treated as the average expected life of all members of the group. This means that we use the average to represent the group in computing depreciation, but that we expect some items to vary from the average in the service life they actually provide. Lives of individual items should vary around the average (some shorter, and some longer) so that the average is a good representation of the group in computing depreciation. To be consistent, we then treat any item that is no longer serviceable as fully depreciated, down to the actual salvage value received for it. Application of the concept of a group rate can be seen in the following example.

Assume that Baker Company had the following transactions involving metal-working machines of similar type and life expectancy:

Purchased for cash:
  Machines 1, 2, and 3 on July 1, 1969, for $2,400 each.
  Useful life expected, ten years; salvage $100 each.
  Machine 4 on October 2, 1970, for $3,000. Life, ten years; salvage $100.
Sold for cash:
  Machine 2 on June 30, 1972, for $1,000 because it has lost precision in some operations sooner than expected.

The following schedule and journal entries show the effects of these transactions and annual straight-line depreciation, recorded on June 30 of each year:

MACHINERY GROUP

Ten-Year Life, Straight-Line Depreciation

Date	Event	Machinery Account		Accumulated Depreciation Account		Book Value of Group	Total Salvage Value
		Change	Balance	Change	Balance		
7/ 1/69	Purchase 1, 2, 3	+ $7,200	$ 7,200			$7,200	$300
6/30/70	Depreciation			+ $ 690	$ 690	6,510	
10/2/70	Purchase 4	+ 3,000	10,200			9,510	400
6/30/71	Depreciation			+ 980	1,670	8,530	
6/30/72	Depreciation			+ 980	2,650	7,550	
6/30/72	Sale of 2	− 2,400	7,800	− 1,400	1,250	6,550	300
6/30/73	Depreciation			+ 750	2,000	5,800	300

Date	Account	Debit	Credit
July 1, 1969	Machinery	7,200	
	Cash		7,200
	Purchase of machines 1, 2, and 3.		
June 30, 1970	Depreciation Expense	690	
	Accumulated depreciation on Machinery		690
	Depreciation for the year based on ten-year life and $100 salvage		
Oct. 2, 1970	Machinery	3,000	
	Cash		3,000
	Purchase of machine 4.		
June 30, 1971	Depreciation Expense	980	
	Accumulated Depreciation on Machinery		980
	Depreciation for the year (cost, $10,200 minus salvage, $400) times 10 percent straight-line rate.		
	Note: It is customary to depreciate additions and deletions to the nearest full period, although other procedures can be followed.		
June 30, 1972	Depreciation Expense	980	
	Accumulated Depreciation on Machinery		980
	Depreciation for the year (cost, $10,200 minus salvage, $400) times 10 percent.		
June 30, 1972	Cash	1,000	
	Accumulated Depreciation on Machinery	1,400	
	Machinery		2,400
	Sale of machine 2.		
	Note: For any disposition of a unit from the group, it is assumed that the concept of *average* life for the group allows for variances from the average; therefore, the disposition is treated as fully depreciated to the salvage realized.		
June 30, 1973	Depreciation Expense	750	
	Accumulated Depreciation on Machinery		750
	Depreciation for the year (cost, $7,800 minus salvage, $300) times 10 percent.		

If additions to the group continue, depreciation will continue beyond the initial ten-year life period. If there are no more additions, depreciation will be recorded until the book value is reduced to the expected salvage from the remaining items in the group.

Composite depreciation rate Operating groups composed of many units having different useful lives may be depreciated as heterogeneous groups. For example, all units making up a steam-turbine, electric-generation plant might be treated as a heterogeneous group. It is assumed that the group will be kept intact by replacement of short-life items as their full utility is consumed. For such a group a weighted-average (composite) depreciation rate is used. Computation of a composite depreciation rate for a heterogeneous operating group of assets is accomplished as follows:

COMPUTATION OF COMPOSITE DEPRECIATION RATE

Steam-Turbine, Electric-Generation Plant

Items	Cost	Expected Life	Salvage	First Year Depreciation
Boilers	$ 300,000	20 years	500	$14,975
Firing units	100,000	15 years	500	6,633
Pressure and flow controls	150,000	10 years	-0-	15,000
Turbines	500,000	15 years	10,000	32,667
Pipe and tubing	80,000	30 years	1,000	2,633
Valves	10,000	5 years	-0-	2,000
Pumps	20,000	10 years	-0-	2,000
Motors	12,000	5 years	1,000	2,200
Miscellaneous small items	6,000	3 years	-0-	2,000
	$1,178,000			$80,108

Composite straight-line depreciation rate:

$$\$80,108 \div \$1,178,000 = 6.8\%$$

Straight-line depreciation has been illustrated in the application of both the group and composite depreciation rates. Declining balance depreciation may be used with groups, also. Because of the likelihood of changes in a group it is doubtful that use of the sum-of-years'-digits computation is appropriate.

Changes in Expected Useful Life of Assets

The projected useful life of an asset is an estimate, and it often becomes apparent that the original projection no longer represents the best estimate of the asset's usefulness. When this situation occurs, the depreciation computation can be changed. In the new computation of depreciation, the book value at the time of the change and the remaining useful life are used instead of the original cost and the original estimate of total life.

To illustrate the change in expected life and the resulting change in depreciation, assume the following:

Asset cost: $26,000.

Original expected useful life: ten years.

Original expected salvage value: $2,000.

Depreciation per year: ($26,000 − $2,000) ÷ 10 years = $2,400.

Straight-line depreciation for four years: $2,400 × 4 = $9,600.

Change of estimated total life at end of the fourth year to a total life of fifteen years (eleven remaining years), and estimated salvage $1,000.

New depreciation, straight-line for eleven remaining years (book value is now $26,000 − $9,600 = $16,400):

($16,400 − $1,000) ÷ 11 = $1,400 per year.

Depreciation on this asset was recorded at $2,400 per year for the first four years of its use. Upon changing the estimate of its useful life and salvage value, depreciation was recomputed. Beginning with the fifth year of use, depreciation is recorded at $1,400; this will depreciate the asset to its salvage value during the remaining years of its life.

If depreciation recorded in the past were considered materially excessive, grossly distorting net income, and if the recomputed depreciation for the future were considered materially less than the amount that should be reported as expense during those periods, then a correcting entry might be made reducing (debiting) Accumulated Depreciation and increasing (crediting) earned capital in the Retained Earnings account. The amount of this correction would be the amount by which depreciation recorded in the past exceeded the amount not considered correct. It appears that this is seldom done in practice.

Disposition of Depreciated Assets

Assets that are subject to depreciation have a limited life. When these assets are scrapped (no salvage value) or sold, appropriate changes must be made in asset data stored in the system. An asset may be scrapped or sold before or after being fully depreciated.

Disposition of a fully depreciated asset If an asset is not expected to have any salvage value, the full amount of the cost will be depreciated during its life. Assume that a machine costing $10,000 is fully depreciated (book value is $0). As long as this machine is in service, even after the full cost has been expensed by depreciation, data for its cost and accumulated depreciation normally are left in the accounts. However, when such an asset is removed from service and scrapped, all data representing it are removed from the accounts. For the $10,000, fully depreciated machine the appropriate journal entry would be:

Mar. 10	Accumulated Depreciation on Machinery.....	10,000	
	Machinery		10,000
	Scrapped machine 11; no salvage value.		

This journal entry removes the original cost and accumulated depreciation from the accounts, leaving no data in the system for this scrapped machine.

When a fully depreciated asset is sold, the amount received must be treated as gain on the sale, since the asset is represented at zero book value in the data system. Data for the asset must be removed from the accounts, and the cash, or other asset received, and gain must be recorded. The sale of a $10,000, fully depreciated machine for $200 cash would result in the following input of data:

Mar. 10	Cash	200	
	Accumulated Depreciation on Machinery.....	10,000	
	Machinery		10,000
	Gain on Sale of Assets		200

This journal entry removes the cost and accumulated depreciation from the accounts and records the amount received and the gain from the sale.

Disposition of a partially depreciated asset Assets may become inoperative or obsolete before their full cost has been reported as depreciation expense. Assume that a machine which cost $10,000 and for which we have recorded depreciation of $8,000 will no longer operate, is not considered repairable, and is scrapped. Data representing the machine are removed from the accounts, and the book value ($2,000) is reported as a loss. The journal entry would be:

Mar. 31	Accumulated Depreciation on Machinery	8,000	
	Loss on Disposition of Assets	2,000	
	Machinery..		10,000
	Machine 13 scrapped; no salvage.		

When a partially depreciated asset is sold, the same action is needed to remove the cost and accumulated depreciation; however, the gain or loss to be recorded is the difference between book value and the amount received. If the amount received is greater than book value there is a gain; conversely, if the amount received is less, there is a loss. The journal entry for an asset sold at a loss is:

Mar. 31	Cash	1,600	
	Accumulated Depreciation on Machinery	8,000	
	Loss on Sale of Assets	400	
	Machinery		10,000

DEPRECIATION BASED ON PRESENT VALUE

It should be remembered that in financial reporting "depreciation" means the distribution of the cost of an asset over its period of utility by some rational and systematic method. The most appropriate method appears to be the one most closely related to the pattern of consumption of the asset's utility. **Basing depreciation on the asset's present value has been recently argued as the best measure of the resource consumed as the asset is used. This would give depreciation a totally different purpose—measuring the value of resources consumed by the use of long-life assets, rather than distributing the original cost of the asset over periods of its utility.**

Basing depreciation on the present value of assets also appears to assume, although not require, that the assets themselves be reported at their present value. As we saw early in this study, the present financial information, or accounting, system does not accumulate data and report information about the *value* of assets; it reports the financial resources committed to specific assets. Adjusting the system to report the present value of assets would require substantial changes in the procedures for acquiring and inputting data, as well as in the qualitative standards for determining what information is reported and, therefore, what data are selected for input to the system. Current values of assets could be reported, with depreciation based on current values if this information is needed and if reliable data are available from which to develop the information. The question of whether the current value of assets should be reported is treated, along with possible methods of accomplishing this, in chapter 10.

QUESTIONS AND EXERCISES

9-A. As used in financial reporting, what is the meaning of *depreciation*?
9-B. Why does depreciation not measure the decrease in value of an asset?

9-C. Name four methods of computing the periodic depreciation of an asset's cost.

9-D. A building cost $45,000, has an estimated useful life of twenty years, will be razed at a cost of $1,000 after approximately twenty years, and will provide approximately $2,000 from the sale of salvage material from its razing. Compute the annual straight-line depreciation for the building.

9-E. Shop equipment which cost $65,000 is expected to have a salvage value of approximately $5,000 after the firm's planned use of five years.
   a. How much depreciation will be reported each year by the sum-of-years'-digits method?
   b. What will be the depreciation each year if a 40 percent rate is used with declining balance computations?

9-F. In what way are the concepts of "unit of production" and "service hours" computations of depreciation similar to the concept of straight-line depreciation?

9-G. What pattern of annual depreciation expense over the life of an asset will result from the use of each of the following depreciation methods?
   a. Straight-line.
   b. Sum-of-years'-digits.
   c. Declining balance.
   d. Unit of production.

9-H. Under what conditions would one argue that unit-of-production or service hours depreciation computation is most appropriate?

9-I. What is the strongest argument for using an accelerated method for computing depreciation?

9-J. For depreciation purposes, what is a homogeneous group of assets? A heterogeneous group?

9-K. Explain the difference between a group rate and a composite rate for computing depreciation.

9-L. An asset cost $24,000 eight years ago. It has been depreciated on the basis of an expected life of twenty years, with a $4,000 salvage value. The asset is now expected to be used for a total of twenty-five years and to have a salvage value of $2,400. Assuming straight-line depreciation, what is the amount of depreciation expense for the ninth year?

PROCEDURAL PROBLEMS

9-1. The Alamo City Manufacturing Company has just purchased factory equipment costing $60,000 and having a useful life of five years and a salvage value of about $6,000. They want to use an accelerated depreciation method and have asked you to prepare a depreciation schedule for both sum-of-years'-digits and declining balance (40 percent rate) methods.

9-2. The Sinclair Piano and Organ Company has sold three automobiles which had been used by salesmen. Prepare the entry recording the disposition of each car. Depreciation is taken for any full year during which the asset is held for six months or more. No depreciation is recorded for a year in which an asset is held less than six months.

	Car No. 1	Car No. 2	Car No. 3
Date purchased	4/1/65	9/1/65	3/1/68
Cost	$3,200	$2,600	$3,800
Estimated salvage value	$ 400	$ 200	-0-
Estimated life	4 years	5 years	5 years
Depreciation method	straight-line	S/L	D/B 40 percent rate
Date sold	3/1/69	10/30/69	5/30/69
Cash received	$ 480	$ 750	$1,200

9-3. James R. Wheat, Inc., takes depreciation on its delivery trucks as a group. They use an estimated life of five years and compute depreciation on a straight-line basis. Use the data in the following illustrations to prepare an asset and depreciation table similar to the one illustrated in the chapter.

Apr. 1, 1965	Purchased three delivery trucks on account for $4,000 each, with a salvage value of $600 each.
July 1, 1965	Purchased truck number 4 for $3,000 cash; truck has a salvage value of $400.
Dec. 31, 1965	Recorded depreciation for the year. Company policy is to take full year depreciation on assets acquired during the year and no depreciation on those disposed of during the year.
Feb. 2, 1966	Purchased truck number 5 for $3,500 on account. Truck has a salvage value of $400.
Dec. 31, 1966	Recorded year's depreciation.
May 11, 1967	Sold truck number 2 for $800 cash.
Dec. 31, 1967	Recorded depreciation for the year.
Dec. 31, 1968	Recorded depreciation for the year.
Sept. 10, 1969	Purchased truck number 6 for $5,000 on account. The salvage value is estimated to be $800.
Dec. 31, 1969	Recorded depreciation for the year.

9-4. On January 1, 1967, Acme Corporation purchased some factory equipment at a cost of $40,000 with no salvage value. The declining balance method of depreciation with a rate of 40 percent is used to record depreciation each December 31.

On January 1, 1969, the company examines the equipment, determining that it has a remaining useful life of five years and a salvage value of $800. They also decide to change to straight-line depreciation at this time.

Prepare the December 31, 1969, journal entry to record depreciation for the year and prepare a partial balance sheet as of December 31, 1969, showing the equipment and related accumulated depreciation.

9-5. On January 1, 1967, the Rhine Manufacturing Company purchased two machines:

	Cost	Salvage Value	Estimated Life
Machine A	$14,000	$ 500	Ten years or 135,000 units
Machine B	$ 9,000	$1,000	Eight years or 160,000 units

Depreciation expense is recorded each December 31.

a. Using straight-line depreciation prepare the journal entry to record depreciation for the year 1967. Prepare a partial balance sheet to show the machinery and accumulated depreciation as of December 31, 1969.

b. Assume the following production schedules:

	Machine A	Machine B
1967	16,000	12,000
1968	11,000	21,000
1969	12,000	15,000

Prepare the journal entry to record depreciation for the year 1969 and prepare a partial balance sheet for December 31, 1969, presenting machinery and accumulated depreciation. Use unit-of-production method.

9-6. The Stewart Manufacturing Company takes depreciation on its entire plant by computing a composite straight-line depreciation rate based on the five machines in use.

Complete the following table to compute first year depreciation and the straight-line depreciation rate.

Item	Cost	Expected Life	Salvage	First Year Depreciation
A	25,000	4 years	1,000	
B	15,000	5 years	-0-	
C	40,000	8 years	2,000	
D	20,000	5 years	2,000	
E	35,000	6 years	1,000	

9-7. The Rehfield Company uses the group depreciation method on its machinery. On May 1, 1969, the balance of the Machinery account was $72,000, and the Accumulated Depreciation-Machinery balance was

$24,500. Depreciation is computed using the straight-line method, with an estimated useful life of ten years and no salvage value.

Journalize each of the following events.

May 31 Record depreciation for the month.
June 14 Received $600 when we sold one of our machines which had cost $6,000.
June 30 Record depreciation for the month.
July 6 Purchased a new machine for $9,000 cash.
July 23 Scrapped one machine which had cost $4,000.
July 31 Record July depreciation.

9-8. On January 1, 1969, Horne Industrial Products put into operation two machines. Machine A was purchased for $26,000, has a salvage value of $2,000, and is expected to produce 80,000 units before it is scrapped. Machine B cost $31,000, with a salvage value of $3,000 and an estimated production of 400,000 units.

The company had the following production:

1969...........	30,000 units
1970...........	24,000 units
1971...........	19,000 units

a. Compute depreciation expense for 1970.
b. Compute the book value of the machines after the December 31, 1970, entry to record depreciation.
c. What is the balance of Accumulated Depreciation account after recording depreciation expense for 1971?

9-9. Dial Furniture, when it began operations in January 1966, purchased four delivery trucks at a total cost of $32,000. The company computed depreciation each year using the straight-line method, with an estimated life of five years and estimated total salvage value of $2,000.

In January 1971 the company examined the trucks and decided that they could all be used an additional three years with no salvage value remaining.

a. Compute the amount by which depreciation has been overstated during the five years due to the company's incorrect estimates of useful life.
b. Assuming the company does not correct prior years' earnings, what is the depreciation expense for 1971?

9-10. The Tanner Manufacturing Company has assembled a group of four assets which are used to manufacture a special product. The company will take depreciation on the assets by computing a composite declining balance rate based on the four assets. The declining balance rate for each of the four assets is to be twice the straight-line rate.

Complete the following table to compute first year depreciation and the declining balance depreciation rate.

Asset	Cost	Estimated Life	Declining Balance Rate	First Year Depreciation
1	$12,000	4 years		
2	7,000	5 years		
3	10,000	10 years		
4	15,000	3 years		

9-11. Complete the schedule for each independent situation below. For this problem all machines are considered to be purchased on January 1 of the year and sold on December 31, with a full year's depreciation taken in year of purchase and year of sale.

Machine Number	Date Acquired	Depreciation Method	Estimated Life	Cost	Estimated Salvage Value	(Date of Sale) Accumulated Depreciation	Date Sold	Cash Received	Gain (Loss)
1	1/1/65	Straight-line	10 years	?	$2,000	$15,200	12/31/68	?	$ 400
2	1/1/63	Declining balance 40 percent	5 years	$60,000	None	$47,040	?	$11,400	?
3	1/1/66	Sum-of-years'-digits	6 years	$45,000	$3,000	?	12/31/70	?	$4,400
4	1/1/65	Units of Manufacture	200,000 units	$34,000	$2,000	$17,000	12/31/67	?	None
5	1/1/67	Straight-line	6 years	$42,000	?	$13,000	12/31/68	$31,000	?
6	1/1/68	Straight-line	?	$20,000	$2,000	$10,800	12/31/70	$ 9,000	?

9-12. On January 1, 1971, McGowan Corporation owned three delivery trucks:

	Number 1	Number 2	Number 3
Purchased	11/14/70	4/1/69	5/3/69
Cost	$7,800	$21,500	$10,000
Estimated salvage value	$600	$1,200	$ 1,000
Estimated life	6 years	4 years	5 years
Depreciation method	S/L	Sum-of-years'-digits	D/B 40 percent

The company maintains a separate Accumulated Depreciation account for each truck. Depreciation is not recorded in a year in which an asset is held less than six months, but is recorded for a full year when a truck is held for more than six months.

a. What is the annual depreciation for truck number 1?
b. What is the January 1, 1971, book value of truck number 2?
c. Truck number 2 was sold on March 19, 1971, for $7,420 cash. Prepare the journal entry.
d. On April 4, 1971, the company purchased a new truck for $8,000 cash. The truck has an estimated life of four years and salvage value of $700. Journalize the purchase.
e. Truck number 3 was destroyed in an automobile wreck on May 27, 1971. The company sold it to a scrap metal dealer for $70. Journalize.
f. Prepare the December 31, 1971, entries to record depreciation, assuming truck number 4 is depreciated using declining balance rate of 50 percent.

9-13. The Atlas Aviation Company manufactures parts for missiles and other aviation products. When they purchase plant assets they want to recover cost (through accelerated depreciation methods) as rapidly as possible because these contracts are sometimes cancelled.

Assuming an asset cost of $100,000, prepare the depreciation schedules for declining balance and sum-of-years'-digits method with no salvage value for the cases below.

a. Three-year estimated useful life and declining balance with a 67 percent rate.
b. Four-year estimated life and declining balance rate of 50 percent.
c. Five-year estimated life and declining balance rate of 40 percent.

CONCEPTUAL PROBLEMS

9-14. The X-Cel Company has just purchased a piece of equipment that is expected to produce approximately the same number of units of product each year until it is retired. Company management sees no reason to expect prices of the products sold to either increase or decrease during the machine's productive life. Operating and repair costs are expected to increase by about the same amount each year, however, and economic life of the equipment is expected to end seven years from now, when the cost savings from a new machine will be adequate to justify replacement.

What method would you use to calculate annual depreciation charges on this equipment? Give reasons for your answer.

9-15. Elmor Corporation purchased a major item of equipment fifteen years ago at a cost of $300,000. At that time it was estimated that the economic life of the equipment would be twenty years and that its scrap value would be $30,000. The company has used straight-line depreciation for this equipment.

For each of the following events, indicate whether a revision of the original depreciation rate is necessitated, and give reasons for your answer.

a. Due to recent price increases, the present replacement cost of the same type of equipment is $500,000.
b. For the same reason (increase in prices), the final scrap value is expected to be $50,000.

c. The company could sell the equipment now at a price of $100,000.
d. At the end of last year a major breakdown occurred. After extensive repairs, the equipment now has a productive capacity of 90 percent per year of its production before the breakdown. Management still expects to use the equipment for five more years, retiring it after a total life of twenty years.

9-16. The Air-Go Air Freight Lines has purchased a new cargo plane for $1,200,000. All the company's equipment has been depreciated in the past by the straight-line method, but since experience indicates that operating expenses and repairs and maintenance will become heavier as the plane gets older, the controller suggests that some accelerated method of depreciation should be considered. The plane is expected to be operative for about ten years and to have a salvage value of about $128,000 at the end of that time.

A special study of past operating and repair expenses, made by the controller's office, reports that on aircraft such as this the expenses increase year by year. The results of that study, applied to the new plane, provide projections of operating, repair, and maintenance expenses the first year of $400,000, increasing by the formula $p + f \times .12\,(.8)^{n-1}$, where p is the preceding year's expense, f is the first year's expense, and n is the number of years' service at the beginning of that year. Using this computation, expenses are projected for the second year of

$$\$400,000 + \$400,000 \times .12(.8)^0, \text{ or } \$448,000.$$

For the third year the expense estimate is

$$\$448,000 + \$400,000 \times .12(.8)^1, \text{ or } \$486,000.$$

For the fourth year the expense is projected as

$$\$486,400 + \$400,000 \times .12(.8)^2, \text{ or } \$517,120.$$

Expenses for the following years are projected by like computations.

The maximum rate allowed by the Internal Revenue Code for this kind of asset is 15 percent declining balance. It is suggested that 20 percent declining balance or sum-of-years'-digits procedure might provide a more realistic depreciation amount.

Using the controller's data, compute the projection of operating, repair, and maintenance expenses for the aircraft for the ten years. Also, compute depreciation on the three bases suggested above. Prepare a chart to show the levels of the total of the projected expenses plus depreciation, using depreciation for the three methods computed.

What method of depreciation appears to be most reasonable for this particular aircraft? Why?

10 Asset Values

Preview Questions

As you study look for the answers to the following questions:

- **What information about assets is provided by the accounting system and financial reports?**
- **Are funds-committed data always relevant? Why or why not?**
- **What are capital expenditures?**
- **What are revenue expenditures?**
- **How are present values related to return-on-investment ratios?**
- **How is present value computed?**
- **How is the price of bonds computed?**
- **What is involved in maintaining data about a bond investment?**
- **How can the present value of a business or segment of a business be computed?**
- **What are price indexes and when are they used in financial information?**

Information needed about assets differs for various decisions. It is important to understand exactly what kind of information is currently provided by the accounting system so that it can be used correctly. Also, it is important to understand the potential need for other information and how that information might be generated.

FUNDS-COMMITTED INFORMATION

From study in prior chapters it should be clear that **data in the accounting system and, therefore, information on the balance sheet do not provide a measure of the value of assets.** Rather, these data indicate the funds that management has committed to specific types of properties, minus any portion of the total price of assets that has already been allocated as depreciation expense. The remaining amount is not value, but undistributed cost, or funds that are considered still tied up or committed in the assets. **The financial information system provides funds-committed information.**

Background of the System

Financial information has been reported in an organized and rather formal manner for centuries. Development of the financial information, or accounting, system began when businesses were proprietary ventures: each business was owned by a proprietor and run by him or by a manager who reported directly to him. The owner's asset and equity information needs for a relatively small business were fairly simple. A report telling him the source of funds for the business (his investment, borrowing, or credit) and where these funds were committed or tied up met his needs quite well.

The complexity of business operations has increased tremendously; the shareholder-investor has replaced the owner-manager in much of the business world; the risks involved in rapid technological change are greater, and decisions are more difficult. However, the information system still provides the same basic data about assets: where the firm's money is committed, and not the worth of various properties. It should be apparent that both kinds of information are needed; one kind comes from the formal system, and the other must be generated by special computations. The danger is that the two kinds of information will be confused. Managers and investors may use the readily available *funds-committed* information in making decisions for which *value* information actually is needed. Decisionmakers must use care in determining the relevance of information provided them, and persons who provide the information must know and distinguish between the kinds of information.

Classes of Assets

The balance sheets illustrated in chapter 4 and discussed in detail in chapter 13 both indicate that asset information is separated into categories related to current assets and long-life assets. Information about the latter broad group is further classified into groups such as plant assets or fixed assets, intangible assets, and investment.

Current assets The funds in current assets are available for recommitment by management in the near future. Current assets consist of cash and other items that will be converted into cash or consumed in operation of the business within the next fiscal year. Such assets include cash, of course, accounts receivable, short-term notes receivable, temporary investment, merchandise, supplies, and short-term prepaid expenses.

Among the current assets, cash, receivables, and temporary investments are considered available for commitment almost as quickly as if they were all in the form of cash. These are often called "quick assets." Receivables are reported at the amount of funds involved, that is, at the amount of cash one expects to collect. Reference to chapter 6 will help recall the adjustments made to accounts receivable because of expected uncollectible amounts, leaving the receivables at the expected collectible amount.

Temporary investments of funds in marketable securities such as stocks and bonds are reported at the lower of cost or current market price. This is derived from the funds-committed rationale that if the market price of securities rises the amount of money tied up in the investment is not affected, but if the price drops, a part of the funds originally invested is lost. The amount reported for temporary investments, as with other assets, is not the value but the amount of funds committed.

Merchandise inventory is reported at its cost or the current purchase price, whichever is lower. Data for cost of the merchandise are determined by the methods (LIFO, FIFO, and average) used to assign prices as studied in chapter 8.

Plant assets Long-life assets used in business operations are classified as *plant assets* or *fixed assets.* Often one sees the term *plant and equipment* used to report these assets on published annual reports. Plant assets are reported at the funds committed in them. Detailed questions related to measuring an asset's cost are considered later in this chapter; depreciation and its effect on the amounts reported for assets were discussed in chapters 7 and 9.

Intangible assets Long-life assets that do not have physical or tangible form may be reported as *intangible assets* or they may be included in plant assets. Funds committed is the basis for reporting intangible assets; the amount reported is determined by the cost of the asset and the amount that has been amortized as expense.

Among intangible assets are such items as patents, copyrights, trademarks, organization costs, and goodwill. Some of these have limited useful lives while others may not have a discernible limit on the length of their usefulness. The cost of an intangible asset with a limited life is amortized as expense over its useful life; the cost of intangible assets with unlimited lives is not amortized.

Limited life intangible assets Patents and copyrights provide legal protection for their holder for a limited number of years, patents usually for seventeen years and copyrights for twenty-eight years. The revenue-producing life of a patent or copyright may continue for the full period of legal protection, or it may be much shorter. The cost of the asset is amortized over its useful life.

A patent right which was purchased from an inventor for $5,250 when it had a remaining legal life of twelve years, but which was expected to be useful to the firm for only about seven years, would be amortized over the seven-year period. The annual adjusting entry to amortize the patent cost on a straight-line basis would be:

Patent Expense	750.00	
Patents		750.00

After one year the patent is reported on the balance sheet at $4,500 ($5,250 − 750).

Unlimited life intangibles Trademarks normally provide exclusive rights to a name or symbol for an unlimited period. The cost of such assets cannot be amortized because there is no measurable service period over which to spread the cost.

Organization costs are the cost of obtaining a corporate charter and organizing the firm. These cannot be identified with any period short of the full expected life of the firm, which normally is indefinite. Organization costs often are arbitrarily amortized over a five-year period, probably because this is permitted in computing federal income taxes.

Goodwill is the ability of a firm to earn an exceptionally high net income; it is recorded as the amount paid for a business in excess of the fair value of all the identifiable assets, minus liabilities of the purchased firm. Goodwill is recorded and reported on the standard basis of the funds committed and, therefore, it is reported only when it has been purchased. For example, if a firm purchases all the shares in AB Company for $110,000 when the fair value (not the book value) of AB Company's identifiable assets totals $140,000 and its liabilities are $50,000, the firm is paying $20,000 [$110,000 – ($140,000 – 50,000)] for goodwill.

It is quite difficult to relate purchased goodwill to a specific number of years. This topic is argued strongly by representatives of both business firms and public accountants, some contending that goodwill is of short duration, having to be renewed constantly by management and employee effort, and some contending that with continued success of the firm the goodwill relates to an indefinite period. Proponents of a short-life interpretation of course favor goodwill amortization over a relatively few years. The opposition argues that goodwill is not amortizable at all and that its cost should be retained unamortized until some event clearly demonstrates that the purchased goodwill has been dissipated. It should then be recorded as an extraordinary loss. Financial reporting is clearly divided on the treatment of goodwill, but the position of the American Institute of Certified Public Accountants is that goodwill should be amortized over a reasonable number of years.

Information Needs Identified

To illustrate the need for specific kinds of information, assume that your firm owns a large tract of land which you bought as an investment several years ago. Since you purchased it, new roads have been built along two sides of the tract, and industrial and commercial building has developed around the property. Another firm now would like to acquire your property for expansion and offers you shares of its stock in exchange for your land. What information do you need in order to determine the desirability of this trade? Surprisingly to some, the basic comparison is not between the value of the shares offered and what you paid for the land. Rather, it is between the value of the shares offered and the value of the best alternative use for the land.

For example, if the value of the shares offered amounts to $2,000 per acre for the land, and if it cannot be foreseen that a better offer will be available relatively soon or that the value of the land will increase substantially in the future, then the offer of stock apparently should be accepted, regardless of how much the firm paid for the land originally. The data about what the firm has committed or tied up in the land aids in computing the profit or loss on the venture and in computing the income tax consequences, but it does not help directly in deciding whether to accept the offer. For that decision, one compares alternatives to find the best among them; information is needed which will indicate the relative value of alternatives – not the value of an alternative compared with the original cost of the land.

The use of different kinds of information may be seen in the decision about replacing an operating asset. Assume that your firm purchased a machine for $50,000 three years ago. This machine was expected to last about ten years with no scrap value. Operating expenses, including labor and materials, are about $10,000 per year, and the product sells for about $25,000 each year. The firm has recorded straight-line depreciation for three years and reduced the *book value* of the machine to $35,000. A new processing innovation has made it possible to double the production, using a machine with an estimated five-year life that costs only $30,000 to purchase and about $6,000 per year to operate. Should the firm scrap its old machine after only three years' use and purchase one of the new machines? This decision does not hinge on how much the firm still has committed in the old machine; it relates instead to how the firm will benefit from purchasing and using the new equipment compared to continuing with the old. Relevant data are

BENEFIT FOR NEXT FIVE YEARS

Using old equipment:		Using new equipment:		
Cash inflow	$125,000	Cash inflow		$250,000
Cash outflow	50,000	Cash outflows:		
Net benefit	$ 75,000	Purchase price	$30,000	
		Operation	30,000	60,000
		Net benefit		$190,000

These data show clearly that in the next five years the firm will benefit by the amount of $115,000 ($190,000 – $75,000) by scrapping the old equipment and using the newly developed equipment instead. The unexpired cost of the old equipment is not relevant to the decision, because the value of the old equipment was lost when the new process was developed. The funds still committed in the old equipment (unexpired cost) would be used in measuring the profit made from operations if the equipment were still used; such data are relevant primarily for computation of profit, rate of return on investment, and other performance measures.

Capital Expenditures versus Revenue Expenditures

A firm may make many expenditures in connection with the purchase and operation of an asset. Some such expenditures are illustrated in the following list:

a. Invoice price of machine	$12,000
b. Marine transportation charge	800
c. Marine insurance	120
d. Import duties	600
e. Packing and transfer for rail shipment	440
f. Railway shipping and storage	230
g. Local delivery and uncrating	90
h. Preparing special foundation because of machine weight	510
i. Extension of 220 volt wiring to the machine location	120
j. Installation and engineering check of component performance	315
k. Test and adjustment run, including material and labor	100
l. Training of operators	220
m. Insurance to protect operators, one-year premium	75
n. Engineering fee for weekly preventive maintenance inspections and tests for the first quarter of use	150
o. Major repair after six months' use	280

Expenditures which logically should be recovered from machine production over some long period of time are thought of as committed or tied up in the machine; these are recorded in an asset classification and depreciated over the life of the asset. Expenditures which logically should be recovered from current machine production or which relate to current operations qualify as expenses and are classified as such. The criteria for reporting expenses studied in chapter 7 aid in determining which expenditures to report as expenses and which as asset cost.

The expenditures in the preceding list might be treated as follows:

1. Items (a) through (g) clearly are commitments of funds to be recovered through future use of the machine.
2. Items (h) and (i) are expenditures to be recovered through use of the machine or use of the building. If these add value (utility) to the building, that is, if they will serve beyond the life of the machine just purchased and are expected to be used with later machines, they will be

classified as committed to the building (additional cost of the building) and will be depreciated over the remaining life of the building as a whole. If, however, the modifications to the building are solely for this special machine and are not expected to be used with any later machines, the costs should be classified as machine cost and amortized with other costs over the productive life of the machine. At any rate, the expenditure clearly is to be classified as an asset (capitalized) rather than as an expense or revenue expenditure.

3. Items (j) and (k) are additional investments in the machine which are required before any utility can be derived. They are capitalized and are a part of the total machine cost, to be depreciated over the useful life of the machine.

None of the items discussed thus far has met the expense criteria discussed in chapter 7; they are classified as assets because they relate rather directly to the future production of revenue. The last four items in the list are different:

4. The expenditure in item (l) results in a resource (trained employee) which certainly should relate to future revenue. However, an employee is not owned; the resource is not under the control of the firm, and, therefore, the relationship to future revenue is considered less than direct. Most accountants and financial managers would argue that this expenditure meets the expense criteria and should be reported in this period as an expense.
5. The insurance premium in item (m) clearly meets the expense criteria and should be reported as an expense, since it expires (is consumed) in the current year.
6. Items (n) and (o) clearly do not relate to future revenues and, meeting the expense criteria, they are classified as expenses (revenue expenditures) and reported as such this year.

When evaluating a proposed project to decide how profitable it should be, management determines how much funds would have to be committed to the project before revenue could be produced. This concept of committed funds, coupled with the expense criteria, provides the standards for classifying expenditures for the acquisition and use of an asset as either capital or revenue expenditures. Capital expenditure amounts become the basis for depreciation and for reporting the assets on future balance sheets.

ASSET VALUE INFORMATION

Asset information reported on the balance sheet serves principally as a basis for measuring net income. Most of the amounts are depreciated, depleted, or otherwise amortized as expense, providing an imprecise and sometimes arbitrary measure of resource consumption through use of the asset. This is used as an expense in computing net income for each period. The amounts reported as undepreciated cost of assets are not intended to represent the value of those assets; these are the amounts of funds committed in the purchase of the assets which will be distributed to future periods as expense.

Needs for Present Value Information

We have already seen some specific decisions for which information about the present value of assets is needed. There are other needs for present value information.

Purchase or sale of a firm or segment When management is faced with the decision as to whether to purchase another firm or a segment (division or operating plant) of a firm, **it needs to know what the properties are worth.** The amount of the present owners' original investment not yet depreciated is not directly related to the decision about what price to offer. The same is true of information needed by management of the firm selling a segment or whole subsidiary operating company. Alternative uses and benefits are not measured by the undepreciated cost of the assets involved; information about alternative opportunities must be obtained through special inquiry, computation, and estimates.

The decision about selling an asset (including a subsidiary firm) can be improperly influenced by the practice of reporting undepreciated cost of the assets involved. Gain or loss on the sale transaction is measured as the difference between the undepreciated cost and the price obtained by sale. A professional manager (not owner-manager) could feel that reporting a large loss on such a sale would reflect poorly on his ability as a manager, even though the firm would benefit in the future from the transaction. Therefore, he might prefer to wait on the slimmest hope for a better offer or improved operations rather than sell a machine or other asset at a large loss. The fact that the loss has already occurred, even though there has been no sale to prove it, may not be reported by the "funds committed" information system until the asset is consumed or disposed of. The manager may therefore be encouraged to wait, even unwisely, in order to prevent reporting a substantial loss which may be hidden in the long run in slightly lower profits rather than reported as a special item. Such actions which benefit the manager rather than the firm may be encouraged by the way in which data are reported.

Measures of performance The degree of success achieved in the operation of a firm or a segment of a firm is often measured by the return (profit) on investment. The elements of this computation may vary, depending upon exactly what is being measured.

Return on total capital If one wants a measure of operating performance, excluding the effects of the way in which the operation is financed, he compares earnings and total capital used. This would be stated as follows:

$$\frac{\text{Income before deducting interest}}{\text{Total assets of the firm or segment}}$$

Interest is not deducted in computing this income because interest is the return to the providers of debt capital. If the percent of return on all capital is to be determined, the earnings used must be the total earnings before deduction of payment for the use of any capital. This kind of computation is often made with estimated or forecast data to determine the degree of probable profitability of a proposed project. The performance trend of a firm or division can be seen by comparing the ROI (return on investment) percents for several years. Of course, the performance of one firm or division can be compared with others by comparing the ROI rates.

Return on shareholders' equity A measure of performance for a firm, including the effects of various financing methods, can be found by comparing the net income with the equity of shareholders. Stated in computation form, this is

$$\frac{\text{Net income}}{\text{Shareholders' equity}}$$

This computation for a segment of a firm or specific project would be the net income of the segment or project (actually, its contribution toward overall company profit) divided by the amount of company funds required (excluding borrowed funds). It is easy to see that if funds can be borrowed at a rate less than the earnings rate, the rate of return to shareholders can be improved by using more borrowed funds and less of shareholders' investments. The effect of this leverage on financing is included in the ratio for return on shareholders' equity; the effect is excluded by the preceding computation to obtain return on total capital.

The effect of the financing leverage is apparent in the following illustration. Assume that two small companies operate in similar fashion. However, the funds for Company A are all provided by shareholder investment of $100,000, while $50,000 of Company B's funds are provided by borrowing at 7 percent and $50,000 by investment. If the firms make a return on total investment of 10 percent (before deducting payment for any capital used), the following comparison can be made of returns on shareholders' investment:

	Company A	Company B
Profit before deduction for interest	$ 10,000	$10,000
Interest on borrowed funds	-0-	3,500
Net income (shareholders' portion)	$ 10,000	$ 6,500
Amount of shareholder investment	$100,000	$50,000
Ratio of net income to shareholder investment	10 percent	13 percent

It should be clear that the return on total capital measures management's performance in operating the firm, excluding its performance in financing the operation, while the return on shareholders' investment measures the performance of both operating and financial management.

Using values in ROI computation When one computes the return on investment using amounts from the income statement and balance sheet, **the result is return on the funds committed.** This may be quite different from return on the present value of the assets used; values of assets may be quite different from the funds committed to their purchase. This situation is demonstrated in the following illustration.

Assume that two companies are using assets of almost identical nature and value and that their profits are the same. The only significant difference between the firms is that Company X purchased its assets for $100,000 and began operations fifteen years ago, while Company Y purchased similar assets this year for $80,000 from a firm that has been in operation about fifteen years. Company X has depreciated its assets on a straight-line basis and an expected life of twenty-five years [computation: ($100,000 ÷ 25) × 15 = $60,000], reducing the book amount to $40,000. If both firms made a net income of $8,000 this year, rates of return on total capital would be 20 percent for Company X and only 10 percent for Company Y. These rates do not measure performance of present management; rather, the difference in rates is the result of inflation and the depreciation policy of Company X. If Company X had used a longer life in depreciating its assets, the difference in ROI rates would have been less, measuring more closely the effect of inflation. If an accelerated depreciation method had been used by Company X the rates would have differed even more, reflecting the effects of inflation and the more rapid depreciation.

The preceding situation demonstrates that if a rate of return on investment is to be used to compare management performance, adjustments in the computation must be made so that the values of assets used are stated on the same basis—either the values at the same time in the past with similar depreciation computations, or present values for all assets. It is hardly conceivable that unadjusted ROI rates would be helpful in comparing managers' performances in companies with assets of significantly different ages. To measure performance, these rates must be based on similar valuations of the assets involved.

PRESENT VALUE INFORMATION

Accounting and financial management literature indicate that the need for present value information has been recognized for decades; however, the financial information system has not been adapted to provide this information. One reason that the funds-committed information is consistently reported to management and investors and that the present values of assets are not reported is the ready availability of objectively measured data about the funds committed by purchase of assets, and the difficulty of arriving at objectively supportable data about present values of properties. Of course, data about funds committed are useful and important, but they cannot be used instead of current values where the latter are needed.

Market Price as Current Value

Market price measures quite well the value of marketable assets. If the purpose of purchasing and holding an asset is to sell it at a gain, then the market price is the value relevant to the firm's operations. The value of an asset still in inventory would apparently be measured by the market price minus the expected costs of selling the item (including something for the risk of failing to sell and return on investment for the time anticipated to elaspse before sale). For many standard products sale may be virtually assured, the amount of risk may be very little, and adjustments from market price to value might be only the additional costs of selling the item and a return on investment for the waiting period.

For assets which are not to be sold, it has been argued that the market price states the value of the asset's future utility for persons who normally would purchase it. This could not be the value for *all* persons who might purchase the product; it would be the value for the small incremental group providing a market for an adequate number of additional items so that the total purchased roughly equals the supply at that price. Use of the market price in computing a value implies that the relevant value is that of the marketplace. It is true that in almost any situation, one alternative for management is to sell an asset rather than to use it in continued operations. However, determination of a market value for some properties would be very difficult. The market price of a steel plant, chemical plant, or any segment of a plant is not as easy to determine as the market price of a new item appearing on a supplier's price list.

In summary, it has to be acknowledged that market price may not be useful as a measure of value because market price can be obtained only by sale and that may not be a reasonable alternative for management, and a market price may not be available for many assets that are in use in a firm. However, it must be recognized that selling an asset should be treated as an alternative to continued use whenever it appears that selling offers the greater benefit to the firm. This means that for management use, market price information should be available when its need is indicated. For computing the rate of return on investment, it may be that a most realistic rate for measuring management performance would be obtained by using the proceeds from a possible sale (market price) as the "investment" against which to measure the actual return. The difficulty of obtaining reliable market prices for most plant assets has precluded the general use of market value in financial reporting and in measuring management performance.

Discounted Cash Flow Valuation

The value of an asset is based upon its expected future benefit to the firm. When one can identify and project future benefits and assign a value to them, he can place a value on the asset providing those benefits.

Future net benefits Future benefits normally are composed of inflows of cash or other resources to the firm from the sale of an asset's products or services. The production or delivery of these products or services may require that the firm spend cash or consume other resources. The excess of the projected cash inflows over the outflows is the future net benefit. Actually, all inflows and outflows are discounted from their expected date of occurrence to the present at the minimum acceptable rate of earning; the excess of the resulting present values of inflows over present values of outflows is the present value of an asset to the firm.

Present value of a bond investment The present value of future net benefits is computed as the normal means of arriving at the investment value of (amount which would be offered for) a bond. A $10,000 bond which pays 6 percent annually and matures in five years will provide the investor with the following cash inflows:

At the end of each year	$ 600
At the end of the fifth year..	10,000

Computing present value of each benefit If we assume that an investor demands a return of 7 percent then we can raise the question, "What is the value of the $10,000, 6 percent bond to this investor?" The value of the bond is the present value of all the benefits to be derived from it (amounts discounted to the present at 7 percent). There are no projected cash outflows in this case.

Each future benefit is discounted to the present by use of the formula

$$\frac{b}{(1+r)^n}$$

where b is the future benefit, r is the interest rate demanded, and n is the number of periods until receipt of the benefit. The present value of the $600 to be received one year from now is

$$\frac{\$600}{(1+.07)}$$

or $560.75. This means that if you were buying only that one separate benefit you would pay $560.75, because that amount with 7 percent added to it ($39.25, for earnings during the year) equals the $600 which would be collected at the end of the year. The present value of the second receipt of $600 is

$$\frac{\$600}{(1+.07)^2}$$

or \$524.06. Computation of the present value of all the benefits is shown below:

First interest payment:	$\frac{\$600}{(1+.07)}$	or	\$ 560.75
Second interest payment:	$\frac{\$600}{(1+.07)^2}$	or	524.06
Third interest payment:	$\frac{\$600}{(1+.07)^3}$	or	489.78
Fourth interest payment:	$\frac{\$600}{(1+.07)^4}$	or	457.74
Fifth interest payment:	$\frac{\$600}{(1+.07)^5}$	or	427.79
Face amount at maturity:	$\frac{\$10{,}000}{(1+.07)^5}$	or	\$7,129.87
Total present value of all benefits, or value of the bond to an investor at 7 percent			\$9,589.99

Computing present value of an annuity This present value for the bond may be computed by finding the present value of an annuity of \$600 per year for five years (combination of the first five items in the above computation), plus the present value of \$10,000 to be received five years in the future. These computations are

Present value of a future benefit b in the form of an annuity of \$600 for five years, at 7 percent:

$$\frac{b - \frac{b}{(1+r)^5}}{r} \quad \text{or} \quad \frac{\$600 - \frac{\$600}{(1+.07)^5}}{.07} = \$2{,}460.12$$

Present value of the face amount at maturity on a 7 percent earning basis:

$$\frac{b}{(1+r)^5} \quad \text{or} \quad \frac{\$10{,}000}{(1+.07)^5} = 7{,}129.87$$

Total present value of bond \$9,589.99

Earnings on present value of bond investment A thorough understanding of this concept of present value can be achieved by computing the earnings at 7 percent and adjusting the investment for the amount received periodically. These computations are as follows:

Present value of bond		$ 9,589.99
7 percent earned the first year	$671.30	
Minus $600 cash received, end of first year	600.00	
Amount earned but not collected		71.30
Value at beginning of second year		$ 9,661.29
7 percent earned the second year	$676.29	
Minus $600 cash received, end of second year	600.00	
Amount earned but not collected		76.29
Value at beginning of third year		$ 9,737.58
7 percent earned the third year	$681.63	
Minus $600 cash received, end of third year	600.00	
Amount earned but not collected		81.63
Value at beginning of fourth year		$ 9,819.21
7 percent earned the fourth year	$687.34	
Minus $600 cash received, end of fourth year	600.00	
Amount earned but not collected		87.34
Value at beginning of fifth year		$ 9,906.55
7 percent earned the fifth year	$693.45	
Minus $600 cash received, end of fifth year	600.00	
Amount earned but not collected		93.45
Value at maturity, end of fifth year		$10,000.00
Collection of maturity value, end of fifth year		10,000.00
		$ -0-

DATA FOR BOND INVESTMENT AND EARNINGS

Data for an investment such as the one illustrated in the preceding section should indicate the funds committed in the investment (initial amount plus the adjustment each year) and the annual earning (income) from the investment. Data for the purchase of the bond investment would be input by the following journal entry (assuming the purchase date to be July 1):

July 1	Investment in XY Bonds	9,589.99	
	Cash		9,589.99

During the first year, the amount earned was $671.30, but the amount received in cash was only $600. This means that $71.30 of the amount earned was not received during that year and, therefore, became part of the investment to be collected later. This classification of data can be shown in journal entry form as follows (assuming the year end to be June 30):

June 30	Cash	600.00	
	Interest Income		600.00
	To record cash received from bond investment.		
30	Investment in XY Bonds	71.30	
	Interest Income		71.30
	To record earning in excess of cash received from bond investment.		

Data are recorded each year in this pattern, with the amount earned above the cash actually received being added to the investment account. Examination of the computations in the preceding section will reveal that the full $410.01 gained during the five years will be added to the investment account in this way. This means that at maturity the investment account will have a balance of $10,000, the amount that will be collected.

Discount on Bond Investment

When an investor buys a bond at less than maturity value, he is said to have bought it at a discount. In the preceding illustration, when the $10,000 bond was bought for $9,589.99, the discount was the difference, $410.01. Since the bond investment normally is recorded at cost, this discount does not appear as a separate item, but it is the amount added to the investment and to income over the life of the bond. This spreading of the discount over the life of the bond is called *amortizing* the discount. The second journal entry in the preceding section, in which $71.30 is debited to Investment in XY Bonds and credited to Interest Income, was made to amortize the portion of the discount applicable to that year. When all of the discount has been amortized, the amount in the investment account will be the maturity value of the bond.

Premium on Bond Investment

Earlier in this chapter we found that the present value of a bond purchased to yield more than the face rate is less than the maturity value.

It would be purchased at a discount. In contrast, a bond purchased to yield less than the face rate has a present value greater than the maturity value. Such a bond would be purchased at a premium.

Using the tables on the following pages, one can compute the present value of a $10,000, 7 percent bond on the basis of a 6 percent yield. This value is found as follows:

Present value of $10,000 to be received five years in the future, discounted at 6 percent	$ 7,472.60
Present value of $700 (7 percent of $10,000) to be received at the end of each year for five years, discounted at 6 percent	2,948.61
Present value of the bond investment, at 6 percent yield	10,421.21

This $10,000 bond would be bought for $10,421.23 if the investor demanded only 6 percent return, or earning, on his investment. The bond would be purchased at a premium of $421.23. The amount earned during the first year would be 6 percent of $10,421.23, or $625.27. This is $74.73 less than the $700 which the investor will receive at the end of the year as an interest payment. The amount received above the earned amount ($74.72) is considered a return of a part of his investment, and is credited to the Investment in XY Bonds account.

Journal entries for the receipt of the $700 payment and for amortization of bond premium at the end of the first year would be:

June 30	Cash	700.00	
	Interest Income		700.00
	Receipt of Interest on XY bonds.		
30	Interest Income	74.73	
	Investment in XY Bonds		74.73
	Amortization of bond premium to reclassify part of amount collected as return of investment.		

The premium will be amortized year by year, until the Investment in XY Bonds account has a balance of $10,000 at maturity of the bonds. Interest income would be reported as $625.27; this is the balance in the Interest Income account ($700.00 − 74.73). The investment would be reported as $10,346.50, the balance in the Investment in XY Bonds

Table A

PRESENT VALUE OF ONE DOLLAR DUE AT THE END OF *N* PERIODS

Interest Rates (in percents)

N	2½	3	3½	4	5	6	7	8	9	10	*N*
01	0.97561	0.97087	0.96618	.96154	.95238	.94340	.93458	.92593	.91743	.90909	01
02	0.95181	0.94260	0.93351	.92456	.90703	.89000	.87344	.85734	.84168	.82645	02
03	0.92860	0.91514	0.90194	.88900	.86384	.83962	.81630	.79383	.77218	.75131	03
04	0.90595	0.88849	0.87144	.85480	.82270	.79209	.76290	.73503	.70843	.68301	04
05	0.88385	0.86261	0.84197	.82193	.78353	.74726	.71299	.68058	.64993	.62092	05
06	0.86230	0.83748	0.81350	.79031	.74622	.70496	.66634	.63017	.59627	.56447	06
07	0.84127	0.81309	0.78599	.75992	.71068	.66506	.62275	.58349	.54703	.51316	07
08	0.82075	0.78941	0.75941	.73069	.67684	.62741	.58201	.54027	.50187	.46651	08
09	0.80073	0.76642	0.73373	.70259	.64461	.59190	.54393	.50025	.46043	.42410	09
10	0.78198	0.74409	0.70892	.67556	.61391	.55839	.50835	.46319	.42241	.38554	10
11	0.76214	0.72242	0.68495	.64958	.58468	.52679	.47509	.42888	.38753	.35049	11
12	0.74356	0.70138	0.66178	.62460	.55684	.49697	.44401	.39711	.35553	.31683	12
13	0.72542	0.68095	0.63940	.60057	.53032	.46884	.41496	.36770	.32618	.28966	13
14	0.70773	0.66112	0.61778	.57747	.50507	.44230	.38782	.34046	.29925	.26333	14
15	0.69047	0.64186	0.59689	.55526	.48102	.41726	.36245	.31524	.27454	.23939	15
16	0.67362	0.62317	0.57671	.53391	.45811	.39365	.33873	.29189	.25187	.21763	16
17	0.65720	0.60502	0.55720	.51337	.43630	.37136	.31657	.27027	.23107	.19784	17
18	0.64117	0.58739	0.53836	.49363	.41552	.35034	.29586	.25025	.21199	.17986	18
19	0.62553	0.57029	0.52016	.47464	.39573	.33051	.27651	.23171	.19449	.16351	19
20	0.61021	0.55367	0.50257	.45639	.37689	.31180	.25842	.21455	.17843	.14864	20
21	0.59539	0.53755	0.48557	.43883	.35894	.29415	.24151	.19866	.16370	.13513	21
22	0.58086	0.52189	0.46915	.42195	.34185	.27750	.22571	.18394	.15018	.12285	22
23	0.56670	0.50669	0.45329	.40573	.32557	.26180	.21095	.17031	.13778	.11168	23
24	0.55288	0.49193	0.43796	.39012	.31007	.24698	.19715	.15770	.12640	.10153	24
25	0.53939	0.47760	0.42315	.37512	.29530	.23300	.18425	.14602	.11597	.09230	25

Table A (continued)

PRESENT VALUE OF ONE DOLLAR DUE AT THE END OF *N* PERIODS

Interest Rates (in percents)

N	11	12	13	14	15	16	17	18	19	20	*N*
01	.90090	.89286	.88496	.87719	.86957	.86207	.85470	.84746	.84034	.83333	01
02	.81162	.79719	.78315	.76947	.75614	.74316	.73051	.71818	.70616	.69444	02
03	.73119	.71178	.69305	.67497	.65752	.64066	.62437	.60863	.59342	.57870	03
04	.65873	.63552	.61332	.59208	.57175	.55229	.53365	.51579	.49867	.48225	04
05	.59345	.56743	.54276	.51937	.49718	.47611	.45611	.43711	.41905	.40188	05
06	.53464	.50663	.48032	.45559	.43233	.41044	.38984	.37043	.35214	.33490	06
07	.48166	.45235	.42506	.39964	.37594	.35383	.33320	.31392	.29592	.27908	07
08	.43393	.40388	.37616	.35056	.32690	.30503	.28478	.26604	.24867	.23257	08
09	.39092	.36061	.33288	.30751	.28462	.26295	.24340	.22546	.20897	.19381	09
10	.35218	.32197	.29459	.26974	.24718	.22668	.20804	.19106	.17560	.16151	10
11	.31728	.28748	.26070	.23662	.21494	.19542	.17781	.16192	.14756	.13459	11
12	.28584	.25667	.23071	.20756	.18691	.16846	.15197	.13722	.12400	.11216	12
13	.25751	.22917	.20416	.18207	.16253	.14523	.12989	.11629	.10420	.09346	13
14	.23199	.20462	.18068	.15971	.14133	.12520	.11102	.09855	.08757	.07789	14
15	.20900	.18270	.15989	.14010	.12289	.10793	.09489	.08352	.07359	.06491	15
16	.18829	.16312	.14150	.12289	.10686	.09304	.08110	.07078	.06184	.05409	16
17	.16963	.14564	.12522	.10780	.90293	.08021	.06932	.05998	.05196	.04507	17
18	.15282	.13004	.11081	.09456	.08080	.06914	.05925	.05083	.04367	.03756	18
19	.13768	.11611	.09806	.08295	.07026	.05961	.05064	.04308	.03669	.03130	19
20	.12403	.10367	.08678	.07276	.06110	.05139	.04328	.03651	.03084	.02608	20
21	.11174	.09256	.07680	.06383	.05313	.04430	.03699	.03094	.02591	.02174	21
22	.10067	.08264	.06796	.05599	.04620	.03819	.03162	.02622	.02178	.01811	22
23	.09069	.07379	.06014	.04911	.04017	.03292	.02702	.02222	.01830	.01509	23
24	.08170	.06588	.05322	.04308	.03493	.02838	.02310	.01883	.01538	.01258	24
25	.07361	.05882	.04710	.03779	.03038	.02447	.01974	.01596	.01292	.01048	25

Table A (continued)

PRESENT VALUE OF ONE DOLLAR DUE AT THE END OF *N* PERIODS

Interest Rates (in percents)

N	21	22	23	24	25	26	27	28	29	30	*N*
01	.82645	.81967	.81301	.80645	.80000	.79365	.78740	.78125	.77519	.76923	01
02	.68301	.67186	.66098	.65036	.64000	.62988	.62000	.61035	.60093	.59172	02
03	.56447	.55071	.53738	.52449	.51200	.49991	.48819	.47684	.46583	.45517	03
04	.46651	.45140	.43690	.42297	.40960	.39675	.38440	.37253	.36111	.35013	04
05	.38554	.37000	.35520	.34111	.32768	.31488	.30268	.29104	.27993	.26933	05
06	.31863	.30328	.28878	.27509	.26214	.24991	.23833	.22737	.21700	.20718	06
07	.26333	.24859	.23478	.22184	.20972	.19834	.13766	.17764	.16822	.15937	07
08	.21763	.20376	.19088	.17891	.16777	.15741	.14776	.13878	.13040	.12259	08
09	.17986	.16702	.15519	.14428	.13422	.12493	.11635	.10842	.10109	.09430	09
10	.14864	.13690	.12617	.11635	.10737	.09915	.09161	.08470	.07836	.07254	10
11	.12285	.11221	.10258	.09383	.08590	.07869	.07214	.06617	.06075	.05580	11
12	.10153	.09198	.08339	.07567	.06872	.06245	.05680	.05170	.04709	.04292	12
13	.08391	.07539	.06780	.06103	.05498	.04957	.04472	.04039	.03650	.03302	13
14	.06934	.06180	.05512	.04921	.04398	.03934	.03522	.03155	.02830	.02540	14
15	.05731	.05065	.04481	.03969	.03518	.03122	.02773	.02465	.02194	.01954	15
16	.04736	.04152	.03643	.03201	.02815	.02478	.02183	.01926	.01700	.01503	16
17	.03914	.03403	.02962	.02581	.02252	.01967	.01719	.01505	.01318	.01156	17
18	.03235	.02789	.02408	.02082	.01801	.01561	.01354	.01175	.01022	.00889	18
19	.02673	.02286	.01958	.01679	.01441	.01239	.01066	.00918	.00792	.00684	19
20	.02209	.01874	.01592	.01354	.01153	.00983	.00839	.00717	.00614	.00526	20
21	.01826	.01536	.01294	.01092	.00922	.00780	.00661	.00561	.00476	.00405	21
22	.01509	.01259	.01052	.00880	.00738	.00619	.00520	.00438	.00369	.00311	22
23	.01247	.01032	.00855	.00710	.00590	.00491	.00410	.00342	.00286	.00239	23
24	.01031	.00846	.00695	.00573	.00472	.00390	.00323	.00267	.00222	.00184	24
25	.00852	.00693	.00565	.00462	.00378	.00310	.00254	.00209	.00172	.00142	25

Table B

PRESENT VALUE OF ONE DOLLAR PER PERIOD FOR *N* PERIODS

Interest Rates (in percents)

N	2½	3	3½	4	5	6	7	8	9	10	*N*
01	.9756	.9709	.9662	.9615	.9524	.9434	.9346	.9259	.9174	.9091	01
02	1.9274	1.9135	1.8997	1.8861	1.8594	1.8334	1.8080	1.7833	1.7591	1.7355	02
03	2.8560	2.8286	2.8016	2.7751	2.7233	2.6730	2.6243	2.5771	2.5313	2.4868	03
04	3.7620	3.7171	3.6731	3.6299	3.5459	3.4651	3.3872	3.3121	3.2397	3.1699	04
05	4.6458	4.5797	4.5151	4.4518	4.3295	4.2123	4.1002	3.9927	3.8896	3.7908	05
06	5.5081	5.4172	5.3286	5.2421	5.0757	4.9173	4.7665	4.6229	4.4859	4.3553	06
07	6.3494	6.2302	6.1145	6.0020	5.7863	5.5824	5.3893	5.2064	5.0329	4.8684	07
08	7.1701	7.0196	6.8740	6.7327	6.4632	6.2098	5.9713	5.7466	5.5348	5.3349	08
09	7.9709	7.7861	7.6077	7.4353	7.1078	6.8017	6.5152	6.2469	5.9852	5.7590	09
10	8.7521	8.5302	8.3166	8.1109	7.7217	7.3601	7.0236	6.7101	6.4176	6.1446	10
11	9.5142	9.2526	9.0016	8.7604	8.3064	7.8868	7.4987	7.1389	6.8052	6.4951	11
12	10.2578	9.9539	9.6633	9.3850	8.8632	8.3838	7.9427	7.5361	7.1607	6.8137	12
13	10.9832	10.6349	10.3027	9.9856	9.3935	8.8527	8.3576	7.9038	7.4869	7.1034	13
14	11.6909	11.2960	10.9205	10.5631	9.8986	9.2950	8.7454	8.2442	7.7861	7.3667	14
15	12.3814	11.9379	11.5174	11.1183	10.3796	9.7122	9.1079	8.5595	8.0607	7.6061	15
16	13.0550	12.5610	12.0941	11.6522	10.8377	10.1059	9.4466	8.8514	8.3125	7.8237	16
17	13.7122	13.1660	12.6513	12.1656	11.2740	10.4772	9.7632	9.1216	8.5436	8.0215	17
18	14.3534	13.7534	13.1897	12.6592	11.6895	10.8276	10.0591	9.3719	8.7556	8.2014	18
19	14.9789	14.3237	13.7098	13.1339	12.0853	11.1581	10.3556	9.6036	8.9501	8.3649	19
20	15.5892	14.8774	14.2124	13.5903	12.4622	11.4699	10.5940	9.8181	9.1285	8.5136	20
21	16.1845	15.4149	14.6980	14.0291	12.8211	11.7640	10.8355	10.0168	9.2922	8.6487	21
22	16.7654	15.9367	15.1671	14.4511	13.1630	12.0416	11.0612	10.2007	9.4424	8.7715	22
23	17.3321	16.4435	15.6204	14.8568	13.4885	12.3033	11.2722	10.3710	9.5802	8.8832	23
24	17.8850	16.9355	16.0584	15.2469	13.7986	12.5503	11.4693	10.5287	9.7066	8.9847	24
25	18.4244	17.4131	16.4815	15.6220	14.9039	12.7833	11.6536	10.6748	9.8226	9.0770	25

Table B (continued)

PRESENT VALUE OF ONE DOLLAR PER PERIOD FOR *N* PERIODS

Interest Rates (in percents)

N	11	12	13	14	15	16	17	18	19	20	*N*
01	.9009	.8929	.8850	.8772	.8696	.8621	.8547	.8475	.8403	.8333	01
02	1.7125	1.6901	1.6681	1.6467	1.6257	1.6052	1.5852	1.5656	1.5465	1.5278	02
03	2.4437	2.4018	2.3612	2.3216	2.2832	2.2459	2.2096	2.1743	2.1399	2.1065	03
04	3.1024	3.0373	2.9745	2.9137	2.8550	2.7982	2.7432	2.6901	2.6386	2.5887	04
05	3.6959	3.6048	3.5172	3.4331	3.3522	3.2743	3.1993	3.1272	3.0576	2.9906	05
06	4.2305	4.1114	3.9976	3.8887	3.7845	3.6847	3.5892	3.4976	3.4098	3.3255	06
07	4.7122	4.5638	4.4226	4.2883	4.1604	4.0386	3.9224	3.8115	3.7057	3.6046	07
08	5.1461	4.9676	4.7988	4.6389	4.4873	4.3436	4.2072	4.0776	3.9544	3.8372	08
09	5.5370	5.3282	5.1317	4.9464	4.7716	4.6065	4.4506	4.3030	4.1633	4.0310	09
10	5.8892	5.6502	5.4262	5.2161	5.0188	4.8332	4.6586	4.4941	4.3389	4.1925	10
11	6.2065	5.9377	5.6869	5.4527	5.2337	5.0286	4.8364	4.6560	4.4865	4.3271	11
12	6.4924	6.1944	5.9176	5.6603	5.4206	5.1971	4.9884	4.7932	4.6105	4.4392	12
13	6.7499	6.4235	6.1218	5.8424	5.5831	5.3423	5.1183	4.9095	4.7147	4.5327	13
14	6.9819	6.6282	6.3025	6.0021	5.7245	5.4675	5.2293	5.0081	4.8023	4.6106	14
15	7.1909	6.8109	6.4624	6.1422	5.8474	5.5755	5.3242	5.0916	4.8759	4.6755	15
16	7.3792	6.9740	6.6039	6.2651	5.9542	5.6685	5.4053	5.1624	4.9377	4.7296	16
17	7.5488	7.1196	6.7291	6.3729	6.0472	5.7487	5.4746	5.2223	4.9897	4.7746	17
18	7.7016	7.2497	6.8399	6.4674	6.1280	5.8178	5.5339	5.2732	5.0333	4.8122	18
19	7.8393	7.3650	6.9380	6.5504	6.1982	5.8775	5.5845	5.3176	5.0700	4.8435	19
20	7.9633	7.4694	7.0248	6.6231	6.2593	5.9288	5.6278	5.3527	5.1009	4.8696	20
21	8.0751	7.5620	7.1016	6.6870	6.3125	5.9731	5.6648	5.3837	5.1268	4.8913	21
22	8.1757	7.6446	7.1695	6.7429	6.3587	6.0113	5.6964	5.4099	5.1486	4.9094	22
23	8.2664	7.7184	7.2297	6.7921	6.3988	6.0442	5.7234	5.4321	5.1668	4.9245	23
24	8.3481	7.7843	7.2829	6.8351	6.4338	6.0726	5.7465	5.4509	5.1822	4.9371	24
25	8.4217	7.8431	7.3300	6.8729	6.4641	6.0971	5.7662	5.4669	5.1951	4.9476	25

Table B (continued)

PRESENT VALUE OF ONE DOLLAR PER PERIOD FOR *N* PERIODS

Interest Rates (in percents)

N	21	22	23	24	25	26	27	28	29	30	*N*
01	.8264	.8197	.8130	.8065	.8000	.7937	.7874	.7813	.7752	.7692	01
02	1.5095	1.4915	1.4740	1.4568	1.4400	1.4235	1.4074	1.3916	1.3761	1.3609	02
03	2.0739	2.0422	2.0114	1.9813	1.9520	1.9234	1.8956	1.8684	1.8420	1.8161	03
04	2.5404	2.4936	2.4483	2.4043	2.3616	2.3202	2.2800	2.2410	2.2031	2.1662	04
05	2.9260	2.8636	2.8035	2.7454	2.6893	2.6351	2.5327	2.5320	2.4830	2.4356	05
06	3.2446	3.1669	3.0923	3.0205	2.9514	2.8850	2.8210	2.7594	2.7000	2.6427	06
07	3.5079	3.4155	3.3270	3.2423	3.1611	3.0833	3.0087	2.9370	2.8682	2.8021	07
08	3.7256	3.6193	3.5179	3.4212	3.3289	3.2407	3.1564	3.0758	2.9986	2.9247	08
09	3.9054	3.7863	3.6731	3.5655	3.4631	3.3657	3.2728	3.1842	3.0997	3.0190	09
10	4.0541	3.9232	3.7993	3.6819	3.5705	3.4648	3.3644	3.2689	3.1781	3.0915	10
11	4.1769	4.0354	3.0918	3.7757	3.6564	3.5435	3.4365	3.3351	3.2388	3.1473	11
12	4.2785	4.1274	3.9852	3.8514	3.7251	3.6060	3.4933	3.3868	3.2850	3.1903	12
13	4.3624	4.2028	4.0530	3.9124	3.7001	3.6555	3.6381	3.4272	3.3224	3.2233	13
14	4.4317	4.2646	4.1082	3.9616	3.8241	3.6949	3.5733	3.4587	3.3507	3.2487	14
15	4.4890	4.3152	4.1530	4.0013	3.8593	3.7261	3.6010	3.4834	3.3726	3.2682	15
16	4.5364	4.3567	4.1894	4.0333	3.8874	3.7509	3.6228	3.5026	3.3896	3.2832	16
17	4.5753	4.3908	4.2890	4.0591	3.9099	3.7705	3.6400	3.5177	3.4028	3.2948	17
18	4.6079	4.4187	4.2431	4.0799	3.9279	3.7861	3.6536	3.5294	3.4130	3.3037	18
19	4.6345	4.4415	4.2627	4.0967	3.9424	3.7985	3.6642	3.5386	3.4210	3.3105	19
20	4.6567	4.4603	4.2786	4.1103	3.9539	3.8083	3.6726	3.5458	3.4271	3.3158	20
21	4.6750	4.4756	4.2916	4.1212	3.9631	3.8161	3.6792	3.5514	3.4313	3.3198	21
22	4.6900	4.4882	4.3021	4.1300	3.9705	3.8223	3.6844	3.5553	3.4356	3.3230	22
23	4.7025	4.4985	4.3106	4.1371	3.9764	3.8273	3.6885	3.5592	3.4384	3.3254	23
24	4.7128	4.5070	4.3176	4.1428	3.9811	3.8312	3.6981	3.5619	3.4406	3.3272	24
25	4.7213	4.5139	4.3232	4.1474	3.9849	3.8342	3.6943	3.5640	3.4423	3.3286	25

account. The full effect of amortizing the premium is seen in the following schedule:

BOND PREMIUM AMORTIZATION

$10,000, 7 Percent Bond to Yield 6 Percent

(a) Date	(b) Cash Debit	(c) Interest Income Credit	(d) Investment Credit (Premium Amortization)	(e) Investment Balance
7/ 1/71	–	–	–	$10,421.21
6/30/72	$700	$625.27	$74.73	10,346.48
6/30/72	700	620.79	79.21	10,267.27
6/30/72	700	616.04	83.96	10,183.31
6/30/72	700	611.00	89.00	10,094.31
6/30/72	700	605.69	94.31	10,000.00

(b) Cash collected, 7 percent of face amount of bond.
(c) Interest earned on the basis of the purchase price, 6 percent of column (e) on the preceding line, last amount adjusted for rounding in tables and computations.
(d) Amount collected in excess of earnings, (b) minus (c).
(e) Amount of investment not yet collected, on the basis of 6 percent earning. Preceding amount in (e) minus (d).

Straight-line Amortization of Premium and Discount

The method of amortizing bond discount and premium illustrated in the preceding sections is normally called the *scientific* or *actuarial* method (presumably because actuaries use compound discount in computing the present value of future amounts). This method is exact in the measurement of income and is most appropriate in providing data about a bond investment. However, it does involve substantial calculations. Before the days of the electronic computer, it was quite burdensome to compute the interest earned and premium or discount amortized on a large portfolio of bond investments. Straight-line amortization was widely adopted as a method which adequately approximated the earning and amortization, and which required little computation. In straight-line amortization, the total discount or premium on a bond investment is spread evenly over the periods before maturity of the bond. This procedure provides a good measure of the total income from the investment, but it does provide only an approximation of the amount earned each year. In the following schedule, compare the discount amortization and the annual interest income provided by the two methods of amortization. The investment balance begins with the same figure in both methods, because this is the price of a 6½ percent, $100,000 bond yielding 7 percent five years before maturity.

AMORTIZATION AND INCOME SCHEDULE

$100,000 6½ Percent Bond to Yield 7 Percent

		Actuarial, or Scientific			Straight-Line		
Date	Cash Debit	Interest Income Credit	Investment Credit (Discount Amortization)	Investment Balance	Interest Income Credit	Investment Credit (Discount Amortization)	Investment Balance
7/ 1/71	—	—	—	$ 97,950	—	—	$ 97,950
6/30/72	$6,500	$6,857	$357	98,307	$6,910	$410	98,360
6/30/73	6,500	6,881	381	98,688	6,910	410	98,770
6/30/74	6,500	6,908	408	99,096	6,910	410	99,180
6/30/75	6,500	6,937	437	99,533	6,910	410	99,590
6/30/76	6,500	6,967	467	100,000	6,910	410	100,000

Bond Investment Balance and Value

Amortizing the premium or discount on a bond investment actually adjusts the balance in the investment account to the present value of the bond each year, based on the interest rate which the bond was purchased to yield—*not* on the interest rate at which such investment would be bought or sold at the time the adjustment is made each year. This means, of course, that the investment balance at the end of any year is not the actual present value, but the present value which "might have been" if the interest rate had stayed the same as when the investment was purchased.

The point just made emphasizes that bond investments are reported on the basis of funds committed to the investment, as are other assets. They are not adjusted to actual market value each year. This can be demonstrated by the fact that a bond investment may be sold at a considerable gain or loss, based on the investment balance.

Assume that the bond investment in the preceding section (a $100,000, 6½ percent bond purchased to yield 7 percent) was sold for $97,400 after collecting the second year's interest. Based on the amortization and income schedule for this investment, data from the sale would be classified as follows, depending upon whether actuarial or straight-line amortization had been used:

Assuming actuarial amortization:

June 30	Cash	97,400	
	Loss on Sale of Investments	1,288	
	Bond Investment		98,688

Assuming straight-line amortization:

June 30	Cash	97,400	
	Loss on Sale of Investments	1,370	
	Bond Investment		98,770

If the purpose of the annual adjustment were to report the bond at its present value, it would have been adjusted to the market value of $97,400 at the end of the year, and there could have been no gain or loss on the sale. Clearly, the amortization of premium or discount on bond investments is done in order to measure the income for each year based on the investment's purchase price, not to measure the current value of the asset. The asset is reported each year at the amount of financial resources still committed or tied up in the investment, according to the original investment plan.

PRESENT VALUE OF A BUSINESS OR BUSINESS SEGMENT

The discounted present value of future benefits can be computed for a business firm, or for any segment of a business for which a specific inflow and outflow of resources can be measured. The computation involves the present value of two sets of items, as follows.

1. Present value of future inflows of benefits: revenue inflow, discounted to present date; market value, or other residual value, of assets at the end of a specified time or action (a number of years, or completion of a project), discounted to the present date.
2. From (1) subtract the present value of future outflows required: additional investments to be required at future periods, discounted to the present date; expenditures required for operating the firm, discounted to the present date. These may be subtracted from revenues and only the difference discounted to the present date.

Choice of Discount Rate

The concept of discounting future amounts indicates that time is a factor in determining value. But what rate should be used in recognizing the time factor? For any firm, *the rate to be used in determin-*

ing value clearly should be the minimum rate of earning that would persuade the firm to purchase the asset. This can be measured best by considering the best alternative use of money by the firm. If a firm can use its money to earn a return of 11 percent, then apparently its management would be unwise to buy any asset that would provide less than this rate of earning. Therefore, this best alternative use of funds is widely used as the rate for determining the value to a business firm of an asset, a project, or another business. The managements of large business firms quite often use the average rate of return on total assets on the premise that no new asset that will reduce the rate of earnings should be acquired. This may be a questionable premise on which to work blindly, but as a short-run rule of thumb it provides a reasonable basis for measuring value.

Elements of Present Value

The technique of computing the present value of a business is similar to that used for computing the present value of a bond investment. Compound discount formulae or tables are used to find the present value of future benefits and costs. The difference between the present values of these is the present value of the firm, or business segment of a firm.

Assume that an earth-moving contractor owns the assets and owes the liabilities in the following list, and he has just received final approval of the contract described below the list.

Assets		Liabilities	
Cash	$ 4,000	Note payable to the bank in sixty days	$6,000
Accounts Receivable	3,000		
Supplies	3,000		
Equipment	90,000		
	$100,000		

The contract requires the construction of highway embankments over the next three years. Expenditures required for supplies and equipment in addition to those now on hand amount to $500,000 immediately, $200,000 at the beginning of the second year, and $250,000 at the beginning of the third year. Collections are estimated to be as follows:

At end of the first year, for that portion of embankments completed	$350,000
At end of the second year, for additional construction completed by that date	400,000

At end of the third year, for completion of contract	$550,000
Market value of supplies and equipment at end of the construction	150,000

Assume that a prospective purchaser of the firm has a continuing opportunity to buy "working interests" in contracts of other earth-moving contractors at a return of 10 percent. Very probably he would use 10 percent as the minimum earning rate in computing a value for a firm in that business.

Factors to be used in computing the present value of the firm are

1. Amounts of future benefits
2. Time, or dates, of future benefits
3. Amounts of future expenditures
4. Time, or dates, of future expenditures
5. Discount rate

Computation of Present Value

The discounting of future benefits and costs to find the present value of the firm is done as follows:

Present value of future benefits:

Collection at end of first year:	$\frac{\$350{,}000}{1.10} =$	$ 318,182
Collection at end of second year:	$\frac{\$400{,}000}{(1.1)^2} =$	330,580
Collection at end of third, plus market value of supplies and equipment left at that time:	$\frac{\$700{,}000}{(1.1)^3} =$	525,917
Total		$1,174,679

Present value of future expenditures:

Immediate expenditures for supplies and equipment:		$ 500,000
Expenditure at beginning of second year:	$\frac{\$200{,}000}{1.1} =$	181,818
Expenditure at beginning of third year:	$\frac{\$250{,}000}{(1.1)^2} =$	206,613
Total		888,431
Present value of the firm		$ 286,248

This computation indicates that if an investor pays $286,248 for the construction firm, and if the contract provides benefits and requires expenditures as projected, the investor will earn 10 percent on his investment.

Use of Present Values in Business

The discounted present value computation is used by management in evaluating proposed business projects within the firm and possible purchases of other firms. In some instances, it may be used to evaluate specific equipment, but only when the benefits expected from the equipment can be identified and measured in money amounts. Special automatic metal-tooling equipment which will produce specific items at a predetermined rate can be evaluated by this method. It is doubtful that future benefits of additional tables and seating for the employee cafeteria can be specified accurately enough for use of the discounted present value technique. This method of computing the present value is often called the *discounted cash flow method;* its use is fairly widespread in business, and frequent attention is given to it in business journals.

Use of Present Values in Financial Reporting

Authoritative voices in financial reporting have almost consistently upheld reporting as it is currently done on the "funds-committed" basis for assets. The discounted cash flow method is used to compute the original price of bond investments, but not for computing a new value for bond investments each year. Rather, the bonds are reported at the original amount of funds committed to them, adjusted by the amortization of premium or discount. Purchase prices, which are less accurately related to value, measure the funds committed to other assets; these amounts, with some adjustments, are used for reporting the assets through their useful lives.

Arguments against reporting computed discounted present values on the balance sheet have included some very poor and some very valid ones:

1. One relies heavily on a rather intuitive sense that "original cost" has some special qualities. The expression, "But it didn't cost that much," is one form of this argument.
2. The position that the most useful information relates to the commitment and freeing up of financial resources is a valid argument for the funds-committed basis of reporting. It is not an argument against reporting present values in addition to those data traditionally provided.

3. The argument that discounted present value of assets must be computed for each investor because each would demand a different earnings (discount) rate has some validity. The chief value of this argument is that it raises the question of "discounted present value to whom?" Apparently, the best response is that the firm's discount rate (based on its best alternative use of funds), rather than the earnings rate demanded by any investor, should be used. On this basis, rates (and values) would be different for different firms, and at different times.
4. Perhaps the soundest argument has been that a discounted present value cannot be determined on a fully objective basis. Opinions enter into projections of benefits and required expenditures, and there is some subjectivity involved in arriving at the rate that could be earned by the best alternative use of funds.
5. Discounted present value requires the determination of a financial measure of future benefits. It is not possible to determine this for all assets, especially for assets which contribute indirectly to production.

Apparently the second, fourth, and fifth arguments in the above incomplete list have been most effective in preventing the use of computed present values in financial reporting. Such values would apply to major segments of assets directly related to production and not to many separate assets. This kind of value computation could be used to form an opinion of value as the basis for bargaining for a firm's purchase. Within the last decade dissatisfaction with the present basis of reporting has increased, but it does not appear that this will lead to the use of present values within the forseeable future.

Differences Between Original Cost and Present Value

The original cost of assets, less depreciation to date, represents the funds still considered committed in the specific properties. Present values of assets are not likely to be the same as the original cost less depreciation. The difference can be explained by several factors:

1. The original cost might not represent value by the same measure used in determining present value, market value, or discounted present value of future benefits.
2. Inflation could have caused a general upward change in prices and, therefore, in values in terms of money.
3. Changing technology and accompanying social changes could have caused a change in the relative supply and demand for specific assets, including the cost to produce the assets.

In the preceding sections of this chapter present value relates to changes in individual and group asset values from inflation and from social and technological influences. Changes in value due to general inflation are actually changes in the general value of money, rather than changes in value of specific assets. Adjustment could be made for inflation without attacking the problem of computing values for specific assets.

ADJUSTMENTS FOR PRICE CHANGES

When the original cost of assets is adjusted for changes in the general price level (inflation or deflation), the resulting amount is still the original cost. It is expressed in terms of the present value of the monetary unit rather than of monetary value at the time the asset was purchased. **The amount still represents the funds committed in the asset, stated in the number of current dollars equivalent to the original dollars of cost.**

Price Indexes

When the prices of most goods rise, money is worth relatively less because the same amount of money will buy less goods. Of course, as prices generally fall, money is worth more because the same amount of money will buy more goods. The device used to measure the amount of price change and, therefore, the amount of change in the value of money, is a price index. Prices prevailing at some specified period are used as a base of 100; increases and decreases from those prices result in a computed index above or below 100 in proportion to the amount of price change. When prices have risen 20 percent, the price index will be 120; when prices have risen 42 percent above the base period, the price index will be 142.

Choice of an index One difficulty in adjusting the asset cost for the changing value of the monetary unit is choosing the index. Many indexes are available: they may measure changes in prices of steel and related products, changes in prices of household appliances, changes in a broad group of items at wholesale level, changes in prices of items commonly purchased by the average family. Indexes such as the latter two appear to be more appropriate for most price level adjustment of financial data. The Bureau of Labor Statistics regularly publishes a wholesale price index and a consumer price index. The consumer price index is commonly referred to in the press as the cost of living index since it measures changes in prices of items that families consume in daily living. An even broader based index is the gross national product implicit price deflator index published quarterly by the Office of Business Economics of the Department of Commerce.

As we shall see, the use of a price index is not difficult. However, the computation of the index is exceedingly complex. Criteria must be established for selecting the products whose prices will be included. Also, a means must be found for giving appropriate weight to each price that is included. For example, in the consumer price index, things that are used commonly and in large quantity are weighted more heavily than items purchased less frequently and in smaller volume. In index preparation each item's price is weighted in proportion to the dollar volume of that item in the total of all purchases included.

Difficulties in selecting a price index appropriate for measuring changes in the general price level center around the problem of which prices to include in the index. If the index is to be used for adjusting the cost of a steel company's assets, should the index include only the prices of goods used in the steel industry? Would an index to be used for adjusting the cost of a shipping company's assets include only the prices of those assets commonly used in shipping? Or would a very broadly based index be better for all such use? Arguments for specific indexes are very persuasive. Nevertheless, an index including prices of a wide range of products, such as the GNP explicit price deflator index recommended by the AICPA in its APB Statement no. 3, dated June, 1969, may be preferred for general use for reasons such as the following:

1. The basis for adjusting cost prices by a price index is the argument that the value of the monetary unit has changed. A general understanding of the adjustment is thought to be more likely if the value referred to is the *general* value of the dollar (or peso, pound sterling, etc.).
2. Rapid changes in industrial technology and the resulting changes in goods used in various industries and companies suggest that a broadly based index is more appropriate than a specialized index which may no longer be exactly applicable.
3. Diversification of even small companies and the growth of large conglomerate companies, including activity in a wide range of industries, suggests that a broad index is appropriate.

Use of the price index To state the cost of an asset at the current price level, one adjusts the original cost in proportion to the change in price level since the asset was purchased. A small warehouse building completed five years ago at a total cost of $85,722 would be reported unadjusted as follows if it has an expected life of thirty years with no expected salvage value:

Building (at cost)	$85,722	
Less accumulated depreciation, computed on a straight-line basis	14,287	71,435

If the general price index was 157 at the time this building was constructed and is now 182, the cost of the building might be adjusted to the appropriate number of today's dollars by this computation:

Adjusted cost of building:

$$\$85{,}722 \times \frac{182}{157} = \$99{,}372$$

Adjusted amount of accumulated depreciation:

$$\$14{,}287 \times \frac{182}{157} = \$16{,}562$$

This building would be reported on a price index adjusted basis as follows:

Building (at cost adjusted to the current price level by ——— index)	$99,372	
Less accumulated depreciation on a straight-line basis (adjusted for price level by ——— index)	16,562	82,810

Meaning of Price Index Adjusted Cost

The original cost of an asset that has been adjusted for general purchasing power changes of the monetary unit is still the original cost; it is stated in the number of dollars of current value equivalent to the dollars originally spent. This is still reporting the funds committed in the asset rather than attempting to report the value. Reporting asset value rather than cost in terms of today's purchasing power of money would involve changing to the present market price, discounted present value of future benefits, or some other measure of value.

Cost of plant assets adjusted for price changes Data for long-life assets are more seriously misstated because of general price level changes than are data for more short-term assets. With inflation of 5 percent per year, a highly material change occurs in a period of ten years. A building which cost $250,000 when the general price index was at 120 would be reported at $500,000 when the price index rises to 240. This means that the funds committed in the building represented a general buying power equal to $500,000 today. It does not mean that it would cost that amount to duplicate the building today; it does mean that it would take $500,000 to buy today what could be bought generally for $250,000 when that amount was expended for the building. It should be clear that adjusting cost for price level changes does not state assets at present value, but one would normally expect the adjusted amount to be closer to present value than the unadjusted cost.

Cost of inventories adjusted for price changes The methods of assigning cost to inventories (LIFO, FIFO, and average) were developed because prices change enough to affect noticeably the measure of expenses and net income. To the extent that prices of specific goods in inventory change in concert with the general price level, adjusting inventory cost for price level changes would make unnecessary the different methods of cost assignment. For example, a LIFO-priced inventory with a substantial adjustment to the present price level would be stated at the same amount as a FIFO-priced inventory with a lesser adjustment to current prices. Of course, if all costs were adjusted to the current level, averaging the prices would not be meaningful.

Adjusting the inventory cost by a general price index would not necessarily state those inventories at present costs. It would express the funds committed in the inventories in dollars of current purchasing power. If the price of a specific item moved opposite to the general change in prices, if it dropped in price while the general price level was rising, adjusting the cost of that item by a general price index would provide a good statement of funds committed, but it would depart even more than the original cost from the present value of the item.

Assume that two different items in inventory were purchased for $800 each six months ago when the price index was 160. Assume further that demand and technology have effected changes in prices to $790 for one item and $820 for the other, and that the present general price index is 163. Adjustment of the cost of the two items would provide the following:

$$\$800 \times \frac{163}{160} = \$815 \quad \text{cost adjusted for general price level change.}$$

The original cost is adjusted toward present market price for one item but away from present market price for the other. A general price index is itself an average of selected prices and, therefore, is not applicable to individual items in inventory. It may, however, be applicable to the whole of mixed inventory. One would expect adjustment toward present value when a price index is applied to an aggregate inventory. Such adjustment should be considered an adjustment of funds committed in the inventory rather than a meaningful expression of present value.

SPECIAL PROBLEMS OF ADJUSTED ASSET REPORTING

Concepts and techniques of financial reporting are based on the fundamental ideas of measuring the funds committed in acquiring resources received and consumed on the assumption that the monetary unit is a stable factor. When present values of real-value assets or of the monetary unit are introduced into the financial information system, some rather significant changes may be required.

Depreciation, as it is used in current financial reporting, is the spreading of the cost of assets as expense over their useful lives. This concept of depreciation could remain the same if a price index were adjusted to express original cost in dollars of current purchasing power. If cost were adjusted to present value of the assets, the concept of depreciation apparently would refer to the value of resources consumed.

Depreciation of Price Index Adjusted Cost

With price index adjusted cost data, depreciation might still be computed as the spread of the original cost (now in terms of its current purchasing power) as expense over the useful life of the asset. Any of the methods traditionally used to compute depreciation might still be used. The change caused by adjusting the asset cost is that depreciation to date would be computed on the adjusted cost, and current depreciation expense logically would be reported on an adjusted basis, also.

For an example of sum-of-years'-digits depreciation on price adjusted cost, assume that equipment with an expected life of twenty years and an expected salvage value of $3,500 was purchased nine years ago for $35,000. The price index then was 140; it is now 170. Unadjusted data for this asset would be reported for the ninth year as follows:

Balance sheet:		
Equipment	$35,000	
Less depreciation to date	21,600	13,400
Income statement:		
Depreciation expense	$ 1,800	

Adjusted from a price index of 140 to an index of 170, the data would be reported as:

Balance sheet:		
Equipment, at cost adjusted by the price index	$42,500	
Less depreciation to date adjusted to same price basis as cost	26,229	16,271
Income statement:		
Depreciation expense	$ 2,186	

Each amount based on original cost was adjusted to the current price level by multiplying by the fraction $^{170}/_{140}$. If data had already been adjusted to the price level prevailing at the end of the preceding (eighth) year, the current adjustment would have been from that index, perhaps 167, to the current index of 170.

Depreciation of Present Values

If long-life assets were reported at their present values, depreciation apparently might be used to express the amount of value lost during the period. Assets for which a new value could be determined at the end of each year might have depreciation reported as the change in value from one date to another. Depending upon how the values were determined, this "depreciation" might be a negative amount, or appreciation. If discounted present value of projected future benefits were used for reporting, in a year in which expectations of future benefits increased, there might be a greater value at the end of the period than there was at the beginning.

It appears more likely that with current value reporting, the value at the end of the year plus the benefits derived during the year might be input as the value of the asset at the beginning of the year. Then depreciation could be taken as the value of the benefits actually derived from the asset during the year. This is a great departure from present asset reporting and current measurement of net income, and it is largely conjectural whether current values of assets will be used as the basis for financial reporting in the forseeable future.

Related Adjustments in Equity Accounts

In a preceding section, an illustration showed equipment adjusted for change in price levels from $35,000 to $42,500, with accumulated depreciation adjusted from $21,600 to $26,229, and the book amount (undepreciated cost) of the equipment adjusted from $13,400 to $16,271. Data for this increase in dollars reported for the asset must be reflected in equity accounts of the firm, also. Some of the major problems of financial reporting might be overcome and some confusion prevented if only major assets were adjusted for changes in price levels. If this were done, the data might be most easily understood if a special owners' equity account were added to reveal the source of the additional dollars reported for the firm's resources (assets). Such an account might be called Price Level Adjustments to Assets; it would contain positive data during inflation and negative data during periods of deflation. Such data could be reported as an adjustment to the total of other owners' equity accounts.

In case of full adjustment of all data (all assets and all equities) the original equity accounts would be adjusted by price indexes, and no additional equity data would be needed. Further comments are provided on this topic in the next paragraphs.

Full Price Level Adjustment (Stabilized Accounting)

If all data in the system were adjusted for the effect of changes in the monetary unit's purchasing power, the following adjustments would be included:

1. Real-value assets (not dependent for their value on the value of money), such as inventories, plant assets, and investments in land and buildings, would be adjusted from the price level at which they were acquired to the present level.
2. Monetary assets (cash and other assets for which a specified amount of money will be collected) would not be adjusted, but a loss would be acknowledged from holding these assets. The dollars in which they are stated will not buy as much after a period of inflation as before, and this loss in real value of the assets is a financial loss to the firm.
3. Liabilities would not be adjusted, since they will be paid in the number of dollars indicated, regardless of the purchasing power of a dollar. Since the firm received high-value dollars and will repay the claims of creditors with low-value money after a period of inflation, it has gained financially by carrying the debt. This gain from liabilities would be computed and reported in terms of current dollars.
4. Owners' equity accounts would be adjusted for price level changes from the date of inputs to these accounts to the present.
5. Revenues and expenses would all be adjusted to the price level prevailing at the end of the year.
6. Net income computation would include special items for holding gains and losses derived from the carrying of liabilities and holding monetary assets during periods of inflation. Of course, the opposite effects would occur during periods of deflation.

It is beyond the scope of this text to illustrate the computation of all the price level adjustments suggested above. However, in addition to price level adjustments for assets illustrated in earlier sections of this chapter, attention will be given to holding gains and losses.

The loss suffered by holding money during inflation can be illustrated by assuming that the sum of $34,000 was held for four years, during which time the price level advanced from an index of 170 to 190. Currently, the amount of money needed to have the purchasing power of $34,000 four years ago is computed as:

$$\$34{,}000 \times \frac{190}{170} = \$38{,}000.$$

Purchasing power of $38,000 is needed today to equal the purchasing power held four years ago, and, since the money that was held did not increase in purchasing power, it is clear that the firm has purchasing power of only $34,000 currently. This leaves a clear loss of $4,000 in purchasing power suffered by the firm during the four years it held the cash. This same kind of loss is effective for holding any kind of receivable which is collectible in a specified amount of money.

The gain achieved by carrying liabilities during a period of inflation is a very real financial gain. Assume that a firm has owed a long-term note for $405,000 for a period of six years and that the price index six years ago was 135 compared to 166 today. The amount of money needed currently to pay back the real (purchasing power) amount of the debt as of its inception is computed as:

$$\$405{,}000 \times \frac{166}{135} = \$498{,}000.$$

Since the firm received funds with a current purchasing power of $498,000 but can repay the debt currently with $405,000, it appears that the firm has gained $93,000 in current dollar purchasing power during the period it has owed the debt. This amount would be reported as a financial gain from carrying the liability if full adjustments were made for effects of price changes.

The result of full price level adjustments to financial data is that all nonmonetary items on the balance sheet and the income statement are reported in the number of dollars currently equivalent in general purchasing power to the dollars originally committed to the items. Financial gains and losses from inflation and deflation are recognized and reported.

STATUS OF PRESENT-VALUE AND PRICE LEVEL REPORTING

Sections of this chapter may have implied that data reflecting present asset values and the effects of price level changes are not used in current financial reporting. This is not altogether true; such data are reported in some instances.

Current Use of Price Level Reporting

The American Institute of Certified Public Accountants (AICPA) has not sanctioned through its Accounting Principles Board the use of price level adjusted data for financial reporting. Therefore, this cannot be said to be within the scope of "generally accepted accounting principles" in the United States. The Securities Exchange Commission (SEC) has not approved the reporting of such data to stockholders by companies subject to its reporting requirements.

In some other countries where inflation has been more extreme than it has been in this country, financial data have been adjusted for the effects of price changes. In most instances the adjustments have been only for the cost of assets; no country appears to have attempted to reflect all the measurable effects of inflation in financial data.

Current Use of Present-Value Reporting

As with price level adjusted data, present-value reporting has not been approved as a generally accepted accounting principle by the AICPA, nor for public reporting to stockholders by the SEC. However, many balance sheets for individuals and smaller firms are prepared on a current-value basis at the request of banks and other lending organizations. Since the firm's assets serve as direct or indirect security for credit or loans granted to it, the present value of those assets is much more relevant to the loan decision than is the original price paid for them. Certified public accountants generally may not associate their names and the weight of their opinions with statements reflecting the current value of assets rather than cost.

Prospects for Future Approval

There is not sufficient agreement or objectivity in the determination of present asset values to suggest that this basis of reporting will be generally accepted in the foreseeable future. There are too many unresolved questions concerning the meaning and measurement of value for this standard of reporting to gain acceptance quickly.

There are many voices in the United States saying that inflation is great enough and is sufficiently projected for the future to warrant adjustment for its effects. The AICPA has sponsored a special study on this subject; their researcher concluded that adjustments for price level changes should be made in financial data. The Accounting Principles Board of the AICPA is studying this subject and has issued a statement indicating that they do not judge inflation in the United States to be serious enough to require price adjusted information. However, they do suggest that such information may be presented in addition to the unadjusted basic financial statements (APB Statement no. 3, June, 1969).

Whether the board will recommend in the future that the reporting of price adjusted data be required is quite uncertain. It appears reasonable to expect, however, that any positive recommendation on the subject would involve reporting adjusted data as supplemental information first, on a trial basis to determine how much it is used and desired by those receiving the published annual reports of corporations.

QUESTIONS AND EXERCISES

10- A. At what amount are assets normally reported, their value or the amount of funds committed in them? What are the major reasons for reporting in this way?

10- B. What use is made of the information about the amount of funds committed in a long-term asset when the decision is made to replace the asset?

10- C. What is the general purpose for which funds-committed information about assets is used?

10- D. Inventories are listed in financial reports at cost (funds committed), but receivables and cash are listed at their cash value rather than cost. Why is this?

10- E. Dianne Jay's Credit Company will purchase receivables to be collected in the future by discounting them at 12 percent compounded annually. What will the company pay for a $10,000 receivable due at the end of three years? For $10,000 due at the end of six years?

10- F. If Dianne Jay's Credit Company changes its discount terms to 12 percent compounded semiannually (6 percent semiannual rate), what will it pay for a $10,000 receivable due at the end of three years? For $10,000 due at the end of six years?

10- G. When Mr. Hein Bartow retired from an executive position with a large business firm, he received an annuity contract providing a payment of $10,000 each six months for the next ten years. Mr. Bartow would like to sell the annuity contract for cash. At a discount of 10 percent per annum compounded semiannually, how much would he receive for the annuity contract?

10-H. Compute the price of a $100,000 bond with a face rate of 7 percent per annum, paid semiannually, if the bond is issued five years before its maturity at a price to yield 8 percent per annum compounded semiannually.

10-I. Define "present value." What figures are used in calculating present value?

10-J. Distinguish between tangible and intangible assets.

10-K. What is business goodwill? Under what circumstances would you expect to see goodwill listed on a company's balance sheet?

10-L. If you are willing to accept all investment proposals that you expect will yield an annual return of 12 percent or more, which of the following investment opportunities would you accept?

a. Cost: $ 35,000 on January 1, 1971.
   Return: $100,000 on January 1, 1981.

b. Cost: $80,000 on January 1, 1971 and
   $20,000 on January 1, 1976.
   Return: $10,000 on each January 1, 1972 through 1977, and
   $20,000 on each January 1, 1978 through 1987.

c. Cost: $ 20,000 on each January 1, 1971 through 1981.
   Return: $250,000 on January 1, 1983.

10-M. Mr. A finds a house that can be bought for $21,000 cash. However, the seller will accept a down payment of $10,000 and a series of payments of $2,000 at the end of each of the next seven years.

a. If Mr. A can invest his money to earn 8 percent compounded annually, which of these alternatives provides him the better price?
b. If the seller can invest his money at 6 percent, what price is the deferred payment plan on the house worth to him?

10-N. Brown owns some commercial property which he leased to White for $10,000 per year on a fifteen-year lease. After the lease had run for five years, Black offered to sublease the property from White for $30,000 per year. White offered, instead, to transfer the original lease to Black for a cash payment of $160,000, with Black then responsible for making the ten annual payments of $10,000 to Brown. Assume that money is worth 6 percent compounded annually to Black and that he will prefer the arrangement with the smaller present discounted value. Should he accept White's counteroffer or should he try to get White to accept his offer to sublet for $30,000 per year?

PROCEDURAL PROBLEMS

✓ 10-1. The Stuart Corporation incurred the following costs to construct its new office building. Compute the costs applicable to the Building account.

1. Contract price (labor and materials), $1,400,000. Bldg.
2. Architect's fees, $220,000. Bldg.
3. Cost of the land, $340,000. Land

4. Proceeds from a mortgage issued to pay for the building, $1,400,000.
5. Landscaping costs, $1,100.
6. Building permit fee, $600.
7. $4,000 paid for cleaning services during first year of occupancy.
8. Excavation costs for basement of building, $22,000.
9. Cost of a temporary fence around the construction site, $400.
10. $700 interest paid on the mortgage during the construction period.
11. Salary paid to company officials during period of construction, $44,000 (not directly related to the construction).
12. Insurance premium on building during construction period, $400.

10-2. The Saxton Brothers Company is considering three possible bond purchases. They have asked you to compute the present value of each of the described bonds.
 a. A $20,000, 7 percent bond maturing at the end of seven years, to be discounted at 8 percent.
 b. A $10,000, 6 percent bond to be discounted at 8 percent, maturing at the end of four years.
 c. A $10,000, 9 percent bond to be discounted at 7 percent, maturing at the end of five years.

10-3. The Community Development Company intends to purchase a $100,000, 7 percent bond, with a remaining life to maturity of five years, to yield 6 percent.
 a. Compute the present value.
 b. Assuming the bond is purchased for the present value to yield 6 percent on October 1, 1969, with interest paid on September 30 each year, prepare an amortization and income schedule using both actuarial and straight-line amortization.

10-4. The Weyman Manufacturing Company purchased on January 1, 1969, a $100,000 maturity value bond. Six years remain to maturity with 7 percent paid each December 31 to yield 8 percent.
 a. Compute the purchase price and prepare an amortization and income schedule using the actuarial tables.
 b. Prepare the journal entries to record the purchase and interest income for 1969.
 c. Assuming the bond is sold on January 1, 1973, for $101,800, prepare the journal entry to record the gain or loss.

10-5. The Gulf Coast Shipbuilding Company is considering the purchase of the Bayside Marine Construction Company's assets. Bayside Marine Construction Company has a contract for the construction of a barge. Expenditures required to complete this contract are estimated to be $400,000 immediately, $300,000 at the beginning of the second year, and $100,000 at the end of the second year. Expected collections are $200,000 at the end of the first year, $600,000 at the end of the second year, and $250,000 at the end of the third year. No supplies are expected to remain at the end of construction. If Gulf Coast Shipbuilding Company intends to realize 10 percent on this purchase, what will be its bid price?

10-6. On January 2, 1963, the Ames Corporation purchased a building for $120,000 with a salvage value of $12,000 and an estimated useful life of twenty years. The company uses straight-line depreciation. The price index at time of purchase was 120.

a. When preparing financial statements on December 31, 1969, the company wants to adjust the building and depreciation account to current price levels. The price index is now 140. Compute the price adjusted values for December 31, 1969, including depreciation expense for the year.

10-7. Compute the return on investment for Company A and Company B on each of the following two independent cases.

a. In 1970 Company A had stockholders' equity of $200,000 and a net income of $20,000. Company B had stockholders' equity of $50,000 and also had $50,000 borrowed at 7 percent annual interest. Net income for Company B was $10,000 before the interest payment.

b. In 1971 Company A had assets of $80,000. All assets were purchased in 1933. Company A had a 1971 net income of $25,600. Company B had a 1971 income of $24,000 earned on assets of $150,000, all purchased in 1971. The price index has changed from 100 in 1933 to 140 in 1971. Compute the rate of return on total assets based on 1971 dollar value.

10-8. Purnell Construction is considering bidding on two projects. Both projects will require an immediate expenditure of $500,000. Additional expenditures will be $1,500,000 for project A and $1,100,000 for project B. Total revenues will be $2,700,000 for project A and $2,100,000 for project B. Supplies worth $200,000 will be left after completion of project B. No supplies will be left after project A.

For making computations the company assumes that expenditures will be made at the beginning of the year and collections at the end of the year, both based on the percentage of work completed during that year. Production schedules are:

	Percent Completed During Year	
Year	Project A	Project B
1	10	10
2	40	20
3	50	30
4		40

The company expects to earn 8 percent on project A and 10 percent on project B. Compute the bid price for each project.

10-9. On January 1, 1970, Crowe Incorporated purchased a $100,000, 5 percent bond with interest payable on December 31. The bond has a life of ten years. The company uses straight-line amortization.

a. Crowe Incorporated purchased the bond to yield 7 percent. Compute the purchase price.

b. Compute the annual amortization of discount or premium and the annual interest income.

c. The bond is sold on June 30, 1973, for $90,600 plus interest. Prepare the entry to record the amortization and interest income for January 1 through June 30 and the entry to record the sale.

10-10. On January 1, 1970, the Hodges Tool Company purchased a $200,000 par value bond, 5 percent stated interest with a remaining life of five years. Interest is paid each December 31.

a. The bond was purchased to yield 7 percent. Prepare the journal entry to record the purchase and prepare an income and amortization schedule using scientific amortization.
b. Prepare the entry to record the 1971 income.
c. The bond is redeemed on January 1, 1975, for its maturity value. Journalize.

10-11. On January 1, 1970, Mr. James Kelly purchased a $100,000, 7 percent bond with a four-year life, to yield 6 percent; interest is paid on December 31.

a. Compute the present value on January 1, 1970, and journalize the purchase.
b. Prepare an income and amortization schedule using straight-line amortization.
c. The bond is sold on January 1, 1972, for $101,600. Journalize.

10-12. In 1955 the Keystone Corporation purchased factory equipment for $300,000 with no salvage value and an estimated useful life of thirty years. The company used straight-line depreciation. On December 31, 1970, the company decided to adjust the equipment and depreciation accounts to reflect the price level change from an index of 120 in 1955 to 150 in 1970.

a. Prepare the journal entry to record the price level change.
b. Prepare a partial balance sheet showing the plant asset and owners' equity sections (assume capital stock of $200,000 and retained earnings of $300,000).

CONCEPTUAL PROBLEMS

10-13. Last month Energy, Incorporated was in need of some especially accurate transducers. When he found a small firm in New Jersey that produced transducers with adequate precision, the director of production for Energy, Inc., instructed the purchasing agent to obtain seven of the instruments. The purchasing agent was to obtain the best price possible on the assumption that if these seven transducers proved satisfactory, a continuing demand might result; however, he was limited to paying at most $1,100 for each.

The New Jersey producer was not aware of the price restrictions placed on Energy, Inc.'s purchasing agent and, wanting to increase its production volume, it priced six of the transducers at $800 each and the seventh, because of highly intricate requirements, at $1,200. The purchasing agent objected to the $1,200 price, but obtained permission to accept it because of the low price required for the other six instruments.

The seven transducers were shipped and billed at a total of $6,000 with a 2 percent discount available for payment within ten days. The bill was paid within a week by a check for $5,880. Separate fixed asset records were set up on the transducers, with the first amount entered on each being the net price paid.

Currently, an international conglomerate corporation is discussing with the board of directors of Energy, Incorporated the possibility of merging EI into their company and the terms under which such a merger might occur. A question of critical importance is the value of EI's assets.

a. What arguments support the position that the prices paid for the transducers ($784 each for six and $1,176 for one) represent their values?
b. What arguments support the position that the prices paid for the transducers do not represent their values, but that some other amounts would better represent values?
c. Assuming that the arguments in (b) above prevailed, how would you describe what is represented by the transducer prices of $784 and $1,176?

10-14. Venture Capital Corporation invests in several categories of risk ventures. One such category is a group of "high technology" new businesses which are estimated to have approximately an 83 percent probability of success. Venture Capital makes such new businesses "loans" with conditions that will allow the company to convert the loans into capital stock at a gain of 8 percent compounded annually, plus a substantial additional gain to compensate for the high risk involved. Venture Capital's investment manager explains the company's contracts with this particular category of investments as follows, using an amount of 100 to represent all such loans.

"Loan" plus 8 percent for one year		108
Original amount	100	
Probable losses at 17 percent	17	
Probable remainder of original value		83
Gain required to provide for losses plus 8 percent return		25

25/83 = .3012 Rounded to nearest ½ percent, 30 percent

The discount rate of 30 percent per annum is used to compute the amount that can be lent for a specified possible future return. The rate is used also to compute the future return demanded in conversion to shares of stock for a loan of a specified amount.

a. Compute the amount that Venture Capital Corporation will lend a new business in the 17 percent failure risk category in exchange for an agreement to convert the debt after five years into capital stock estimated to have a market price of $100,000.
b. What market value of stock to be received by conversion of notes to stock at the end of one year would Venture Capital demand for a loan of $100,000?
c. What is the present value to Venture Capital of $100,000 of stock (at its market value) in a new company in the 17 percent risk category, to be received four years from now, if the company has not failed by that time?

10-15. The X-T Company purchased three high-precision, convertible PL-7 ALCO lathes at the beginning of the year for $89,000 each. These were the first of a new line of lathes with pluranium alloy cutting tools and position controls that make possible precision work within much closer tolerances than other equipment.

During the past year the supply of pluranium has become limited, and the price has risen substantially. Lathes of the type purchased a year ago by the X-T Company are now priced at $107,500, and the company has had a tentative offer of $95,000 each for its used machines. The X-T Company does not plan to sell its lathes "at any price" according to the production superintendent because they make it possible for the company to do very profitable high-precision tooling work. The superintendent says the lathes are worth "twice the price we paid for them."

a. In response to a request from a group of X-T Company creditors for a report showing the present value of all assets, at what amount would you show the three PL-7 ALCO lathes? Why would you use that amount?
b. A security analyst wishes to predict future benefits to the stockholders by projecting a matching of revenues (measured by the funds received) and expenses (measured by the funds committed in the resources consumed) as seen in financial statements prepared in accord with "generally accepted accounting principles." What amount would you use as the basis for computing depreciation expense for this purpose? Why this amount?

10-16. The firm of Doon Bodwoks, Inc. has just received the report of a market survey predicting the national market demand it might expect for its new, high-pressure bodwok. This device can be manufactured in large volume at an amazingly low cost; it can be operated manually by an unskilled person, and it is compatible with a number of robot devices for use in areas of high danger to human beings. A demand-price curve developed as a part of the market report indicates the following relationships:

Price	Number of New Bodwoks Sold	Use
$200	100	Highly restricted use.
150	200	" " "
100	400	
50	2,000	Aircraft market added here.
40	2,600	
30	4,000	
25	10,000	Luxury auto market added.
20	13,000	
18	18,000	
16	25,000	
14	50,000	Use with pleasure vehicles.
13	60,000	
12	70,000	
11	80,000	
10	88,000	

Assume that business firms and individuals purchase bodwoks for use and not for resale. Assume further that, because of the low manufacturing cost, Doon Bodwoks, Inc. decides to market the new item at a price of $11.

a. What is the value of a bodwok to a purchaser who plans to operate it by robot in dangerous and generally inaccessible places (highly restricted use)?
b. What is the value of a bodwok to a purchaser who plans to use it in an aircraft? In a luxury automobile? In a pleasure vehicle?
c. For how many potential purchasers does a bodwok have a value of $11 or more?
d. For how many potential purchasers does a bodwok have a value of $11, but not as much as $12?
e. What is the general relationship between the cost of a bodwok and its value to a purchaser?

11

Liabilities

Preview Questions

As you study look for the answers to the following questions:

- **What are liabilities?**
- **Differentiate between current and long-term liabilities.**
- **What are payroll liabilities?**
- **How are sales taxes handled by the firm?**
- **What are bonds payable?**
- **What are bond sinking funds?**
- **What is the origin of deferred income tax liability?**
- **When are liabilities and expenses for pensions reported?**

Liabilities are claims against the firm which require the payment or consumption of resources. Often liabilities are referred to as claims against the resources of the firm; in this definition there is implied a restriction on the use or disposition of resources. Ordinary liabilities do not provide any such restriction; that would require a special provision, such as a pledge or mortgage, which gives the creditor a claim against specific properties and prevents their disposal without his consent. Liabilities generally are not claims directly against resources of the firm, but against the firm itself.

The claims of creditors may arise because they provided credit capital to the firm, or because the firm became committed to pay out or consume resources for their benefit. The concept of liabilities as the debt source of the firm's resources is especially helpful in understanding the nature of the balance sheet. From this view, *equities* (liabilities, owners' investment, and earnings) *represent sources of the firm's resources; assets indicate the form in which the resources are committed.*

LIABILITY RECOGNITION: LEGAL AND ECONOMIC BASES

The question of which claims against a firm to recognize as liabilities in reporting financial information normally is resolved by requiring that claims be legally valid. However, there are a number of claims based on economics rather than legally enforceable agreements. These must be considered in the study of liabilities.

Legal Basis for Liability Recognition

Liabilities such as notes, accounts, salaries, and taxes payable are based on commitments of the firm legally enforceable through contracts or provisions of the law. Historically the legal validity of a claim has been the controlling criterion in its recognition as a liability.

Most liabilities stem from creditors' providing resources (money, materials, or services) to the firm and agreeing to accept payment at some later date. Under such agreements, the firm's obligations clearly have a legal basis. On interest-bearing notes a liability is recognized for the face amount, plus any interest that has accrued; this is the amount which is legally enforceable at this time. Liability is not recognized for the full amount of future interest accruing before the note is paid; payment of the future interest is not now enforceable.

Taxes imposed on the firm by law result in a legally enforceable claim by the governmental unit. The amount of such a claim is recognized as a liability when it becomes enforceable. Other claims imposed by law, such as damages awarded by a court, are recognized as liabilities. All claims such as these clearly have a legal basis for recognition.

In recent years, the complexities of financial operations and of tax and regulatory law have resulted in a new type of obligation of the firm which may be based more on economic considerations than on strict legal enforceability.

Economic Basis for Liability Recognition

In the ordinary course of its operations a firm may develop needs for future expenditures which must be met if it is to continue operating. An example is routine maintenance and repairs on machinery. The wear on the machinery during the operating period necessitated the needed repairs, and operations can be continued for only a limited time without having the maintenance and repair work done. Is there an economic liability at the end of a reporting period for ordinary maintenance and repairs that have been postponed until the next period? The general answer has been that, for interim reporting within a year, such deferred maintenance may be reported as a liability; however, generally accepted standards do not condone this practice for annual financial reporting. Annual reports normally would not include a liability for deferred maintenance and repair.

In recent years a liability with similar characteristics has been recognized by the Accounting Principles Board of the AICPA. Briefly, a future obligation to pay greater taxes develops when a firm takes deductions earlier on its income tax reports than it does on its income statement. A firm may deduct depreciation by an accelerated method in computing its current income tax but may use straight-line depreciation in computing net income on its income statement. As a result, the tax which must be paid is abnormally low relative to net income in early years of the life of major assets and abnormally high relative to the net income in later years. The Accounting Principles Board has said that income tax expense should be related to the net income reported on the income statement, and that if a smaller amount than this is currently due, the remainder should be shown as a liability payable some years later when the accelerated depreciation computation provides a smaller tax deduction. This situation is presented in detail below, with long-term liabilities. The point, however, is that while the liability is imposed by law, the amount currently recognized is entirely based on the economic situation and economic assumptions rather than on current legal enforceability.

By and large, liabilities are recognized on the basis of legal validity. Some obligations, although not enforceable, may be accepted by the firm; these are recognized because they have been accepted, and management intends to treat them as other obligations. A few liabilities, such as deferred income taxes, are recognized on an economic basis—probably because they are a material amount in the income computation rather than because of any great sentiment to report them on the balance sheet.

LIABILITY CLASSIFICATION

Liabilities normally are divided into two general classes, current and long term. Sometimes a third class of liabilities is used for reporting obligations which represent amounts already collected but which will not be reported as revenue until later periods; liabilities of this type were seen as *unearned collections* in the earlier study of revenue. They are sometimes reported under the heading of Deferred Credits, following long-term liabilities, on the balance sheet.

Current Liabilities

Liabilities due to be paid within the next operating cycle of a business (normally, one year) are reported as current liabilities. Included are accounts payable, interest payable, salaries and wages payable, taxes payable, dividends payable, and other amounts.

Trade accounts payable Accounts payable indicate the amount of goods and services that have been provided with payment deferred for several days or a few months. At the consumer level, ninety-day credit sometimes can be obtained at the same price afforded on a cash transaction. However, the retailer and wholesaler often are offered a 1 percent or 2 percent discount for payment within ten days; passing this discount in order to obtain credit becomes expensive. Passing a 2 percent discount for ten-day payment in order to use thirty-day credit terms is the equivalent of about 36 percent per annum. This is extremely high credit cost. However, if no discounts are allowed for cash payment, accounts payable may be a very inexpensive means of financing at least a part of the firm's operations.

Notes payable Short-term notes payable usually indicate a supplier's extension of credit beyond the time normally allowed on accounts, or the borrowing of funds from a commercial bank. These notes normally bear interest at the prevailing rate. Suppliers usually do not favor providing the extension of credit indicated by notes, but banks welcome the opportunity to provide commercial credit to good bank customers.

Accrued liabilities Interest, salaries, wages, taxes, and other items payable at the end of a period occur because payment does not coincide with the end of the reporting period. These are obligations that have accumulated and normally are not yet due to be paid. Resources in the form of goods or services have been received and, in many cases, consumed, but there has been no billing or payment; no data has been input to the system. Many of these liabilities are recorded in the accounting system by adjusting entries such as those included in the earlier study of expenses.

Unearned collections In some instances resources, usually in cash form, are received before they are earned. Until they are earned, these amounts are reported as liabilities because they represent claims of the customers against the firm. These claims normally will be satisfied by the delivery of goods or providing of service, but if these are not properly provided a refund might be demanded. It is generally accepted that the proper measure of the liability is the amount of the collection not yet earned. These liabilities usually require adjusting entries, as was seen in the study of revenues.

Long-term Liabilities

Many medium-sized and large corporations obtain great sums of long-term capital from lenders. Often long-term borrowing can be done at interest rates which allow the firm and its shareholders to benefit from using relatively low-cost financing to produce earnings at a substantially higher rate.

Long-term notes payable If a firm borrows from a commercial bank, directly from an institution such as an insurance company, or by purchasing long-life assets on credit, it may give a long-term note for the full amount of each loan or the credit part of a purchase. Quite often such notes include mortgages on assets of the firm. They may be due in installments or in full amount at maturity. If the firm's financial and credit standing are good, the interest rate on long-term notes may be relatively low.

Bonds payable When the firm borrows on the money market it issues bonds which are offered for sale through established bond market channels. Bonds are another type of long-term note; they are printed in denominations to suit the market (type of lender) to which they will be offered, with face amounts ranging from $1,000 to perhaps $100,000 per bond. The rate of interest payable in cash is stated on the bond. *Coupon* bonds have coupons for all the interest payments printed and attached to the bonds. Each coupon is detached (clipped) on the due date indicated and deposited like cash by the lender. More details concerning the classification and reporting of bond payable data are included in a later section of this chapter.

Other long-term liabilities The firm may incur other types of long-term liabilities through agreements such as pension plans and by its treatment of deductions for tax computation and financial reporting. The interpretation of the kind and amount of liability involved in various pension plans is becoming more standard; however, there is not full standardization, and varied interpretations are acceptable. Deferring income tax as a long-term liability has grown out of an attempt to match tax expense to revenue and other expenses as they are reported on the income statement. More attention will be given these topics in later sections of this chapter.

PAYROLL LIABILITIES

The firm's use of personal services creates a liability to the employees for payment of cash salary or wages and for payment of amounts withheld for insurance premiums, savings, and bonds. Tax liabilities to various governmental agencies are also created.

Payroll Taxes

Taxes based on the firm's payroll are the FICA (Federal Insurance Contributions Act) tax and the unemployment compensation taxes. Local governmental units (larger cities, for example) may tax a firm on the basis of its payroll. Only the two nationally applicable payroll taxes are illustrated here; others would be treated in a similar manner.

FICA taxes Federal taxes to finance retirement, health, and other benefits for a large part of the working public are assessed on both the employee and employer. The employer is responsible for withholding the employee's tax from his pay and for paying this amount, plus an equal amount as his own tax, to the federal government.

The FICA tax currently is 5.2 percent of the first $7,800 of each employee's yearly earnings. This rate is applicable to both the employee and his employer, making the total tax 10.4 percent of the first $7,800 of earnings. If an employee earned $200 per week, the tax withheld from his pay would be $10.40 ($200 × .052) each week until he had earned $7,800 within the year; then there would be no further tax withheld. The employer would pay the $10.40 withheld, plus a like amount as his tax, or a total of $20.80, to meet his responsibility.

The FICA tax rate and the amount of earnings on which it is levied have increased through the years. Currently, only the rate is definitely scheduled to change; the following schedule indicates the planned increases:

Year	Percent
1973–75	5.65
1976–79	5.7
1980–86	5.8
1987	5.9

Payment of FICA taxes is made monthly or quarterly, depending on the total amount owed for FICA taxes and for federal income taxes withheld from employees' earnings.

Unemployment compensation taxes The unemployment compensation program in the United States is federally enacted, but state operated. The basic tax is levied by the federal government, but credit is given against this tax for the amount of tax levied by the state in which employees work. The gross federal tax rate is now 3.1 percent of the first $3,000 earned by any employee, levied on the employer only. The employee is not responsible for any of this tax. Although the gross federal tax rate is 3.1 percent, the effective rate is only .4 percent (4/10 of 1 percent) because credit is given against the gross rate up to 2.7 percent for taxes levied by the different states; all states have an unemployment compensation tax of at least 2.7 percent.

Many states have merit-rating systems which allow employers to reduce their state unemployment tax rate by having very few separated employees who claim unemployment compensation. These employers who earn a lower state rate still get credit for the full 2.7 percent against the federal tax. In some states a successful, or fortunate, employer may have a state unemployment compensation tax as low as .1 percent of the first $3,000 paid each of his employees.

Plans for computing and paying the state tax vary among the states, but in all cases it must be computed and paid in at least once each year. The tax liability accrues as wages are paid and is classified and recorded with data related to the payroll.

Employees' income tax withheld Federal income taxes on employees' earnings must be withheld by the employer and paid to the federal government. The amount withheld is determined by the amount of the earnings and the number of "exemptions" the employee claims for income tax purposes. Tax withholding tables are available for employer use; the amount to be withheld can be read from the table for any combination of earnings and dependency exemptions. The amounts withheld must be paid in, along with FICA taxes, either monthly or quarterly. A liability is established when taxes are withheld from the employee's pay; the liability is recorded as a part of data related to the payroll. The income tax withheld from employees' pay is entirely separate from the computation and payment of the employer's own income taxes.

In many areas there are additional local income taxes which must be withheld from employees' earnings and paid in to the state and local governments. These are not illustrated here, but they would be handled similarly to the withholding, recording, and paying of the federal income tax.

Other payroll deductions Employers may be authorized to withhold various amounts from employees' pay for specific purposes. Group insurance premiums often are withheld and paid to the insurance company by the employer. Employees may have savings withheld to purchase savings bonds or deposited with credit unions and other savings organizations. Dues for labor unions and other organizations may be withheld and paid in by the employer. All of these deductions from employees' pay are treated in the same manner. A liability is recognized at the time the payroll is computed. Payments are made at agreed intervals.

Payroll Data Illustrated

To illustrate the identification and classification of payroll data, especially the data related to liabilities, the following situation is presented.

Assume that five employees are to be paid on the two-week payroll ending November 14, based on the following data:

Name	Earnings in Prior Periods	Earnings This Period	Income Tax Exemptions
Abner, Joe K.	$2,000	$400	1
Azul, Maria C.	2,900	300	2
Bahwu, Uhni Q.	4,000	450	5
Mann, Jack V.	7,700	400	4
Wolfe, Ann L.	8,000	450	3

Each employee has authorized a $15 deduction to purchase savings bonds and a $3 deduction for group insurance premiums. Mr. Bahwu and Miss Wolfe have authorized a $10 deduction for a special, voluntary savings "thrift plan." The employer has a state merit plan unemployment compensation tax of 2 percent.

The following data are computed or identified for each employee:

1. Amount of earnings subject to FICA tax and amount of the tax on the employee.
2. Amount of earnings subject to unemployment compensation tax.
3. Amount of federal income tax to be withheld.
4. Amount of other payroll deductions.
5. Net amount of pay.
6. Amount of FICA tax and state and federal unemployment compensation tax on employer.

These data normally are accumulated on a payroll record similar to the following if the payroll check and records are kept manually. If the

(a)	(b) Earnings in Prior Periods	(c) Earnings This Period	(d) Subject to FICA	(e) Amount of FICA Tax	(f) Income Tax Withheld
(1) Abner, Joe K.	$2,000	$ 400	$400	$20.80	$ 65
(2) Azul, Maria C.	2,900	300	300	15.60	35
(3) Bahwu, Uhni Q.	4,000	450	450	23.40	35
(4) Mann, Jack V.	7,700	400	100	5.20	35
(5) Wolfe, Ann L.	8,000	450	–	–	55
		$2,000		$65.00	$225

	(g)	(h)	(i)	(j)	(k)	(l)	(m)	(n)
	Other Deductions							
	Savings Bonds	Insurance Premiums	Thrift Plan	Total Deductions	Net Pay	Subject to U. C. Tax	State U. C. Tax	Federal U. C. Tax
(1) ...	$15	$ 3		$103.80	$ 296.20	$400	$ 8	$1.60
(2) ...	15	3		68.60	231.40	100	2	.40
(3) ...	15	3	$10	86.40	363.60	–	–	–
(4) ...	15	3		58.20	341.80	–	–	–
(5) ...	15	3	10	83.00	367.00	–	–	–
	$75	$15	$20	$400.00	$1,600.00		$10	$2.00

payroll is computed and checks written by computer, this manual type of record may be omitted; a printed record may be obtained for each employee, providing a cumulative record of his earnings and deductions. Of course, the cumulative data may be kept on punched cards, on tape, or on discs to be printed out or transferred on tape or cards to a governmental agency as needed.

Payroll Data Classified: Journal Entries

Data are classified to indicate the expense of using employees' services and to indicate liabilities incurred as shown in the following journal entry:

Nov. 14	Salary Expense (c)	2,000,00	
	Salaries Payable (k)		1,600
	FICA Tax Payable (e)		65
	Employees Income Tax Payable (f)		225
	Bond Deductions Payable (g)		75
	Insurance Premium Payable (h)		15
	Thrift Plan Deductions Payable (i)		20

The preceding journal entry inputs data for all the liabilities incurred by withholding various amounts from employees' pay and, of course, the liability for employees' salaries on this payday. Expenses and liabilities related to payroll-based taxes imposed on the employer are shown in this journal entry:

Nov. 14	Payroll Tax Expense	77	
	FICA Tax Payable (e)		65
	State U. C. Tax Payable (m)		10
	Federal U. C. Tax Payable (n)		2

It should be noted that after the preceding entries, the FICA Tax Payable account has a balance of $130, the total of the equal amounts withheld from employees' pay and levied on the employer.

When checks are written for the payroll, the Cash account will be credited and the Salaries Payable account will be debited. When payments are made for any other liabilities related to the payroll similar entries are made, with both the liabilities and cash being reduced.

In the preceding illustration all salaries are recorded in a single Salaries Expense account. Depending upon the services various employees perform, the salaries might be divided among several classifications: Selling Expense, Administrative Expense, etc.

SALES TAX LIABILITY

Many states and cities levy a sales tax or use tax on consumers. This tax is collected by retailers when they collect for sales made to their customers. When the tax is collected or charged to customers, a liability to the state or city is generated. Identifying and measuring this liability may be accomplished through either of two patterns of data handling.

Sales Tax Liability Identified at Time of Sale

When a taxable sale is made, the retailer must compute the tax and add it to the amount charged the customer. The data for the retailer's tax liability may be classified and recorded now as follows (assume a 4 percent state sales tax):

Dec. 14	Cash	1,040	
	Sales		1,000
	Sales Tax Liability		40

The liability for sales taxes collected from customers accumulates as sales are made. The Sales Tax Liability account should always indicate the amount owed; this account is debited when payment is made to the state government.

Sales Tax Not Identified at Time of Sale

When the tax is included in a sale made to a customer, the amount of the tax may not be separately identified. If this procedure is followed, a sale for $1,000 plus sales tax of $40 would be recorded as follows:

Dec. 14	Cash	1,040	
	Sales		1,040

The amount of the retailer's liability for sales taxes can be computed later by recognizing that the amount stored in the Sales account actually is 104 percent of the sales amount; that is, the Sales account contains data for sales, plus 4 percent for the sales tax liability. If we assume that the Sales account balance is $312,000 at the end of the month, we can compute the sales revenue and sales tax liability as follows:

$$\$312{,}000 \div 1.04 = \$300{,}000 \text{ (sales revenue)}$$
$$\$312{,}000 - 300{,}000 = \$12{,}000 \text{ (tax liability)}$$

An adjusting journal entry is made to transfer the $12,000 from the Sales account to the Sales Tax Liability account:

Dec. 31	Sales	12,000	
	Sales Tax Liability		12,000

This entry leaves a balance of $300,000 in the Sales account and, as indicated, stores the amount of the tax, $12,000, in the Sales Tax Liability account.

The sales tax must be paid in at frequent intervals by the retailer. The liability for this tax is classified, therefore, as a current liability in financial reporting.

BONDS PAYABLE

Bonds payable are long-term notes issued in compliance with rather strict governmental standards. The face amounts, due date, and interest rate of bonds are decided before the bonds are approved and printed. Of course, the interest rate demanded by lenders can be expected to differ from the rate specified for the bonds, at least by a fractional percent. The amount that a lender can invest in the bond and earn the rate of interest he demands is computed as the present value of the future proceeds from the investment. The investor will collect the regular interest payments, plus the face amount at maturity; the present value of these amounts, discounted to the present date at the demand rate, is the price of the bond. The details of this computation were presented in chapter 10.

Recording Bonds Payable

The amount of the bonds payable liability is reported on the assumption that the bonds will be paid at maturity and that the amount of the liability in the interim should be measured by the conditions under which the bonds were issued. Interest rate changes demanded by lenders after the bonds are issued cannot affect the actual rate paid by the firm, nor can they affect the amount that the firm will pay in canceling the liability at maturity. If the bonds are paid before maturity, then some amount other than the maturity value or the recorded amount of the bonds may be paid. Details of data classification and reporting will be seen in the following paragraphs.

Issue of bonds When bonds are issued, data must be classified to indicate the amount of cash received and the amount of liability. The issue of $100,000 face amount of 6 percent, ten-year bonds to yield the lender 7 percent with interest paid semiannually, would be recorded in journal form as follows:

Dec. 1	Cash	92,897	
	Discount on Bonds Payable	7,103	
	Bonds Payable		100,000

The liability is recorded at full face amount, but the discount recorded separately is always deducted from this face amount in reporting the actual amount of the liability.

The issue of a $100,000, 7 percent, ten-year bond to yield the lender 6 percent, with interest paid semiannually, would be recorded as shown in the following journal entry:

Dec. 1	Cash	107,441	
	Premium on Bonds Payable		7,441
	Bonds Payable		100,000

Again, the liability is recorded at face amount of the bonds, but the premium received on the bonds is added to this amount when reporting the amount of the liability.

Payment of interest Interest expense is incurred daily as the resource (availability of the money) is consumed. Interest is paid semiannually or annually on most bonds, as indicated on the bond itself. When interest checks are written, or when interest coupons are charged by the bank against the firm's account, the payment is recorded as an expense and a decrease in cash:

June 1	Interest Expense	3,000	
	Cash		3,000

Accrual of interest At the end of the fiscal year, any interest expense that has been incurred but not yet paid is accrued. The expense and a liability for the unpaid interest are recognized. If we assume that the fiscal year ends on November 30, interest for a full six months ($3,000) would have accrued since the last interest payment on the $100,000, 6 percent bonds discussed above. This interest of $3,000, due to be paid on the following day, is classified as expense and liability by the following journal entry:

Nov. 30	Interest Expense	3,000	
	Interest Payable		3,000

When the payment is made on the following day, December 1, the classification of data will be:

Dec. 1	Interest Payable	3,000	
	Cash		3,000

Amortizing bond discount At the end of the year, accounts are adjusted to show interest cost according to the terms under which bonds were issued.

The issue of $100,000, 6 percent, ten-year, semiannual interest bonds to yield the lender 7 percent was illustrated in a preceding section. These bonds are issued to cost the firm 7 percent per year on the amount of the debt. The computation of periodic interest and the amortizing of discount are shown in the following partial schedule, which contains the first three years of the ten-year period.

If the fiscal year of the firm ends on November 30, the interest expense for the year ended November 30, 1971, is the total of the interest expense amounts for the two six-month periods making up the year, or $6,511. Interest actually paid or accrued during the year is $6,000. The additional $511 is interest expense that will not be paid until maturity of the note, when the firm will pay the lender $7,103 more than was received at the issue of the bond. The firm received $92,897, but will pay back $100,000 in addition to the regular interest payments. The $511 interest incurred but not paid this year is added to interest expense and to the balance of the bond liability, as shown in the following journal entry.

INTEREST AND AMORTIZATION SCHEDULE

$100,000, 6 Percent, Ten-year, Semiannual Interest Bonds
Issued to Yield 7 Percent

Date	(a) Interest Payment— Cash Credit	(b) Interest Expense Debit	(c) Bond Discount Credit	(d) Bond Liability Balance
Dec. 1, 1970	–	–	–	$92,897
June 1, 1971	$3,000	$3,251	$251	93,148
Dec. 1, 1971	3,000	3,260	260	93,408
June 1, 1972	3,000	3,269	269	93,677
Dec. 1, 1972	3,000	3,279	279	93,956
June 1, 1973	3,000	3,289	289	94,245
Dec. 1, 1973	3,000	3,299	299	94,544

(a) Actual cash paid.
(b) $\frac{1}{2} \times$ 7 percent $\times$ preceding amount in (d).
(c) Column (b) minus (a).
(d) Preceding amount in (d) plus (c) on current line.

Nov. 30	Interest Expense..................................	511	
	Discount on Bonds Payable		511

The preceding entry amortizes $511 of the original discount on the bond. The balance in the Discount on Bonds Payable account is now $6,592 ($7,103 − 511); the face of the bond minus this amount ($100,000 − 6,592) gives the bond liability a balance of $93,408, which is the same as that shown on the December 1, 1971, line of the preceding schedule. Amortizing the bond discount will increase the bond liability to $100,000 by the maturity date.

Amortizing bond premium The $100,000, 7 percent, ten-year, semiannual interest bond issued to yield the lender (or to cost the firm) 6 percent, the issuance of which was recorded in a preceding section of this chapter, is the basis for the interest and premium amortization table on the following page.

If we again assume that the fiscal year of the firm ends on November 30, the interest expense for the year ending November 30, 1971, would be the total of the two interest expense amounts shown on the schedule on June 1, 1971, and December 1, 1971. The total of these is $6,437, while the cash interest payments total $7,000. The difference of $563 is the amount of payments in excess of the scheduled interest; this amount is classified as a reduction in the recorded interest ex-

INTEREST AND AMORTIZATION SCHEDULE

$100,000, 7 Percent, Ten-year*, Semiannual Interest Bonds
Issued to Yield 6 Percent

Date	(a) Interest Payment— Cash Credit	(b) Interest Expense Debit	(c) Bond Premium Debit	(d) Bond Liability Balance
Dec. 1, 1970	—	—	—	$107,441
June 1, 1971	$3,500	$3,223	$277	107,134
Dec. 1, 1971	3,500	3,214	286	106,848
June 1, 1972	3,500	3,205	295	106,553
Dec. 1, 1972	3,500	3,197	303	106,250
June 1, 1973	3,500	3,188	312	105,938
Dec. 1, 1973	3,500	3,178	322	105,616

(a) Actual cash paid.
(b) ½ × 6 percent × preceding amount in (d).
(c) Column (a) minus (b).
(d) Preceding amount in (d) minus (c) on current line.
* Seven years are omitted to shorten this schedule illustration.

pense and as a reduction in the liability balance, or a return of a part of the money provided by the lender. The effect of this is recorded in a journal entry as follows:

Nov. 30	Premium on Bonds Payable	563	
	Interest Expense...........................		563

This journal entry amortizes $563 of the original premium of $7,441 on the bond. The balance of the Premium on Bonds Payable account is reduced to $6,848, and the liability balance is the total of this and the face amount of the bonds, or $106,848. Amortizing the bond premium will reduce the amount of the liability to $100,000 by maturity date.

Methods of amortization: scientific and straight-line In the preceding sections the bond premium and discount were amortized by first computing the amount of interest expense according to the interest yield indicated by the issue price of the bonds. The difference between this computed interest and the actual interest payments was amortized as a reduction in bond discount or premium. This procedure results in an accurate measurement of interest income in accordance with the conditions under which the firm borrowed the funds. It is called the scientific, or actuarial, method of amortization.

A simpler procedure, which results in a reasonable approximation of interest expense, is straight-line amortization of premium and discount. This method amortizes an equal amount of the premium or discount each year. The discount of $7,103 on the $100,000, 6 percent bond issued to yield 7 percent would be divided by the number of years to maturity of the bond (ten, in this instance) to determine the amount of the annual discount amortization. The following tables show semiannual interest payments with annual straight-line amortization of discount and premium for the same bonds shown in the preceding schedules.

INTEREST AND AMORTIZATION SCHEDULE

$100,000, 6 Percent, Ten-year, Semiannual Interest Bonds—Straight-line Amortization of Discount

Date	Interest Payment—Cash Credit	Interest Expense Debit	Bond Discount Credit	Bond Liability Balance
Dec. 1, 1970	–	–	–	$92,897
June 1, 1971	$3,000	$3,000		
Dec. 1, 1971	3,000	3,000		
Dec. 1, 1971		710	$710	93,607
June 1, 1972	3,000	3,000		
Dec. 1, 1972	3,000	3,000		
Dec. 1, 1972		710	710	94,317
June 1, 1973	3,000	3,000		
Dec. 1, 1973	3,000	3,000		
Dec. 1, 1973		710	710	95,027

INTEREST AND AMORTIZATION SCHEDULE

$100,000, 7 Percent, Ten-year, Semiannual Interest Bonds—Straight-line Amortization of Premium

Date	Interest Payment—Cash Credit	Interest Expense Debit (Credit)	Bond Premium Debit	Bond Liability Balance
Dec. 1, 1970	–	–	–	$107,441
June 1, 1971	$3,500	$3,500		
Dec. 1, 1971	3,500	3,500		
Dec. 1, 1971		(744)	$744	106,697
June 1, 1972	3,500	3,500		
Dec. 1, 1972	3,500	3,500		
Dec. 1, 1972		(744)	744	105,953
June 1, 1973	3,500	3,500		
Dec. 1, 1973	3,500	3,500		
Dec. 1, 1973		(744)	744	105,209

Payment of bonds at maturity By a bond's maturity date, all premium and discount should be amortized. On that date the balance of the bond liability, as shown by data in the accounting system, should be the face amount of the bonds. When the bonds are paid, the data are classified to reduce the Bonds Payable account and to reduce the Cash account. In journal form, this entry for the $100,000 of bonds used in prior illustrations is as follows:

Dec. 1	Bonds Payable	100,000	
1980	Cash		100,000

Redemption of bonds before maturity When bonds are paid they are said to be *redeemed.* A firm may find it financially advantageous to redeem bonds before maturity. If interest rates have dropped since the bonds were issued, they can be redeemed only by paying more than the scientific carrying value, or balance, of the bonds. If interest rates have risen, the bonds can be redeemed at less than their scientifically computed balance, because a lower bond value yields a higher rate of interest.

When bonds are redeemed before maturity, the amount paid is compared with the balance of the liability according to the firm's records, and the difference is classified as a gain or loss from early redemption of the bonds. Assume that the $100,000 of 6 percent bonds, issued for $92,897 (to yield 7 percent), were redeemed for $94,800 on December 1, 1973. If the firm has used scientific amortization, the balance of the liability is $94,544 (from the scientific amortization schedule) on the redemption date. The journal entry to record the redemption is:

Dec. 1	Bonds Payable	100,000	
1973	Loss on Bond Redemption	256	
	Discount on Bonds Payable		5,456
	Cash		94,800

If the firm has used straight-line amortization of bond discount, the balance of the bond liability according to the records is $95,027 (see the straight-line amortization schedule). This balance, compared with the amount paid, indicates a gain on redemption. The journal entry recording the redemption for $94,800 is:

Dec. 1	Bonds Payable	100,000	
1973	Discount on Bonds Payable		4,973
	Gain on Bond Redemption		227
	Cash		94,800

It should be noted that the data classification for the bond redemption cancels all data from the accounts representing the liability (Bonds Payable, and Discount on Bonds Payable) and reflects the changes in assets and the gain or loss. If only a part of the bonds were redeemed, the appropriate fraction of all of the data would be involved.

BOND SINKING FUND

As part of the agreement when bonds are issued, the firm may annually set aside money for a fund to be used to redeem the bonds at maturity. Such a fund is called a *sinking fund.* Money and other assets accumulated in a bond sinking fund are reported as long-term assets under the balance sheet heading of Investments or Other Assets.

Payments into the bond sinking fund are recorded as an increase in the asset account, Bond Sinking Fund. The following entry records an annual payment into a sinking fund which is to accumulate $100,000 in ten years at 6 percent:

Dec. 1	Bond Sinking Fund	7,600	
1971	Cash		7,600

Assume that at the end of the following year the fund has earned $456 and another payment is to be made into it. The journal entries for these two events are:

Dec. 1	Bond Sinking Fund	456	
1972	Sinking Fund Income		456
Dec. 1	Bond Sinking Fund	7,600	
	Cash		7,600

The sinking fund should accumulate enough, through earnings and payments, so that $100,000 will be available in it to redeem the bonds at maturity. To redeem the bonds the fund is transferred back into the Cash account so that a check can be written for the full amount; then the maturity amount of the bonds is paid. Journal entries for these events are:

Dec. 1	Cash	100,000	
1980	Bond Sinking Fund		100,000
Dec. 1	Bonds Payable	100,000	
	Cash		100,000

The sinking fund is not an essential element of the bond issue. The fund may be required by some bond agreements. In other cases it may be set up voluntarily by management as a reasonable way of accumulating funds with which to redeem the bonds.

REPORTING BONDS PAYABLE

Bonds payable normally are long-term liabilities and are reported under that heading on the balance sheet. Usually bonds are redeemed with funds accumulated in a sinking fund or in various investments. Even when bonds will mature within a year they normally are reported as long-term liabilities because they will be paid with funds reported among the long-term, rather than current, assets. In the rare case in which the amount of bonds maturing within the year is small and will be paid from cash accumulated in the ordinary operating Cash account, bonds currently maturing will be reported as current liabilities.

Reporting Bond Premium on the Balance Sheet

Premium on bonds payable is the amount exceeding the face amount which the firm received when it issued the bonds. A lender (investor) is willing to pay more than the face amount for a bond because the regular interest payments are more than the amount he demands as interest. A portion of each interest payment is considered a payment of principle; the bond premium will be paid back to the lender through these regular interest payments. The final installment of principle will not be paid until the last interest payment is made. At any time the amount of premium on bonds payable is reported with the face amount of the bond as an additional long-term liability. This reporting might appear as follows:

Long-term Liabilities		
Bonds payable (7 percent, semiannual interest payments, maturing in December, 1980)............	100,000	
Unamortized premium on 7 percent bonds payable...	5,616	$105,616

Reporting Bond Discount on the Balance Sheet

Discount on bonds payable is the amount by which the maturity value of the bonds exceeds the amount the firm received when the bonds were issued. This amount that will be paid, in addition to the regular interest payments, for the use of the borrowed money is additional cost of using money, or additional interest. It is interest which is being incurred, but which will not be paid until maturity of the bonds. At the time bonds are issued, the interest represented by the discount has not been used, and the discount is not considered a part of the debt; it is deducted from the face amount of the bonds in reporting long-term liabilities. As the interest is used and the discount is amortized, the amount of unamortized discount decreases year by year. Since the unamortized discount is deducted from the face amount of the bonds each time it is reported, the amount of the reported liability increases as the unamortized discount becomes smaller. At maturity, the liability on the bonds would be reported at its full maturity value.

Bonds payable and the related unamortized discount would be presented on the balance sheet under the heading of Long-term Liabilities as follows:

Long-term Liabilities		
Bonds payable (6 percent, semiannual interest payments, maturing in December, 1980)	$100,000	
Unamortized discount on 6 percent bonds payable ...	5,456	$94,544

DEFERRED INCOME TAXES

The business firm is not required to use the same depreciation rate for computing its federally taxable income and for reporting net income on the income statement. If an accelerated depreciation method is used for tax purposes with straight-line depreciation used for financial reporting, the resulting data may mislead the reader of the income statement. Under these conditions it would be possible for a series of income statements to misrepresent the firm substantially if the income tax actually paid were reported as the tax expense on the income statement.

Effect of Varying Taxes on Net Income

The following series of four annual income statements is based on the assumptions that operations are stable and that tax expense should be reported as the income tax actually paid; the only yearly change is in the depreciation, computed by the sum-of-years'-digits method for tax purposes.

	First Year		Second Year		Third Year		Fourth Year	
	Income Statement	Tax Reported	Income Statement	Tax Reported	Income Statement	Tax Reported	Income Statement	Tax Reported
Revenue	$600*	$600	$600	$600	$600	$600	$600	$600
Operating expense	$300	$300	$300	$300	$300	$300	$300	$300
Depreciation	100	160	100	120	100	80	100	40
	$400	$460	$400	$420	$400	$380	$400	$340
Taxable income		$140		$180		$220		$260
Net income before taxes	$200		$200		$200		$200	
Income tax (50 percent)	70		90		110		130	
Net income	$130		$110		$ 90		$ 70	

* All figures in table represent thousands of dollars.

It appears that net income decreases from $130,000 to $70,000 in the four years. Note that depreciation in the computation of taxable income begins at a high of $160,000 compared with the straight-line depreciation of $100,000. The tax depreciation decreases to $120,000 the second year, and then to $80,000 and $40,000, while the straight-line depreciation on the income statement remains at $100,000. The accelerated depreciation has a decided effect on the timing of the tax payments. The tax paid in the illustration varies from a low of $70,000 the first year to a high of $130,000 the fourth year. If straight-line depreciation had been used for tax purposes, the same total tax ($400,000) would have been paid in the four-year period, but it would have been paid at the level of $100,000 each year.

Improved Reporting of Tax Expense

The Accounting Principles Board of the AICPA has indicated that **the income tax expense used on the income statement should relate to the net income reported and should not necessarily be the income tax actually paid for the year.** In the preceding illustration, this would result in reporting as expense some income tax which would not be paid for two more years. Study the following schedule to see that the amount of tax reported as an expense but not paid is classified as a liability. In later years, when the amount of tax actually paid is greater than the expense for the year, the excess is applied as a payment of the deferred income tax liability.

Journal entries recording data for the income tax expense, the

	First Year		Second Year		Third Year		Fourth Year	
	Income Statement	Tax Reported	Income Statement	Tax Reported	Income Statement	Tax Reported	Income Statement	Tax Reported
Revenue	$600*	$600	$600	$600	$600	$600	$600	$600
Operating expense	$300	$300	$300	$300	$300	$300	$300	$300
Depreciation	100	160	100	120	100	80	100	40
	$400	$460	$400	$420	$400	$380	$400	$340
Taxable income		$140		$180		$220		$260
Net income before taxes	$200		$200		$200		$200	
Income tax	100		100		100		100	
Net income	$100		$100		$100		$100	
Income tax expense	$100		$100		$100		$100	
Income tax paid	70		90		110		130	
Deferred income tax liability	$ 30		$ 10		−$ 10		−$ 30	

* All figures in table represent thousands of dollars.

deferred income tax, and the payment of taxes are presented below for the four years.

First Year:

Dec. 31	Income Tax Expense	100,000	
	Income Tax Payable		70,000
	Deferred Income Taxes		30,000
Mar. 15	Income Tax Payable	70,000	
	Cash		70,000

Second Year:

Dec. 31	Income Tax Expense	100,000	
	Income Tax Payable		90,000
	Deferred Income Taxes		10,000
Mar. 15	Income Tax Payable	90,000	
	Cash		90,000

Third Year:

Dec. 31	Income Tax Expense	100,000	
	Deferred Income Taxes	10,000	
	Income Tax Payable		110,000
Mar. 15	Income Tax Payable	110,000	
	Cash		110,000

Fourth Year:

Dec. 31	Income Tax Expense	100,000	
	Deferred Income Taxes	30,000	
	Income Tax Payable		130,000
Mar. 15	Income Tax Payable	130,000	
	Cash		130,000

Not all situations in the business world are as simple as the preceding illustration, but the same basic procedures apply. The deferred income tax liability is not legally enforceable and depends upon the firm's continuing at a profitable level of operations. It is based much more on economic argument than on legal affirmation of the debt. The deferred income taxes are normally reported as a long-term liability.

LIABILITY FOR PENSIONS

Recognition and measurement of a firm's liability under its employee pension plan may be more difficult than for most other liabilities. Pension plans may vary greatly as to when employees obtain rights and as to patterns of employer payment. The employer may pay into a fund out of which pensions will be paid, or he may assume the responsibility of setting up a fund at the retirement of the employee, or he may make the pension payments directly.

The most common attribute of pension plans is probably the employer's responsibility for developing a fund, which will be turned over to an insurance company when the employee retires and will pay the employee a lifelong annuity. If the plan is operating when the employee is hired, then at the end of the first year the employer has developed a liability for the agreed percent of the employee's wages. If we assume that the employee earned $10,000 and that the percent of earnings to be accumulated as a retirement fund is 5 percent, the expense and liability at the year's end would be recorded by this journal entry:

Dec. 31	Pension Expense	500	
	Pension Liability		500

The employer's liability for pension payments, based on wages earned after the plan is adopted, is not a difficult concept; however, requirements of some plans are difficult to interpret and apply. When a plan is adopted the pensions promised to employees often are based on the total wages earned since employment, not since adoption of the plan. Measuring the employer's liability for service of employees prior to the plan's adoption has been most difficult. The Accounting Principles Board of the AICPA did not take a strong position in its Opinion no. 8, issued in November, 1966. It indicated that employers might accrue the liability for prior services over a period of at least ten years, charging the amounts to expense as they become a liability over this period of time. Also, the APB Opinion no. 8 indicated that employers might not accrue the liability for prior services at all, based on what appears to be faulty reasoning. It specifies that under no circumstances should the cost of the pension plan related to service of employees prior to adoption of the plan be charged against retained earnings; all benefits of the plan are received after its adoption and, therefore, all cost should be reported as expense after the adoption date.

The liability of some firms for pension plans is substantial. Standards for reporting this significant liability are not yet clearly specified, although considerable progress has been made in clarifying the pension situation and preparing the way for more standardization in reporting.

QUESTIONS AND EXERCISES

11-A. Define liabilities. What part of this definition distinguishes liabilities from other claims against the firm?

11-B. What are unearned collections? Are these liabilities that will be paid in cash? How will they be paid?

11-C. How do notes payable and accounts payable differ from unearned collections?

11-D. The face amount of a long-term note or bond that will be paid in the future is reported as a liability. Why are the amounts of interest that will be paid on such a note in the future not reported as liabilities?

11-E. If $221.40 of FICA taxes are withheld from employees' wages by a firm, how much total FICA taxes will be paid by the firm on that payroll?

11-F. Explain the difference between the coupon or face rate and the yield rate on a bond. Under what conditions will the two rates be equal?

11-G. Why might a firm use the actuarial or scientific amortization of premium or discount on bonds payable?

11-H. How does a liability for deferred income taxes arise? How should it be reported on the balance sheet?

11-I. A $7\frac{1}{2}$ percent bond due 12 years from now is selling to yield $7\frac{1}{4}$ percent. What does this statement mean? Is the selling price greater than, equal to, or less than the face amount?

11-J. How would you describe discount on bonds payable to make it understandable to a person who has not studied long-term liabilities in detail?

11-K. Why is discount on bonds payable reported as a deduction from long-term liabilities and premium as an addition to such liabilities?

11-L. On what basis might some argue that discounts on bonds should be reported as assets?

11-M. Why is a firm's liability for employee pensions more difficult to measure than most other liabilities?

11-N. What is the distinction between current liabilities and long-term liabilities?

11-O. Explain warranty liabilities. Why should they be reported on the balance sheet?

11-P. How much could your firm obtain upon the issue of a $1,000, ten-year bond with a coupon rate of 8 percent paid semiannually, priced to yield 7 percent paid semiannually?

PROCEDURAL PROBLEMS

✓11-1. The information below is taken from the payroll records of Wilson Paper Company for the pay period ended April 20.

Employee	Earnings in Prior Periods	Earnings This Period	Income Tax Withheld	Group Insurance Withheld	Savings Bonds Withheld
A	$11,400	$ 900	$220	$21	$ 0
B	7,400	600	100	8	20
C	2,600	450	60	0	20
D	4,700	550	85	0	0
E	4,800	400	40	4	0
F	2,800	300	45	11	20
		$3,200	$550	$44	$60

a. Prepare the journal entry to record salary expense and liabilities for employee withholding. Show supporting computations.

b. Prepare the journal entry to record employer's payroll taxes. The state unemployment tax rate is 2 percent.

11-2. Simmons Corporation has established a bond sinking fund to retire $200,000 of bonds in ten years. Each year the corporation makes a contribution of $17,000. All money in the fund is invested at 5 percent interest.

a. If the sinking fund is started December 31, 1960, prepare the journal entries for 1960, 1961, 1962 to record the contributions to the fund and the fund income.

b. If at the end of ten years the balance of the sinking fund is $197,000, prepare the entry to record the additional required contribution and the entry to retire the bonds.

✓ 11-3. Shackleford, Inc., had the following revenue, operating expenses, and depreciation charges. The tax rate is 50 percent for each year. Prepare the computations of tax expense and liability, and prepare the journal entry for each year.

	1967		1968		1969	
	Income Statement	Tax Return	Income Statement	Tax Return	Income Statement	Tax Return
Revenue............	$600,000	$600,000	$800,000	$800,000	$600,000	$600,000
Operating Expenses......	200,000	200,000	300,000	300,000	300,000	300,000
Depreciation.......	80,000	160,000	80,000	100,000	80,000	60,000

11-4. The Hines Corporation issued on January 1, 1969, a $100,000, 6 percent, four-year bond with interest payable on June 30 and December 31.

a. Compute the amount Hines Corporation will receive if the bond is sold to yield 8 percent, and prepare the journal entry to record the issuance.
b. Prepare an interest and amortization schedule for the four years using scientific amortization.
c. Prepare the entry recording the redemption of the bonds on June 30, 1971, for $97,100.
d. Prepare a partial balance sheet for December 31, 1971, showing the long-term liability section.

11-5. The Hines Corporation, on October 1, 1969, issued a $100,000, 8 percent, eight-year bond with interest payable on September 30 and March 31.

a. Compute the amount Hines Corporation will receive if the bond is issued to yield 6 percent, and prepare the journal entry to record the issuance.
b. Prepare the interest and amortization schedule from date of issuance through the interest payment of March 31, 1972, using scientific amortization.
c. Prepare the September 30, 1970, entry to record the payment of interest and the amortization of premium for the fiscal year ended September 30.
d. Assuming the company pays $104,000 to redeem the bonds on March 31, 1972, prepare the journal entry.

11-6. Linne, Incorporated issued on January 1, 1970, a five-year, 8 percent stated interest, $100,000 par value bond. Interest is paid each June 30 and December 31. The discount or premium amortization is journalized only at the end of the year.

a. The bond is issued to yield 6 percent. Compute the present value, and prepare the entry to record the issuance.
b. Prepare an interest and amortization schedule for the bond using scientific amortization based on six-month interest periods.
c. Journalize the June 30, 1971, interest payment.
d. Journalize the amortization on December 31, 1972.
e. The bond was redeemed on January 1, 1973, for $103,420.00. Journalize.

11-7. Peterson Sales Corporation divides its employee compensation into sales commissions and office salaries. Sales commissions are 6 percent of total sales; office salaries are $2,000 per week. An average of 20 percent of the sales commissions and office salaries are withheld as the employees' income tax. The state unemployment tax rate is 3 percent. The stock purchase plan is a 2 percent contribution of gross salary from all employees, matched by the corporation. The corporation works a normal Monday through Friday week. Sales for the week ended Friday, July 2, were $150,000 spread equally through the week. Prepare the entries to record payroll expenses and the corporation's payroll taxes as of June 30. (Ignore possible limitations on FICA and state unemployment tax.)

11-8. On October 1, 1968, the Tapley Corporation issued a $100,000, 5 percent bond with a five-year life for $104,000. Interest is paid each March 31 and September 30. The company uses straight-line amortization. The company has a sinking fund for bond retirement to which it contributes $16,000 each September 30.

a. Prepare the March 31 and September 30 entries to record the payment of interest and the September 31, 1969, entry to record amortization for that year and sinking fund contribution.
b. The company redeems the bonds on October 1, 1971, for $103,800. The balance of the sinking fund is $51,100. Journalize.

✓ 11-9.

Bond Issue	Par Value	Interest Rate (in percent) Stated	Effective	Date Issued	Date of Maturity	Interest Paid	Amortization Method
A	$100,000	6	7	January 1, 1970	December 31, 1975	Annually	Scientific
B	$200,000	7	6	January 1, 1970	December 31, 1979	Semi-annually	Scientific
C	$ 50,000	4	6	January 1, 1970	December 31, 1977	Semi-annually	Straight-line
D	$100,000	6	5	January 1, 1970	December 31, 1974	Annually	Scientific

a. For each of the four bond issues extend the schedule to show the proceeds, the amount of the discount or premium, and the periodic cash interest payment.
b. If bond issue C is amortized using the straight-line method, what is the annual interest expense?
c. Prepare the entry to record the issuance of bond D.
d. Prepare the entry to record the June 30, 1970, interest payment and amortization of bond B.
e. If bond C is redeemed on January 1, 1973, for $52,000, prepare the entry.

f. Considering each bond to be a separate issue of Volpe Construction Company, prepare the long-term liability section of their January 1, 1970, balance sheet.

11-10. The Maritime Construction Company normally does subcontracting for other shipyards. Its revenue from this service was $1,200,000 each year for 1968–71, with expenses of $900,000 each year. During 1968 the company accepted a special project, collecting revenue of $1,600,000 in cash and incurring expenses of $1,000,000 evenly over four years. The company was required to report all revenues for this project on its 1968 tax return, but decided to allocate revenue over a four-year period for its income statement. It charged prepaid income taxes for the excess payment for 1968.

a. Prepare a tax allocation schedule for 1968–71, assuming a 50 percent tax rate.

b. Prepare the December 31 entry for each of the four years to record the tax expense and tax liability.

11-11. The August sales summary for Meyerson Drug Store shows that total recorded for the month's sales was $120,000. The state sales tax rate is 4 percent.

a. If the store collects and records sales tax as each sale is made, compute the sales tax liability for August.

b. If the store does not identify sales tax at the time of the sale, compute the sales tax liability and prepare the adjusting entry.

c. Using the amount computed in (a) above, prepare the entry to record the payment to the state.

11-12. On January 1, 1967, the Porter Corporation issued a five-year, 6 percent, $100,000 par value bond with interest paid each June 30 and December 31. The bond discount or premium is amortized each interest payment date. Each December 31 the company transfers $18,000 to a sinking fund for bond redemption.

a. The bond is issued to yield 7 percent. Journalize.

b. Prepare an interest and amortization schedule for the five years using scientific amortization method.

c. Journalize the December 31, 1967, transfer to sinking fund for bond redemption.

d. Prepare the December 31, 1968, entry to record fund income for the year of 1970.

e. Prepare the January 1, 1972, entries to close the sinking fund for bond redemption and redeem the bonds. The sinking fund income for the five years was $10,700.

CONCEPTUAL PROBLEMS

11-13. The Danbar Corporation has a noncontributory employee pension plan to provide pensions for employees who retire at age 65 or later. The amount of pension is based on each employee's length of service and total earnings before retirement. The expense to the company computed for this year is 4 percent of the payroll, or $610,000; this amount is recorded also as an addition to pension liability. Cash in this amount is transferred to a special fund which, with its accumulated earnings, will be used to pay pensions. The company's contributions to the fund for each employee will "vest" with him after ten years' service; if he leaves the company after ten years' service but before he reaches age 65, he receives a pension at age 65 on the basis of the contribution for him while he was employed by Danbar.

The marketing manager is disturbed by the company's lack of funds for long-term market development. In searching the company's finances for available funds, he finds that of the $610,000 paid into the pension fund this year, approximately $280,000 is for employees with less than ten years' service. He argues that many of these relatively new employees will not remain long enough for their funds to vest and, therefore, that the company should reduce the amount of the expense and liability and, also, reduce the amount in the special pension fund. Danbar's controller disagrees and argues that the full $610,000 should be shown as an addition to the company's liabilities and that the full contribution should remain in the pension fund.

a. How should the probability that many employees will not remain with the company for the required ten years have been taken into account in computing or estimating the amount of expense and liability for the year's payroll? Do you know that it was not taken into account in arriving at the 4 percent contribution?
b. Would it be appropriate to report no expense and no liability for an employee until he has been employed by Danbar for ten years? What rationale supports your position?

11-14. Sandford, Incorporated is planning to expand its manufacturing plant, but the expansion will require $5,000,000 of new, long-term capital. The proposed expansion is expected to increase net income before taxes (and before deducting additional interest, in case bonds are issued) to $2,700,000 from the present net income of $1,600,000. It appears feasible to obtain the additional funds by issuance of 7 percent, twenty-year bonds or additional capital stock. The company currently has no long-term debt. The stock of Sandford, Inc. is currently selling for $8 per share, and there are one million shares outstanding as seen from current balance sheet information:

Capital stock, 1,000,000 shares at $4 par value	$4,000,000
Premium on capital stock	800,000
Retained earnings	2,300,000
Total	$7,100,000

a. What effect on net income per share of capital stock would occur, if (assuming 50 percent income tax rate):
   1. The funds are borrowed.
   2. The funds are obtained by issue of stock.
b. Under which plan is Sandford, Inc. most firmly bound to make payments of cash for use of the funds? For repayment?

11-15. DeSalCo, Inc. built a seawater desalinization plant near an island military base for a total cost of $20,000,000. A special income tax provision allows DeSalCo to depreciate the plant at 20 percent per year (on a straight-line basis) for tax purposes. The plant has an expected life of twenty years with no salvage value beyond dismantling costs. Straight-line depreciation will be used for financial reporting. The corporation was organized especially to operate this plant, which is its only depreciable asset. Income before depreciation and 50 percent income taxes is expected to be $8,000,000 each year from January 1, 1971, when the plant went into operation.

a. Compute the company's net income after taxes for the years 1971 and 1976 as it would appear on income statements for those years.
b. Compute the balance in the Deferred Income Taxes account at the end of each year, 1971 through 1977.

12 Reporting Owners' Equity

Preview Questions

As you study look for the answers to the following questions:

- **How is owners' equity information reported?**
- **What are the three legal statuses of firms?**
- **How do the claims and rights of shareholders differ from those of proprietors and partners?**
- **What is book value per share?**
- **How is paid-in capital received by a corporation?**
- **How may shares be issued?**
- **What is capital stock?**
- **What is meant by "splitting" stock?**
- **What is a cash dividend?**
- **What is a stock dividend?**
- **What is treasury stock? How is it related to retained earnings?**
- **What are executive stock options?**
- **What are convertible bonds?**

Information about the equity, or claims, of owners of the firm is reported according to the legal status of the firm as a proprietorship, partnership, or corporation. The amount of owners' equity is not measured by the present value of the firm's assets, but by the amount of funds invested in the firm and the amount of earnings (net income) accumulated by it.

LEGAL STATUS OF THE FIRM

The combination of capital and people that makes up a business firm may operate with the legal status of a sole proprietorship, a partnership, or a corporation. Within these various legal structures the rights and claims of the owners are different. We will examine these differences in some detail.

Sole Proprietorship

A firm may operate with all its properties belonging to one person and without the firm's having any legal rights or responsibilities. In such a situation the owner, or proprietor, owns the assets personally and owes to creditors the amounts indicated as liabilities. The sole-proprietorship firm is not a legal entity; it has no existence as a unit in matters of property ownership, rights, and obligations. Such a firm is made up of the persons and properties identified with some economic endeavor such as a retail store, a movie theatre, a parking garage, etc. The sole proprietorship is an economic entity, not a legal entity.

The equity of a sole proprietorship's owner is reported as his capital in the firm. Normally an account with a title such as *Jack Jones, Capital* is used to accumulate all data reflecting changes in the owner's capital. These changes might involve his resources invested in the firm (increases), periodic net income (increases) or net losses (decreases), or withdrawals of capital (decreases). In a sole proprietorship the effects of all these changes normally are summarized in one capital account. In the summarizing process other accounts are used for partial summaries, as seen in the following series of transactions and data transfers.

Income summary account Revenue and expense accounts contain data reflecting the inflow of earned resources and the consumption of resources for a period of time. At the end of the period, these data are summarized by transferring them from the various revenue and expense accounts to one Income Summary account (alternatively called Profit and Loss account, P & L account, or Revenue and Expense Summary account). The following entries illustrate this process.

To close revenue accounts (transfer data to the summary account):

Dec. 31	Sales Revenue	50,000	
	Service Revenue	20,000	
	Income Summary		70,000

To close merchandise accounts and record new inventory:

Dec. 31	Income Summary	48,600	
	Merchandise Inventory (new)	20,000	
	Purchase Discounts	1,400	
	Purchase Returns and Allowances	1,000	
	Purchases		48,000
	Merchandise Inventory (old)		23,000

To close expense accounts (transfer data to the summary account):

Dec. 31	Income Summary	13,000	
	Salaries Expense		8,000
	Rent Expense		2,000
	Depreciation Expense		1,800
	Miscellaneous Expenses		1,200

After these transfers of data to the Income Summary account, all revenue and expense accounts are balanced; positive and negative inputs to these accounts are equal, and the accounts, therefore, have balances of zero. All revenue and expense data are summarized in the one account, Income Summary. In the preceding illustration, this account has a credit balance of $8,400, indicating a net income of this amount.

When all revenue and expense accounts are summarized in the Income Summary account, the balance of this account is transferred to the owner's capital account. The balance of the Income Summary account is the amount of the net income for the period; this amount is used as a negative input to the Income Summary account and a positive input to the Capital account. The journal entry for this transfer is:

Dec. 31	Income Summary	8,400	
	Jack Jones, Capital		8,400

Proprietor's drawing account The sole proprietor of a business firm may have the firm pay him (he may *draw* from the firm) amounts that represent compensation to him or that are expected to be offset by earnings of the firm. The reduction of his equity in the firm, occasioned by his drawing funds, normally is reflected by debits to a special account such as Jack Jones, Drawing. The total of data accumulated in this account is compared later with the amount of the net income and is transferred as a reduction in capital. The journal entry to close a drawing account with accumulated data totaling $7,200 is:

Dec. 31	Jack Jones, Capital	7,200	
	Jack Jones, Drawing		7,200

Proprietor's capital account A proprietor's capital account contains data showing all changes in the proprietor's equity in the firm. The following is an account containing examples of the basic changes:

Jack Jones, Capital

Dec.	31	Drawings		7200 00	Jan.	2	Investment		20000 00
					Dec.	31	Net Income		8400 00

The journal entry for a cash investment in the firm indicates the increase in cash and the owner's equity in the firm, as follows:

Jan. 2	Cash	20,000	
	Jack Jones, Capital		20,000

Journal entries for other changes in the capital account have been illustrated in connection with the income summary and proprietor's drawing accounts. Note that the proprietor's capital account summarizes the proprietor's equity in the firm that is derived from his investment and from net income exceeding the amount he has withdrawn from the firm.

Interpreting data from the capital account The balance in the proprietor's capital account does not indicate how much of his equity was derived from investment and how much from accumulated earnings of the firm. The proprietor's capital account, therefore, does not indicate with any precision the source of the firm's resources; it indicates only the total amount of the owner's equity in the firm. The amount of this equity is developed from flows of resources into and out of the firm, with resources measured by the amount of funds committed in them.

The capital account does not provide information about the present value of the proprietor's equity in the firm; the information provided is the total of funds invested and net resources added, as measured by the excess of profits over the proprietor's drawing.

Partnership

A partnership is a firm formed by two or more persons agreeing to share in the profits of an operation. Profits may be shared equally among partners, or each partner's share may be determined by such steps as computing interest on his investment, allowing an amount for his services, and distributing any remaining income or loss (deficit) by an agreed ratio. When a partnership is dissolved, each partner's share in the assets (after paying liabilities) usually is the amount in his capital account.

It should be noted that the partnership firm can own property, whereas the properties used by a sole-proprietorship firm are owned by the proprietor. In some states partnerships may own only personal property, and real estate must be owned by the partners personally; in other states partnerships may own both personal and real property. A partnership is both a legal and an economic entity; it is recognized by law, and its purpose is to perform an economic activity.

A partnership has been described as a continuously consensual relationship. This indicates that the firm can be dissolved by any partner's withdrawal from the firm. The withdrawing partner normally has the right to withdraw his share of the capital; this, of course, creates problems for the other partners if they want to continue business operations. Many articles of co-partnership (partnership agreements) provide for the remaining partners to operate the firm and to have a reasonable time (several months, or longer) to pay the withdrawing partner his share of the capital.

Partners' capital accounts The financial information (accounting) system will contain a capital account for each partner, showing the total of his investment and his share of profits that he has not withdrawn. When the partnership receives an investment from a partner, the amount is recorded as an increase in cash (or some other asset) and an increase in that partner's capital account. An investment of $6,000 by Mr. Jones and $8,000 by Mr. Sanchez would be recorded as follows:

Date	Account	Debit	Credit
Mar. 1	Cash	14,000	
	Jack Jones, Capital		6,000
	Simon Sanchez, Capital		8,000

When the partnership's revenues and expenses are closed into the Income Summary account, the net income (profit) is then transferred to the partners' capital accounts. This is accomplished by closing the Income Summary account with a debit for the amount of the net income (or a credit for the amount of the net *loss*) and crediting each partner's capital account for his share of the net income. Assume a net income of $9,000 and a specification in the partnership agreement that Mr. Sanchez shall have $6,000 for his service to the firm with the remaining net income divided equally between the partners. Closing of the Income Summary account and distribution of the net income to the partners' capital accounts would be accomplished by the following journal entry:

Mar. 31	Income Summary	9,000	
	Jack Jones, Capital		1,500
	Simon Sanchez, Capital		7,500

When this entry is posted, the capital accounts will contain amounts for partners' investments and their shares in the net income. Of course, any withdrawals of money from the firm will reduce the capital accounts.

Partners' drawing accounts As with the sole proprietorship, a partner's withdrawal of funds as compensation or in anticipation of net income will result in a reduction of his capital. The withdrawals might be made regularly (equal monthly amounts, for example), or at any time a partner needs the funds and it is agreed that the firm can afford the withdrawal. Payment of cash to a partner as withdrawal is recorded as follows:

Mar. 31	Simon Sanchez, Drawing	1,000	
	Cash		1,000

At the end of the fiscal period, partners' drawing accounts are closed into their capital accounts so that the capital accounts will show the amount of each partner's capital currently in the firm. Transfer of Mr. Sanchez' drawing to his capital account would be done as follows:

Mar. 31	Simon Sanchez, Capital	1,000	
	Simon Sanchez, Drawing		1,000

After the investments, income distribution, and drawing illustrated for Jones and Sanchez, their capital accounts would appear as follows:

Jack Jones, Capital

			Mar.	1	6000 00
			Mar.	31	1500 00

Simon Sanchez, Capital

Mar.	31	1000 00	Mar.	1	8000 00
			Mar.	31	7500 00

Interpreting data from partners' capital accounts Capital accounts contain data showing investments, plus shared profits, minus amounts drawn out of the firm. The resulting amount is not a measure of what the partner can take out of the firm if he dissolves it by withdrawing from the partnership. Upon dissolution of the firm its assets would be sold, perhaps to a successor firm belonging to the other partner or partners. Any gain or loss on this sale of assets is distributed to the partners' capital accounts; the new balance in the withdrawing partner's capital account would then indicate the value of his share in the firm. A partner's capital account normally does not show the present value of his interest in the firm until liquidating gains and losses are recorded. A partner might sell his interest in a firm for much more or much less than the balance in his capital account. If the firm is unprofitable and assets cannot be sold for their book value, then his interest probably is not worth as much as his capital account shows. If the firm is very profitable or if assets are worth more than their book value, a partner's interest probably is worth much more than the balance of this capital account.

It is important to recognize that, whereas the proprietor's capital account indicated his investment in the assets of the firm and his direct claim on the assets, a partner's capital account indicates his claim against the firm, but normally does not give an exact measure of the amount of that claim. The partner does not own any of the assets of the firm; he owns a claim against the firm for his share in the assets.

Corporation

From the preceding paragraphs it should be clear that the partnership is a legally recognized association of persons for the purpose of engaging in economic activity. The partnership is an association of certain specific individuals, and apart from those specific persons the partnership does not exist. However, a group of persons may associate themselves in such a way as to form a more permanent entity that can continue even though the persons who formed it transfer their interests and are no longer connected with it. When formed in accord with the appropriate state laws, this separate legal entity is termed a corporation.

Characteristics of the corporation The corporation is referred to and treated legally as a person. Important legal characteristics of the corporation are:

1. Separate legal existence; it may own property, enter into contracts, bring suit and be sued, and take other legal actions separate and apart from any of its shareholders.
2. Transferable investment units; investment in the corporation entitles the investors to transferable *shares* in the corporation. One may receive a fractional share or thousands of shares, depending on the amount of his investment. An investor's sale of his shares to another is an independent transaction between the investors; it does not affect the corporation financially.
3. Continued existence; the corporation continues in existence independently of its individual shareholders. So long as the corporate charter is not surrendered or forfeited, the corporation continues, even though none of the original investors may continue to own shares.
4. Limited liability of shareholders; as a separate legal entity, a corporation is responsible for its own obligations. Normally the property of a shareholder cannot be claimed by creditors for debts of the corporation. The potential loss of a shareholder, therefore, may be limited to the amount of his investment.
5. Governmental regulation; corporations are subject to more legal regulations and control than are sole proprietorships and partnerships. This is because corporations are created by law and investors in corporations have limited liability. States may restrict the corporate ownership of some kinds of property, control the distribution of earnings to shareholders and exercise other restrictions.
6. Corporation taxes; a filing fee must be paid to the state at the time of incorporation, and a franchise tax is paid annually thereafter. Also, federal and state income taxes are paid by corporations. Corporate earnings that are distributed to shareholders as dividends are taxable income to the shareholders for federal and state income tax purposes. State franchise taxes and corporation income taxes are additional costs of doing business as a corporation; these are offset by advantages, one of which is the ease of assembling a large amount of capital in the corporate structure.

Classes of capital stock Shares in the corporation may be all of one type, with each share giving its holder the same voting and dividend rights as afforded by every other share. However, the corporate charter can provide for some shares to confer advantages, or preferences, to their holders. The stock made up of these shares is called *preferred* stock, in contrast to the *common* stock, which carries no preferences.

Commonly the right to vote is withheld from holders of preferred stock. The preferences given can be one or more of those described below. Preferences normally are described in the corporate charter and on the preferred stock certificates.

Dividend preference Preferred stock usually has this preference, which requires that the board of directors declare a dividend of a stated rate or amount on preferred stock before a dividend can be declared on common stock. Preferred stock often carries the dividend rate or amount in its description. For example, 6 percent preferred and $3 preferred would give holders the right to a dividend of 6 percent of the par value of the stock in one case and the right to a dividend of $3 per share in the other.

Cumulative preference An additional preference may be that if a dividend is not declared on preferred stock during a year, the dividend accumulates and a two-year dividend must be paid the next year before any dividend to common stockholders. During a prolonged period of passing dividends, the cumulative feature can provide substantial financial protection to preferred shareholders.

Participating preference In some cases, especially in high-risk and high-profit potential companies, preferred stock may carry the right to participate with common stock in any dividend above a specified level for common. For example, a 6 percent participating preferred stock might participate equally per share with common stock in any dividend declared after the required 6 percent to preferred and a 10 percent divident to common.

Preference at liquidation Upon liquidation of the corporation preferred stockholders normally have the right to receive the full par value of their shares before common stockholders receive any payments. This is meaningful in cases in which there have been severe corporate losses.

Par value of shares An application for a corporate charter must specify the capital structure of the proposed corporation, giving the number and par value (if any) of shares which the state is asked to authorize for issue to investors. The par value becomes the measure of legal capital, as discussed in later paragraphs. Also, it serves as a basis for declaring dividends; a 6 percent dividend is 6 percent of the par value of shares outstanding. Par value of preferred shares indicates the amount of preferred shareholders' preferred claims in case the corporation liquidates. Par value does *not* indicate what the shares are worth.

Stated value of shares Sometimes one sees stock described in a corporate charter as no-par value, but with a *stated value* of a specified amount. *Stated value* has most of the attributes of par value; therefore, for data classification purposes, the two terms are treated alike. Stated value measures the legal capital (the amount recorded in a Capital Stock account) and serves as the basis for measuring dividends.

Shareholders' equity accounts Some of the restrictions and controls imposed on corporations necessitate specific information about the shareholders' equity in the corporation. This, in turn, determines the classifications of data (accounts) related to shareholders' equity.

Capital stock account Various states describe a part of the capital invested in a corporation as *stated capital,* or *legal capital.* These synonyms are used to indicate the part of invested capital which the corporation's board of directors cannot, by its own authority, diminish or dissipate. A dividend cannot be paid if it would reduce the capital of the corporation below this amount. The corporation cannot buy back some of its own shares if this action would reduce the capital below the legal capital amount. Normally, legal capital is measured by the *par value* of shares that have been issued. In case of shares without par value, the amount the corporation receives for such shares normally is designated as legal capital. There is not absolute uniformity among the states, but there is a general similarity of laws on this point. *Legal capital* (par value of shares issued, or amount received upon issue of no-par shares) is recorded in the Capital Stock account. If the corporation has more than one class of capital stock (or shares), a separate account may be used for each class, for example, Common Stock and Preferred Stock.

Paid-in capital in excess of par value A part of the capital paid in as investments by shareholders is classified as legal capital, and data measuring this are accumulated in a Capital Stock account. The remainder of the capital paid in by shareholders (amount exceeding the par value of shares issued to them) has a different legal significance. Data for this part of the paid-in capital are accumulated in an account, Paid-in Capital in Excess of Par. Alternate, simpler titles are Additional Paid-in Capital, Premium on Capital Stock, or Paid-in Surplus.

"Surplus" is a term apparently becoming outmoded. It was used to mean all capital in excess of legal capital, either paid in or earned by the corporation; thus the two terms, paid-in surplus and earned surplus (now, retained earnings) were used almost consistently, but are used less widely now.

Paid-in capital in excess of legal capital is restricted differently in the various states. In some states the board of directors can designate as dividends a return of this part of the original investment; in others this is not permitted. In all cases, this account and the Capital Stock account (or accounts) indicate the amount of corporate resources that were invested by shareholders.

Retained earnings account Part of the shareholders' equity in a corporation is developed by earnings of the company. When a corporation's earned inflow of resources (revenue) exceeds the consumption of resources (expenses), the result is a net increase in corporate resources. The equity in the increase in resources is indicated in the Retained Earnings account.

In the process of closing revenue and expense accounts, the balances are transferred to the Income Summary account. The balance in this account, which is the net income for the period, is transferred to the Retained Earnings account. The journal entry to accomplish this, and the resulting amounts in the Income Summary and the Retained Earnings accounts are as follows:

		Debit	Credit
Mar. 31	Income Summary	8,400	
	Retained Earnings		8,400

Income Summary

Debit	Credit
Mar. 31 Expense 61,600	Mar. 31 Revenue 70,000
31 Net income 8,400	
70,000	70,000

Retained Earnings

Debit	Credit
	Mar. 1 Balance 80,000
	31 Net income 8,400

Interpreting data from shareholders' equity accounts Amounts in the Capital Stock, Additional Paid-in Capital, and Retained Earnings accounts indicate how much of the firm's resources came from the shareholders and how much from the company's earnings. Although these accounts are called shareholders' equity accounts, it is doubtful that this is a good description in a large, widely held corporation. The rights of the shareholders are clearly limited. The shareholders cannot claim a return of their investments without dissolving the corporation. They cannot claim the retained earnings as a distribution of corporate earnings; shareholders receive a distribution of earnings as dividends when the board of directors declares a dividend. The nature of shareholders' rights makes it doubtful that their equity can be described as the total of the "shareholders' equity" accounts. Perhaps it would be more accurate to describe the amounts in the Capital Stock and Additional Paid-in Capital accounts as equity from shareholders, or paid-in equity, and to describe the amount in the Retained Earnings account as equity from earnings, or earned equity, rather than to refer to both equity classes as simply shareholders' equity.

In smaller, closely held corporations the shareholders are closer to the position of owners, in that they exercise greater control. This is possible not because they have more legal power, but because that power is concentrated in fewer shareholders, sometimes in one shareholder. In such corporations the term shareholders' equity, or even owners' equity, would be descriptive of paid-in and earned equity. All corporations may have the same legal status, but closely held and widely held corporations differ markedly in the degree of authority and control exercised by the shareholders.

Information about a corporation's invested and earned capital can be interpreted in a more strictly legalistic way. The total of this equity can be seen simply as the firm's capital, distinguished from debt capital. The three basic divisions of this capital, the Capital Stock, Additional Paid-in Capital, and Retained Earnings accounts, can be considered as the legal divisions of the capital. Legal capital is the more permanent part of the capital structure, the disposition of which is outside the authority of the board of directors. The additional paid-in capital (paid-in capital in excess of par value) is less restricted, with the board having somewhat different authority over its disposition in different states. The earned capital can be retained for company growth or paid out as dividends to shareholders at the discretion of the board of directors; the board has greatest control over this part of the capital.

To use information about the structure of corporate equity accounts intelligently, all the preceding interpretations and views must be recognized. The terms used on a specific financial report should not lead one to overemphasize or ignore any meaning of this information.

Book value per share The *book value* of shares is the shareholders' equity as indicated by the data in the accounting system. The book value per share for a company having only one class of stock is the shareholders' equity divided by the number of shares outstanding.

Shares outstanding The number of shares outstanding is the number owned by shareholders. This number could be determined by obtaining the total from the record of shares owned by individual shareholders, or from the stockholders' ledger. A simpler computation is to deduct any shares reacquired by the corporation (see treasury stock later in the chapter) from the number of shares issued. The result is the shares issued and still outstanding, or in the hands of shareholders. This number of shares for both common and preferred stock is used in computing the book value per share.

Preferred stock book value The shareholders' equity of preferred stockholders involves the specific rights and preferences of the preferred stock in a particular corporation. The par value (or liquidating or redemption value, if one is given) of the preferred stock, plus any dividend claims that have not been paid, usually make up the book value of preferred stock. This total, divided by the number of preferred shares outstanding, gives the book value per share. This is illustrated in the book value computations below.

Common stock book value The common stockholders have a residual equity in earnings (secondary to preferred stockholders) and in assets in case the company dissolves. This equity is most easily found by subtracting the preferred shareholders' claims from the total shareholders' equity of the corporation; the remainder, or residual equity, is appropriately claimed by the common stockholder. This amount, divided by the number of common shares outstanding, provides the book value per share of common stock.

Book value per share illustrated Assume that we are to compute the book value per share of both preferred and common stock from the following corporate data.

Preferred stock:	
Shares authorized	10,000
Par value per share (no redemption or liquidating value specified)	$100
Shares issued	5,000
Preferred treasury shares (reacquired by the company)	500
Shares outstanding	4,500
5 percent cumulative dividend—no dividend paid in two preceding years nor in current year.	
Common stock:	
Shares authorized	100,000
Par value per share	$10
Shares issued	80,000
Common treasury shares (reacquired by the company)	1,000
Shares outstanding	79,000

Shareholders' equity:		
Common stock	$800,000	
Preferred stock	500,000	$1,300,000
Premium on common stock	$300,000	
Premium on preferred stock	10,000	310,000
Retained earnings		562,500
		$2,172,500
Treasury stock, common	$ 19,500	
Treasury stock, preferred	55,500	75,000
		2,097,500

In computing the book value per share for preferred stock we must attribute to preferred stockholders the following claims:

Par value of shares outstanding (4,500 × $100)	$450,000
Dividends for three years at 5 percent (total, 15 percent)	67,500
Total book value of preferred stock	$517,500
Book value per share of preferred stock (4,500 shares)	$ 115

Note that, in attributing to preferred stockholders the claims for cumulative dividends in arrears, there is a question of whether such dividends do accumulate for years in which net income is less than the dividend amount and whether such dividend claims can be enforced if there is not sufficient retained earnings to provide for them. Answers to these questions appear to differ from state to state. They are omitted from consideration in this illustration.

The book value of common stock is computed as follows:

Total shareholders' equity	$2,097,500
Less total book value of preferred stock	517,500
Total book value of common stock	$1,580,000
Book value per share of common stock (79,000 shares)	$ 20

It is vitally important to remember that book "value," in fact, does not indicate value at all. Because assets may be worth more or less than the funds committed in them, the present worth of the net assets per share might be substantially different from the book value per share. Also, because the stock market is influenced by many factors, including predictions of the firm's future profits, the market value might be quite unrelated to the book value per share. Thus, the book value per share is best interpreted as an index, not a measure, of value. If the book value increases from year to year, the index is rising, and this is a good indicator of growing financial strength.

CHANGES IN CORPORATE EQUITY

Many events create changes in the amount and structure of a corporation's equity. These range from the initial issue of capital shares to such things as stock splits and convertible debentures (bonds). These changes in corporate equity are examined in the following paragraphs.

Issue of Shares

Stock is issued as evidence of investments in the corporation. The amount of investment the corporation receives may be the par value of the shares or some amount greater than par value. In many states, the board of directors may be penalized if it approves issue of shares at any price below par.

Issue of shares at par value When the par value of shares is received and the shares are issued, the changes in assets and equity can be described by the following journal entry:

Mar. 1	Cash	12,000	
	Common Stock		2,000
	7 percent Preferred Stock		10,000
	To record cash received and the issue of 100 shares common stock (par value $20) and 100 shares of 7 percent preferred stock (par value $100).		

Issue of shares at a premium If common and preferred shares are issued at a price above par value, part of the equity is classified as paid-in capital in excess of par value. This part of the capital is recorded in the accounts, Premium on Common Stock and Premium on Preferred Stock, as illustrated in the following journal entry:

Mar. 1	Cash	13,500	
	Common Stock		2,000
	Preferred Stock		10,000
	Premium on Common Stock		1,000
	Premium on Preferred Stock		500
	Issue for cash of 100 shares common stock at $30 (par $20) and 100 shares of 7 percent preferred at $105 (par $100).		

The accounts for premium on common and preferred stock might carry other titles, such as Additional Paid-in Capital, Common Stock and Additional Paid-in Capital, 7 percent Preferred Stock. Whatever account titles are used, this capital is the paid-in capital in excess of par value, or paid-in surplus.

Subscriptions for capital stock Investors may subscribe for shares of stock, that is, purchase the shares and agree to pay within a specified period of time. Shares normally are not issued until fully paid for. While the shares are subscribed but not yet fully paid, the corporation has a claim against the subscriber and has committed itself to issue the shares. This is shown in the journal entry to record the subscription:

Mar. 1	Stock Subscriptions Receivable	3,000	
	Common Stock Subscribed		2,000
	Premium on Common Stock		1,000
	Subscription for 100 shares common stock at $30 per share, to be paid at $500 per month for six months.		

As payments are received from the subscriber, cash is increased and the claim against the subscriber is decreased. This is shown in journal entry form as follows:

Apr. 1	Cash	500	
	Subscriptions Receivable		500

When the subscription is fully paid, the shares are issued. This cancels the data classified under Common Stock Subscribed and increases data under Common Stock, as follows:

Sept. 1	Common Stock Subscribed	2,000	
	Common Stock		2,000

The last journal entry is for only the par value of the shares involved. The premium (paid-in capital in excess of par) was recorded in the Premium on Common Stock account when the subscription was received. Firms may use variations of the above procedure, but the final effect upon issue of the shares will always be the same.

During the time the subscription is in effect, the amount due from the subscriber is reported as a current asset on the balance sheet. The amount in the Common Stock Subscribed account is reported as a special item in the corporate equity section of the balance sheet, along with the amount in the Common Stock account. This might appear as follows:

SHAREHOLDERS' EQUITY

Common stock (10,000 shares authorized; 6,000 issued; $20 par value)		$120,000	
Plus 100 shares common stock subscribed		2,000	
Preferred stock (5,000 shares authorized; 2,000 shares issued; $100 par value)		200,000	
Additional paid-in capital			
Premium on common stock issued and subscribed	$61,000		
Premium on preferred stock	10,000	71,000	
Retained earnings		308,000	
Total shareholders' equity			$701,000

Stock Split

When the market price of a stock rises above $100 per share, and especially when it reaches several hundred dollars, trading in that stock may be slowed because of the price. Smaller investors may find it difficult to buy the stock, and investors who like to buy in round lots (one hundred shares or more) likewise may find it difficult. This may act as a brake, preventing the price from rising higher. If the company is planning an additional issue of stock, or if it is bargaining to acquire another company with a trade of its own shares for the shares of the other company, it may be important financially that the market price be allowed to rise to its full potential. To counteract the effect of its stock's high market price, the company may amend its charter to substitute a greater number of shares for those then authorized. For each share previously authorized, there might be substituted two, three, or even ten shares. This is called a stock split.

In a three-for-one split, the investor who owned one hundred shares finds himself owning three hundred shares, each share with a par value equal to one-third that of the original shares. The market price responds immediately to a stock split, dropping in almost exact proportion to the size of the split. Shares selling at $240 before a three-for-one split would sell for about $80 per share afterward. However, with the lower price per share, trading probably would increase, bringing the price upward again, perhaps to $85 or $90 per share. Ninety dollars per share on the new shares would be the equivalent of $270 per share on the stock before the split. The company's market position is much better for an additional issue or a stock trade in a merger (acquisition) transaction.

It is important to note that in a stock split the total par value of the authorized shares remains unchanged. For example, one million shares with a par value of $15 per share provide the same total as five million shares (after a split) with a par value of $3 per share. The significant point is that there is no change in resources in a stock split, and the legal capital does not change. The only change needed in the corporate data system is the number of shares authorized and issued and the par value per share—no change in total amounts is needed. To clearly show the change in data, one might move the amount of legal capital from Common Stock, $15 Par Value, for example, to a new account: Common Stock, $3 Par Value. Assuming a legal capital for common stock of $1,500,000, this change could be entered with a journal entry like the following:

Aug. 1	Common Stock, $15 Par Value	1,500,000	
	Common Stock, $3 Par Value		1,500,000

It is not essential that a journal entry like the preceding actually be made. One might simply change the heading on the Common Stock account, making a note of the change of par value and number of shares authorized and outstanding.

Cash Dividend: Declaration and Payment

Corporate earnings are distributed to the shareholders as dividends. The board of directors may declare dividends quarterly, annually, or at irregular intervals. In large, widely held corporations, one expects to find dividends declared at regular intervals, with extra dividends possible when profits are higher. A dividend declared by the board, if it is to be paid in cash, becomes a liability of the company. A cash dividend, once declared, cannot be cancelled. Invariably, dividends are paid shortly after declaration and are, therefore, classed as current liabilities until payed.

Dividends are declared in terms of a percent of the outstanding shares' par value, or at some amount per outstanding share. If a company has 600,000 shares of $40 par value stock outstanding and declares a 6 percent dividend, the amount to be paid is 6 percent of (600,000 × $40), or $1,440,000.

There are three dates involved in a normal dividend. The dividend is declared on one date, to be paid to shareholders "of record" on some date a few days to a few weeks later, with actual payment to be made several days after the "of record" date to allow time for writing and mailing checks. The dividend is a liability from the declaration date to the payment date. Use of the record date enables the company to record share transfers in time for the new owner to receive the dividend, or late enough for the seller to retain the dividend, according to their agreement.

For a 6 percent dividend on 600,000 outstanding shares of $40 par value stock, declared on August 5 and payable on August 31 to shareholders of record on August 20, the journal entries would be as follows:

Aug. 5	Dividends	1,440,000	
	Dividends Payable		1,440,000
	Declaration of 6 percent dividend on 600,000 shares of $40 par stock.		
Aug. 31	Dividends Payable	1,440,000	
	Cash		1,440,000
	Payment of Aug. 5 dividend.		

In very closely held corporations, the declaration, record, and payment dates may all be the same day. In such situations one may find that no indication is made of a monetary liability, and the journal entry may simply record the dividend data and the cash paid out, as follows:

Nov. 15	Dividends	80,000	
	Cash		80,000
	4 percent dividend on 200,000 outstanding shares of $20 par value stock.		

Dividends are normally described as distributions of corporate earnings to stockholders. Although in some states dividends may be declared from paid-in capital in excess of par value, the normal basis for the dividend is company earnings. Declaration of a cash dividend reduces the amount of capital from earnings remaining in the company and establishes a liability for this amount instead. This reduction of retained earnings may be recorded in a Dividends account, as was illustrated in the above examples. At the end of the year, the Dividends account is closed into the Retained Earnings account to reduce the balance in that account. This has the same general effect as closing the Drawing account of a sole proprietor or partner and is accomplished as follows:

Dec. 31	Retained Earnings	5,760,000	
	Dividends		5,760,000
	To transfer the data for quarterly dividends for the year to Retained Earnings.		

The amount of the dividends for the year is not a consumption of resources involved in the production of revenue; it is not reported as an expense, therefore, in computing the amount of net income. Rather, dividends are a distribution of part of net income to shareholders, and data for this distribution are reported as changes in the retained earnings of the company not in the computation of net income on the income statement.

Stock Dividend: Declaration and Issue

A corporation's board of directors may wish to provide the investors some return on their investments but may not wish to dissipate the cash of the company. To accomplish both of these ends, they may declare a dividend payable by the issue of additional shares of stock. This stock dividend is interpreted as a distribution of earnings to shareholders, with the resources represented by the earnings kept in the firm and shares of stock substituted. The result of this transaction is the reclassifying of a part of retained earnings as paid-in capital and the issue of shares of stock.

Assume that a corporation has 600,000 shares of $20 par value stock outstanding and that the present market price is $30. A 5 percent stock dividend would amount to 5 percent of the 600,000 shares outstanding, or 30,000 shares. These would be recorded at the current market price of $30 per share, reducing the retained earnings (through the Dividends account) and increasing the Capital Stock and the Premium on Capital Stock accounts. The journal entry would be

Jan. 20	Dividends	900,000	
	Stock Dividend Payable		600,000
	Premium on Capital Stock		300,000
	5 percent stock dividend on 600,000 shares outstanding, recorded at $30 per share.		

The Dividends account will be closed at the end of the year into Retained Earnings, making effective the reduction in that class of equity. Stock Dividends Payable is a temporary account, used until the stock actually is issued.

When the stock is issued some days later, the temporary capital account, Stock Dividends Payable, is cancelled by a negative input, and the Capital Stock account is increased to indicate the legal capital for the shares issued. The journal entry for this stock issue on a stock dividend is

Feb. 5	Stock Dividend Payable	600,000	
	Capital Stock....................................		600,000
	Issue of 30,000 shares for stock dividend declared on Jan. 20.		

The reaction of the stock market to a stock dividend appears difficult to predict. If the company is regarded favorably, a small stock dividend may attract interest and cause a rise in the stock's market price; if the company is considered weak or if a cash dividend was expected, the stock dividend may be interpreted as evidence of financial weakness and may cause a drop in the price. A large stock dividend normally results in at least a temporary drop in the market price because there are more shares (as in a stock split) to participate in the Company's earnings and growth. When the market price remains stable or rises, it appears that the investors do receive a return on their investment, not from the company but from the market place. If the additional shares can be sold and the investor retain a total market price as great as before the stock dividend, he clearly has benefited. However, if the price drops roughly in proportion to the dividend, no benefit to the investor has resulted from the stock dividend.

Treasury Stock

For a variety of reasons, the board of directors may authorize officers of the company to purchase some of its own shares from stockholders. Shares thus purchased and held for reissue are termed *treasury shares*, because they are held "in the treasury" or by the treasurer. Payments for the purchase of treasury stock actually are decreases in the firm's total capital, normally interpreted and reported as temporary decreases in capital.

At the time the shares are purchased, a decrease is shown in cash and in the shareholders' equity. The temporary reduction in shareholders' equity is recorded in the Treasury Stock account, as shown in this journal entry:

Oct. 17	Treasury Stock	10,000	
	Cash..		10,000
	Purchase of 500 shares of company stock for treasury at $20 per share.		

Treasury shares may be resold or issued for a number of purposes: bonuses for outstanding employee performance, awards in contests, etc. Treasury stock may be resold at a price either above or below the price of acquisition; this results in an addition to or a deduction from the paid-in capital in excess of par value (additional paid-in capital). The following entry records the resale of 100 shares (purchased at $20 per share) for $25 per share.

Dec. 11	Cash	2,500	
	Treasury Stock		2,000
	Paid-in Capital from Treasury Stock		500

Treasury stock is reported as a general reduction in the shareholders' equity section of the balance sheet. The four hundred shares purchased on October 17 in the preceding illustration and still on hand at the end of the year would be reported on the balance sheet as follows:

STOCKHOLDERS' EQUITY

Common stock (10,000 shares authorized; 6,000 issued; $20 par)		$120,000	
Preferred stock (5,000 shares authorized; 2,000 shares issued; $100 par value)		200,000	
Additional paid-in capital			
Premium on common stock	$61,000		
Premium on preferred stock	10,000	71,500	
Paid-in capital from treasury stock	500		
Retained earnings		308,000	
Total		701,500	
Less treasury stock at cost (400 shares)		8,000	
Total shareholders' equity			$693,500

Restriction of Retained Earnings for Treasury Stock Purchased

We saw above that the board of directors may not reduce the total capital below the amount specified as legal capital. The company cannot purchase treasury stock if the purchase would reduce total capital below the legal capital limit. For example, if a company has a total shareholders' equity of $102,000 (composed of $90,000 in the Capital Stock account, $8,000 in the Premium on Capital Stock account, and $4,000 in the Retained Earnings account) and is offered a large block of shares at a good price by a major shareholders' estate, it could spend only $12,000 for the purchase. An expenditure of more than the $12,000 would reduce total capital below the $90,000 legal minimum and would not be permitted by law in most states.

To be sure that the restriction on permitted expenditures is evident, many states legally restrict retained earnings for the amount expended for treasury stock. This restriction prevents the declaring of dividends for the restricted amount until the treasury stock is sold. The restriction on retained earnings for treasury stock purchased is applied as shown in the following entries:

Date	Account	Debit	Credit
Oct. 17	Treasury Stock	10,000	
	Cash		10,000
	Purchase of 500 shares of company stock for treasury at $20.		
Oct. 17	Retained Earnings	10,000	
	Retained Earnings Restricted for Treasury Stock		10,000
	To record retained earnings' restriction because of purchase of treasury stock.		

The restriction on retained earnings may be removed as the treasury stock is sold. For example, the entry for the December 11 sale of one hundred shares purchased on October 17 would be accompanied by an entry cancelling a part of the restriction:

Date	Account	Debit	Credit
Dec. 11	Cash	2,500	
	Treasury Stock		2,000
	Paid-in Capital from Treasury Stock		500
	Sale of 100 shares of treasury stock at $25.		
11	Retained Earnings Restricted for Treasury Stock	2,000	
	Retained Earnings		2,000

The amount recorded in the account, Retained Earnings Restricted for Treasury Stock, is still a part of retained earnings, but is set apart in a separate account so that the balance in the unrestricted Retained Earnings account will be reduced to the smaller unrestricted amount.

The account title, Retained Earnings Restricted for Treasury Stock, has been used here because it describes the status of that part of the corporate equity. Other titles that one may see are Retained Earnings Appropriated for Treasury Stock, Appropriation for Treasury Stock, and Reserve for Treasury Stock Purchased.

Other Restrictions on Retained Earnings

Management may restrict retained earnings as a means of communicating company plans and intent to stockholders, labor, governmental agencies, and the financial world in general. Especially when the company holds large amounts of rather liquid investments, management may feel the necessity of indicating that the resources are being held for a specific purpose.

A good example of management's purpose for holding large investments is the accumulation of resources to build additional plants. If such were the case, management might restrict retained earnings in the amount of the resources currently being held for expansion. This restriction might be recorded with the following journal entry:

Dec. 31	Retained Earnings	4,000,000	
	Retained Earnings Restricted for Plant Expansion....................		4,000,000
	To record retained earnings restriction to match investments being held for plant expansion.		

Perhaps years later, when the investments have been liquidated and the funds used for plant expansion, the restriction on retained earnings would be removed. The investments would then no longer appear on the report and the restriction would no longer be needed to communicate the reason for holding the investments. The entry for this removal of the restriction would be

Dec. 31	Retained Earnings Restricted for Plant Expansion...........................	4,000,000	
	Retained Earnings		4,000,000
	To remove the restriction on retained earnings upon completion of plant expansion project.		

Of course, the retained earnings restriction would be removed if the plant expansion project were cancelled and the reason for the resource accumulation no longer existed.

Sometimes restrictions on retained earnings are agreed to as a part of a bond indenture (agreement). Because the restriction often is matched to the resources accumulated in the bond sinking fund, the retained earnings restriction is commonly referred to as a sinking fund reserve. This unfortunate title has caused considerable confusion because of the words "sinking fund" and because the word "reserve" implies to some that the Sinking Fund Reserve account measures funds set aside; the Sinking Fund account actually represents those funds. The Sinking Fund Reserve account might better be called Retained Earnings Restricted by Bond Indenture. Often, it is increased each year by an entry such as the following:

Dec. 31	Retained Earnings	100,000	
	Sinking Fund Reserve (or Retained Earnings Restricted by Bond Indenture)		100,000

The addition to the restricted retained earnings might continue as in the preceding entry for twenty years until the bonds matured and were paid; the total restriction accumulated would then be returned to unrestricted retained earnings. This would be accomplished by a journal entry as follows:

Dec. 31	Sinking Fund Reserve (or Retained Earnings Restricted by Bond Indenture)	2,000,000	
	Retained Earnings		2,000,000
	To remove retained earnings restrictions upon payment of bond liability.		

Reporting Data for Retained Earnings Restrictions

Retained earnings are reported on the balance sheet at the total amount, including both the restricted and the unrestricted portions. On a detailed balance sheet the retained earnings presentation might appear as follows:

Stockholders' Equity			
Capital stock			$3,000,000
xxxxxxxxx			xxxxx
Retained Earnings:	Unrestricted	$1,022,000	
	Restricted (Note H)	610,000	1,632,000

Note H for this balance sheet would include a detailed listing of the amounts restricted for all purposes, making up the $610,000 total. On a condensed balance sheet the retained earnings might appear without any indication of restrictions except for the footnote reference:

Retained earnings (Note H)	$1,632,000

Balance sheets of companies with operations in war zones and in countries undergoing considerable civil disturbance or guerrilla activity contain restrictions, or "reserves" for war losses, property loss and damage, and other similar eventualities. The retained earnings restrictions may often be misunderstood, but they are used frequently in an effort to communicate a variety of conditions.

Executive Stock Options

The combination of high executive salaries and high personal income tax rates has made executive stock options a popular type of compensation. For many executives, salary in excess of about $50,000 per year is subject to at least 50 percent federal income taxes. This means that an executive's company must more than double his salary in order to increase his effective income by one-half. The stock option can provide greater income to the executive, taxable at the favorable long-term capital gains rate (maximum rate 25 percent) and, at the same time, include a direct incentive for the executive to work for the firm's success. The more successful his firm is, the more he will gain from his stock option.

The executive stock option plan works as follows. The executive is granted an option, probably as part of the inducement for him to join the company, to buy stock up to a specified limit over several years at the market price existing when the option is granted. If the executive succeeds in increasing the firm's income and growth, the stock will be worth much more than he has to pay for it, perhaps many times that amount. He can purchase the stock, hold it for a required time, and sell it for the profit, taxable at a long-term capital gains rate. If he does not hold the stock for the required time, his gain on the sale is taxed at the full rate applicable to ordinary income; he loses the tax advantage that normally is one of the reasons for the stock option plan.

Another aspect of compensating key executives with stock options appeals to some smaller companies that expect to grow rapidly. When an executive accepts the option, a significant part of his compensation is not paid from company funds. Therefore, funds that otherwise would be used for payments to executives can be used for financing the company's growth.

Purchasing stock at less than the current market price dilutes the value of the stock outstanding at that time. However, if the options are not large relative to the total stock outstanding, this dilution may not have an immediate effect on the market price, and the stockholders may not feel that they have lost anything. Of course they have; the net income per share will be lower because of the greater number of shares outstanding and, in time, this will affect the market price to some degree.

The financial effect on the company of granting executive stock options can be argued from several viewpoints. The generally accepted reporting is based on the proposition that there is no measurable compensation to the executive in the granting of an option at the current market price. He has an opportunity to benefit from the unknown and indeterminable future success of the company, and then by a diluting of the benefits to other stockholders rather than payments directly from the company. When the options are granted, no financial effect is identified and no input to the accounting system is made. When the executive exercises his option and purchases shares, the transaction is interpreted as are other issues of shares for cash. If an executive has an option to purchase shares at $72 per share and exercises this option by purchasing one thousand shares when the price is $154 per share, the price of $154 is ignored, and the issue of stock ($20 par) for $72 per share is recorded as follows:

Oct. 6	Cash	72,000	
	Capital Stock		20,000
	Premium on Capital Stock		52,000
	Issue of 1,000 shares to P. T. Black at option price in the Jan. 16, 1969, option to key executives.		

It is generally conceded that the full financial effects of large executive stock options cannot be measured accurately. The above simple, limited interpretation of stock option granting and exercising should make the data understandable and available for use in special analyses.

Convertible Bonds

Corporations often issue bonds giving bondholders the right to exchange their bonds for common stock at a predetermined price. The period during which the bondholder may make the exchange (convert bonds to stock) often extends from issue date to from three to ten years after their issue. This gives the investor (or lender) the ability to remove some uncertainty in choosing the type of investment, for he can postpone the choice and base his decision on actual events rather than on his projection of events.

Convertible bonds usually are convertible *debentures*, which are unsecured bonds; *that is, no property is pledged as security for them.* The use of convertible debentures defers the lender's decision as to whether he will claim the rights of a creditor or a shareholder. It also delays the corporation's final classification as to the source of the capital obtained by issuing the bonds and, therefore, the kind of claim that exists against the corporation. When the bonds are issued, the basic claim is that of the creditor; the bonds are recorded, therefore, as liabilities of the corporation. This classification remains until the bondholder requests their conversion to stock. His rights then become those of a stockholder, and he gives up the right to interest and repayment of his loan. When this occurs, the data in the corporation's accounting system are changed to reflect the new situation. Data for the bonds are cancelled, and new data for the shares of stock are entered. If the bonds converted were $1,000,000 in face value and had $21,000 unamortized premium at the time of conversion, and if $500,000 par value of common stock was issued in the conversion, the journal entry to accomplish the change in data is:

Sept. 7	Bonds Payable	1,000,000	
	Premium on Bonds Payable	21,000	
	Capital Stock, Common		500,000
	Premium on Common Stock		521,000

Until the end of the conversion period, during which time it is not known whether the final status of the equity holder will be that of creditor or shareholder, the convertible bonds are reported as liabilities of the company. However, a full description is given on the face of the balance sheet or in a footnote, including the conversion period and the terms of conversion, so that real and potential creditors and investors will have full information about the company's status.

Convertible bonds present another problem in computing earnings per share for the corporation. Should convertible bonds be counted as shares of stock for this computation? Since earnings-per-share amounts usually are used in predicting future performance, the shares to be issued upon conversion of the bonds normally are treated as currently outstanding for this computation if it appears that the bonds probably will be converted. Even if there currently is no evidence that the bonds will be converted, an earnings-per-share figure is computed on a *fully diluted* basis, showing the net income before interest deductions, divided by the total shares outstanding and to be issued if all convertible bonds are converted. One should expect to see in published financial statements two earnings-per-share amounts, one based on the shares currently outstanding plus those that quite apparently will be issued in forthcoming conversions of bonds, and another (the *fully diluted* earnings per share) based on the shares currently outstanding plus all shares that could be issued upon conversion, whether likely or unlikely, of all outstanding convertible bonds. The effect of this is presented in detail in the following chapter.

QUESTIONS AND EXERCISES

12- A. What are the three basic forms of legal ownership of firms?

12- B. Explain the meaning of the balance in a proprietor's capital account; in a partner's capital account.

12- C. A corporation is said to be a legal entity. What is meant by this?

12-D. Why are the names of stockholders normally of little importance to creditors of a corporation?

12- E. What is meant by common stock? What is meant by 7 percent, cumulative, participating, convertible, $100 par value preferred stock?

12- F. Corporate resources come from three principal sources. Explain.

12-G. What accounts are used for classifying and storing corporate equity data? What kind of data goes into each?

12-H. Is book value of stock really the "value" of the shares? What "value" of assets is used in computing book value of shares?

12- I. Are "book value" and "market value" of shares the same? What factors influence the market price of shares?

12- J. Kitirik, Inc. received its charter on November 1, authorizing the issue of 10,000 shares of $50 par value stock. On November 6, 5,000 shares were issued at par value. Give the needed journal entry or entries.

12- K. What is premium on stock? Discount on stock?

12- L. Does a corporation earn a profit by issuing stock at a premium?

12-M. On November 21 the D-A Corporation received subscriptions to 500 shares of its $100 par value common stock at $105 per share. The subscription contracts provided for a down payment of $21 per share to accompany the subscription contracts and the payment of the remainder in two equal payments in thirty and sixty days from the subscription date. Give the journal entries to record
a. the subscription,
b. the down payment,
c. the two installment payments,
d. issue of the stock.

12- N. Distinguish between a stock split and a stock dividend. Do they serve the same purpose or do they have different objectives?

12- O. Company X's board of directors declared a stock dividend of one share of common stock for each ten shares outstanding. Prior to the stock dividend, 30,000 shares with a par value of $10 each were outstanding. It was decided to record the stock dividend at $25 per share. Give the needed journal entries.

12- P. On November 28, Company Y repurchased 100 shares of its $10 par common stock at $30 per share. These shares were held as treasury stock until January 14, when they were sold at a price of $40 per share. Give journal entries for both dates.

12- Q. Should a firm report a profit or loss on the purchase and sale of treasury stock? On the purchase and retirement of its own stock? Give reasons for your answers.

12- R. What is the purpose of restrictions on retained earnings?

12- S. The OHO Corporation transferred $100,000 to Restricted Retained Earnings for the contingency of an expected lawsuit arising from the injury suffered by one of its customers through the use of its product. The suit was settled for $110,000 in the following year. Give the appropriate journal entries for the two years.

12- T. It has been said that stock options provide a means of compensating the company's officers without cost to the company. Whom does it cost? Discuss.

PROCEDURAL PROBLEMS

12-1. The Garret Manufacturing Company had the following account balances at April 30, 1969:

Inventory April 1, 1969	$ 32,000
Sales	145,000
Purchases	126,000
Sales returns	2,500
Purchases discounts	400
Interest earned	1,100
Depreciation expense	6,500
Rent expense	12,000
Supplies expense	4,100
Dividends (James Garret, drawing, for Requirement B)	4,000

(Inventory on April 30, 1969, was $34,000)

a. Prepare the closing entries.
b. Assuming these accounts were for James Garret, a sole proprietor, prepare the closing entries. Note that the Dividend account is assumed to be a drawing account for this requirement.

12-2. On August 1, 1969, William Ames and James Stewart agree to form a partnership. Ames contributes land worth $20,000 and $20,000 in cash. Stewart contributes equipment and machinery worth $10,000 to the partnership. The partnership agreement states that each partner is to work in the partnership and that each will receive 15 percent of the net income, with the remainder to be divided between the partners according to their initial contributions. Withdrawals made by the partners were

William Ames, on September 30	$2,000
James Stewart, on November 1	$1,000
William Ames, on December 1	$2,000
James Stewart, on December 1	$3,000

Net income for the five months ended December 31 was $12,000.

Prepare journal entries to record the investments of the partners, the partners' withdrawals, closing of partners' drawing accounts, and the distribution of net income between the partners.

12-3. The Lary Manufacturing Company has two classes of capital stock. The common stock has a stated value of $10 per share with 100,000 shares authorized and issued. There is a $50,000 balance in the Premium on Common Stock account. Preferred stock is $20 par value, 6 percent cumulative; 10,000 shares are authorized; 8,000 have been issued. There is a $16,000 premium on preferred stock. No dividends have been paid during the current year. The company has purchased 4,000 shares of its common stock for $48,000, and 600 shares of preferred stock have been purchased at a total cost of $12,800. The company has retained earnings of $380,000.

Compute the book value per share of both common stock and preferred stock.

12-4. The S. A. Marsh Company has declared both a cash dividend and a stock dividend on March 31, 1969, for the quarter ended that day. There are 1,200,000 shares of $20 par value common stock outstanding and 400,000 shares of $20 par value, 8 percent, noncumulative preferred stock outstanding. The quarterly cash dividend is $20 per share on the common stock. In addition to the cash dividend, a stock dividend of common stock equal to 5 percent of the preferred stock outstanding is to be issued to preferred stockholders. The current market price is $25 per share for the common stock. All dividends are to be paid on April 15. The company has adequate cash and retained earnings.

a. Prepare the March 31 entries to record the cash dividends on both common and preferred stock and the stock dividend. Also, prepare the April 15 entries to record the payment.
b. Assuming the preferred stock was 8 percent, cumulative, and that no dividends had been paid in 1968, prepare the entry to record cash dividends at March 31, 1969, on preferred stock to date and on common stock.

12-5. The W. R. Weyman Corporation was formed on July 1, 1969. Both common stock with a par value of $50 per share and preferred stock with par value of $50 per share were authorized. The company was authorized to issue 20,000 shares of each class of stock.

a. Prepare journal entries to record all transactions in the stock accounts.
b. Prepare the stockholders' equity section of the balance sheet as of July 31, 1969.

July 1 The company issued 2,000 shares of common stock for $65 a share.

6 The company issued 3,000 shares of common stock for land worth $60,000 and cash of $100,000.

14 The company issued 800 shares of preferred stock for $40,000.

16 The company received a subscription for 500 shares of common stock at $55 per share, to be paid at $2,500 on the last day of each month for eleven months.

23 The company issued 400 shares of common stock in exchange for the right to use certain patents. Since the patents did not

have an established market value the stock was issued at par value.

27 The company repurchased 100 shares of common stock for a total price of $4,600.

31 The company collected the monthly amount from stock subscribers.

12-6. The Saxton Toy Company has one Capital Stock account with $200,000 shares, par value $10, all issued and outstanding; $20,000 in the Premium on Common Stock account; and Retained Earnings of $720,000. Of the Retained Earnings, $100,000 is Restricted for Plant Expansion and $310,000 is Restricted for the Payment of Bond Liability. The remainder is unrestricted. Each time the company purchases or sells treasury stock it restricts or removes from restriction Retained Earnings equal to the cost of the treasury stock involved.
a. Prepare journal entries for each transaction below.
b. Prepare the stockholders' equity section of the balance sheet as of October 31, 1969.

Oct. 4 The company purchased 1,000 shares as treasury stock for $18 per share.

11 The company sold 300 of the treasury shares for $6,300.

17 The company cancelled the proposed plant expansion.

31 The company made a $10,000 additional restriction of retained earnings for the retirement of the bond liability.

Net income for the month was $70,000; transfer to retained earnings.

12-7. Britton Corporation has an executive stock option plan. The option price is $30 per share for stock with a par value of $10. The stock is selling for $42 when the option for 200 shares is exercised.
Prepare the journal entry to record the issuance of the stock.

12-8. On April 1, 1968, Croft, Inc. issued $500,000 of convertible bonds at a $20,000 discount. On April 1, 1969, the bondholder converted his bonds into common stock, receiving 40,000 shares of $10 par value common stock. During the year that the bonds were outstanding, $2,000 of the discount was amortized.
Prepare the journal entries to record the issuance of the bonds and the conversion of bonds into stock.

12-9. In February 1969 William Matters and Steve Axel organized the A-M partnership. Capital contributions were Matters, $60,000 and Axel, $30,000. Twenty percent of the partnership net income is given to Matters for his work in managing the partnership; 60 percent of the remainder is allocated to Matters and 40 percent to Axel. Partnership net income and withdrawals were

	1969	1970	1971
Net income	$32,000	$44,000	$48,000
Matters withdrawals	6,000	14,000	17,000
Axel withdrawals	3,000	4,000	5,000

The partnership uses a calendar year.

a. Prepare a schedule showing the balance of the partners' capital accounts at the close of each year.
b. Prepare the December 31, 1971, entries to record the closing of the partners' drawing accounts and the distribution of net income.

12-10. Presented below are account balances taken from the accounting records of Waymandt Corporation as of December 31, 1971.

Using any information necessary, prepare a partial balance sheet showing the details of stockholders' equity. Note that some items shown below may not be required.

Common stock (authorized 20,000 shares, issued 6,000 shares, par value $10)		$ 60,000
Preferred stock (authorized 10,000 shares, issued 3,000 shares, 5 percent cumulative, $50 par value)		150,000
Treasury stock (2,000 shares of preferred at cost)		120,000
Stock subscription receivable		30,000
Retained earnings		
Unrestricted	$320,000	
Restricted for treasury stock	120,000	
Restricted for payment of preferred dividends in arrears	15,000	455,000
Preferred stock subscribed		2,500
Premium on common stock	22,000	
Paid-in capital from treasury stock	14,000	
Premium on preferred stock	50,000	86,000

12-11. The following account balances were taken from the January 1, 1971, trial balance of Granger, Inc.

Preferred stock (6 percent, 5,000 shares authorized 2,000 shares issued, $50 par value)	$100,000
Common stock ($10 stated value, 50,000 shares authorized, 10,400 shares issued)	104,000
Premium on common stock	6,000
Premium on preferred stock	14,000
Treasury stock, common (at cost, 800 shares)	16,000
Retained earnings (unrestricted)	444,000
Retained earnings restricted for treasury stock	16,000

The company restricts retained earnings equal to the cost of treasury stock held.

a. Journalize each of the following transactions.

b. Prepare the December 31, 1971, stockholders' equity section of the company's balance sheet.

Mar. 1	The company declared and paid a cash dividend to preferred shareholders.
Apr. 14	The preferred stock was split 2 for 1.
July 11	200 shares of treasury stock were sold for $24 each.
Sept. 22	The company declared and paid a 5 percent stock dividend on both classes of stock. The market value was $50 per share for preferred stock and $30 per share for common stock.
28	Mr. Brown subscribed to 200 shares of common stock for $16 per share.
Dec. 1	The company declared a cash dividend of $.20 per share on common stock.
14	The company repurchased 100 shares of its preferred stock for $7,000.
31	Net income for the year was $77,000.

12-12. The Winborn Corporation has two capital stock accounts. The common stock is $5 par value with 200,000 shares issued and outstanding. The preferred stock is $20 par value, 6 percent, cumulative and participating with 10,000 outstanding. Dividends payments were

1970.........	$ 4,000
1971.........	100,000

Compute the dividend payment to each class of stock for the two years.

12-13. On December 31, 1968, the Axon Corporation had the following account balances:

Common stock ($10 stated value, 10,000 shares authorized, 8,000 shares issued)................................	$ 80,000
Preferred stock ($50 par value, 8 percent, cumulative, 10,000 authorized, 2,000 issued)	100,000
Retained earnings	306,000

All shares were originally issued in 1966. Dividends were declared each December 31 and paid on January 3 of the next year. Total cash dividends declared were

1969.........	$ 4,000
1970.........	11,000
1971.........	16,000

The following transactions occurred:

1. On June 4, 1969, the corporation purchased 500 shares of its preferred stock, holding it until February 14, 1970.
2. On September 22, 1969, the company purchased 600 shares of its common stock. Two hundred shares were sold again on November 3 of the same year.
3. The company declared and paid a 10 percent stock dividend of common stock during August 1970 when the stock price was $22 per share.
4. The preferred stock was split 2 for 1 on July 1, 1971.

Net income for the years was

1969.........	$ 7,000
1970.........	38,000
1971.........	27,000

a. Compute the cash dividends declared for each class of stock for each of the three years.

b. Compute the December 31, 1971, balance of retained earnings.

12-14. The Hayworth Corporation has the following capital stock account balances on December 31, 1971:

Class A preferred (20,000 shares authorized, 20,000 shares issued in 1969, 8 percent, cumulative, $20 par value)

Class B preferred (50,000 shares authorized, 20,000 shares issued in 1969, 6 percent, noncumulative, $20 par value)

Common stock ($10 stated value, 10,000 shares authorized and issued)

Treasury stock consists of 200 shares of Class B preferred and 200 shares common, both purchased in 1969.

Cash dividends paid were

1970	Class A preferred.........	$20,000
	Class B preferred.........	20,000
1971	Class A preferred.........	32,000
	Class B preferred.........	23,760

The net assets at December 31, 1971, are $3,000,000.

Compute the December 31, 1971, book value of each class of stock.

12-15. Butex Corporation had the following trial balance.

BUTEX CORPORATION
Trial Balance
June 30, 1971

Cash	$ 11,200	
Accounts receivable	23,500	
Subscriptions receivable	2,000	
Inventory, July 1, 1970	29,300	
Building	73,600	
Accumulated depreciation		$ 14,000
Accounts payable		9,100
Stock dividends payable		3,500
Preferred stock		50,000
Common stock		5,000
Common stock subscribed		2,000
Retained earnings		58,900
Dividends	3,000	
Sales		114,600
Sales discounts	400	
Purchases	71,500	
Purchase returns and allowances		200
Depreciation expense	3,000	
Rent expense	12,000	
Salary expense	27,800	
	$257,300	$257,300

Its inventory on June 30, 1971, was $33,400. Prepare the closing entries.

CONCEPTUAL PROBLEMS

12-16. The stockholders' equity section of Steve's Reed Products, Inc. on December 31, 1970, was as follows:

Capital stock, 400,000 shares, par value $1	$ 400,000
Additional paid-in capital	3,000,000
Retained earnings	2,700,000
	$6,100,000

The following changes took place during 1971, in the sequence listed:
1. A cash dividend of fifty cents per share was declared.

2. A stock dividend of 10 percent was declared and issued; the dividend was recorded at $40 per share.
3. 5,000 shares of stock were purchased at $42 per share, to be held as treasury shares.
4. 3,000 of the treasury shares were resold at $45 per share.
5. A restriction was placed on $400,000 of retained earnings because of possible future losses on overseas investments.
6. 40,000 shares of previously unissued stock were issued at a price of $48 per share.
7. A charter amendment was obtained, splitting all shares 2 for 1.
8. Net income for 1971 was $900,000.

Required:

a. What was the total stockholders' equity on December 31, 1971?
b. How many shares had been issued as of December 31, 1971?
c. How many shares were outstanding on December 31, 1971?
d. What was the book value per share on December 31, 1971?
e. Prepare the stockholders' equity section of the corporation's balance sheet for December 31, 1971.

12-17. Comparative information from the shareholders' equity section of the balance sheet of Richtime, Inc. for December 31, 1970 and 1971 is presented below:

	December 31	
	1971	1970
Capital stock (120,000 shares, 1971; 100,000 shares, 1970) par value $5.....	$ 600,000	$ 500,000
Additional paid-in capital	1,763,800	1,200,000
Retained earnings*	1,700,000	1,550,000
Treasury stock (at cost; 2,000 shares, 1971; 1,200 shares, 1970)..................	(60,000)	(30,000)
	$	$3,220,000

* Restrictions totaling $330,000 were effective at December 31, 1970, for bond retirement and treasury stock. Restrictions of $410,000 were effective at December 31, 1971, for the same purposes.

Required:

a. How many shares of stock were issued as of December 31, 1970? December 31, 1971?
b. How many shares of stock were outstanding on December 31, 1970? December 31, 1971?
c. If all treasury shares on hand at December 31, 1970, were purchased at the same price, and if all shares on hand at the end of 1971 were purchased at the same price, were any shares carried over from 1970 to the end of 1971?
d. There was a 10 percent stock dividend in 1971, with the shares recorded at $27 at a date when there were 1,500 shares of treasury stock. All additional shares of stock were issued later for $29 per

share. If the only other transaction affecting Additional Paid-in Capital was the sale of the 1,200 shares of treasury stock on hand at the end of 1970, at what price were those shares sold?

e. In addition to the stock dividend stated in (d), there was a $73,000 cash dividend. Using these data and the assumption that there were no other significant equity transactions, compute the amount of net income for 1971.

12-18. On December 10, 1970, the Baroon Corporation issued 200,000 shares of $4.00 dividend, no par, convertible preferred stock at an issue price of $55, collected in cash for all shares. These shares were convertible into common stock (par value, $5) at the rate of two and one-half shares of common for each share of preferred. Earnings of the company increased markedly during the next two years and, during the second quarter of 1973, all of the preferred stock was converted into common. Additional data about the Baroon Corporation are

	December 10, 1970	Second Quarter 1973
Market prices:		
Baroon common stock	$ 20	$ 40
Baroon $5 preferred stock	55	110
General index of common stock prices	100	110
Book value per Baroon common share before conversion of preferred	28	35

Required:

a. What effect did the conversion have on book values and earnings per common share? One million shares of common stock were outstanding prior to the conversion. If the conversion had not taken place, the company's earnings for 1973 would have been $2 per share of common stock.

b. Did the conversion of the preferred shares into common shares amount to a dilution (weakening or dissipating) of the common shareholder's equity? Give reasons for your answer.

c. Prepare journal entries for the issue and conversion of the preferred stock.

13 Financial Statements

Preview Questions

As you study look for the answers to the following questions:

- **What are the principal information models, or financial statements, of the firm?**
- **What are the information categories of the balance sheet?**
- **What are the information categories of the income statement?**
- **What are the information categories on the statement of retained earnings?**
- **How does one set up a combined statement of income and retained earnings?**
- **What two types of financial analysis are used on financial statements?**
- **What are the elements of the worksheet, and how is the worksheet used?**
- **What is meant by consolidated financial statements?**

The financial information system is planned to provide information for decisions; this is the basic premise on which we began this study of accounting. The hundreds of decisions which necessitate financial information about a firm are not always accompanied, however, by their needed information. Instead, certain summary information in the form of financial models of the firm and of the firm's activities is presented. From these one can choose the information needed for a specific decision, or obtain it by analyzing the information in the models. These information models, or financial statements, are

Balance sheet. Often called the statement of financial position, it presents the firm's present position as to funds committed or tied up in different types of resources and the sources which provide corporate resources.

Income statement. Sometimes called the operating statement (or, formerly, the profit and loss statement), it presents information about the firm's earnings, both ordinary and extraordinary.

Statement of retained earnings. Contains information about changes in retained earnings (earnings, dividends, and other changes) during the year. For a sole proprietorship or partnership, the *statement of capital* gives all changes in the proprietor's or partners' capital during the year.

Funds statement. Often called the statement of source and application of funds, presents information about the flow of financial resources into and out of the firm. Because of the detailed analysis needed for this statement, it is presented separately in chapter 14.

Keeping in mind the various aspects of financial information studied in the preceding chapters we shall now view each kind of information in relation to other financial information in the statements, noting the significance of the various formats in which it is presented, and performing some basic analyses.

BALANCE SHEET

The balance sheet is composed of two lists. One shows the kinds of resources or properties owned by the firm and the amount of funds committed in these properties; these are the firm's assets. The other list shows the sources of the firm's funds and the kinds of claims their providers can exert against the firm; this is the list of equities (liabilities and investors', or owners', equity).

The balance sheet lists show the status of items at the close of business on the date of the statement. The balance sheet does not cover a period of time, but presents the status at a specific moment.

Assets

Properties of the firm, or assets, are presented in groups according to the length and kind of fund commitment involved. The most common groupings are *current assets, plant assets* (also called *fixed assets,* or *plant and equipment*), and a miscellaneous group called *other assets.* A substantial number of firms have enough investments in other firms to use a fourth group called *investments.* Also, some firms prefer to show certain of their intangible assets under the heading *intangible assets* on the balance sheet. However the assets are grouped, they indicate by group and in total the amount of funds committed in the assets.

Current assets Assets in this group include cash and items that are expected to be converted to cash or used in the firm's operations during the next operating period, almost always one year. These assets are cash, accounts and notes receivable from customers, inventories of merchandise and supplies, and some services paid for in advance. In Figure 13-1 these classifications of assets are grouped under the heading, Current Assets.

Plant assets Assets used in the production of goods or services that are expected to have a long, useful life are grouped under this heading. Such assets could include land, buildings, machinery, stationary and mobile equipment, automobiles, trucks, aircraft, ships, trains, furniture, and other long-life properties used in the business. In Figure 13-1 this group is shown under the heading Plant Assets, which is in common use. The heading Fixed Assets is not seen as frequently as it was some years ago; the headings Plant Assets and Plant and Equipment are used more frequently now.

Investments Funds invested in other companies, usually evidenced by notes, bonds, or shares of stock, and funds invested in assets not used in operations but held for growth or production of income may be presented on the balance sheet under this heading. If investments are small in amount they may be included in the miscellaneous grouping, Other Assets. Firms may hold large amounts of investments for the income they produce, or so that the funds will be readily available for acquiring other types of assets or paying off long-term liabilities.

Figure 13-1

DETAILED BALANCE SHEET

Crown Electronics, Inc.
Balance Sheet
December 31, 1970

ASSETS			
Current assets:			
Cash		$ 18,350	
Accounts receivable		17,800	
Merchandise inventory		37,400	
Store supplies		1,380	
Office supplies		680	
Prepaid insurance		1,608	
Total current assets			$ 77,218
Plant assets:			
Store and warehouse equipment	$23,400		
Less depreciation to date	11,300	$ 12,100	
Office equipment	$ 6,800		
Less depreciation to date	2,040	4,760	
Building	$56,000		
Less depreciation to date	8,400	47,600	
Land		6,000	
Total plant assets			70,460
Investments:			
Shares in Dow Electric Company			9,550
Other assets:			
Officers' and employees' notes		$ 11,000	
Utility and other deposits		1,025	12,025
Total assets			$169,253

LIABILITIES AND SHAREHOLDERS' EQUITY		
Current liabilities:		
Trade accounts and notes payable	$ 18,440	
Notes payable to banks	5,000	
Mortgage note payable (current payment)	2,000	
Commissions payable	1,128	
Salaries payable	424	
Income tax payable	9,519	
Other accrued liabilities	755	
		$ 37,266
Long-term liabilities:		
Mortgage notes payable (final maturity in 1978)		16,500
Total liabilities		$ 53,766

Figure 13-1 (continued)

Shareholders' equity:		
Common stock (10,000 shares, $10 par value authorized; 5,000 shares issued)	$ 50,000	
Additional paid-in capital (premium on common stock and sale of treasury stock)	24,000	
Retained earnings	44,487	
	$118,487	
Less treasury stock (150 shares at cost)	3,000	
Total shareholders' equity		115,487
Total liabilities and shareholders' equity		$169,253

Intangible assets When a firm has a substantial amount of funds committed in long-lived, intangible assets, this grouping may be used on the balance sheet. Assets normally presented here are patents, copyrights, franchises, other exclusive rights, and goodwill. Exclusive rights to use or sell specific goods or services are provided by patents, copyrights, trademarks, franchises, licenses, etc. These rights are obtained by purchasing them or by developing items or processes and applying for patents or copyrights. Goodwill is described as the extraordinary profit capacity of a firm or a person; in order to purchase a very profitable firm, one may find it necessary to pay for this profitability in addition to all other assets of the firm. Intangible assets are reported at the amount invested in them. Usually they are amortized over the period of time the firm expects to benefit from them.

Observe that certain current assets and investments actually are intangible. The intangible assets reported as a separate group are those of long life that are involved in the firm's operations. The term "intangible fixed assets," used occasionally, is very descriptive. If intangible assets of this type are not material in amount they may be reported as a part of fixed assets or in the "other assets" group.

Other assets As the title of this grouping indicates, it is of a miscellaneous nature. If there are not large amounts of investments and long-term intangible assets, these may be included in this miscellaneous group as mentioned above. Notes that the firm holds on officers and other employees usually are presented in this group. Land held for future use (future plant site, for example) is included here, along with any other property that does not fit well in another group.

Deferred charges This group of assets is not found on all balance sheets because it includes only special items not found in all firms. The title means "deferred charges to income," and the group includes items that have been recorded but that will be reported as expenses in later periods. Long-term prepayment of rent might be included in this category. Discount on bonds payable, when the questionable interpretation of prepaid expense is used for the item, is reported as deferred charge.

Equities

The sources of funds or resources provided to the firm are grouped according to the kinds of claims that can be exercised against the firm. Amounts received from creditors, who can claim repayment at specified times, are shown under the general heading, Liabilities. Amounts invested and amounts earned by the firm are presented as Shareholders' Equity; naturally, "owner" is substituted for "shareholder" in reports for sole proprietorships and partnerships.

Current liabilities Usually these result from the purchase of goods or services or the borrowing of money on short-term credit. Repayment is to be made within the next operating period of the firm, which almost always is one year. As can be seen in Figure 13-1, current liabilities include trade accounts and notes payable, notes payable to banks, the current portion of long-term notes (mortgage notes, for example), and debts that accrue from operations, such as commissions, salaries, and taxes.

Long-term liabilities Liabilities to be paid at some time beyond the next year are reported in this category. Such liabilities normally are incurred by purchasing property financed by mortgage notes or by borrowing money on long-term notes. Bonds payable are long-term notes and are reported in this group. Because current liabilities are frequently matched with current assets in analyzing information on financial statements (as we shall do later in this chapter), the payments on long-term notes and bonds due within a year are classified as current liabilities if funds to pay them will come from the current asset group. If funds for paying the current portion of these long-term liabilities are to come from investments or other assets, then amounts due currently will be reported as long-term liabilities, so that they will be matched in ratio analysis with the assets to be used in paying them.

Deferred credits This is a special category of long-term liabilities often reported separately because of their special nature. Collections of rents or other revenue several years in advance sometimes are presented as deferred credits. The group title is understood to mean "deferred credits to income"; it includes any amounts already recorded but which will be reported as revenue or reductions in expenses in future periods. Items in this group do not require payment in cash as do most other liabilities. The obligation may be to allow the tenant to occupy a building in the future as a means of earning the revenue collected in advance. Some rather complicated financing plans may result in liabilities of this "deferred credits to income" type.

Shareholders' or owners' equity Funds received from investors, either shareholders of a corporation or owners of a partnership or proprietorship, give rise to this kind of equity. Also, earnings of the firm that are not paid out to shareholders or owners are reported as additions to this equity.

Capital stock This grouping is used to report the par value of the shares issued by a corporation. This amount has a legal significance, being the legal, or stated, capital of the corporation. Capital stock, both common and preferred, that has once been issued is reported in this category until the shares are returned to the corporation and their issuance is legally cancelled. Shares purchased and held as treasury stock do not reduce this classification, but their cost is deducted from total shareholders' equity.

Additional paid-in capital Amounts collected from investors above the par value of shares issued are reported in this classification. This includes premiums on common and preferred stock, additional capital from treasury stock transactions, and capital derived from a few other investor transactions such as forfeited subscriptions to capital stock. The heading for this information grouping may be Paid-in Capital in Excess of Par Value, or Premium on Capital Stock if this is the only item involved.

Retained earnings As was seen in the preceding chapter, this is the amount of earnings retained in the firm. Usually this amount is analyzed in the statement of retained earnings, an example of which is found in Figure 13-5. Descriptive titles such as Earnings Retained in the Business or Earnings Reinvested in the Business are seen frequently on balance sheets, as well as the older title, Earned Surplus.

Donated capital Some corporations receive permanent capital as donations from persons or organizations other than shareholders. For example, a corporation may receive a free plot of land from a governmental unit or community organization if it will build and operate a plant at that location. The land is reported as an asset by the corporation, and Donated Capital is credited with this portion of the firm's capital.

Partners' or owner's equity The source of capital for a partnership or a sole proprietorship, or the partners' or owner's capital in such a firm, is reported as one figure, rather than being reported in the categories for corporations seen in the preceding paragraphs. Details about the owner's or partners' equity are reported in a Statement of Capital for the sole proprietorship or partnership.

Balance Sheet Illustrated

The balance sheet in Figure 13-1 is a detailed statement such as might be prepared for management or submitted to a bank with a loan application. In this detailed balance sheet, specific items are given for all groups of information. In a condensed balance such as the one in Figure 13-2, only selected individual items (if any at all) are included as details of the general categories of information. Note that some details of current assets are given, but that plant assets and other categories are described without any detailed amounts being reported. This condensed balance sheet is often used in reporting to stockholders of widely held corporations, especially in interim reports (quarterly or monthly) between more formally audited annual reports.

Figure 13-2

CONDENSED BALANCE SHEET

Crown Electronics, Inc.
Balance Sheet
December 31, 1970

ASSETS		
Current assets:		
Cash and receivables	$36,150	
Merchandise inventory	37,400	
Supplies and prepaid expenses	3,668	
Total current assets		$ 77,218
Plant assets, at cost less depreciation to date – Schedule A*		70,460
Investment in shares of an associated company		9,550
Other assets (deposits and loans to employees)		12,025
Total assets		$169,253

*Schedules A and B (lists of detailed items) are not reproduced in this example of a condensed balance sheet.

Figure 13-2 (continued)

LIABILITIES AND SHAREHOLDERS' EQUITY

Current liabilities (accounts, notes, and accrued liabilities) – Schedule B	$ 37,266
Mortgage notes payable (final maturity in 1978)	16,500
Shareholders' equity:	
Common stock (10,000 shares, $10 par value authorized; 5,000 shares issued)	50,000
Additional paid-in capital	24,000
Retained Earnings	44,487
Treasury stock (150 shares at cost)	(3,000)
Total liabilities and shareholders' equity	$169,253

INCOME STATEMENT

The income statement presents the amount of revenues and expenses for the period. Revenues are earned inflows of resources, and expenses are consumed resources; the combination of these on the income statements results in net income, the net increase in earned resources of the firm.

Revenue

All revenue that meets the criteria for revenue recognition, or reporting, is included on the income statment. The part that comes from ordinary operations of the firm is reported first; the amount from extraordinary events is reported separately in the last section of the statement. These items can be seen clearly in Figures 13-3 and 13-4.

Expenses

All consumption of resources in the conduct of business is reported as expense on the income statement. As with revenue, expenses related to the firm's ordinary operations are listed in the computation of net income from operations (before extraordinary items); expenses or losses which are classed as extraordinary are presented in the last section of the statement. Expenses are the consumption of resources; they may be related to current expenditures, such as for services of employees (salaries), supplies, and some merchandise, or they may be related to expenditures made years before, such as use of buildings and equipment (depreciation). The flow of funds, in contrast to the consumption of resources, is seen in the funds statement presented in the following chapter.

Extraordinary Items

Earned inflows and consumption (or losses) or resources not related to ordinary operations of the firm are reported in this section of the income statement. These items may be extraordinary because they simply are not derived from the kind of thing that the firm has done and is expected to do in the future, or because they represent events that are not recurring. Examples of the first might be a gain from holding investments or a loss from storm damage. Although gains and losses of such nature may be expected to occur from time to time, they are not a planned part of the firm's operations. An example of an event that is not expected to recur is a gain or loss from the sale of a plant building. Although the building is used in operations and the gain or loss may be interpreted as an adjustment of occupancy costs (maintenance and depreciation) of prior years, it is not expected to recur and, therefore, is excluded from ordinary expenses of this period. Opinion no. 9 of the Accounting Principles Board (of the American Institute of Certified Public Accountants) is generally the controlling guide for income presentation.

Income taxes

Federal and local income taxes usually are considered the consumption of company resources legally required as a part of producing earnings for distribution to shareholders or for use in company growth. As ordinary expenses, income taxes would be reported as they relate to operations and extraordinary items, as shown in Figure 13-3. There is a widespread interpretation of income taxes, however, as a distribution of a part of net income to governmental units rather than an ordinary expense. For this reason, one often sees the last part of the income statement arranged as follows:

Net income before extraordinary items and before income taxes		$100,000
Income taxes		42,000
Net income before extraordinary items		$ 58,000
Extraordinary gains and losses:		
Gain on sale of plant building	$80,000	
Less income tax on this gain	20,000	60,000
Net income		$118,000

If revenue or deductions reported for tax computations differ from those for financial reporting on the income statement, taxes on reported net income may either be paid after or before income is reported. In such cases, the income tax expense on the income statement may show both the amount to be paid currently and the amount applicable to prepayments or to be deferred to later years. Such a presentation of income taxes might appear on the income statement as follows:

Income taxes to be paid currently	$30,000	
Deferred income taxes	12,000	
Income taxes applicable to this year		$42,000

Refer to the earlier study of liabilities for a review of the problem of deferred income taxes.

Net Income per Share of Common Stock

Income reporting includes the earnings per average share of common stock outstanding during the year. When there are extraordinary items on the income statement, two earnings per share are computed, one for net income from operations (or net income before extraordinary items) and one for net income. The divisor in the computation is the average number of common shares outstanding, giving weight to the time during which newly issued and repurchased (treasury) shares were outstanding during the year.

When there are convertible preferred shares or convertible bonds outstanding, and when the convertibility clearly is a valuable aspect of these securities, then they, too, are included in the computation of average common shares outstanding. This is done because the convertible securities are considered the equivalent of common shares if there is strong indication that they will be converted. There have been significant differences of opinion among industrial accountants, investment analysts, and public accountants concerning the best presentation of earnings-per-share information. The figure is used widely by investors and investment analysts and is important in investment decisions.

Income Statement Illustrated

Figures 13-3 and 13-4 illustrate a detailed income statement and a condensed income statement. Some differences in arrangement and format may be found in practice, but the contents and information disclosed should be generally the same as seen in the illustrations.

Figure 13-3

DETAILED INCOME STATEMENT

CROWN ELECTRONICS, INC.

Income Statement

For the Year Ended December 31, 1970

Revenue from sales:				
Sales of goods		$138,448		
Sales of services		85,303	$223,751	
Less: Returns and allowances		$ 1,601		
Discounts on sales		2,069		
Estimated credit losses		1,312	4,982	
Net sales of goods and services				$218,769
Cost of merchandise and services sold:				
Merchandise inventory, Jan. 1, 1970		$ 34,200		
Purchases of merchandise	$79,403			
Less: Returns and allowances $ 568				
Discounts on purchases 1,410	1,978			
Net purchases		$ 77,425		
		$111,625		
Less merchandise inventory, Dec. 31, 1970		37,400		
Cost of merchandise sold			74,225	
Service labor costs		$ 26,601		
Service supplies used		9,777		
Miscellaneous service expenses		6,096		
Cost of services sold			42,474	
Total cost of merchandise and services sold				116,699
Gross profit on sales of goods and services				$102,070
Operating expenses:				
Selling expenses:				
Sales salaries		$ 26,324		
Sales commissions		12,862		
Advertising		3,760		
Depreciation of store equipment		2,000		
Delivery expenses		1,926		
Store supplies used		1,160		
Insurance expense, selling		840		
Miscellaneous selling expense		1,448		
Total selling expenses			$ 50,320	

Figure 13-3 (continued)

General and administrative expense:			
Administrative and office salaries	$ 21,838		
Property and operating taxes	3,524		
Federal income taxes	4,810		
Depreciation of office equipment	680		
Depreciation of building	1,400		
Office supplies used	480		
Insurance expense, general	592		
Interest expense	960		
Miscellaneous general expense	426		
Total general and administrative expenses		$ 34,710	
Total operating expenses			$ 85,030
Net income before extraordinary items			$ 17,040
Extraordinary gains and losses:			
Gain on sale of Erie Building		$ 21,404	
Less income tax on gain		4,709	16,695
Net income			$ 33,735
Income per share of common stock before extraordinary items			$3.47
Net income per share of common stock			$6.88

Figure 13-4

CONDENSED INCOME STATEMENT

CROWN ELECTRONICS, INC.

Income Statement

For the Year Ended December 31, 1970

Net revenue from sales of goods and services	$218,769
Operating expenses:	
Cost of goods and services sold	$116,699
Selling expenses	50,320
General and administrative expenses	34,710
Total operating expenses	$201,729
Net income before extraordinary items	$ 17,040
Extraordinary gains (net of income tax effects)	16,695
Net income	$ 33,735
Net income per share of common stock before extraordinary items*	$3.47
Net income per share of common stock*	$6.88

*Treasury shares were purchased May 1, 1970. Average shares outstanding for the year are 4,900.

STATEMENT OF RETAINED EARNINGS

Changes in the capital derived from earnings during the period are reported on this statement. This information tells one about the amount of dividends and any exceptional items considered so unrelated to events of the current period that they were interpreted as adjustments to retained earnings rather than part of the income computation. Such exceptional items would appear on the retained earnings statement rather than on the income statement.

Statement of Retained Earnings Illustrated

A statement of retained earnings in good form is illustrated in Figure 13-5. This statement contains a highly exceptional item from an event of a prior year, shown as an adjustment of the opening amount of retained earnings.

Figure 13-5

CROWN ELECTRONICS, INC.

Retained Earnings Statement

For the Year Ended December 31, 1970

Retained earnings balance, January 1, 1970		$47,402
Loss from expropriation of foreign assets*		(22,100)
Adjusted retained earnings, January 1, 1970		$25,302
Net income for the year	$33,735	
Dividends declared	(14,550)	19,185
Retained earnings balance, December 31, 1970		$44,487

* Real estate holdings of the company in Merzanzia were expropriated by decree of the president of that country on November 1, 1968. It was not known at that time whether any compensation would be received for these properties. Officers and attorneys of the company now conclude that the full book value of these properties ($22,100) may be lost. Petitions for reimbursement have been filed, and agents of the Company are in contact with the State Department for its assistance.

Combined Statement of Income and Retained Earnings

The managements of many firms apparently prefer a single statement showing both net income and a summary of income retained in the business rather than separate income and retained earnings statements. Such a combined statement contains all the information that would be included on separate statements, arranged in a continuous computational or reporting format. The statement illustrated in Figure 13-6 would be used instead of those in Figure 13-5 and either Figure 13-3 or 13-4. Some proponents of this report form like the fact that it tends to de-emphasize net income since that is not the last figure on the report.

Figure 13-6

CROWN ELECTRONICS, INC.

Statement of Income and Retained Earnings
For the Year Ended December 31, 1970

Net revenue from sales of goods and services		$218,769
Operating expenses:		
Cost of goods and services sold		$116,699
Selling expenses		50,320
General and administrative expenses		34,710
Total operating expenses		$201,729
Net income before extraordinary items		$ 17,040
Extraordinary gains (net of income tax effects)		16,695
Net income		$ 33,735
Retained earnings balance, January 1, 1970		$ 47,402
Loss from expropriation of foreign assets (see footnote to Figure 13-5)		(22,100)
Adjusted retained earnings, January 1, 1970		$ 25,302
		$ 59,037
Dividends declared		(14,550)
Retained earnings balance, December 31, 1970		$ 44,487
Net income before extraordinary items per share of common stock	$3.47	
Net income per share of common stock	$6.88	

STATEMENTS FOR SOLE PROPRIETORSHIPS AND PARTNERSHIPS

Income statements and balance sheets for sole proprietorships and partnerships are identical in many respects to those for corporations, illustrated in Figures 13-1 through 13-4.

Balance Sheet for the Unincorporated Firm

The one significant difference from a corporation's balance sheet is seen in the invested equity section. For a corporation this section is termed the stockholders' equity section, but for an unincorporated firm it is called the *owner's equity* section (*owners'*, for a partnership), or the *capital* section. If the Crown Electronics firm were not incorporated but, instead, were owned by two partners, the equities half of the condensed balance sheet in Figure 13-2 might appear as follows:

LIABILITIES AND OWNERS' EQUITY

Current liabilities	$ 37,266
Mortgage notes payable	16,500
Partners' capital	115,487
Total liabilities and owners' equity	$169,253

For a sole proprietorship owned by Mr. Ralph Sleng, the line for partners' capital might read Ralph Sleng, Capital.

Other than the owners' equity section, all information in the balance sheet could be the same regardless of the legal status of the firm as a corporation, partnership, or sole proprietorship.

Income Statement for the Unincorporated Firm

Income is measured in virtually the same fashion regardless of the legal structure of the firm. The only significant differences are that in a sole proprietorship and in some partnerships salary for the proprietor or partners is not deducted as an expense, and there are no income taxes on the unincorporated firm, only on owners individually. Both differences stem from the fact that in such firms the assets and liabilities are considered to be those of the owner, or owners. It would follow that all revenue is an earned inflow of funds to the owner; any compensation he might receive must be paid by himself, and income taxes are levied directly on him. Traditionally, the entrepreneur's gain has included the direct results of his personal efforts as well as the earnings of his properties; whatever he withdraws from the firm has been interpreted as a withdrawal of profits or of capital. In corporate reports the costs of all service, from shareholders and others alike, are included in expenses.

For items other than these one would expect income statements of corporations, sole proprietorships, and partnerships to be very much alike.

Statement of Capital

For a proprietorship or partnership, information about the source of capital is found in the statement of capital, or statement of partners' capital. This statement gives the changes that have occurred in the owners' capital during the year. If the Crown Electronics firm had been unincorporated and owned by partners Burr Fleming and Anthony Monito, the statement of partners' capital for the firm might have appeared as illustrated in Figure 13-7. Similar information could be reported for a sole proprietorship by omitting the columns for the individual partners and reporting the information in the total column for the one owner.

Figure 13-7

CROWN ELECTRONICS (A PARTNERSHIP)
Statement of Partners' Capital
For the Year Ended December 31, 1970

	Burr Fleming	Anthony Monito	Total Capital
Capital at January 1, 1970	$51,202	$60,200	$111,402
Additional investments during year		10,000	10,000
Net income distributed	13,868	19,867	33,735
	$65,070	$90,067	$155,137
Partners' withdrawals	(4,500)	(13,050)	(17,550)
Extraordinary, nonoperating loss	(11,050)	(11,050)	(22,100)
Capital at December 31, 1970	$49,520	$65,967	$115,487

FINANCIAL ANALYSIS

Analysis of financial information usually involves comparing information for one year with that of other years. Also, it includes the computation of ratios from information for the year and the comparison of these with ratios of prior years.

Comparative Financial Statements

Financial statements illustrated earlier in this chapter were shown for only one year because the emphasis was on the form and content of the statements. Normally, annual financial statements for corporations are prepared in comparative form; that is, the information for two years is reported in parallel columns so that basic comparisons can be made readily.

Comparative income statements for Crown Electronics, Inc., are found in Figure 13-8. Comparative balance sheets and statements of retained earnings are arranged in parallel columns similar to income statements.

Comparative statements prepared for use within the company often have the changes from one year to the next (increases or decreases) shown in a third column, with the percent of change indicated in a fourth column. This arrangement is most informative; it allows one to find easily the changes of greatest absolute amount and those of greatest proportionate significance. Normally, the amount and percent of changes are not included on published comparative statements.

Figure 13-8

CROWN ELECTRONICS, INC.

Income Statements

For the Years Ended December 31, 1969 and December 31, 1970

	1970	1969
Net revenue from sales of goods and services...	$218,769	$201,661
Operating expenses:		
Cost of goods and services sold	$116,669	$112,227
Selling expenses	50,320	53,198
General and administrative expenses	34,710	30,041
Total operating expenses	$201,729	$195,466
Net income before extraordinary items	$ 17,040	$ 6,195
Extraordinary gains or losses, net of income tax effects..................................	16,695	(4,140)
Net income	$ 33,735	$ 2,055
Net income before extraordinary items per share of common stock............................	$3.47	$1.24
Net income per share of common stock	$6.88	$ .41

Ratio analysis

Early in this study of financial information we emphasized that the two primary things an investor needs to know about a firm are its financial strength and its profitability. Having information about the firm's financial strength helps one assess the degree of risk involved in investing in that firm. Knowing the firm's potential profitability gives one a basis for estimating the probable return on his investment, either through dividends or growth of the firm and increased market price of his stock. Information about financial strength and profitability can be presented in the form of ratios.

Ratios indicating financial strength Part of a firm's financial strength is related directly to its profits and, therefore, information about financial strength and about profitability becomes intermingled. A company with strong and steady profits can obtain needed capital by borrowing more easily than a firm with a poorer record, proving that it has greater financial strength. One normally does not attempt to evaluate this specific borrowing potential by ratio analysis. Ratios are more often used to evaluate present financial strength and stability as factors separate from profitability and as an ultimate protection for creditors. Many ratios are used for financial strength analysis; the following are used quite frequently.

Current ratio This ratio of current assets to current liabilities gives an index of the firm's short-run financial strength. In computation form, it is stated as follows:

$$\frac{\text{Current assets}}{\text{Current liabilities}} = \text{Current ratio}$$

Using data from the balance sheet of Crown Electronics, Inc., in Figures 13-1 or 13-2, the computation is

$$\frac{\$77{,}218}{\$37{,}266} = 2.07 \text{ to } 1$$

It is difficult to compare firms in different industries on the basis of current ratios; a ratio of a specific size does not give a definite good or bad measure. A retail jewelry firm, because of an expensive and slow turning inventory, might normally have a much higher current ratio than a wholesale produce broker, for example. The ratio does serve as an index to compare a given firm's annual performance, however; if the current ratio is higher this year than last, the firm is in a stronger short-term financial position. One of the best uses of the short-term financial strength ratios is in the index capacity.

Acid-test ratio A sterner index of current financial strength, the acid-test ratio, compares *liquid* (or quick) assets with current liabilities.

Liquid assets are cash and receivables; merchandise and supply inventories and prepaid expenses are excluded because it is difficult to obtain immediately any significant amount of cash from them. Receivables are included with cash because they can be collected, used as collateral in borrowing, or factored to obtain ready cash.

$$\frac{\text{Quick assets}}{\text{Current liabilities}} = \text{Acid-test ratio}$$

$$\frac{\$36,150}{\$37,266} = .97 \text{ to } 1$$

This ratio and the current ratio are used in judging whether a firm is a good risk for a short-term loan or credit extension. If a firm is acceptably profitable but has weak current and acid-test ratios because of using funds for equipment purchase, short-term credit may be granted on the assumption that the funds will be repaid from future operations. However, if a firm has both a weak profit record and weak current position, as indicated by very low current and acid-test ratios, it may present too great a risk to obtain the needed credit.

Debt to equity ratio Often referred to simply as the debt-equity ratio, this financial strength indicator shows how the capital from creditors compares in amount to the capital from shareholders and earnings. It compares the capital that must be repaid (debt) to the permanent capital. The computation, using the Crown Electronics, Inc., data, is

$$\frac{\text{Total liabilities}}{\text{Stockholders' equity}} = \frac{\$53,766}{\$115,487} = .466, \text{ or } 46.6\%$$

For a firm which is undercapitalized, that is, that has inadequate invested capital, it might be critically important that this ratio show a decreasing trend to indicate that the firm is developing greater financial stability.

Debt to total assets ratio This ratio serves about the same purpose as the preceding debt to equity ratio. The comparison is different, but the ratio still indicates the relative degree of reliance on debt capital as opposed to invested, or equity, capital. From the Crown Electronics, Inc., data, the ratio is

$$\frac{\text{Total liabilities}}{\text{Total assets}} = \frac{\$53,766}{\$169,253} = .318, \text{ or } 31.8\%$$

This ratio for Crown Electronics indicates that 31.8 percent of the firm's capital comes from using credit and from borrowing. If the firm had been highly capitalized in the past, with little benefit derived from leverage on borrowed funds and with a debt to assets ratio of 22 percent last year, the increase of the ratio to 31.8 percent this year might indicate more profit potential because of better balanced financing.

Ratios indicating profitability Investors and investment analysts are very interested in means of measuring and comparing firms' profit capacity and potential. Following are some of the ratios more popularly used for this purpose.

Return on total assets This ratio often is called the *return on total capital.* It compares the total return before payment for the use of any capital with the total capital used in the firm. The total return would be a net income figure computed without deducting interest expense; this normally is computed by adding interest expense back to net income. For valid results in a comparison it is essential to use the same figures: use either income from operations (before extraordinary gains and losses) or final net income amount (after extraordinary items), but use it consistently. Since ratios are used to compare and predict, it seems reasonable to use the net income before extraordinary items as the amount earned on the resources available, the average total assets. Thus, the formula for computing this ratio is

$$\frac{\text{Net income before extraordinary items, plus interest expense}}{\text{Average total assets}}$$

Using the data for Crown Electronics, Inc., and assuming total assets to have been $168,747 at the beginning of the year, the computation becomes:

$$\frac{\$17{,}040}{\$169{,}000} = .101, \text{ or } 10.1\%$$

For management use, this ratio indicates the maximum rate of interest that the firm can afford to pay on borrowed funds; of course the lowest available rate would be paid up to this level. Also, this rate indicates the amount of leverage available on borrowed funds. If Crown Electronics, having a 10.1 percent return on total capital, can borrow funds at 7 percent, it has a 3.1 percentage spread for gain on the borrowed capital, or leverage.

In outside analysis by investment analysts, for example, one of the most important uses for this ratio is as an index of earnings to compare different-sized firms and different financial structures. If firms have different amounts of borrowed capital costing different rates of interest, the return on total assets ratio eliminates the effects of these differences and allows comparison of a variety of firms' earning power.

Return on shareholders' equity The ratio that measures the success of both financial management (advantage from leverage, for example) and operating management is the rate of return on shareholders' equity. There are no adjustments to be made in computing this ratio; it is simply

$$\frac{\text{Net income}}{\text{Average shareholders' equity}}$$

Again, there is a question of which net income figure to use. If the rate is being computed to obtain an average rate of return on shareholders' equity for the same company for several years, it appears that the final net income figure should be used. However, if the computation is made to compare the current performance of one company with that of another, then the net income from operations (before extraordinary items) appears more appropriate. Using net income before extraordinary items from the Crown Electronics data, the computation is

$$\frac{\text{Net income from operations}}{\text{Average shareholders' equity}} = \frac{\$17{,}040}{\$118{,}455^{*}} = .144, \text{ or } 14.4\%$$

The same yearly ratio for Crown Electronics, but using the final net income figure, would be

$$\frac{\$33{,}735}{\$118{,}455} = .285, \text{ or } 28.5\%$$

This rate is much more meaningful to investors in common stock than to preferred stockholders, since it indicates the degree of growth that can be expected in shareholders' equity in the firm. When both classes of stock are outstanding, analysis for the common stockholder is some-

* Average of beginning and ending shareholders' equity.

times refined by computing a *return on book value of common stock* as follows:

$$\frac{\text{Net income minus preferred dividends}}{\text{Book value of common stock outstanding}}$$

This rate could be used in comparing the growth of common stockholders' equity in various companies.

Earnings per share of common stock This is not so much a ratio as a measurement. Earnings of the company which should benefit the common stockholders are expressed in a dollar amount per share rather than as a percent of common stock book value as was illustrated in the preceding paragraph. The computation is

$$\frac{\text{Net income minus preferred dividends}}{\text{Average number of common shares outstanding}}$$

This figure expresses in a dollar amount per share the earnings which should benefit the common stockholders, either in dividends or growth of the firm, and a corresponding increase in market value of the shares.

Number of times bond interest earned This rate indicates to the bond investor (lender) the relative assurance that the firm can make interest payments. This is of critical importance because, if an interest payment is passed over or defaulted, there is the danger that the firm will not be able to pay the interest or the principal and there is a corresponding loss of market value for the bonds. The lender may not be able to collect interest currently and may not be able to liquidate his investment without a serious loss. Thus, he may become locked into a longer term investment than originally planned or be faced with a loss of interest and a large part of the principal of his investment. The number of times interest is earned provides a ready index by which to compare the safety margin of bond investments in different companies. Since bond interest is deductible in computing income taxes, the best comparison is to divide net income before either income taxes or bond interest expense, by bond interest for the period. The rate is computed as follows:

$$\frac{\text{Net income plus bond interest expense and income taxes}}{\text{Bond interest paid and accrued for the period}}$$

Net income to sales By using this ratio, along with other indicators, one may compare management performance in different companies within an industry or sector of commerce. Because extraordinary items on the income statement may not represent current management performance but simply cause sporatic variations in the rate, it is suggested that net income before extraordinary items be used in this computation. The computation, using data from the Crown Electronics income statement, is

$$\frac{\text{Net income before extraordinary items}}{\text{Net sales}} = \frac{\$17,040}{\$218,768} = .078, \text{ or } 7.8\%.$$

This ratio, along with other ratios of management performance, can be used to analyze certain areas of operations for strengths and weaknesses. For example, if this ratio increases while sales are increasing, it may be the result of lower incremental expenses for additional units of goods sold, or it may be the result of a tortuous rise in sales prices. However, if the ratio increases while sales are decreasing, management apparently is doing a magnificent job in maintaining prices or in controlling expenses. Ratios of other facets of management performance follow.

Inventory turnover The number of times per year that the equivalent of the firm's average inventory is sold has become a standard in expressing the vigor and speed of merchandising activity. Within an industry, the firm with the more rapid inventory turnover has a continuing financing and merchandise storage advantage. The turnover rate is computed by comparing the cost of merchandise sold during the period with the average inventory at cost. Using Crown Electronics' data, the computation is

$$\frac{\text{Cost of merchandise sold}}{\text{Average inventory}} = \frac{\$74,225}{\$35,800} = 2.1 \text{ times}$$

Within industries, average or normal rates of inventory turnover may be used to determine whether a particular company is suffering or benefiting from its speed of inventory turnover. This aspect of a firm's performance is easy to compare from year to year.

Accounts receivable turnover This ratio, often referred to simply as the number of times receivables are collected, is computed by comparing sales on credit with the average accounts receivable. For Crown Electronics, assume that accounts receivable at the beginning of the year were $18,200 and that out of the total sales of $223,751 the amount of net credit sales was $161,780. Using these data and the reported amount of accounts receivable at the end of the year, the computation of accounts receivable turnover for Crown Electronics is

$$\frac{\text{Net credit sales}}{\text{Average accounts receivable}} = \frac{\$161{,}780}{\$18{,}000} = 9.0 \text{ times}$$

A better average for accounts receivable can be computed if monthly or quarterly data are available. The two year-end amounts could both be exceptionally low or abnormally high because of merchandise and collection cycles. An average of four or twelve amounts from throughout the year would be a much more representative figure.

The accounts receivable turnover can be used to compute the *average collection period for receivables* by dividing this ratio into 365 days. For Crown Electronics this period would be

$$\frac{365 \text{ days}}{9} = 41 \text{ days}$$

If this company extends credit to the end of the month of sale, this is a good collection record; if it extends a full thirty-day credit, this is an exceptionally good collection record. The turnover rate or the average collection period can be used to compare the performance of one firm with others and with industry averages.

THE WORKSHEET

At the end of each fiscal period there are several specific tasks which must be performed as a part of the operation of the accounting system. These tasks have been discussed in prior topics, but they are briefly reviewed below as orientation for study of the worksheet:

1. Updating, or adjusting, data contained in the system. As was discussed in connection with the study of revenue and expenses, no change in data may have been recorded during the period for supplies that have been used, for salaries, interest, and other expenses that have accrued but have not been paid, for revenue that has been earned but not yet billed, and for other similar financial changes. To obtain accurate data about operations for the period and about the current status of resources and equities, one must input data for the unrecorded changes.
2. Preparing information reports or financial statements from data in the system. To do this, one must match revenues and expenses properly to

report net income, and one must match assets and equities to report the status of the firm. From study in the current chapter, it should be recognized that this means the preparation of the standard financial statements (income statement, balance sheet, and statement of retained earnings).

3. Readying the information system for the next period's data inputs. The closing entries, which transfer data balances from revenue, expense, special gain and loss, and dividend accounts to the Retained Earnings account, accomplish this task of getting the system ready for the use during the next period. The accounts in which changes are accumulated annually are given zero balances so that changes for the following period can be accumulated separately from prior changes.

Purpose of the Worksheet

In accomplishing these end-of-period tasks, the worksheet provides efficiency and convenience in a manual system or a less sophisticated punched card or electronic system. In more sophisticated electronic systems, the worksheet provides the general pattern for block diagramming and flow charting the procedures to be programmed into the computer.

In systems in which the end-of-period tasks are done manually, the worksheet functions as a well-organized scratch pad. Here the accountant works through all the steps on one sheet. He changes data on the worksheet without disturbing the ledger accounts until he is certain that worksheet data are correctly computed, complete, and ready for input to the ledger. On the worksheet, the accountant classifies data in columns indicating the financial statement on which they will be reported. He can be certain that the statements are completed and accurate and, therefore, that the information on one statement relates properly to that on the others.

When it has been determined that period-end adjustments are accomplished properly and that the data for financial statements are classified correctly, journal entries for adjusting and closing the appropriate accounts can be prepared by taking the data directly from the worksheet. Financial statements can be prepared, also, by copying data from the worksheet, rather than by obtaining these data from the separate accounts.

Worksheet Illustration

The worksheet is illustrated in Figure 13-9; the notations Step A, Step B, and Step C across the top of the worksheet are not a part of the worksheet itself but were added to this illustration to indicate the steps in its preparation.

Figure 13-9

CROWN ELECTRONICS, INC.

Worksheet

For the Year Ended December 31, 1970

Account	(Step A) Trial Balance		(Step B) Adjustments		(Step C) Income Statement		Balance Sheet	
	Debit	Credit	Debit	Credit	Debit	Credit	Debit	Credit
Cash	$ 18,350						$ 18,350	
Accounts receivable	19,200						19,200	
Allow. for uncol. accts.		$ 88		(a) $ 1,312				$ 1,400
Merchandise inventory	34,200				$ 34,200	$ 37,400	37,400	
Store supplies	2,540			(j) 1,160			1,380	
Office supplies	1,160			(e) 480			680	
Prepaid insurance	3,040			(f) 1,432			1,608	
Store and wh. equipment	23,400						23,400	
Depreciation to date		9,300		(b) 2,000				11,300
Office equipment	6,800						6,800	
Depreciation to date		1,360		(c) 680				2,040
Building	56,000						56,000	
Depreciation to date		7,000		(d) 1,400				8,400
Land	6,000						6,000	
Dow Electric stock	9,550						9,550	
Notes-officers and employees	11,000						11,000	
Deposits-utility, etc.	1,025						1,025	
Accounts payable		15,400						15,400
Notes payable-trade		3,040						3,040
Notes payable-banks		5,000						5,000
Commissions payable				(i) 1,128				1,128
Salaries payable				(h) 424				424
Income tax payable				(k) 9,519				9,519
Misc. payables				(g) 755				755
Mortgage notes payable		18,500						18,500
Common stock		50,000						50,000

Add. paid-in capital		24,000						24,000
Retained earnings		47,402						47,402
Dividends	14,550						14,550	
Treasury stock	3,000							
Sales of goods		138,448				138,448		
Sales of services		85,303				85,303		
Sales returns and allow.	1,601				1,601			
Sales discounts	2,069				2,069			
Credit losses			(a) $ 1,312		1,312			
Purchases	79,403				79,403			
Purchase ret. and allow.		568				568		
Purchase discounts		1,410				1,410		
Service labor	26,601				26,601			
Service supplies used	9,777				9,777			
Misc. service expense	6,096				6,096			
Sales salaries	26,064		(h) 260		26,324			
Sales commissions	11,734		(i) 1,128		12,862			
Advertising	3,760				3,760			
Depreciation of S.E.			(b) 2,000		2,000			
Delivery expense	1,026				1,926			
Store supplies used			(j) 1,160		1,160			
Insurance exp., selling			(f) 840		840			
Misc. selling expense	1,448				1,448			
Admin. and office salaries	21,674		(h) 164		21,838			
Property and operating taxes	3,524				3,524			
Federal income taxes			(k) 4,810		4,810			
Depreciation of O.E.			(c) 680		680			
Depreciation of bldg.			(d) 1,400		1,400			
Office supplies used			(e) 480		480			
Insurance exp. general			(f) 592		592			
Interest expense	205		(g) 755		960			
Misc. general expense	426				426			
Extraordinary gains		21,404	(k) 4,709		4,709	21,404		
Extraordinary losses	22,100						22,100	
	$428,223	$428,223	$20,290	$20,290	$250,798	$284,533	$232,043	$198,308
Net income					33,735			33,735
					$284,533	$284,533	$232,043	$232,043

Trial balance The first step in preparing a worksheet is the listing of all accounts in the ledger with their balances placed in the appropriate debit or credit column. From early in our study of the financial information system, you should recognize this step as taking a trial balance. This step provides the quantitative proof that all data changes for the period have been recorded correctly, at least to the extent of maintaining an equality of debits and credits. This step also sets up the worksheet in preparation for the two steps remaining in its completion.

Adjustments Step B on the worksheet in Figure 13-9 shows how adjustment data are entered. The source of data for each expense and revenue account on the trial balance is examined to determine if there are unrecorded data for those accounts. Also, asset and liability accounts, both those with balances and those without, are examined to determine if there are unrecorded changes in data which might not have been revealed by examining sources for revenue and expense data. From these examinations, data for credit losses, depreciation, use of supplies, expiration of insurance, accrual of commissions, salaries and interest, and federal income taxes were computed and recorded in the adjustments columns of the illustrated worksheet. Related data are keyed with letter notations so that adjusting journal entries may be taken from the worksheet without further analysis.

Financial statements The final phase (Step C) of the worksheet preparation is classifying data according to whether they will be reported on the balance sheet or the income statement, and entering each amount in the appropriate column under the heading for one of these statements. This step calls attention to special items for which reporting decisions must be made. Examples in Figure 13-9 are the extraordinary gains and extraordinary losses, listed as the last items on the worksheet. In this case it was decided that the extraordinary gains should be reported on the income statement (in conformity with Opinion no. 9 of the AICPA's Accounting Principles Board), minus the income tax effect of this transaction, and that the extraordinary loss (described in a footnote to the statement of retained earnings) should not be reported as a part of income for the current year, but as an adjustment of retained earnings and, therefore, a part of the data for the balance sheet. Columns for the statement of retained earnings could be added to the worksheet in order to indicate clearly those items which would be reported on that statement. On the illustrated worksheet all items that would go on the statement of retained earnings are listed in the balance sheet columns, because the retained earnings statement is commonly considered secondary or subsidiary to the balance sheet.

When all items have been classified and entered in the columns for the income statement and the balance sheet, the amount that does not appear in either set of columns is the net income. This is added as the last item on the worksheet, the amount being the difference between debits and credits in the income statement data. This also equals the difference between debits and credits to this point in the balance sheet data. When the net income is entered, it balances both these sets of columns. This step provides additional information, but it also provides a convenient quantitative check of the accuracy of all data manipulation on the worksheet.

Using information from the worksheet In order to expedite financial reporting, the financial statements illustrated earlier in this chapter would next be prepared from the data in the last four columns of the worksheet. After these statements are prepared in good form or, perhaps, simultaneously with their preparation, journal entries would be prepared for all adjustments, (a) through (k), with these journal entries being posted to the ledger accounts immediately. Then journal entries would be prepared from the income statement columns to close all revenue and expense accounts into the Income Summary account. From the worksheet this can be accomplished by entering the total of the Income Statement, Debit column as a debit to the Income Summary account and crediting each account with its balance appearing in that column. Then debit each account with its balance from the Income Statement, Credit column and credit the total to the Income Summary account. The balance of the Income Summary account after the above entries (net income, $33,735) would then be debited to Income Summary and credited to Retained Earnings. Finally, the Dividends and the Extraordinary Losses accounts would be closed to Retained Earnings. These closing entries are presented below:

Dec. 31	Income summary	250,798	
	Merchandise inventory		34,200
	Sales returns and allowances		1,601
	Sales discounts		2,069
	Credit losses		1,312
	Purchases		79,403
	Service labor		26,601
	Service supplies used		9,777
	Miscellaneous service expense		6,096
	Sales salaries		26,324
	Sales commissions		12,862
	Advertising		3,760
	Depreciation of sales equipment		2,000
	Delivery expense		1,926
	Store supplies used		1,160

Date	Account	Debit	Credit
Dec. 31	Insurance expense, selling		840
	Miscellaneous selling expense		1,448
	Administrative and office salaries		21,838
	Property and operating taxes		3,524
	Federal income taxes		4,810
	Depreciation of office equipment		680
	Depreciation of building		1,400
	Office supplies used		480
	Insurance expense, general		592
	Interest expense		960
	Miscellaneous general expense		426
	Extraordinary gains		4,709
	Closing entry from the worksheet for the year 1970.		
31	Merchandise inventory	37,400	
	Sales of goods	138,448	
	Sales of services	85,303	
	Purchase returns and allowances	568	
	Purchase discounts	1,410	
	Extraordinary gains	21,404	
	Income summary		284,533
	Closing entry from the worksheet for the year 1970.		
31	Income summary	33,735	
	Retained earnings		33,735
	Closing entry from the worksheet for the year 1970.		
31	Retained earnings	36,650	
	Dividends		14,550
	Extraordinary losses		22,100
	To close the Dividends and Extraordinary Losses accounts.		

Closing entries arranged as shown above accomplish their purpose efficiently and easily. They have the same final result, although arranged differently, as the closing entries illustrated in the preceding chapter.

By now it should be clear that the worksheet is not an essential element of the financial information system, but a device for convenience and efficiency. The techniques of its use are applicable at the end of the period and at other times to arrange data clearly and to work with them efficiently.

Read to here- not on test

Consolidated Financial Statements

When one corporation owns the controlling shares in another, it can control all the resources and operations of that firm through its power to elect the board of directors and officers of the second company. In many cases the subsidiary (controlled) company operates virtually as a department of the parent (owning) company. This means that with a high-percent ownership of another company's stock a firm has available all the assets of that company and the economic responsibility to see that its liabilities are paid. In this situation the two firms are one economic entity, and financial information models (financial statements) should indicate this.

Consolidated Balance Sheets

A consolidated balance sheet prepared for a parent company and one or more subsidiary companies should include all the assets and equities of all the companies. Care must be taken that assets reported for the consolidated companies do not include duplicate reporting. For example, after AB Company has paid $100,000 for all the capital stock in XY Company, a separate balance sheet for AB Company would include a $100,000 asset for its investment in XY Company stock. The consolidated balance sheet of the two companies, however, does not include an asset of this type; instead, it includes all the assets and liabilities of XY Company replacing the investment account of AB Company. Inclusion of the investment of one company in the other would result in duplicate reporting of their combined assets.

Examine Figure 13-10 to see how the duplication of asset and equity reporting is prevented by eliminating from the consolidated balance sheet the investment asset of the parent company and shareholders' equity accounts of the subsidiary. In this illustration it is assumed that there have been no earnings since the stock was purchased by AB Company.

In the following illustration, if AB Company had purchased only 80 percent of the shares of XY Company for $80,000, the investment account of $80,000 would have been eliminated, along with 80 percent of the shareholder equity accounts of XY Company. This 80 percent elimination is made as elimination (a) in Figure 13-11. Note that the remaining 20 percent of XY Company's corporate equity accounts is transferred by entry (b) from the three accounts to a separate line to be reported as one amount, "minority interest in XY Company." This equity of minority shareholders is not a liability of the consolidated entity, but neither is it equity in which the shareholders of the parent company have a direct interest. The shareholders' equity section of the consolidated balance sheet would include, in addition to the three normal equity items (capital stock, additional paid-in capital,

Figure 13-10

AB COMPANY AND 100-PERCENT-OWNED CONSOLIDATED SUBSIDIARY

Worksheet for Consolidated Balance Sheet

December 31, 197_

	AB Company	XY Company	Eliminations	Consolidated
	ASSETS			
Cash	$ 20,000	$ 10,000		$ 30,000
Accounts receivable	150,000	60,000		210,000
Plant assets	300,000	80,000		380,000
Investment in XY Co.	100,000		($100,000)	
	$570,000	$150,000	($100,000)	$620,000
	LIABILITIES			
Accounts payable	$130,000	$ 50,000		$180,000
	SHAREHOLDERS' EQUITY			
Capital stock	200,000	60,000	($ 60,000)	200,000
Additional paid-in capital	95,000	30,000	(30,000)	95,000
Retained earnings	145,000	10,000	(10,000)	145,000
	$570,000	$150,000	($100,000)	$620,000

and retained earnings), a special classification for equity of minority shareholders.

Another problem in the preparation of consolidated balance sheets arises when one of the consolidated companies has a debt to another. For example, assume that AB Company has lent its subsidiary, XY Company, $10,000 as operating funds. The $10,000 would be included among receivables in the information for the parent company and among payables for the subsidiary, but there is no receivable nor debt for the entity that includes both companies. Such intercompany accounts are eliminated when a consolidated balance sheet is prepared. Note elimination (c) in Figure 13-11 to see the effect of offsetting or eliminating intercompany receivables and payables.

Consolidated Income Statements

A consolidated income statement presents the revenue and expenses of the combined entity made up of the parent company and its subsidiaries. This statement may be simply the totals from income statements for all the individual companies. However, if the parent com-

Figure 13-11

AB COMPANY AND 80-PERCENT-OWNED CONSOLIDATED SUBSIDIARY

Worksheet for Consolidated Balance Sheet

December 31, 197_

	AB Company	XY Company	Eliminations	Consolidated
	ASSETS			
Cash	$ 40,000	$ 10,000		$ 50,000
Accounts and notes receivable	150,000	60,000	(c) ($10,000)	200,000
Plant assets	300,000	80,000		380,000
Investment in XY Co.	80,000		(a) (80,000)	
	$570,000	$150,000	($80,000)	$630,000
	LIABILITIES			
Accounts and notes payable	$130,000	$ 50,000	(c) ($10,000)	$170,000
	SHAREHOLDERS' EQUITY			
Capital stock	200,000	60,000	(b) ($12,000)	
			(a) (48,000)	$200,000
Additional paid-in capital	95,000	30,000	(b) (6,000)	95,000
			(a) (24,000)	
Retained earnings	145,000	10,000	(b) (2,000)	145,000
			(a) (8,000)	
Minority interest in XY Co.			(b) (20,000)	20,000
	$570,000	$150,000	($80,000)	$630,000

pany and one or two subsidiary companies carry on business between themselves, then there may be revenue, expenses, and net income reported for the individual companies that would not be reported for the consolidated entity because the transactions were within the entity.

Consolidation of income statements is illustrated in Figure 13-12. In this illustration it is assumed that AB Company collected $24,000 rent from its subsidiary, XY Company. This amount appears as a part of the total revenue for AB Company and as a part of the operating expenses for XY Company. On consolidated statements, the two companies are treated as one, and there would be no revenue or expense derived from a firm's occupying its own building. The revenue and expense items are eliminated on the worksheet. The expenses related to maintaining the building are a part of AB Company's expenses and would remain as such for consolidated reporting.

Figure 13-12

AB COMPANY AND CONSOLIDATED SUBSIDIARY

Worksheet for Consolidated Income Statement

For the Year Ended December 31, 197–

	AB Company	XY Company	Eliminations	Consolidated
Revenue:				
Sales	$810,000	$140,000		$950,000
Rent revenue	64,000	–	$(24,000)	40,000
	$874,000	$140,000		$990,000
Expenses:				
Cost of goods sold	$415,000	$ 85,000		$500,000
Operating expenses	205,000	39,000	(24,000)	220,000
	$620,000	$124,000		$720,000
Net income	$254,000	$ 16,000		$270,000

Complexities of Consolidated Reporting

Situations that complicate the consolidation of financial reports occur commonly among companies making up a consolidated entity. If one company sells merchandise to another at a profit and if the merchandise is still in inventory, the sales revenue and cost of goods sold must be eliminated along with the markup above cost included in the transfer price of the merchandise. If a fixed asset is sold at a gain within the consolidated companies, the gain on the sale is eliminated from income and from the cost of the asset, and depreciation for the period is adjusted to eliminate that part of the depreciation that is based on the gain. These and more involved situations make the consolidation of financial information an intricate and challenging task. The resulting consolidated statements represent the companies as one entity.

Mergers: Pooling of Interests versus Purchase

The study of consolidated statements requires attention to the conditions under which the companies were joined or merged. When one company's controlling stock is purchased by another company, the former company is normally considered to have been purchased by the latter. This results in an adjustment on the worksheet for a consolidated balance sheet, changing the amounts reported for the subsidiary's assets from their book values to their valuation in determining the purchase price of the firm's controlling stock. For example, Figure 13-13 shows the result of AB Company's paying $120,000 for all the stock in XY Company, with the price including the following elements:

Cash	$ 10,000
Accounts receivable at amount expected to be collected	57,000
Plant assets at current value	88,000
Current value of total assets	$155,000
Minus liabilities	50,000
Value of net assets of the firm	$105,000
Additional amount in total price of $120,000 for goodwill	15,000
Price for all of XY Company stock	$120,000

Note that in Figure 13-13 the assets are adjusted to the fair values by (a) entries, including the recording of $15,000 goodwill which will

Figure 13-13

AB COMPANY AND CONSOLIDATED SUBSIDIARY

Worksheet for Consolidated Balance Sheet
with Revaluations and Purchased Goodwill
December 31, 197–

	AB Company	XY Company	Adjustments and Eliminations	Consolidated
		ASSETS		
Cash	$ 20,000	$ 10,000		$ 30,000
Accounts receivable	150,000	60,000	(a) $(3,000)	207,000
Plant assets	300,000	80,000	(a) 8,000	388,000
Investment in XY Co.	120,000		(b) (120,000)	
Goodwill			(a) 15,000	15,000
	$590,000	$150,000		$640,000
		LIABILITIES		
Accounts payable	$130,000	$ 50,000		$180,000
		SHAREHOLDERS' EQUITY		
Capital stock	220,000	60,000	(b) (60,000)	220,000
Additional paid-in capital	95,000	30,000	(b) (30,000)	95,000
Retained earnings	145,000	10,000	(b) (10,000)	145,000
Equity from adjusting assets to current value			(a) 20,000 (b) (20,000)	
	$590,000	$150,000		$640,000

appear on the consolidated balance sheet. After the assets are adjusted, the investment is eliminated by (b) entries along with the corporate equity items for XY Company, including the equity recorded from adjusting the assets to current values.

In the situation illustrated in Figure 13-13, if AB Company had issued its own stock to shareholders of XY Company in exchange for their XY Company shares, the merger of the companies might have been interpreted as a pooling of interests. This is a merger in which two or more companies merge their resources without an identifiable purchase of one by the other. The pooling interpretation results in all assets of both firms being reported at their book values with no adjustment to current values. The net book value of XY Company's assets would be treated as the price of the AB Company shares issued, and AB Company's entry for the issue of the shares would be based on that amount. Since in a pooling-of-interests merger there is no restatement of assets, a consolidated balance sheet can be prepared with the same kind of elimination shown in Figure 13-10 where XY Company stock was purchased at book value.

The real difference in reporting a merger of companies as a purchase and as a pooling of interests is that:

1. In a purchase the acquired firm's assets are restated at their current values, and any additional amount paid above this is reported as goodwill purchased, and
2. In a pooling of interests assets are not restated, and the net book value of the acquired firm's assets is treated as the price received for the shares issued in exchange for its stock. In some mergers the two methods of reporting make substantial differences in the resulting consolidated balance sheets and in the amount of amortization of asset cost on the consolidated income statements.
3. In a purchase, only the net income of the acquired company earned after the acquisition date is reported on the consolidated income statement. In a pooling of interests, the net income of both firms for the full year is reported on the consolidated income statement for the year.

Although many mergers have been reported as poolings of interests in the past, the generally accepted interpretation of most mergers now appears to be the purchase of one firm by the other. To the extent that this is true, adjustments of the type shown on Figure 13-13 will be used in preparing consolidated financial statements.

QUESTIONS AND EXERCISES

13- A. What is the relationship between the income statement and the balance sheet?

13- B. Why is the period of time covered by the income statement so significant?
13- C. Which financial statement reports the results of the firm's operations for the period?
13- D. Which financial statement presents the firm's financial status or position? Does the financial position mean the worth of the firm?
13- E. What is the relationship between the income statement and the statement of retained earnings? Between the statement of retained earnings and the balance sheet?
13- F. Explain the function of the worksheet in the preparation of financial statements.
13- G. If routine bookkeeping has been done correctly during the year, why is it necessary to adjust the accounts (make adjusting entries) at the end of the year?
13- H. What do the closing entries accomplish?
13- I. What are the criteria for classifying an item as a current asset?
13- J. Why is land held for resale not a fixed asset?
13- K. What is the greatest number of asset classifications one would expect to see on a balance sheet? What are these classifications?
13- L. What are deferred charges? Deferred credits?
13-M. On the income statement for a wholesale hardware firm, the gain on the sale of a large investment in the capital stock of one of its suppliers would appear under what heading?
13- N. Indicate in which of the following sections of the financial statements each of the listed items would most likely be shown: (a) current assets, (b) fixed assets, (c) current liabilities, (d) long-term liabilities, (e) owners' equity, (f) revenue, (g) expense, (h) none of these.

Accounts receivable
Cash
Loss on sale of equipment
Advances to salesmen
Sales returns and allowances
Allowance for uncollectible accounts
Credit losses
Notes receivable from customers
Depreciation of office equipment
Fees collected in advance
Income taxes withheld
Investments in short-term government securities
Office salaries
Additional paid-in capital
Petty cash
Product warranty expense
Purchase discounts
Raw materials for factory
Royalties earned
Sales equipment
Interest earned

13- O. Data reported on financial statements reflect the past. A person interested in investing in a company wants to forecast its future profits and strength. How can analysis of financial information be useful to him?
13- P. A company reported net income of $15,000 for 1971, but its cash balance at the end of the year was $10,000 less than it had been at the beginning of the year. How can this be explained?
13- Q. A B Company's return on total assets is 14 percent, but its net income as a percent of sales is only 2 percent. How can this be true?
13- R. X Y Company's return on total assets is 5 percent; its return on common shareholders' equity is 3.5 percent. What is indicated?

PROCEDURAL PROBLEMS

13-1.

LAYNE MANUFACTURING COMPANY

Trial Balance
December 31, 1969

	Debit	Credit
Cash	$ 7,800	
Accounts receivable	17,400	
Allowance for uncollectible accounts		$ 1,100
Merchandise inventory, Jan. 1, 1969	41,000	
Prepaid expenses	2,900	
Investment in ABC bonds	48,800	
Automotive equipment	38,000	
Accumulated depreciation, automotive equipment		8,400
Land	51,000	
Accounts payable		11,600
Accrued payables		900
Interest payable on bonds		-0-
Bonds payable (6 percent, due December 31, 1979)		50,000
Discount on bonds payable	4,000	
Common stock ($10 par authorized 8,000 shares)		50,000
Preferred stock (6 percent, $20 par value, 5,000 shares authorized)		20,000
Premium on common stock		2,000
Treasury stock	1,500	
Retained earnings		25,400
Dividends		-0-
Sales		170,600
Interest income	-0-	
Sales discounts	350	
Credit losses	650	
Purchases	98,900	
Purchases returns		400
Salary expense	30,000	
Depreciation expense		
Advertising expense	6,600	
Payroll taxes expense	2,700	
Interest expense	-0-	
Loss on sale of automotive equipment	200	
Gain on sale of land		11,400
	$351,800	$351,800

1. Merchandise inventory on December 31, $44,000.
2. Depreciation of automotive equipment is straight-line. The equipment has a ten-year useful life and no salvage value.
3. The bond investment is being amortized $200 per year. The bonds are par value of $50,000 with a stated interest rate of 6 percent. Interest is accrued for the year each December 31.
4. On December 31, the company declared a cash dividend of 6 percent to preferred stockholders and $.20 per share on the common stock.
5. On extraordinary gains and losses the federal income rate is 25 percent, and is to be applied against the net gains after subtracting any losses.
6. Federal income tax rate on operating income is 50 percent.
7. Interest payable is accrued on the bonds each December 31. The discount is amortized, using the straight-line method, at $400 each year.

Using the Layne Manufacturing Company's trial balance and additional data provided:

a. Prepare a worksheet.
b. Prepare a condensed combined statement of income and retained earnings for the year 1969.
c. Prepare a condensed balance sheet as of December 31, 1969.
d. Compute book value per share of common stock.

13-2.

WILLIAMS, INC.
Trial Balance
December 31, 1969

	Debit	Credit
Cash	$ 3,100	
Accounts receivable	19,200	
Allowance for uncollectible accounts		350
Note receivable, due Jan. 31, 1970	4,000	
Merchandise inventory, Jan. 1, 1969	26,500	
Supplies	700	
Prepaid insurance	1,100	
Factory equipment	55,800	
Accumulated depreciation on factory equipment		17,100
Building	40,000	
Accumulated depreciation on building		6,700
Land	32,000	
Investment in XYZ stock	48,300	
Accounts payable		10,600
Salaries payable		1,400
Interest payable		450
Rent payable		800

13-2. (continued)

	Debit	Credit
Bonds payable		20,000
Premium on bonds payable		1,200
Common stock ($10 par, 10,000 authorized)		70,000
Preferred stock ($50 par value, 1,000 shares authorized and issued, 5 percent)		33,000
Premium on common stock		7,000
Premium on preferred stock		3,000
Retained earnings		49,350
Dividends	7,400	
Sales		152,500
Sales discounts	400	
Credit losses	950	
Purchases	86,000	
Purchase discounts		725
Purchase returns and allowances		125
Salaries	22,000	
Interest	1,600	
Rent	8,000	
Insurance	4,500	
Taxes	5,200	
Depreciation, building	700	
Depreciation, factory equipment	950	
Interest income		300
Flood loss	6,200	
	$374,600	$374,600

January 1, 1969, inventory	$ 28,000
Accounts receivable (net) on January 1	16,700
Total assets on January 1	188,000
Credit sales	128,000
Income taxes	4,000

a. Prepare a detailed income statement for the year ended December 31, 1969.
b. Prepare a detailed statement of retained earnings for the year ended December 31, 1969.
c. Prepare a detailed balance sheet as of December 31, 1969.
d. Compute the following ratios:
   current ratio
   acid-test ratio

debt to equity
debt to total assets
return on total assets
return on stockholders' equity
earnings per share on common stock
net income to sales
inventory turnover
accounts receivable turnover

e. Compute book value per share of common stock.

13-3. On September 1, 1969, Mr. Charles M. Reddick formed the Land-Mart Corporation to take over his real estate agency. He transferred the following assets (at fair market value) in exchange for 2,500 shares of $100 par value stock.

Land	$200,000
Commercial buildings	165,000
Truck	7,000

On September 30, 1969, he attempted to prepare a trial balance but made several errors, resulting in the following:

LAND-MART CORPORATION
For the Month Ended September 30, 1969
Trial Balance

Cash	$ 35,000	
Accounts receivable	19,000	
Dividends receivable	400	
Inventory of land and buildings held for sale	386,300	
Prepaid insurance on buildings	14,000	
Investments owned by Mr. Reddick	11,000	
Truck	7,000	
Accounts payable (includes $200 owed by Mr. Reddick for repairs to his personal residence)		9,700
Salary payable		13,400
Capital stock		372,000
Sales		421,200
Sales commission expense	29,800	
Cost of land and buildings sold	311,000	
Salary paid to Mr. Reddick as president of corporation	12,000	
Insurance expense	2,000	
Dividends income (from Mr. Reddick's investments)		400
	$827,500	$816,700

All capital stock is held by Mr. Reddick and was issued when the corporation was formed.

Prepare a corrected trial balance, an income statement, and a balance sheet for Land-Mart Corporation.

13-4. The J-M Market is operated as a partnership owned by Ted R. Jensen and Fred R. Mitchell. Presented below is a trial balance representing the operations for the year ended December 31, 1970.

a. Prepare a condensed balance sheet and condensed income statement for the market and a statement of partners' capital.
b. Prepare closing entries.
c. Compute the following ratios:
   acid-test
   debt to equity
   return on total assets
   return on partners' equity
   net income to sales

J-M MARKET
Trial Balance
December 31, 1970

Cash	$ 11,400	
Accounts receivable	29,300	
Inventory, January 1, 1970	16,400	
Prepaid expenses	2,300	
Plant assets	110,000	
Accumulated depreciation		$ 21,000
Accounts payable		4,600
Bonds payable		50,000
Jensen, capital		58,400
Mitchell, capital		36,400
Jensen, drawings	7,100	
Mitchell, drawings	15,900	
Sales (net)		146,000
Purchases (net)	84,000	
Operating expenses	29,000	
Extraordinary loss	11,000	
	$316,400	$316,400

Inventory on December 31, 1970, was $18,100. Ted Jensen made a $10,000 additional investment on April 4, 1970. Net income is allocated 60 percent to Jensen and 40 percent to Mitchell.

13-5. Given the following information and trial balance for 1970 transactions: All services were performed on account. The total assets at

December 31, 1969, were $44,300, and the December 31, 1969 stockholders' equity was $20,300.

KIRBY CORPORATION
Trial Balance
December 31, 1970

Account	Debit	Credit
Cash	$ 6,300	
Accounts receivable (net)	8,100	
Repair parts inventory	5,200	
Prepaid rent	1,200	
Tools and equipment	33,100	
Accumulated depreciation		$ 6,200
Accounts payable		5,200
Salary payable		1,700
Income tax payable		
Note payable (due in 1976)		10,000
Common stock		10,000
Retained earnings		10,300
Service revenue		47,300
Cost of repair parts used	10,900	
Salary expense	19,000	
Depreciation expense	2,300	
Rent expense	3,600	
Interest expense	1,000	
	$90,700	$90,700

a. Prepare an income statement and balance sheet. The income tax expense will be 50 percent of the net income for the year.
b. Compute the following ratios: debt to total assets, return on total assets, and return on stockholders' equity.

13-6. The following trial balance was prepared as of December 31, 1970, the last day of the company's business year. Enter this trial balance on a worksheet, record the adjustments, and complete the worksheet.

Adjustment data:

1. The accrued interest income is $220.
2. The remaining prepaid insurance is $8,000.
3. Depreciation expense is $2,100.
4. The salary payable is $3,400.
5. The warranty liability should be $1,750.
6. A 2 percent dividend was declared but not yet paid.
7. December 31, 1970, inventory is $44,100.

HAYES, INC.
Trial Balance
June 30, 1970

Cash	$ 16,000	
Accounts receivable	43,100	
Interest receivable		
Allowance for uncollectible accounts		$ 2,100
Inventory, July 1, 1969	47,300	
Prepaid insurance	12,000	
Office supplies	3,700	
Factory building	200,000	
Accumulated depreciation		19,400
Accounts payable		21,700
Salary payable		
Dividend payable		
Warranty liability		
Capital stock		100,000
Retained earnings		148,400
Dividends		
Sales		211,400
Sales discounts	350	
Credit losses	2,700	
Purchases	109,300	
Purchase discounts		750
Salary expense	31,300	
Rent expense	8,000	
Insurance expense	11,000	
Office supplies expense	600	
Depreciation expense, factory building		
Warranty expense		
Interest income		2,600
Loss from storm damage	21,000	
	$506,350	$506,350

13-7. The following information in summary form has been taken from the records of Hager, Incorporated for the year ended June 30, 1970.

Retained earnings, July 1, 1969	$116,000
Net sales	725,000
Cost of goods sold	410,000
Operating expenses	236,000

Equities		
Accounts payable	$1,420,000	$ 800,000
Taxes payable	780,000	320,000
Long-term debt	–	2,800,000
Capital stock	4,400,000	1,600,000
Retained earnings	2,400,000	1,080,000
	$9,000,000	$6,600,000

a. Which company is more liquid?
b. Which offers the most security?
c. Which of the companies is more profitable?
Explain your conclusions and support them with ratio analyses.

13-10. Further examination of the Kawana Corporation and the Johnson Company (see problem 13-9) reveals that Kawana is only two years old and that most of its plant and inventory were purchased new since its organization. Johnson was organized and acquired most of its plant assets twenty years ago, when the general price index was 150. This company has used the LIFO inventory pricing procedure for the past twelve years; $1,500,000 of its present inventory is priced at the original prices, when the price index was 180. At the end of 1971, this general price index was 220.

a. Restate inventory, plant and equipment, and depreciation ($200,000 included in operating expenses), and prepare a revised income statement and balance sheet for the Johnson Company. Use the account Capital from Price-Level Adjustment to report the effect of price-level changes on plant assets and inventory.
b. Analyze the data for the companies again, using the adjusted data for Johnson Company, to determine which company is more liquid, which offers the most security, and which of the companies is more profitable.

14 Funds Analysis and Reporting

Preview Questions

As you study look for the answers to the following questions:

- **What does the word *funds* mean as used in the funds statement?**
- **What is working capital, and how is it measured?**
- **What is the significance of changes in the structure of working capital?**
- **What information is provided by the working capital statement?**
- **What changes may take place in working capital?**
- **What information is provided by the funds statement?**
- **How are changes reported in a funds statement?**
- **What is the general meaning of *funds*?**

Information concerning the movement of financial resources within and into and out of the firm is essential to management for understanding the results of its decisions and actions. This information is also necessary to investors and investment analysts for understanding the firm's financial position as a basis for predicting its future financial strength and profits.

The movement of financial resources is often termed the *flow of funds*. Information about this facet of the firm's activities is reported on the *funds statement* (other titles: Statement of Source and Application of Funds, Funds Flow Statement, and confusingly, Cash Flow Statement). Many companies publish this information annually for their stockholders; it is published in aggregate for the national economy by the federal reserve (bank) system in the *Federal Reserve Bulletin*. The purpose of this chapter is to develop an understanding of the source and utility of the individual firm's financial resource, or fund, information.

WORKING CAPITAL

The most active portion of a company's resources is its current assets; sometimes called *working* assets. A major part of the inflow and outflow of resources is in the form of current assets. Current assets are provided partly by short-term credit (current liabilities) and partly by the firm from other sources; this latter part is the firm's working capital. *Working capital* is, therefore, the amount of capital for current assets provided by the firm from long-term sources such as long-term debt and shareholder investment. The common measure of working capital is the excess of current assets over current liabilities.

Importance of Working Capital

Working capital is vitally important for two aspects of the firm's financial activities. First, in planning and providing adequate financial resources for the firm, management must forecast the movement of current assets and the use of short-term liabilities in order to predict the need for resources from long-term sources to finance the firm's current operations. For example, management must know if resources, or funds, from company earnings will be needed in current asset form and whether additional funds from stockholders' investments, long-term borrowing, or the sale of long-term assets will be needed in current asset form for the company's operation.

Second, since adequate working capital is critical to a firm's financial strength, investors include working capital and the flow of resources in their financial analyses. Lack of adequate working capital may pose planning and operational problems for management, and it may significantly affect the market for shares of the company, compounding the problem of providing the needed resources.

Working capital derives some of its importance from the fact that resources in the form of current assets can be used in many ways; they are committed in a specific form (receivables, inventory, etc.) for only a short time. Therefore, rapid changes can be made in the structure and use of these current items. Management has a much greater opportunity for innovation and improvement if it has adequate resources available in this uncommitted form.

Computation

Resources that the firm provides from long-term sources to be used in short-term asset form (working capital) can be computed simply by deducting total current liabilities from the total current assets. Working capital sometimes is *defined* as the excess of current assets over current liabilities; this is like defining cash as the excess of quick assets over receivables! The correct definition of working capital is repeated in the first sentence of this paragraph. The formula for computing the amount of working capital is

Current assets − current liabilities = working capital.

Measurement and analysis of working capital involve both current assets and current liabilities. If current assets total $157,500 and current liabilities total $66,100, the amount of working capital is $91,400.

WORKING CAPITAL ANALYSIS

It is quite common for most of a firm's changes in resources to be reflected in changes in current assets and current liabilities. Relatively few events change the amounts of long-term items alone. Therefore, the greater part of analyzing and reporting changes in funds (resources) is the analyzing and reporting of working capital. In fact, some funds statements present only the changes in working capital.

Changes in the Structure of Working Capital

The first step taken in capital analysis often is the computation of changes in the structure of working capital, in the amount of funds committed in each kind of current asset, and the amount of credit obtained from each kind of current liability. This step in working capital analysis is shown in the schedule below:

	Working Capital Items December 31		Working Capital Increase (Decrease)
	1970	1971	
Current assets:			
Cash	$10,000	$12,000	$ 2,000
Accounts receivable	27,000	30,000	3,000
Notes receivable	2,000	6,000	4,000
Inventory	49,000	45,000	(4,000)
Supplies and other prepaid expenses	2,000	3,000	1,000
	$90,000	$96,000	
Increase in current assets	6,000		$ 6,000
	$96,000	$96,000	
Current liabilities:			
Trade accounts and notes payable	$29,000	$31,000	$(2,000)
Notes payable to bank	10,000	11,000	(1,000)
Accrued liabilities	4,000	3,000	1,000
	$43,000	$45,000	
Increase in current liabilities	2,000		(2,000)
	$45,000	$45,000	
Increase in working capital			$ 4,000

The information revealed by this kind of analysis is helpful to management in deciding whether certain areas, the total of $7,000 increase in notes and accounts receivable, for example, should receive special attention. Perhaps credit has been granted without regard to established criteria; perhaps the criteria need review; or perhaps collection procedures should be revised. Of course, the increase in receivables might have resulted from increased sales; credit granting and collection procedures may be totally acceptable. For the person interested in the firm's financial soundness, the changes in structure of working capital may not be greatly significant. How the firm supplied the additional $4,000 in working capital may be much more important. Did it come from current operations, from additional long-term borrowing, from the sale of long-term assets, or from additional stockholder investments? Further analysis is needed to answer this question.

Changes in the Amount of Working Capital

Funds may be moved within the working capital group without changing the total; for instance, cash is collected from customers, reducing accounts receivable and increasing cash, but not changing the total of working capital. Cash can be paid to creditors, reducing cash and accounts payable, but not changing total working capital. Study of such changes does not provide information about the sources of changes in total working capital. Changes in noncurrent-financial items provide information about the source of changes in total working capital.

Sources of Changes in Working Capital

Funds may be brought into working capital from four basic sources:

1. Excess of funds received over funds expended in current operations;
2. Investments by stockholders;
3. Borrowing from long-term creditors;
4. Sale of long-life assets.

Of course, funds could be received by the firm as gifts from individuals or grants from the government. This occurs so seldom from sources outside the area of "operations" or "investments" that normally it can be ignored.

Interestingly and logically, funds may be removed from working capital by dispositions to the same four sources from which they are received. Funds may be dispensed from working capital to:

1. Operations, as the excess of funds expended over funds received;
2. Stockholders, as dividends or as return of their investments;
3. Long-term creditors, as repayment of loans;
4. Suppliers of long-life assets.

Each of these sources of change in working capital, both provision (source) of funds and disposition (often called application) of funds, will be examined in greater detail.

Operations as source of changes in working capital The inflow of resources identified as revenue is almost invariably in the form of the current assets: cash and accounts receivable. Most resources consumed as expenses are either paid for in cash or purchased on short-term credit; supplies purchased for cash or on credit, services of personnel paid for in cash or represented by accrued liabilities, and rent usually paid for a short time in advance are examples of these. These expenses properly are offset against revenues in computing the funds provided by operations. Expenses that are not the consumption of short-life assets are, of course, the consumption of long-life assets, represented by depreciation, depletion, and amortization; when matching the consumption of short-life resources against the inflow of such resources through revenue, these expenses are omitted. The computation of working capital provided from operations is seen in the following illustration:

	Net Income	Working Capital
Sales	$101,400	$101,400
Expenses:		
Cost of goods sold	$ 56,000	$ 56,000
Salaries	30,000	30,000
Rent	3,600	3,600
Depreciation	4,000	
Amortization of franchise	3,000	
	$ 96,000	$ 89,000
Net income	$ 5,400	
Funds provided from operations		$ 12,400

The preceding illustration demonstrates that funds provided from operations is the excess of the inflow of short-life assets over the consumption of such assets. Often such items as rent and employee services are not considered assets, but expenses. This leads to the description of funds provided from operations as the excess of revenue over expenses other than depreciation, depletion, and amortization. There is a short-cut computation of funds from operations, based on this description, which is accomplished by adding back to net income the amounts deducted as depreciation, depletion, and amortization. For the preceding data this computation would be

Net income		$ 5,400
Add back:	Depreciation	4,000
	Amortization	3,000
Funds provided from operations		$12,400

This is the computation seen most frequently. Normally all of the elements (net income, depreciation, etc.) are reported on the funds statement when the amount of funds provided from operations is reported. Occasionally there is an item of revenue which does not provide working capital. Such items (amortization of discount on bond investment, for example) are deducted from net income in computing working capital provided from operations, just as depreciation is added back to net income. This reporting is illustrated below on the statement of working capital in Figure 14-1.

Obviously, if more current resources are consumed in operations than are provided in revenue, the result is a net consumption of working capital in operations rather than a provision. In Figure 14-1 the working capital from operations is reported under the heading Working Capital Provided by; if there had been a consumption of working capital by operations, this would have been reported in the second section of the report under the heading Working Capital Applied to.

Stockholders as sources and consumers of working capital Cash and other short-term assets (subscriptions receivable, for example) received from stockholders as investments increase working capital. Therefore, investments from stockholders is reported as a source of working capital.

Stockholders can also be the recipients of payments from working capital. Cash dividends declared decrease working capital; so does the purchase of treasury stock. One would report cash dividends and payments for treasury stock as a part of the working capital used, or applied. Both the receipt of working capital from investors and the payment of working capital to them are seen below in the information in Figure 14-1.

Long-term creditors as sources and consumers of working capital Most long-term borrowing increases the firm's cash; this is an increase in working capital. If the full amount of such borrowing is used immediately to purchase long-life assets, the source and use of the funds sometimes are reported in the long-term funds portion of the statement, rather than as changes in working capital. This commonly is done if the money is borrowed for a specific purchase and is transferred directly from the creditor to the supplier, not coming through the firm itself. Money borrowed for use as working capital (payment of creditors, purchase of merchandise, etc.) always would be reported as a source of working capital.

Payments of interest to long-term creditors, as well as short-term creditors, are treated as the payment for a consumed resource (availabile money) and, therefore, become a part of the funds used in operations. However, repayment of principal to long-term creditors clearly is a use of working capital, and this is reported under working capital used, or applied, on the funds statement.

Purchase and sale of long-life assets: effect on working capital Spending cash or incurring short-term liabilities for the purchase of long-life assets is a use of working capital. In analyzing the causes of working capital changes, purchases of long-life assets should be examined to determine the amount of working capital used.

Any cash or short-term receivables obtained when long-life assets are sold are considered working capital provided by that transaction. Sale of investments and other assets is a basic means of obtaining increased working capital. Transactions of this type must be examined for the amount of working capital they provide in an analysis of working capital changes.

Illustration of Working Capital Analysis

Based on the following comparative balance sheets for 1970 and 1971, statements of income and retained earnings for 1971, and the additional information, changes in working capital have been analyzed and a schedule of changes in the working capital structure, plus a working capital statement, have been prepared. Examine the following information and follow each step of the analysis.

BANDY ENTERPRISES, INC.
Balance Sheets
December 31, 1970 and 1971

	1971	1970
ASSETS		
Current assets:		
Cash	$ 225,000	$ 200,000
Marketable securities	100,000	100,000
Accounts receivable (net)	330,000	220,000
Merchandise inventory	720,000	460,000
Prepaid expenses	25,000	20,000
	$1,400,000	$1,000,000
Investments:		
Bond sinking fund	$ 250,000	$ 225,000

Balance Sheets (continued)

	1971	1970
Plant assets:		
Patents	$ 150,000	$ 175,000
Equipment (net)	650,000	550,000
Buildings (net)	1,200,000	900,000
Land	200,000	200,000
	$2,200,000	$1,825,000
Total assets	$3,850,000	$3,050,000
LIABILITIES		
Current liabilities:		
Accounts payable	$ 495,000	$ 274,000
Income tax payable	135,000	126,000
Accrued liabilities	60,000	70,000
	$ 690,000	$ 470,000
Long-term liabilities:		
Mortgage notes payable	$ 500,000	
Bonds payable (including premium)	509,000	$ 510,000
	$1,009,000	$ 510,000
Total liabilities	$1,699,000	$ 980,000
STOCKHOLDERS' EQUITY		
Common stock (par value $100)	$1,200,000	$1,200,000
Additional paid-in capital	400,000	400,000
Retained earnings	551,000	470,000
	$2,151,000	$2,070,000
Total liabilities and stockholders' equity	$3,850,000	$3,050,000

BANDY ENTERPRISES, INC.

Statement of Income and Retained Earnings

For the Year Ended December 31, 1971

Revenue:	
Sales of goods and services (net)	$3,390,000
Sinking fund earnings	14,000
	$3,404,000

Operating expenses:	
Cost of merchandise sold	$2,221,000
Selling expenses	705,000
General and administrative expenses	186,000
Depreciation	110,000
Amortization	25,000
	$3,247,000
Net income before extraordinary items	$ 157,000
Loss on sale of equipment	4,000
Net income	$ 153,000
Retained earnings, January 1, 1971	470,000
	$ 623,000
Dividends (cash)	72,000
Retained earnings, December 31, 1971	$ 551,000
Net income before extraordinary items per share of common stock	$13.08
Net income per share of common stock	$12.75

Additional information:

Depreciation was $65,000 on equipment and $45,000 on buildings.

A new building and equipment were purchased for $520,000, with a cash payment of only $20,000 and a mortgage note for the remainder.

A payment of $11,000, plus sinking fund earnings, increased the sinking fund to its planned balance.

Premium of $1,000 on bonds payable was amortized to interest expense.

Equipment with a book value of $10,000 was sold for $6,000 cash.

Steps in working capital analysis Many devices, such as worksheets and special accounts, are used for organizing the information about working capital changes. Such detailed attention to technique is more appropriate in a professional accounting course. For our purposes the following specific steps should be adequate to understand and perform the analysis.

Schedule of changes in working capital items Examining current assets and liabilities provides information concerning the kinds and amount of changes that occurred during the year; from this a schedule of such changes can be prepared. Such examination also provides the total change in working capital used in preparing the working capital statement.

BANDY ENTERPRISES, INC.

Schedule of Changes in Working Capital Items

For the Year Ended December 31, 1971

	1970	1971	Working Capital Increase (Decrease)
Current assets:			
Cash	$ 200,000	$ 225,000	$ 25,000
Marketable securities	100,000	100,000	
Accounts receivable (net)	220,000	330,000	110,000
Merchandise inventory	460,000	720,000	260,000
Prepaid expenses	20,000	25,000	5,000
	$1,000,000	$1,400,000	
Increase in current assets	400,000		400,000
	$1,400,000	$1,400,000	
Current liabilities:			
Accounts payable	$ 274,000	$ 495,000	$221,000
Income tax payable	126,000	135,000	9,000
Accrued liabilities	70,000	60,000	(10,000)
	$ 470,000	$ 690,000	
Increase in current liabilities	220,000		220,000
	$ 690,000	$ 690,000	
Increase in working capital			$180,000

Sources and uses of working capital Activities which provided additions to working capital or used working capital can be identified under the four categories listed earlier: operations, stockholders, long-term creditors, suppliers of long-term assets. From the comparative balance sheets, the income and retained earnings statement, and the additional information, the following items are obtained.

LIST OF WORKING CAPITAL CHANGES

Operations:		
Funds were provided by:		
(A) Net income		$153,000
Add back deductions in computing net income that did not use working capital:		
Depreciation	$110,000	
Amortization of patents	25,000	
Loss on sale of equipment	4,000	139,000
		$292,000

(B)	Deduct credits to revenue or expense that did not provide working capital:		
	Sinking fund earnings	$ 14,000	
	Amortization of premium on bonds payable	1,000	15,000
Funds from operations			$277,000
Stockholders:			
Funds provided: none (no new investments)			
(C)	Funds used for dividends		$ 72,000
Long-term creditors:			
Funds provided: none			
Funds applied: none			
Long-life asset acquisition and sale:			
(D)	Funds were provided from sale of equipment		$ 6,000
	Funds were applied to:		
(E)	Purchase of building and equipment	$ 20,000	
(F)	Payment into sinking fund	11,000	31,000

This list of the changes that provided or used working capital is obtained by examining each item on the statements and additional information provided to identify the inflows and outflows of working capital. In this list the term *funds* is used to mean working capital, as it is used often in financial reports.

In the group of items designated (A) in the preceding list, notice the $4,000 loss on sale of equipment. In a computation of fund inflows and outflows this item would not appear; the loss of value in a building does not consume working capital. However, this item, along with depreciation and amortization, was deducted in computing net income, and when we start with net income in determining the funds provided by operations we must add back the amount of the item. The sale of equipment actually provided working capital in the amount of $6,000. This is shown in item (D) in the list.

On the income statement there appears a revenue item, sinking fund earnings, in the amount of $14,000. We know that these earnings were added to the sinking fund and did not become a part of current assets. When this item was journalized, the Sinking Fund account (not the Cash account) was debited, and Sinking Fund Earnings was credited. Since the item is included as a part of net income, it is deducted from net income in the funds computation. Amortization of premium on bonds payable has the same effect; when the amortization was recorded, Interest Expense was credited and Premium on Bonds Payable was debited. The $1,000 amount entered into the net income computation, but it did not affect working capital; therefore, it is deducted in computing working capital from operations.

To aid in tracing them from the list to the statement the lettered items in the preceding list retain their letter designations in the working capital statement in Figure 14-1.

Note that the long-term $500,000 mortgage note, given in direct consideration for a building and equipment purchased during the year, did not provide working capital; it therefore does not appear on the list of working capital changes nor on the working capital statement. A funds statement, showing changes in all financial resources, will include this item; that statement appears in the next section of this chapter.

Preparing the working capital statement Organizing data on the informal working capital changes list into a working capital statement makes them more meaningful. This statement contains much of the information appearing on a funds statement, which shows all changes in the firm's financial resources. In fact, the funds statement often contains only working capital changes; therefore, the title "Funds Statement," or "Statement of Source and Application of Funds," often is used for the working capital statement. In this chapter we shall use the titles with some discrimination, but one should be prepared to find them rather loosely used in published financial reports.

In Figure 14-1 a working capital statement presents in more orderly format the same information that appeared earlier on the list of working capital changes. In this statement the major sources and uses of working capital are grouped to compare the total working capital provided with the total used up for various purposes.

Note that the increase in working capital shown on the working capital statement is exactly the same amount as that indicated by the schedule of working capital changes shown earlier in the chapter. The working capital statement provides information to show where the year's operating funds (working capital) came from and where they were used. This information tells creditors and investors a great deal about the firm's financing and indicates the degree of financial soundness to be expected in the future. The working capital statement contains only information relating to the source and use of working capital; other significant financial events of the year which affected the firm's broader financial resources do not appear on this statement. For this reason, working capital information often is included in a broader statement instead of being presented in a separate report as shown here.

Figure 14-1

BANDY ENTERPRISES, INC.
Working Capital Statement
For the Year Ended December 31, 1971

Working capital was provided by:			
Operations:			
(A)	Net income		$153,000
	Plus deductions not requiring working capital:		
	Depreciation	$110,000	
	Amortization of patents	25,000	
	Loss on sale of equipment	4,000	139,000
			$292,000
(B)	Minus amounts not providing working capital:		
	Sinking fund earnings	$ 14,000	
	Amortization of premium on bonds payable	1,000	15,000
	Total working capital from operations		$277,000
(D)	Sale of equipment		6,000
Total working capital provided			$283,000
Working capital was used for:			
(C)	Dividends	$ 72,000	
(E)	Purchase of building and equipment	20,000	
(F)	Payment into sinking fund	11,000	
Total working capital used			103,000
Increase in working capital for the year			$180,000

FUNDS REPORTED AS ALL FINANCIAL RESOURCES

The term *funds* is loosely defined in financial reporting and loosely used. However, the Accounting Principles Board of the American Institute of Certified Public Accountants, in its Opinion no. 3, recommends a funds concept that is broader than working capital, one that can be characterized as *all financial resources of the firm.* For many firms, changes in working capital constitute most of the changes in financial resources; the broader view would include a few additional items such as the issue of company shares in exchange for investment assets and the giving of a long-term note in direct payment for plant assets purchased. Figure 14-2 presents a funds statement prepared on the broader basis.

The few differences between Figures 14-1 and 14-2 are highly

Figure 14-2

BANDY ENTERPRISES, INC.

Funds Statement

For the Year Ended December 31, 1971

FUNDS PROVIDED		
Working capital was provided by:		
Operations:		
Net income		$153,000
Plus deductions not requiring working capital:		
Depreciation	$110,000	
Amortization of patents	25,000	
Loss on sale of equipment	4,000	139,000
		$292,000
Minus amounts not providing working capital:		
Sinking fund earnings	$ 14,000	
Amortization of premium on bonds payable	1,000	15,000
Total working capital from operations		$277,000
Sale of equipment		6,000
Total working capital provided		$283,000
Other funds were provided by:		
Issue of long-term mortgage note		500,000
Total funds provided		$783,000
FUNDS APPLIED		
Working capital was used for:		
Dividends	$ 72,000	
Purchase of building and equipment	20,000	
Payment into sinking fund	11,000	$103,000
Other funds were applied to:		
Increase in working capital		180,000
Purchase of building and equipment		500,000
Total funds applied		$783,000

significant in effect. One additional item is included in both the funds provided and funds applied sections: the provision of resources by the issue of a long-term mortgage note and the application of these resources to the purchase of building and equipment. This transaction did not affect working capital, but it did have a significant effect on the firm's resources. Also, the format of the report in Figure 14-2 is changed so that the increase in working capital is shown as a use of resources (funds), and the report appears as a closed, or balance, report.

Any amount of detail can be included on the face of the funds statement. For example, the changes in the amount of accounts receivable and inventory are highly significant for Bandy Enterprises, Inc., for which the illustrative statements are presented. These changes can be brought into the funds statement by dropping the working capital grouping of items and arranging the information as shown in Figure 14-3.

Figure 14-3

FUNDS STATEMENT SHOWING SIGNIFICANT DETAILS

BANDY ENTERPRISES, INC.

Funds Statement

For the Year Ended December 31, 1971

Funds were provided by:		
Operations:		
Net income		$ 153,000
Plus deductions not requiring working capital:		
Depreciation	$110,000	
Amortization of patents	25,000	
Loss on sale of equipment	4,000	139,000
		$ 292,000
Minus amounts not providing working capital:		
Sinking fund earnings	$ 14,000	
Amortization of premium on bonds payable	1,000	15,000
Total funds from operations		$ 277,000
Increase in accounts payable and other current liabilities		220,000
Sale of equipment		6,000
Issue of long-term mortgage note		500,000
Total funds provided		$1,003,000
Funds were applied to:		
Dividends		$ 72,000
Purchase of building and equipment		520,000
Payment into sinking fund		11,000
Increase in accounts receivable		110,000
Increase in merchandise inventory		260,000
Increase in cash and prepaid expenses		30,000
Total funds applied		$1,003,000

The purpose of the broader funds statement is to reveal the period's significant financial events. The report's structure is loose and flexible, largely because of the loose and varying use of the term *funds*. Information on this less formal report is intended to provide a more detailed understanding of the firm than does information on the more formal balance sheet and income statement.

"CASH FLOW" REPORTING

In recent years there has developed a mislabeled financial item which can be grossly misunderstood. Financial analysts and some financial management have presented a figure termed "cash flow," which normally is computed as net income plus depreciation, depletion, and amortization. This amount does measure approximately the amount of funds generated by the firm's operations, but it is misleading to present it as a measure of total performance. While this computation appears to be an integral part of funds reporting and analysis, reporting it separately and giving it the erroneous title of "cash flow" is a dangerously misinforming process because it is not "cash" and it does not represent a "flow" of anything.

QUESTIONS AND EXERCISES

14-A. What meanings can the word *funds* have when used in a funds statement?
14-B. Working capital is measured as the excess of current assets over current liabilities. How is the excess better described?
14-C. What information does a funds statement provide?
14-D. List the four general sources of working capital and the four general applications of working capital.
14-E. On November 29, a firm borrowed $20,000 on its own ninety-day note. On its December 31 funds statement for the year, will this be shown as the source of $20,000 working capital?
14-F. A firm began the year with a merchandise inventory of $90,000 and reduced this to $80,000 by the end of the year. Was this reduction in inventory a source of working capital?
14-G. A firm issued 1,000 shares of additional stock during the year for $50,000 cash. Was this a source of working capital?
14-H. During the year, 1,200 shares of additional stock were issued in exchange for land to be used as a plant site. Was this issue of stock a source of working capital? Of funds?
14-I. Funds statements often show funds provided as follows:

Funds were provided by:	
Net income for the year	$xxx,xxx
Depreciation, depletion, and amortization	xx,xxx
Funds from operations	$xxx,xxx
Long-term borrowing	xxx,xxx
Total funds provided	$xxx,xxx

a. Does depreciation actually provide funds?
b. What would be a better presentation on the funds statement?

14-J. The Campton Corporation annual report for 1971 shows the following:

	1971	1970
Investments in other companies	$ 44,000	$ 76,000
Retained earnings	190,000	183,000

A footnote to the statements reveals that in 1971 the corporation sold its 10,000 shares in Hedgewood House, Inc. for $53,000. These were reported on the 1970 balance sheet at their cost of $32,000. What sources of funds should one find on the 1971 funds statement from this sale?

PROCEDURAL PROBLEMS

14-1. Discuss the difference between *funds*, as it is used in the funds statement, and *working capital*.

14-2. Explain what the funds statement should contain according to the opinion of the American Institute of Certified Public Accountants.

14-3. The comparative balance sheets for Carolyn Vincent Enterprises, Inc. on December 31, 1970, and December 31, 1971, appear below.

	December 31	
	1971	1970
ASSETS		
Cash	$ 27,400	$ 28,400
Accounts receivable (net)	21,600	33,200
Merchandise inventory	99,100	104,000
Prepaid expenses	2,800	2,960
Plant assets	216,000	170,000
Depreciation to date on plant assets	(64,000)	(94,000)
Liabilities and stockholders' equity	$302,900	$244,560

(continued)

	December 31	
	1971	1970
Accounts payable	$ 36,900	$ 17,280
Notes payable (short-term)	10,000	5,000
Mortgage note payable	–	50,000
Common stock, $10 par value	200,000	140,000
Premium on common stock	6,000	–
Retained earnings	50,000	32,280
	$302,900	$244,560

Additional information:

Net income for the year was $30,320.

Depreciation expense was $10,000.

Cash dividends declared during the year were $12,600.

The mortgage note payable was due in 1977, but the terms permitted the earlier payment without penalty.

An addition to the building was constructed during the year at a cost of $86,000, with $16,000 paid in cash and 1,000 shares of common stock issued for the remainder

Fully depreciated equipment costing $40,000 was sold as scrap for $2,000. This gain was included in net income.

During the year 5,000 shares of common stock were issued for a total of $56,000.

a. Prepare a schedule of changes in current items and working capital.

b. Prepare a statement of working capital.

14-4. For Carolyn Vincent Enterprises, Inc. in problem 14-3, prepare a funds statement for the year 1971.

14-5. Presented below are December 31, 1970, and December 31, 1971, balance sheets for Kimmey, Inc. along with their income statement and retained earnings analysis for the year ended December 31, 1971.

KIMMEY, INC.

Balance Sheet

December 31, 1970 and 1971

	December 31	
	1970	1971
ASSETS		
Cash	$ 19,100	$ 8,200
Accounts receivable	31,000	23,600
Inventory	23,100	24,900

Balance Sheet (continued)

	December 31	
	1970	1971
Prepaid expenses	2,000	2,200
Note receivable (due 1975)	-0-	5,000
Plant assets	241,000	125,000
Depreciation to date	(61,000)	(32,200)
Total	$255,200	$156,700
LIABILITIES AND STOCKHOLDERS' EQUITY		
Accounts payable	$ 3,400	$ 4,900
Income tax payable	6,000	-0-
Bonds payable	50,000	50,000
Capital stock ($10 par value)	50,000	60,000
Retained earnings	145,800	41,800
Total	$255,200	$156,700

KIMMEY, INC.

Income Statement
For the year ended December 31, 1971

Sales		$162,000
Operating expenses	$122,000	
Depreciation	6,000	128,000
Net income		34,000
Retained earnings, January 1, 1971		$145,800
Add operating income		34,000
		179,800
Less: loss from fire damage		138,000
Retained earnings, December 31, 1971		$ 41,800

On August 8, 1971, Kimmey, Inc. extended long-term credit to one of its customers by accepting a note due in 1975 to settle his account.

During November 1971 fire destroyed plant assets with a cost of $172,800 and accumulated depreciation to date of $34,800. The company immediately began purchasing equipment to replace the destroyed assets.

a. Prepare a schedule of changes in working capital items.
b. Prepare a working capital statement.
c. Prepare a funds statement.

14-6. Use information presented below in the December 31, 1970 and 1971 balance sheets and 1971 income statement of Ewing Corporation to prepare
a. Schedule of changes in working capital items.
b. A working capital statement.

EWING CORPORATION

Balance Sheet

December 31, 1970 and 1971

	December 31	
	1970	1971
ASSETS		
Cash	$ 7,100	$ 40,300
Accounts receivable	26,000	19,900
Inventory	21,400	23,100
Prepaid expenses	3,700	1,400
Plant assets	143,000	191,000
Depreciation to date	(39,000)	(46,000)
Bond investment	40,000	-0-
Total	$202,200	$229,700
LIABILITIES AND STOCKHOLDERS' EQUITY		
Accounts payable	$ 3,400	$ 6,200
Note payable (current installment)	10,000	10,000
Note payable, long-term	100,000	90,000
Capital stock	50,000	50,000
Retained earnings	38,800	73,500
	$202,200	$229,700

EWING CORPORATION

Income Statement

For the year ended December 31, 1971

Sales		$103,900
Operating expenses	$ 61,200	
Depreciation expense	10,000	71,200
Net operating income		$ 32,700
Gain on sale of bond investment		8,000
Net income		$ 40,700

Cash dividends were $6,000. Plant assets with a cost of $21,000 and depreciation to date of sale of $3,000 were sold for book value.

14-7. Presented below are the Rowell Corporation's December 31, 1970 and 1971 balance sheets and income statement for the year ended December 31, 1971.

ROWELL CORPORATION

Balance Sheet

December 31, 1970 and 1971

	December 31	
	1970	1971
ASSETS		
Cash	$ 9,100	$ 36,200
Accounts receivable	23,200	26,100
Inventory	14,200	19,600
Prepaid expenses	3,300	4,200
Plant assets	165,000	232,100
Depreciation to date	(62,000)	(71,000)
Sinking fund	40,000	45,500
Patents	12,000	10,000
Total	$204,800	$302,700
LIABILITIES AND STOCKHOLDERS' EQUITY		
Accounts payable	$ 11,100	$ 19,300
Income tax payable	12,000	21,100
Bonds payable	50,000	50,000
Premium on bonds payable	6,000	5,500
Capital stock ($5 par value)	50,000	100,000
Premium on capital stock	-0-	10,000
Retained earnings	75,700	96,800
Total	$204,800	$302,700

ROWELL CORPORATION

Income Statement

For the year ended December 31, 1971

Sales		$148,000
Operating expenses	$91,300	
Amortization of patent	2,000	
Depreciation	11,000	104,300
Operating income		43,700

Income Statement (continued)

Loss from sale of plant assets	$ 2,000	
Sinking fund income	500	1,500
Taxable income		$ 42,200
Federal income taxes		21,100
Net income after taxes		$ 21,100

Plant assets costing $10,000 and with depreciation to date of $2,000 were sold for a $2,000 loss.

a. Prepare a schedule of changes in working capital items.
b. Prepare a statement of working capital.

14-8. Using the comparative balance sheets of Tensin Corporation, prepare a schedule of changes in working capital items and a funds statement for 1970.

TENSIN CORPORATION

Balance Sheet

December 31, 1970 and 1971

	December 31	
	1969	1970
ASSETS		
Cash	$ 14,100	$ 12,800
Accounts receivable	41,200	14,100
Notes receivable (current)	-0-	20,000
Inventory	16,200	13,700
Prepaid expenses	3,600	4,100
Plant assets	183,000	216,000
Depreciation to date	(41,000)	(50,000)
Total	$217,100	$235,700
LIABILITIES AND STOCKHOLDERS' EQUITY		
Accounts payable	$ 9,800	$ 10,300
Mortgage payable	50,000	45,000
Capital stock	50,000	50,000
Retained earnings	107,300	130,400
Total	$217,100	$235,700

TENSIN CORPORATION

Income Statement

For the year ended December 31, 1970

Sales		$193,100
Operating costs	$158,000	
Depreciation	9,000	167,000
Net income		$ 26,100

Cash dividends declared were $3,000. The mortgage was reduced by a cash payment, and plant assets were purchased for cash.

14-9. The December 31, 1970 and 1971 balance sheets and the income statement for the year ended December 31, 1971, for Galloway, Inc. are presented below.

GALLOWAY, INC.

Balance Sheet

December 31, 1970 and 1971

	December 31	
	1970	1971
Cash	$ 23,200	$ 19,400
Accounts receivable	16,100	41,300
Inventory	14,200	19,200
Prepaid expenses	2,000	3,100
Plant assets	167,000	167,000
Depreciation to date on plant assets	(32,000)	(49,000)
Patents	16,000	-0-
Total	$206,500	$201,000
LIABILITIES AND STOCKHOLDERS' EQUITY		
Accounts payable	$ 4,300	$ 3,000
Mortgage payable	80,000	65,000
Capital stock	50,000	50,000
Retained earnings	72,200	83,000
Total	$206,500	$201,000

GALLOWAY, INC.

Income Statement

For the year ended December 31, 1971

Sales		$91,800
Operating expenses	$48,000	
Depreciation	17,000	
Amortization of patent	1,000	66,000
Net income		$25,800

On December 31 the company decided the patent was worthless. They charged $1,000 against current income and the remainder to retained earnings.

a. Prepare a schedule of changes on working capital items.
b. Prepare a statement of working capital.
c. Prepare a funds statement.

Index